# *The Britis..* ~~~~~~ *~~~~ ~~~ ~~~*
# Northern Ireland Crisis, 1969–73

"This volume is a model of lucidity and clarity and a joy to read. Although the particular case study is well known, Smith brings many new insights through an extensive trawl of the archives in London, Dublin, and Belfast, and in his use of private interviews."

—**Paul Arthur,** University of Ulster

"This is an excellent study of a crucial period of British policy towards Northern Ireland. The author has done a very good job in searching the archives and producing a clear and coherent narrative in a detail that has not been matched before. This book is a useful addition to the literature on the Northern Ireland conflict because it is informed by a close understanding of the historical evidence and an acute knowledge of how the British and Irish political systems work."

—**Paul Dixon,** Kingston University

"A highly intelligent, systematic, and original argument about a vitally important subject."

—**Richard English,** University of St. Andrews

"Bill Smith provides us with a unique insight into the use of policy responses by states in managing and resolving violent political conflicts while placing his sharp lens on the unintended consequences of these policy responses. In using a range of case studies from Northern Ireland, dealing with policing, justice, and governance, the author shows how policymakers need to focus on 'the context' for their decisions and be more aware of the choices they make. There are tools here which will help 'peace technicians' heighten their awareness of the policymaking context. You will find solid evidence of what works and what does not in the policymakers' world when dealing with violent political conflict."

—**Monica McWilliams,** Northern Ireland Human Rights Commission

"This is an intelligent and impressive book, with a wealth of detail. Applying useful models from political science, Smith's book is clear and cogent—a very accurate monograph which adds to our knowledge of the formative years of the Northern Ireland conflict. The book is admirably objective and few policy actors are spared criticism."

—**Jon Tonge,** University of Liverpool

# The British State and the
# Northern Ireland Crisis, 1969–73

# The British State and the Northern Ireland Crisis, 1969–73

*From Violence to Power Sharing*

William Beattie Smith

UNITED STATES INSTITUTE OF PEACE PRESS
WASHINGTON, D.C.

The views expressed in this book are those of the authors alone. They do not necessarily reflect the views of the United States Institute of Peace.

United States Institute of Peace
2301 Constitution Ave., NW
Washington, DC 20037
www.usip.org

First published 2011

To request permission to photocopy or reprint materials for course use, contact the Copyright Clearance Center at www.copyright.com. For print, electronic media, and all other subsidiary rights e-mail permissions@usip.org

Printed in the United States of America

The paper used in this publication meets the minimum requirements of American National Standards for Information Science—Permanence of Paper for Printed Library Materials, ANSI Z39.48-1984.

**Library of Congress Cataloging-in-Publication Data**

Smith, William Beattie.
    The British state and the Northern Ireland crisis, 1969–73 : from violence to power-sharing / William Beattie Smith.
        p. cm.
    ISBN 978-1-60127-067-2 (pbk. : alk. paper)
    1. Central-local government relations—Northern Ireland.  2. Central-local government relations—Great Britain.  3. Conflict management—Northern Ireland.  4. Ethnic conflict—Northern Ireland—Prevention. 5. Northern Ireland—Politics and government—1969–1994.  I. United States Institute of Peace.  II. Title.
    JN1572.A56D427 2011
    941.60824—dc22
                                                                        2010052952

*For my wife, Mary,*
*and peacemakers everywhere*

# Contents

# Introduction

*If only we were dealing with reasonable people.*
—Home Secretary Reginald Maudling[1]

On the edge of Europe, paramilitary violence emerged as a lethal threat to the authority of a Western democratic state over thirty years before U.S. president George W. Bush declared war on terror. The Irish Republican Army (IRA) took up arms against the British state in Northern Ireland in 1969 and sustained its insurgency for twenty-six years, defying the determined efforts of successive governments to stop it. The fighting eventually ended with the signing of an international political agreement in April 1998. That document was the outcome of protracted negotiations involving the British and Irish states, IRA representatives, and most of Northern Ireland's political parties.

Northern Ireland's agreement has been celebrated as a model for the resolution of violent political conflicts around the world. Two of the most prominent figures from the Irish peace process, British prime minister Tony Blair and U.S. senator George Mitchell, have been assigned as international peace envoys to the Middle East. Blair has referred to the Irish peace process as an inspiration, saying that "right round the world there are people who have taken heart from it."[2] Mitchell has identified some basic principles of negotiation that apply to both cases.[3]

Political scientists have depicted Northern Ireland as comparable with other cases of ethnonational internal war.[4] But some commentators and negotiators are skeptical about the value of cross-national comparisons.[5] The debate continues over how research can best contribute to the design of workable and sustainable solutions to internal conflicts. But both sides agree on the value of drawing the best possible inferences from these painful experiences. It could be as damaging for governments, negotiators, and mediators to apply inappropriate generalizations out of context as to ignore opportunities for knowledge transfer altogether. This book is a contribution to the collective effort of peacebuilders around the world to learn from and improve our collective understanding.

When the British state first engaged with the Northern Ireland conflict during 1969, the ministers, senior officials, and military commanders assigned to the problem knew little about the place, its people, their turbulent histories, and their ideologies. They learned by trial and error. It took some three years to put in place the essential components of the policy doctrine that eventually resulted in the agreement. This book starts from the premise that there may be as much wisdom to be harvested from the failures of that early formative period as from later successes.

The challenge was not an easy one. British security officials have acknowledged their opponents as "one of the most effective terrorist organisations in history. Professional, dedicated, highly skilled and resilient, it [the IRA] conducted a sustained and lethal campaign in Northern Ireland, mainland United Kingdom (UK) and on the continent of Europe."[6] The IRA's mission was to create an independent all-Ireland socialist republic. To this end, it exploited quasi-religious rhetoric, revolutionary mythology, and patriotic sentiment to legitimize and promote what British ministers at the time denounced as "terrorism" but which its activists called "the armed struggle."[7] In classic guerrilla style, the IRA turned Britain's strengths to its own advantage. Adding political campaigning to paramilitary violence, it secured substantial popular support from the minority community in a deeply divided society.

The IRA campaign did not attain its ultimate objectives. Northern Ireland remains in the United Kingdom, and there is arguably less evidence of socialism throughout Ireland now than when it began. The Republic of Ireland amended its constitution in 1998 so that it no longer declares jurisdiction over the entire island; it is debatable whether this represents progress toward unification.

Nevertheless, the IRA did achieve clear and substantial gains. The British terminated the majority-controlled administration that had run Northern Ireland since its creation in 1920, undertook to work for a united Ireland if a majority of the electorate supported it, introduced new power-sharing arrangements designed to guarantee minority participation in a new devolved administration, promoted new all-Ireland institutions that were presented as a step toward unification, and gave the Irish government substantial influence over British policy decisions. These were considerable achievements for a force of under two thousand fighters confronting one of the world's most experienced and best-equipped armies.

Why did the British yield so much? Did they appease violence or respond pragmatically to the changing elements of an intractable problem with no perfect solution? As events moved on, did they draw the right lessons from experience? This book analyzes and assesses Britain's policy responses to what is euphemistically known locally as "the Troubles." It examines four discrete policy approaches, starting with the decision in August 1969 to reform Northern Ireland's police service and ending with the comprehensive constitutional agreement of December 1973. This was the formative period for Britain's political and security policies, setting the pattern for the next thirty-three years. During 1973, London settled on an approach that subsequently crystallized as the organizational doctrine of the Northern Ireland Office, the department created in 1972 to coordinate security and political development policies.

At the core of the book are six questions. What processes of understanding and reasoning, political pressures, and organizational factors shaped British policies? What principles and interests underpinned them? How were dilemmas and uncertainties resolved? Why did policies evolve as they did? How effective were they? When they failed, what lessons were learned?

The book goes beyond traditional historical narrative to test hypotheses and systematically identify patterns that in theory could recur under comparable conditions in other times and places. It transforms historical events into analytic episodes, distinguishing the universal from the idiosyncratic and setting out its findings in generalizable terms.

A government generally depicts its policies as the products of rational processes of decision-making. In reality, however, they are heavily influenced by the political forces and organizational constraints to which policymakers are subjected. Policy decisions are made under pressure by people who lack essential information and are uncertain about the intentions and capabilities of other players.

In examining the successive policy choices of British ministers, this book draws on four broad models of explanation: economic, psychological, political, and organizational. Each is related to a distinct tradition of policy analysis. The carefully structured application of each of these models in turn structures the analysis, enables robust conclusions to be drawn, and helps to identify lessons for transfer.

Chapter 1 explains how policymakers understand political violence and use the resources at their disposal to tackle it. It defines three broad strategic options—reform, coercion, and power sharing—and identifies factors that influence which of the three are selected in practice. Chapter 2 turns to Northern Ireland, describing the underlying preconditions for the violence in conflicting national aspirations, rooted in Ireland's troubled history and reinforced since the 1880s by a series of mutually reinforcing political, social, economic, and cultural divisions.

Chapters 3 to 6 present four case studies, each of which focuses on a pivotal point in Britain's evolving policy toward Northern Ireland. Chapter 3 looks at the package of reforms that Britain introduced in response to a protest campaign that resulted in rioting and street fighting, particularly the reform of the police service in September 1969. Chapter 4 examines how the role of the British army in Northern Ireland developed from peacekeeping to coercion in response to an increasingly violent insurgency, focusing on the introduction of internment in August 1971. Chapter 5 considers how the perceived failure of this coercive approach led Britain to suspend Northern Ireland's devolved administration in March 1972, replacing it with direct rule, a system of government that persisted, despite short unstable periods of devolution, until 2007. Chapter 6 analyzes the development of what some commentators have depicted as Britain's first comprehensive strategy to address the roots of the conflict, power sharing with an Irish dimension. With occasional deviations and varying interpretations, Labour and Conservative governments have pursued this since then as the most promising formula for a sustainable accommodation.

Chapter 7 compares the findings from the four case studies, traces the evolution of policy, and evaluates the relative importance of rational calculation, patterns of understanding, party politics, diplomatic pressures, organizational structure, and official doctrine in shaping policies and initiating radical change. Chapter 8 looks at what worked, what failed, and why. The last chapter looks at possible lessons for other conflicts, in particular the implications for political development policies.

## Note on Government Sources

In researching this book I consulted official papers at the UK National Archives at Kew, the National Archives of Ireland in Dublin, and the Public Records Office of Northern Ireland in Belfast. The main categories of sources are abbreviated in the endnotes as follows. CAB refers to records of the Cabinet Office, CJ to records created or inherited by the Northern Ireland Office, DEFE to records of the Ministry of Defence, FCO to records of the Foreign and Commonwealth Office and its predecessors, HO to records of the Home Office, MoD to records of the Ministry of Defence, NAI to records of the Government of Ireland (Dublin), PREM to records of the Prime Minister's Office, and PRONI to records of the Government of Northern Ireland (Belfast).

## Notes

1.    UK Public Records Office (PRO) CAB130/522, paper dated November 10, 1971.

2.    Interview, *Belfast Telegraph,* September 4, 2010.

3.    George Mitchell, Dean Acheson Lecture, U.S. Institute of Peace, Washington, DC, May 24, 2010, available at www.usip.org.

4.    See, e.g., J. McGarry and B. O'Leary, *Explaining Northern Ireland* (Oxford: Blackwell, 1995).

5.    See, e.g., D. Trimble, "Misunderstanding Ulster," 2007, available at www.davidtrimble.org (accessed September 16, 2010). Trimble was the leader of the Unionist Party during the 1998 negotiations and subsequently Northern Ireland's first minister.

6.    Ministry of Defence, "Operation Banner: An Analysis of Military Operations in Northern Ireland," Ministry of Defence internal paper, July 2006, paragraph 106c.

7.    The IRA's constitution commits it to five means of advancing its mission, one of which is "to wage revolutionary armed struggle." The document is reprinted as Appendix 3 in E. Moloney, *The Secret History of the IRA* (London: Penguin Press, 2002).

# 1

# Managing Political Violence

## Explaining Policy Choices

*War is a matter of vital importance to the state; the province of life or death; the road to survival or ruin. It is mandatory that it be thoroughly studied.* —Sun Tzu[1]

B roadly speaking, a government faced with a problem of political violence must follow one of two paths: coercion or concession. Coercion entails the use or threat of physical force to suppress or restrain protest. Concessions are of two main types: policy reforms, which offer compliance with the demands of protest leaders, and constitutional reforms, which bring protest leaders into the process of government. The government may direct its actions toward entire population segments, at politically active groups only, or at the few individuals leading identified protest organizations.

## Coercion

In his cross-national study of political violence in ethnically divided societies, Byman has identified three categories of coercive response: police control, selective control, and brute force.[2] All governments routinely use police control. Established systems of criminal law and policing practice provide an array of coercive measures to control disorderly protest. Everyday laws can prevent demonstrations from blocking roads and obstructing business life. In most democratic societies, the population broadly accepts the legitimacy of police control, even when some issues, such as the ethnic composition of the police force, are controversial.

Governments may introduce additional measures into their criminal justice systems to cope with more challenging forms of protest. These include
incremental adjustments to court rules, intrusive arrangements for intelligence gathering, and the deployment of undercover police units. When
such measures are directed at subordinate group leaders in an ethnically
divided society, we enter the realm of what Byman calls selective control,
characterized by such actions as political censorship, harassment, restrictions on political engagement, imprisonment, exile, and even targeted assassination. Finally, brute force entails using coercive measures against an
entire ethnic group irrespective of individuals' political activity. It can range
from petty discrimination, such as legislation preventing people in the target group from living in certain districts, to widespread continuous terror,
as in Saddam Hussein's collective punishments to discourage Kurds from
helping separatist insurgents.

Some commentators, predominantly from a military background, argue
that prompt, robust coercive measures are the most effective response to
the threat of armed insurgency.[3] Those who have studied the comparative history of violent conflicts qualify this argument by adding that any
such response should be proportionate, consistent, and well coordinated
across civilian and security agencies: intelligent selective control rather
than brute force.[4] Hibbs concludes that the mere availability of substantial
coercive resources to a regime tends to deter organized insurgency, even as
it simultaneously intensifies peaceful protest.[5] Gurr likewise finds that the
magnitude of organized violence tends to vary inversely with the perceived
force capability of a political regime.[6] These studies and others suggest that
coercion is most effective when it is overwhelmingly powerful, selective,
consistent, and latent.

Taking the argument further, in a deeply divided society the knowledge
that a strong government will punish violence from any source equitably
can reassure people from all sides, removing their need to organize and
arm themselves for self-defense. The dominant group can feel that its hegemony is secure, and other groups that they will be defended from injustice.[7] The corollary is that if the authorities do not act evenhandedly, the
potential leaders of subordinate group protests will have a source of resentment and fear around which to mobilize support. If the government's
strength is then tested and found wanting, both dominant and subordinate
communities will have cause to resort to paramilitary force to defend their
essential interests.

Coercion, particularly in the form of brute force, tends to generate resentment and exacerbate the status concerns of groups already subject to

discrimination. The level of their disaffection grows in direct proportion to the scale, visibility, and intensity of the measures used against them. Tilly finds that repressive measures tend to transform collective protest—defined as nonfatal riots, strikes, and peaceful demonstrations—into internal war, embracing armed attacks, assassinations, and other lethal incidents.[8] This is consistent with Gurr's conclusion that arbitrary coercion tends to drive sympathetic nonprotesters toward active support for insurgent organizations. Likewise, ineffective, inconsistent, or irresolute coercion can increase disorder by inspiring a combination of disaffection and contempt for the authorities. It may also strengthen protest movements, forcing members to reorganize in underground networks and to rely more heavily on one another. Worst of all may be when a government, having driven its opponents out of sight, inflamed their enmity, and cemented their organization, suddenly relaxes its repressive policies and reverts to conciliation.[9] However disciplined and democratically accountable the state's security forces, coercive actions directed against mass protest may result in deaths and serious injuries. From his analysis of thousands of violent political incidents in Europe since 1800, Tilly concludes that repressive state forces were the most consistent initiators and performers of collective violence, responsible for many more deaths and injuries than were protesters.[10]

The efficacy of coercive responses is directly linked to the legitimacy of the state. The presence of disorder implies a breach in that legitimacy. If that breach is sufficiently large, the power of the state may be insufficient to exercise effective repression without resort to military force.[11] Military coercion risks further undermining the legitimacy of the state, creating a vicious spiral. Special measures against insurgency may constrain or undermine individual and collective liberties, including the right to trial by jury and the freedoms of speech and assembly. Visible, patrolling soldiers are a constant reminder of the lack of consensual support for the authorities. The relaxation of judicial procedures tends to reduce the popular legitimacy of criminal justice institutions, at least in the eyes of the disaffected. When security forces operate outside the law, this gives protesters and insurgents the opportunity to undermine respect for the regime's authority. The cost to the state may be higher if the authorities also fail to prosecute members of the security forces who break the law.[12]

Good gathering and use of information on insurgents are important factors in the success of selective coercion. Intelligence permits security forces to focus on specific individuals rather than on entire communities, avoiding the trap of generating popular resentment.[13] If they can penetrate insurgent organizations with agents and informers, the authorities can prevent planned attacks, disseminate misinformation, exploit internal divisions, weaken or eliminate their most aggressive opponents, and influence the organizations' policies in favor of the regime's or the intelligence services' own interests.

Lustick has argued that the best strategy for containing violent political conflict in a divided society may be one in which the community of potential insurgents passively accepts its own subordination. He has called this the control model.[14] Its distinguishing features are, first, that the superior power resources of the dominant population segment are deployed to constrain the political activities of other segments, and second, that the political system, whether formally democratic or not, promotes the interests of the dominant segment at the others' expense. The most effective way to weaken potential opposition groups is to prevent them from organizing powerfully in the first place. As we shall see, Northern Ireland before 1968 largely fitted Lustick's model. Without having to resort to overwhelming displays of military force, and with an overtly democratic electoral system in place, the largest political party, drawing its support almost exclusively from the majority community, managed to stay in office in an unbroken and apparently unbreakable line of succession.

Byman concludes that in deeply divided societies where a government cannot provide security reliably and evenhandedly for all main ethnic groups, policy reforms and power sharing are unlikely to succeed. In these cases coercive control may be necessary at least for a limited period, until measures can be implemented that transform the political culture. For all their tactical and moral disadvantages, coercive responses can be justified in pragmatic terms if they prevent still worse consequences, such as ethnic cleansing and internal war.[15]

## Reform

Whether reform or coercion appeals more to the authorities depends in part on what is being demanded and the costs to them of granting it. Often, the diverse leaders of a disaffected community vary in their demands. Some ask for small incremental changes, the costs of which are predominantly economic. Others ask for a radical redistribution of power and resources. Protest leaders are likely to differ among themselves over the means to be used and the lengths to which they are prepared to go. An implication of this is that timely concessions may divide moderate protesters from hard-liners, thereby preventing mild collective protest from degenerating into internal war. Hibbs finds such concessions particularly successful where they reduce perceived discrimination on racial or cultural grounds.

Gurr advises policymakers to avoid coercion whenever possible and instead concentrate on minimizing perceived relative deprivation by maintaining current proportions in the distribution of social, economic, and political goods. Discontented groups can be satisfied at least temporarily if they have opportunities to achieve their aspirations unimpeded by discriminatory barriers.[16] Reform is likely to work best when it reduces the frustrations and grievances that gave rise to protest in the first place and enhances government legitimacy. Good timing, presentation, and consistency are essential. Reforms that are slow in coming or that appear to have been extracted by force are less likely to succeed.

Like coercion, reform may pose risks and incur costs. De Tocqueville's well-known maxim is that the most perilous moment for an oppressive government is when it seeks to mend its ways.[17] Concessions may lead to further demands and greater expectations of success. The danger is likely to be greater when reform takes the authorities over some significant symbolic threshold, induces no reciprocity, or shows that the government is prepared to pay a high price to avoid further protest.[18] However equitable, reforms offered in response to violence may undermine the authority of those who offer them, encourage subversion, and provoke counterviolence from loyal but inflexible supporters of the regime. The undesirable consequences are particularly probable in deeply divided societies, where loyalists are likely to feel that they are paying for any concessions to protesters. Few reforms may not be seen in this way, especially in the sensitive areas of constitutional change and security policy. Even at a time of economic growth, a regime may be constrained by opposition within its own ranks from offering sufficient concessions swiftly enough to prevent collective protest from degenerating into internal war. Where controversial policies are perceived in zero-sum terms, a politically acceptable and effective package of concessions may simply not exist.

## Power Sharing

The sharing of power may range from offering subordinate group leaders limited control over their own communities in specified localities or issue areas to the guarantee of full participation in decision-making across all areas of governmental power. Cross-national research suggests that low-level co-optation can foster ethnic peace, soften the grievances of subordinate elites, reduce the status resentment of their constituents, and decrease the risk of armed insurgency, but also that it may not be sufficient to prevent disorderly protest and political violence. Its effect is limited by definition and may decrease over time.[19] Advocates of power sharing claim that, in the right circumstances, it can defuse violence completely and, over time, remove the preconditions for disorder. It is another matter, however, whether shared institutions can reduce the political salience of the ethnic differences in which they are rooted.

Lijphart identifies an important subtype of power sharing, which he calls consociational democracy. He has argued that this may offer the best approach to managing conflict in deeply divided societies, where (according to classic pluralist theory) the absence of cross-cutting cleavages tends to result in political instability.[20] Consociational solutions focus unapologetically on elites. They depart from the normal rules of majoritarian democracy to guarantee the leaders of potentially disaffected population segments a proportionate share of power. The definitive consociational measure is government by a grand coalition, comprising the leaders of all significant ethnic groups. Other definitional elements include a mutual veto over critical public policy decisions, proportionality in the distribution of public sector jobs and resources, and autonomy for each population segment in the administration of its own essential affairs, typically including language, culture, and education. Elements that may also be present are a high degree of federalism, in which power is delegated to the lowest practicable level, and proportional representation voting systems. In practice, as Lijphart has since conceded, there are few examples of fully consociational constitutions that have withstood the test of time. Over the past fifty years attempts to sustain consociational systems have failed in Cyprus, Lebanon, and Northern Ireland.

## Discussion

Reform and power sharing may seem to be more humane responses to violent protest than coercion. Nordlinger has argued that coercion is not a solution at all.[21] Ultimately, however, policies are best assessed by their results. The political predominance of one community over another in a divided society, sustained by the threat of coercion, does not necessarily rule out a high level of equality and human rights in areas that do not impinge on the regime's ultimate political authority. Hegemonic control may be better than civil war or genocide. It may not be possible to manage the conflicting demands of opposing communities within a framework of fully democratic political institutions and processes.

The three strategies outlined above may in practice be blended and pursued simultaneously. Previous research has drawn attention to the value of combining concessions and coercive measures in an integrated strategy covering both the civil and security dimensions of administration.[22] Coercion may be used to buy time for policymakers to implement reforms, engineer agreements among faction leaders, undermine hard-line opponents, or pursue agreement on the specifics of power-sharing institutions. Reforms may be offered to the more moderate faction of a potentially rebellious community to divide it from violent hard-liners. The government of Israel has offered concessions to the Druze community to reduce its identification with the broader Arab cause. From this perspective, the nonviolent political leaders of an ethnic group that includes potential insurgents may be the government's best allies. They offer a source of information on the group's fears and aspirations, an alternative channel for satisfying group demands, a channel of communication with group members, intelligence on their more radical competitors, and a means to obstruct the insurgents' political progress.

The strategies may also be applied sequentially. Comparative research reveals a common sequence of events, in which a state responds initially to peaceful protest with limited reforms. These fail to prevent disorder. The state then resorts increasingly to coercion, with an increasing rhetorical emphasis on law and order. Many of the protesters then yield, but a committed minority organizes clandestinely and attempts to secure popular support for inflating the protest into organized insurgency. A spiral of violence begins in which repression and insurgent violence feed on each other until one side suffers a decisive defeat or loses the will to continue the struggle. This sequencing is illustrated in Townshend's study of the Anglo-Irish War of 1918 to 1921 and in Coyle's account of the conflict in Cyprus in the 1950s.[23] In both cases limited protest spread from a handful of revolutionary intellectuals and eventually attracted sufficient popular support to elicit concessions from the authorities. These were opposed by powerful groups, upon whose acquiescence the government depended. This opposition, combined with the resulting inertia on the part of the authorities, effectively delayed the concessions. In the interim, new protest leaders emerged who built on the success of the earlier peaceful protest to demand more radical concessions, including transfers of power from the incumbent regime. Armed organizations appeared and attacked the police and security forces, directly challenging the authority of the state. They also attacked moderate challengers within their own community and attempted to provoke attack by opposing communities, reducing the authorities' scope for offering further reforms. In an attempt to shore up its authority, Britain in both cases resorted increasingly to coercive measures, including martial law, curfews, military trials, mass house searches, and internment. These were demonstrably counterproductive and contributed to the eventual triumph of the insurgents.

## Models of Explanation

This study hypothesizes that the process of selecting a policy is not simply one of rational decision-making, although governments generally seek to present it as such. Instead, government policies, whether defined as declared statements of intention or as actions repeatedly executed, are determined not primarily by strategic calculation but by policymakers' patterns of understanding, which may be more or less accurate; by political and diplomatic pressures; and by the structures, doctrines, and procedures of the bureaucratic organizations that act on the government's behalf.

We may reasonably expect objective factors, including the nature and level of the violence and the protesters' demands, at least to contribute to the determination of policy. It would be surprising if governments routinely reacted to small, peaceful demonstrations seeking incremental reforms in the same way as to well-organized, sustained terrorist campaigns intended to overthrow the constitution. Yet in practice the international record does not support the proposition that policies for managing political violence are determined primarily by the nature or severity of the opposition. In numerous instances, flagrant violations of the law have been ignored. In others, orderly demonstrations in pursuit of modest demands have been met with harsh brutality.[24]

There are four broad traditions of policy analysis to draw on in identifying and explaining governments' policy choices. For convenience I will use the shorthand terms rational, cognitive process, political, and organizational models. Each is an ideal; none can singlehandedly explain how governments form policies in reality. Each offers insights for those seeking to understand the processes by which policies are made.

### The Rational Model

The rational model focuses on problem solving, treating a government as analogous to an individual decision maker with clearly defined objectives and values. Policymakers identify a problem, survey the resources at their disposal, formulate a series of alternatives for action, systematically assess the costs and benefits of each, and conclude by adopting the most cost-effective policy available. The model is grounded in the rational choice view of behavior, which depicts all human activity as purposive. It assumes that the decision maker has comprehensive knowledge of his environment, clearly defined values and goals, and the ability to integrate competing values through a utility function that permits him to rank alternative courses of action in order of preference. Rational choice consists of selecting the course of action with the highest gross value.[25] In this context, the value of policy options is unlikely to be calculated in monetary terms. But ideally, rational processes of decision-making aspire to apply some form of quantitative scoring to permit tradeoffs between competing goals and principles. Treasury departments typically commend this approach when advising civil servants on best practice in policy formulation. Similarly, ministers like to present their policies publicly as the products of rational calculations. The model is also commonly used in diplomatic contexts, where its dominant pattern of inference is that "if a nation performed a particular action, that nation must have had ends toward which the action constituted a maximizing means."[26]

### The Cognitive Process Model

While the rational model enables the analyst to construct a partial explanation of policy choices out of limited information, it ignores a range of factors that constrain decision-making in the real world, especially when policy is directed toward influencing the actions of other people.[27] Policymakers in practice seldom have all the information they need to meet the requirements of the rational model, in particular reliable probability estimates. In complex problem solving it is, by definition, formulaically impossible to integrate competing values adequately. Uncertainty and confusion are especially likely to surround issues of political conflict and controversy, in which events are unfolding continuously and misinformation is an important weapon in the arsenal of the decision makers' rivals.

Steinbruner offers an alternative model that focuses on how decision makers manage the practical difficulties of their tasks.[28] The distinguishing feature of Steinbruner's model, which he calls cognitive process, is that it expects the mind of the policymaker to impose structure on otherwise highly ambiguous data. Instead of pure rationality, the cognitive process model looks for the patterns of thought and inference that policymakers use to impose order on the random flow of events in their problem field, identify causal relationships, define options, and choose which to implement. These patterns save time and effort, allowing governments to respond to crises quickly. But they do so at the cost of filtering out essential information and simplifying the complexities of the real world. Competing values may not be successfully integrated, and problems may be redefined so that tough tradeoffs can be avoided. The cognitive process policymaker does not need to calculate the estimated values of myriad alternatives because he imposes and then seeks to preserve his own image of the most desirable outcome. Sensitivity to pertinent information varies according to its consistency with his existing preconceptions. When ambiguous, inconsistent, or challenging information arises, he may block it through a variety of simplifying tactics, including ignoring it, discrediting its sources, or reverting to inappropriate analogies, ideological dogma, or abstract principles.[29]

The cognitive process model assumes that policymakers strive for rationality, but also that they do so using predetermined beliefs to resolve value conflicts and uncertainties.[30] It draws our attention as analysts to conflict in policymakers' understandings of the nature, severity, and causes of disorder, their assessments of the parties to the conflict, and their beliefs about their own role and capabilities. It anticipates that policymakers may present themselves as acting more rationally than is in fact the case in their quest for moral authority and popular support.

### The Political Model

Both the rational and the cognitive process model assume that a government tackles problems with the intellectual coherence of a single mind. This neglects the reality that, often, the numerous individuals contributing to policy decisions may disagree among themselves and are subject to outside pressures. The political model assumes that a government consists of many influential people and factions, each with its own interests, objectives, and priorities. Each is subject to pressures from the legislature, the media, interest groups, public opinion, and foreign governments. Within the government machine, players promote their own policy preferences and compete for power resources, including jobs, status, and re-election. They may or may not make rational calculations about the cost-effectiveness of different options, and if they do, their personal political objectives may attract higher scores than public policy outcomes. Their ability to pursue policy goals may be constrained by the need to sustain a supportive coalition.[31]

The political model does not simply measure the relative strengths of the pressures for and against, say, coercion and reform but also accounts for such factors as the locus of decision, the rules of the decision-making game, and the players' skills and tactics. The rational model's metaphor of the calculating individual yields to that of multiple players engaged in a continuous game, where the interests at stake extend wider than any single policy issue.

It expects major policy shifts to occur not directly in response to events but only after these have been mediated through the political system, resulting in a shift in the balance of power such that the coalition against current policy outweighs or can outmaneuver the coalition that supports it. Ministers may be able to build a coalition sufficient to sustain a given policy for years without ever achieving consensus on the underpinning values or goals. Policy may be the lowest common denominator upon which all can agree, and may be accepted as such to avoid criticism and conflict.

## The Organizational Model

The fourth model focuses on the structures, doctrines, and routine behavior of bureaucratic agencies. It explains policies as neither intellectual choices nor the outcomes of political games but as the outputs of complex social machines, the component parts of which may be straining toward competing objectives simultaneously and the actions of which are largely determined by predetermined routines and doctrines.[32] The organizational model works from the premise that the characteristics of public bureaucracies influence policy independently of intellectual and political factors. Students of organizational behavior have identified structure, routine, and doctrine as three sets of factors critical to understanding how public agencies work.

Structure embraces the allocation of responsibilities and tasks among bureaucratic units as well as the arrangements for their control and coordination. The basic features of organizational structure and function mirror the characteristics of human problem solving. Bureaucracies break down decisions involving difficult tradeoffs and uncertainties into discrete elements, which can be assigned to separate administrative units. This enables ministers and senior officials to pursue competing ideas simultaneously without cognitive dissonance. Complex problems are fragmented into separate components, even at the highest levels of the decision-making process, as policymakers focus sequentially on the questions raised and values represented, without having to integrate values and solutions cognitively or organizationally across them.[33] This facility is bought at a price. In a rigid hierarchical structure, information that might damage the interests of the responsible unit can be concealed or distorted. Fragmentation leads to the development of parochial perspectives and interests, diverting resources from the pursuit of shared objectives. Agencies operating toward common broad purposes fail to coordinate their operations. Rivalries develop that seriously impair the system's overall effectiveness and efficiency.

A second group of organizational factors with the potential to shape policies falls under the rubric of routine. Much of what bureaucratic organizations do is laid down in predetermined programs. Routines permit the activities of numerous individuals to be coordinated with minimum fuss and enhance the power of senior managers by reducing the discretion of lower-level officials. They provide stability and permit the organization's members and associates to plan ahead on the basis of reasonably accurate predictions of how the organization will act. The routines may constrain innovation, but they can become the building blocks from which new policies are constructed.

Thus, the organizational analyst seeks to explain today's policies principally by reference to yesterday's, and to predict tomorrow's by teasing out the routines that make up today's.[34] Policy options that can be implemented through existing programs stand a better chance of being adopted than those that require new routines. Problems for which appropriate routines already exist also are less likely to reach the highest political level for decision-making, precluding the possibility of radical solutions. Even when prior programs are abandoned in a search for novel solutions, the search itself is likely to be governed by predetermined routines. Bureaucratic organizations tend not to search systematically for the most cost-effective possible solutions as predicted by the rational choice model but to settle for the first option that satisfies minimal criteria. Simon has described this as satisficing.[35] Consequently, the sequence in which policymakers encounter options can be crucial to the outcome. Cyert and March describe a pattern they call problemistic search, in which decision makers begin with the obvious symptoms of their problem and then, if necessary, move on to review their current policies.[36] Options that can be related immediately either to the problem or to the organization's current policies stand a better chance of selection than those that cannot. Again, the implication is that incremental adjustments to present policies are more likely than radical new departures to be selected in most circumstances.

A third organizational factor that may help determine policy is doctrine, defined as the shared patterns of understanding that underpin the routines of an organization and draw its members together. An agency working in a stable environment over a long period develops a definite philosophy, which helps it to harmonize its present decisions with past ones. Officials see the world in terms of their agency's own unique concepts, which are built into the agency's internal language. The categories and definitions the organization employs become reified for members, appearing to be attributes of the world rather than mere conventions.[37] Like structure and routine, doctrine helps reduce noise and confusion to manageable proportions, offering clarity and consensus where there was doubt and discord.

Like individuals' patterns of understanding, the agency doctrine reduces uncertainties and value conflicts, but does so at the cost of filtering out useful information and neglecting wider values.

At the core of an organization's doctrine is its sense of its essence and capabilities.[38] The organization favors policies that sustain and enhance what it sees as its core mission, and fights hard for the necessary resources; it will equally reject new responsibilities and tasks that fall outside its core mission.[39]

## Learning and Adaptation

Governmental learning can be defined as an improvement in the effectiveness or efficiency of the policymaking process, which the rational model would associate with increases in the intelligence and sophistication of policymakers' thinking.[40] Adaptation, by contrast, implies that policy adjustments are made in response to changes in the problem or its political and organizational context, but these are not necessarily accompanied by improvements in policymakers' understanding.

The rational model assumes that decision makers work energetically over time to reduce uncertainties through research and resolve value conflicts through increasingly sophisticated cost-benefit calculations. Overall intelligence thus increases steadily as new information is accumulated and assimilated into revised value equations. Policymakers produce increasingly accurate and sophisticated explanations of the problem and its causes and incorporate into their value calculations higher, more general objectives.[41]

Under the cognitive process model, learning is constrained by existing structures of belief and strategies of inference. Fresh information and new problems are fitted into already established patterns of thinking without normally causing any structural adjustment. The general pattern of conceptualization remains stable over extended periods. This conforms to Kuhn's account of the evolution of scientific thought. Paradigm shifts occur only in exceptional circumstances and when overwhelming evidence has accumulated to undermine previous doctrine.[42]

Psychological research supports the empirical validity of the cognitive process model of learning. Nisbett and Ross identify a tendency they call belief perseverance—broadly, sticking to fixed beliefs well beyond the point at which logic and empirical evidence fail to sustain them.[43] Decision makers in practice are biased toward new evidence that supports their preconceptions and against evidence that undermines them. They seek out, remember, and interpret evidence in a manner that sustains their established beliefs; derive causal explanations from provisional evidence, in which they then place too much confidence; and act on their theories in a way that makes them self-confirming. Jervis identifies three systematic distortions in the way decision makers learn from history.[44] First, they tend to misread important causal links by failing to distinguish the essential preconditions of events from their ephemeral context. Second, in formulating causal explanations, they pay disproportionate attention to certain types of event, including those experienced personally, those that occurred early in their professional careers, and those that had important consequences for them. Third, they are biased against options similar to others that have recently failed and toward those that appear recently to have succeeded.[45]

The political model suggests additional constraints on learning. While individual policymakers may learn, what they learn may not be translated into policy improvements. The discrete players are likely to draw diverse and possibly conflicting lessons from the same events. They may become more skillful at the game, but this may result only in more tortuous processes with less sharply defined outcomes. On the other hand, the heat of politics may provide the impetus for adaptation in a system that would otherwise succumb to the inertia of routine.[46] Changes in the balance of power may bring fresh minds and patterns of understanding to bear on previously intractable problems.

Finally, the organizational model expects policy developments to be constrained by the tenacity with which agencies adhere to existing routines even in the face of substantial evidence that they are ineffective. Policies normally evolve incrementally through small adjustments to existing programs. Occasionally, a significant failure to meet minimal performance criteria triggers high-level search routines, resulting in such radical organizational transformations as the creation of new agencies. Other changes may appear to be innovative but still bear the heavy influence of established doctrine.

The organizational model draws attention to other aspects of learning in complex bureaucracies. Individuals in different parts of government are exposed to different information and know different things. A government's capacity to learn depends on clear and effective communication channels among its component parts and a willingness to use them. The value of lessons learned at the top of a hierarchy is diluted to the extent that those lower down are not aware of, neglect, or reject them. Organizations process new intelligence depending on senior officials' views about how the intelligence should be used.[47] It should not be assumed that incremental processes of change yield smaller outcomes than sudden dramatic explosions of activity. Stable processes of evolution can produce huge transformations surprisingly quickly.[48]

## Summary

The four studies in this book each examine one case of a discrete policy the British government followed in tackling political disorder in Northern Ireland from 1968 to 1973, seeking to explain why that policy was pursued. Each chapter is structured with a view to identifying the effects of cognitive, political, and organizational factors. The final chapters of the book explore the extent to which valid conclusions may be drawn from systematically comparing the four cases.

It can be argued that the methodology does not satisfy the scientific ideal of controlled comparison. The number of cases is too small and the number of variables too large to allow firm generalizable conclusions to be drawn, and the critical variables fluctuate across the four cases. On the other hand, the strategy of comparison that comes closest to the scientific ideal of experimental control is that of the same political system at adjoining points in time.[49] The large number of background constants can compensate for the paucity of cases. But more generally, the analysis aims primarily not to demonstrate that one of the models invariably offers a better explanation of why governments act as they do but to explore what each has to contribute, and whether the process of combining them produces richer, fuller accounts than any single model on its own.

Those schooled in conventional history making also may argue that it is futile to impose a veneer of scientific method on the random occurrence of unique events, and that good history explains policy decisions very well without needing a superstructure of explanatory models and case comparisons. I disagree. Success in a study of this kind depends on the appropriate transformation of historical events into analytic episodes. This means distinguishing the universal from the idiosyncratic and setting out conclusions in general terms.[50] The underlying logic is that each policy is a dependent variable of sorts, related to a series of potential independent variables as determined by the four models of explanation. Keeping the models separate (see table 1.1) helps to sensitize the analyst to the factors contributing to policymakers' choices and actions, to relate policy failures to deficiencies in policymaking processes, and hence to enable governments to improve those processes.

**Table 1.1   Variables for Analysis**

| | |
|---|---|
| *Rational Model* | |
| Characteristics of problem | Nature and scale of disorder |
| | Levels and trends in violence |
| | Indices of popular disaffection |
| | State of political leadership |
| Policy objectives | Maintaining law and order |
| | Securing cooperation of key players |
| | Minimizing costs |
| | Reducing risks of future violence |
| Possible options | Coercion |
| | Reform |
| | Power sharing |
| *Cognitive Process Model* | |
| Uncertainties | Strength and intentions of key players |
| | Reactions of key players |
| Patterns of understanding | Causes of violence |
| | Protesters'/insurgents' motives |
| | Dynamics of regional political system |
| | State's proper role |
| *Political Model* | |
| Opposition party | Support/opposition to options |
| Government backbenchers | Support/opposition to options |
| Key ministers | Objectives, perceptions and resources |
| Media | Balance of press and television coverage |
| Public opinion | Survey results, protest campaigns |
| International factors | Other governments and diplomatic pressures |
| *Organizational Model* | |
| Structure | Locus of decision |
| | Relationships among agencies |
| | Distribution of powers and functions |
| | Arrangements for coordination and control |
| Routine | Decision-making procedures |
| | Delivery procedures |
| Doctrine | Each agency's mission, priorities, and patterns of understanding |

# Notes

1.   Sun Tzu, *The Art of War* (Oxford: Oxford University Press, 1971), 63.

2.   D.L. Byman, *Keeping the Peace: Lasting Solutions to Ethnic Conflicts* (Baltimore: Johns Hopkins University Press, 2002).

3.  See, e.g., F. Kitson, *Low Intensity Operations* (London: Faber, 1971); R.L. Clutter-buck, *Protest and the Urban Guerrilla* (New York: Abelard-Schuman, 1973).

4.  See, e.g., T.R. Gurr, *Why Men Rebel* (Princeton, NJ: Princeton University Press, 1970), 256.

5.  D.A. Hibbs, *Mass Political Violence* (New York: Wiley, 1973), 185.

6.  T.R. Gurr, "The Genesis of Violence," doctoral dissertation, Department of Politics, New York University, 1965, table 17.

7.  Byman, *Keeping the Peace*, 45.

8.  C. Tilly, "Revolutions and Collective Violence," in F. Greenstein and N. Polsby, eds., *Handbook of Political Science*, vol. 3 (Reading, MA: Addison-Wesley, 1975).

9.  H. Eckstein, "On the Causes of Internal Wars," in E.A. Nordlinger, ed., *Politics and Society* (Englewood Cliffs, NJ: Prentice Hall, 1970), 302.

10. Tilly, "Revolutions," 515.

11. C. Townshend, *Political Violence in Ireland* (Oxford: Clarendon Press, 1983), 409.

12. E. Moxon-Browne, "Terrorism and Northern Ireland: The Case of the Provisional IRA," in J. Lodge, ed., *Terrorism: A Challenge to the State* (London: Martin Robertson, 1981).

13. Byman, *Keeping the Peace*.

14. I. Lustick, "Stability in Deeply Divided Societies: Consociationalism versus Control," *World Politics*, vol. 31, no. 3 (April 1979), 325–44.

15. Byman, *Keeping the Peace*, 80.

16. Gurr, *Why Men Rebel*, 352.

17. The de Tocqueville quote is follows: "Experience teaches us that, generally speaking, the most perilous moment for a bad government is one when it seeks to mend its ways." In the context of the quote, *bad* is shorthand for oppressive. See A. de Tocqueville, *Alexis de Tocqueville on Democracy, Revolution, and Society*, ed. John Stone and Stephen Mennell (Chicago: University of Chicago, 1980), 230.

18. R. Jervis, *Perception and Misperception in International Politics* (Princeton, NJ: Princeton University Press, 1976).

19. Byman, *Keeping the Peace*, 99.

20. A. Lijphart, "Consociational Democracy," *World Politics*, vol. 21, no. 2 (1969), 207–25.

21. E.A. Nordlinger, *Conflict Regulation in Divided Societies* (Cambridge, MA: Harvard University Press, 1972), 11.

22. Gurr, *Why Men Rebel*.

23. J.D. Coyle, *Minorities in Revolt* (East Brunswick, NJ: Associated University Press, 1983); C. Townshend, *The British Campaign in Ireland* (Oxford: Oxford University Press, 1975).

24. For examples see Hibbs, *Mass Political Violence*, and Tilly, "Revolutions."

25. H.A. Simon, *Models of Thought* (New Haven, CT: Yale University Press, 1979).

26. G.T. Allison, *Essence of Decision* (Boston: Little, Brown, 1971), 33.

27. A.L. George, *Presidential Decision-Making in Foreign Policy* (Boulder, CO: Westview Press, 1980).

28. J.D. Steinbruner, *The Cybernetic Theory of Decision: New Dimensions of Political Analysis* (Princeton, NJ: Princeton University Press, 2002).

29. George, *Presidential Decision-Making*. See also Jervis, *Perception and Misperception*, and R. Nisbett and L. Ross, *Human Inference: Strategies and Shortcomings of Social Judgment* (Upper Saddle River, NJ: Prentice-Hall, 1980).

30.    H.A. Simon, "Human Nature in Politics: The Dialogue of Psychology with Political Science," *American Political Science Review,* vol. 79, no. 2 (June 1985), 294.

31.    For a persuasive illustration of the effects of bureaucratic politics, see Allison, *Essence of Decision.*

32.    J.G. March and H.A. Simon, *Organizations* (New York: John Wiley and Sons, 1958).

33.    R.M. Cyert and J.G. March, *A Behavioral Theory of the Firm* (Englewood Cliffs, NJ: Prentice-Hall, 1963). See also Steinbruner, *Cybernetic Theory.*

34.    Allison, *Essence of Decision,* 88.

35.    Simon, *Models of Thought.*

36.    Cyert and March, *Behavioral Theory.*

37.    March and Simon, *Organizations.*

38.    M.H. Halperin, *Bureaucratic Politics and Foreign Policy* (Washington, DC: Brookings Institution Press, 1974), 28.

39.    A. Downs, *Inside Bureaucracy* (Boston: Little, Brown, 1967).

40.    L.S. Etheredge, "Government Learning," in S. Long, ed., *Handbook of Political Behavior* (New York: Plenum Press, 1981).

41.    Steinbruner, *Cybernetic Theory.*

42.    T.S. Kuhn, *The Structure of Scientific Revolutions,* 3rd ed. (Chicago: University of Chicago Press, 1996).

43.    Nisbett and Ross, *Human Inference,* 192.

44.    Jervis, *Perception and Misperception.*

45.    All three types of distortion are illustrated in E.R. May, *Lessons of the Past: The Uses and Misuses of History in American Foreign Policy* (New York: Oxford University Press, 1972).

46.    Etheredge, "Government Learning."

47.    H. Wilensky, *Organizational Intelligence* (New York: Basic Books, 1967).

48.    J.G. March, "Footnotes to Organizational Change," unpublished manuscript, Stanford Gradute School of Business, 1980.

49.    A. Lijphart, "Comparative Politics and the Comparative Method," *American Political Science Review,* vol. 65, no. 3 (September 1971), 688.

50.    A.L. George, "Case Studies and Theory Development: The Method of Structured, Focussed Comparison," manuscript, Department of Political Science, Stanford University, 1979.

# 2

# Preconditions for the Conflict, 1968

*The Irish propensity for violence is well known; at least to the English. And it was of course the English who conceived of the "Irish problem."*
                                                    —Charles Townshend[1]

Numerous studies on the conflict in Northern Ireland treat it as an example of a wider class of disputes, whether ethnic, religious, national, or colonial.[2] To understand British policies and their sources we must first appreciate the complex nature of the conflict and the preconditions for the violence. These preconditions should be distinguished both from the discrete events that triggered specific acts of violence and from paramilitary organizations' deliberate policy of using provocation, disorder, and terror to advance their political objectives. This involves examining the fundamental societal divisions in Northern Ireland that existed in 1968 and identifying a number of structural factors that defined the two sides and intensified the political salience of their differences.

## A Deeply Divided Society

Divisions between distinctive cultural communities within a given polity are a substantial and recurring precondition for political violence and disorder.[3] Societies differentiated by fundamental allegiances—to race, nation, language, or religion—are more likely to suffer conflict than societies in which the primary sources of political differentiation are class, wealth, or status.[4] The risk is further increased when each cultural community has its own network of social organizations, including schools, media, and political parties.

The population of Northern Ireland was in 1968 (and still is today) divided by fundamental allegiances. Lijphart has described it as the most unambiguous example of a deeply divided society in the Western world,[5] arguing that, broadly and with some exceptions, it comprised two culturally differentiated population segments with competing national allegiances. Ulster Unionists insisted that Northern Ireland must remain part of the United Kingdom, Irish nationalists that it must become part of an all-Ireland independent nation-state. Each group had its own political aspirations, social institutions, and historical narratives, a measure of internal solidarity predicated upon opposition to the other, and means of replicating itself through coming generations. Religious affiliation, as Protestant or Catholic, was the primary indicator of community allegiance.

Not everyone accepts Lijphart's analysis, and it requires qualifications. A small proportion of the population in 1968 described itself as not belonging to either of the two main blocs, and there were significant internal differences within the two segments and cross-cutting commonalities between them. Nevertheless, most nonpartisan analysts agree on three main points. First, there was a deep, politically salient division in Northern Ireland between a Protestant population group, which almost entirely considered itself British or Northern Irish, and a Catholic population group, which predominantly (although not so completely) considered itself Irish. Second, since 1920 Northern Ireland's political institutions and party system had entrenched that division and created obstacles to reconciliation. Third, since Northern Ireland's creation there had existed a propensity for conflict between the most aggressive elements in the two communities, and between both of them and the British state.

At the start of what is euphemistically called the Troubles in 1968, Protestants composed 58 percent of a population of just over 1.5 million, Catholics 41 percent.[6] The religious cleavage coincided closely with differences in national allegiance, voting choices, and positions on salient political issues.[7] With few exceptions, Protestants were Unionists; that is, they wanted to retain the union between Northern Ireland and Britain, comprising England, Scotland, and Wales and collectively known as the United Kingdom. A large majority of Catholics were Irish nationalists; that is, they wanted to separate Northern Ireland from Britain and integrate it instead with the Republic of Ireland, the independent state lying to the south and west that originated in a secession from the United Kingdom in 1921.

The Protestant majority had been sufficiently dominant in Northern Ireland since the territory's creation in 1920 to determine which party would govern it. No legal barrier prevented Nationalist elected representatives from holding office, but Nationalists could never in practice form a government as long as the two traditions voted overwhelmingly in line with their national allegiances. This reality was complicated by additional factors. There were politically salient divisions within each tradition based on social class, geography, attitudes toward violence, and socioeconomic issues. A significant minority of Catholics were Unionists in the technical sense that they preferred to be governed as part of the United Kingdom. A number of small political parties gave priority to social and economic issues. Finally, in Ireland as a whole, Catholics outnumbered Protestants by more than three to one. Thus both groups asserted the rights associated with majority status while fearing the discrimination suffered by minorities.[8]

## Historical Background

Townshend has pointed out that resistance to the imposition of British systems of law and order has been intrinsic to Irish politics since the seventeenth century, and that it has not been merely negative but also the assertion and maintenance of an alternative and prior system of social control.[9] The preconditions for today's conflict include its long history, which has helped shape today's allegiances and their meanings for the protagonists. I do not intend to rehearse that history here but will briefly summarize it for those who are not already familiar with it.[10]

### The Plantation

In the political evolution of Britain and Ireland after 1600, as elsewhere in Europe and North America, there occurred intense and prolonged conflict between Protestant and Catholic elites. When the Protestant English defeated the last of the Catholic Irish chieftains in the early 1600s, the northern province of Ulster was the last center of Irish resistance. To prevent further insurrection, the Crown created plantations for Protestant settlers from England and Scotland, who moved onto confiscated land in and around a series of fortified towns. By 1703, Protestants owned over 95 percent of eight of the nine counties of Ulster.[11]

The settlers introduced their own language, values, and practices to the area, including legal and economic customs that radically changed the nature of agriculture and business where they lived. The authorities discouraged them from becoming assimilated, and they maintained close links with their home communities in Scotland and England. Clayton has identified three main characteristics common to the political culture of settler societies that she ascribes to the Protestant tradition in Northern

Ireland: an ideology that devalued the culture of the established inhabitants and justified coercive measures to suppress their protests, solidarity across the settler social classes, and a commitment to a more democratic and egalitarian society than existed in the originating political culture, but excluding the established Irish people, who were seen as a threat.[12]

In 1690, the Protestant Prince William of Orange defeated the Catholic King James II at the battle of the Boyne, near Dublin, so consolidating Protestant supremacy in Britain and Ireland. The deep resentment of the native Irish toward the settlers and the siege mentality of the latter have both been renewed through recurrent periods of conflict since then, persisting as preconditions for further strife.[13] The Protestant parliament passed strict laws to suppress the Irish language and cultural traditions. These cemented the Catholic population and its church in a defiant alliance against the Protestants' attempts to impose their authority.

Economic developments during the nineteenth century reinforced the distinction between the predominantly Protestant northeast and the rest of Ireland. The distinctive geographical characteristics and form of land tenure practiced in the northeast promoted industrialization. The port of Belfast became Ireland's first industrial city, and by 1880 it was an integral part of the trading economy of the British Empire. Meanwhile the rest of Ireland, predominantly rural, declined demographically and economically.[14] Belfast's industrial and commercial growth attracted rural Catholics in search of work. Its population grew from 19,000 in 1801 to 349,000 in 1901. Protestants reacted with hostility to the influx.[15] The first urban riots occurred in the city in July 1835, initiating a pattern of street violence that has persisted into the 2000s.[16]

### Home Rule

The Catholic Irish gradually acquired rights of political expression from the UK parliament after 1830. In 1867, franchise reform paved the way for the growth of the Irish Nationalist Party, which in 1885 won eighty-five of the hundred Irish seats at Westminster. This gave it the balance of power between the Liberals and the Conservatives. In 1886, it persuaded Gladstone's Liberal government to introduce a home rule bill, which would have devolved responsibility for Ireland's internal affairs to a new Irish parliament in Dublin. As a result of opposition to the bill from within its own ranks, Gladstone's government fell and the bill failed.

The demand for home rule did not diminish. A nationalist movement emerged across the island, working to rebuild and promote a distinctive Irish culture in language, literature, the arts, and sports. In 1910, the Irish Nationalist Party again held the balance of power at Westminster. The Liberal government introduced a further home rule bill and, after some delay due to opposition from Conservatives in the House of Lords, completed its passage in January 1913. Protestants throughout Ireland had opposed home rule, believing that the proposed Irish parliament would advance Catholic interests at their expense. In March 1905, following an initiative from some Ulster members of parliament (MPs)—both Conservatives and Liberals—the Ulster Unionist Council (UUC) was created in Belfast to coordinate the resistance in the northeast. Half its planned membership of 200 was to be drawn from local constituency associations and a further 50 from the exclusively Protestant Orange Order, an institution originally established in 1795 to protect the interests of Protestant weavers and farmers against the threat of Catholic competition.

In September 1912 the UUC produced a Solemn League and Covenant, which was signed by 471,414 people. They committed themselves to "using all means necessary to defeat the present conspiracy to set up a Home Rule Parliament in Ireland."[17] Although this was tantamount to a threat of violent rebellion, the Conservative opposition at Westminster supported the UUC, which then created a provisional government to assume control of as large an area as practicable if and when the bill was enacted. To enforce its will, the UUC also created the Ulster Volunteer Force (UVF), a paramilitary organization. As the bill wound its way through Parliament, it became clear that the UVF had the weaponry, capacity, and popular support to render home rule from Dublin unworkable in most of Ulster. In March 1914 a group of officers in the British army and navy made known that they would not comply with any instruction to attack the Unionists. The ministers of the Liberal government then turned their minds to the possibility of permitting the Unionists to opt out of home rule. Their parliamentary allies in the Nationalist Party strongly objected. The impasse remained unresolved when war in Europe intervened.

### The 1916 Rising

Many Irish people joined the British army to fight in World War I, but militant republicans saw Britain's difficulty as Ireland's opportunity. In April 1916, a small group of rebels occupied the main post office and other public buildings in Dublin and proclaimed an independent republic. At first the uprising, later celebrated by republicans as the Easter Rising, had limited popular support. Then, fearing a large-scale rebellion planned in collaboration with the Germans, the British authorities in Ireland applied brute force: 3,400 suspects were arrested and 15 prominent rebels summarily executed.

The coercive response alienated public opinion in Ireland. People were already concerned at the prospect of military conscription. The planned introduction of home rule had undermined Britain's authority. In 1917 the political party Sinn Féin, founded in 1905, committed itself to the rebel cause. The stirring rhetoric of republicanism generated popular support for full national independence, and the incremental moderation of the Nationalist Party was swept aside. In the Westminster election of December 1918, Sinn Féin won seventy-three seats to the Nationalists' six. The successful Sinn Féin candidates boycotted Westminster, meeting instead as the Dáil (Irish parliament) in Dublin. In January 1919 they declared independence and proclaimed themselves to be the legitimate government of the new Irish Republic.

### Partition

On the military front, the Irish Republican Army (IRA) emerged to enforce the declaration of independence. The IRA focused on undermining the legitimacy of the British administration and destroying its police service, the Royal Irish Constabulary (RIC). Mindful of the outcome of the 1916 uprising, IRA tacticians, in particular Michael Collins, determined to destroy Britain's intelligence network and to provoke further acts of state repression.

In many parts of the country, the RIC disintegrated in response to the assassination of individual officers, attacks against isolated police stations, and an orchestrated campaign to ostracize policemen.[18] The British military authorities obligingly played the part Collins had scripted for them. Their methods for dealing with the disorder included reprisals directed at the wider population, mass house searches, curfews, revenge killings, and the destruction of civilian property. As the RIC collapsed, they increasingly depended on irregular soldiers from Britain, the so-called Black and Tans, who lacked appropriate equipment and police training.

Faced with Sinn Féin's unilateral declaration of independence and Unionist resistance to home rule, both backed by the credible threat of force, Westminster passed the Government of Ireland Act in March 1920. This provided for two devolved parliaments in Ireland, one in Dublin for the twenty-six counties with clear Nationalist majorities and one in Belfast for the remaining six. The jurisdiction of the new parliament in Belfast was provisionally defined to encompass four counties in which there was a clear Unionist majority and two in which there was a slight Catholic majority. Unionists argued that these two must be included for the new state to be viable.

The 1920 act also provided for an all-Ireland council as a vehicle for cooperation between the two new jurisdictions, which, the British hoped, would enable them gradually to move toward unification by consent. Unionists rejected the council but accepted the other parts of the act as "a final settlement and supreme sacrifice in the interests of peace."[19] The king opened the first session of the Belfast parliament in June 1920. Forty Unionist members took their seats; all six Nationalists and six Sinn Féiners boycotted it. The parliament moved to purpose-built premises on the outskirts of Belfast in 1932, from which it took its present colloquial name of Stormont.

Westminster delegated legislative and executive responsibility for most internal matters to Belfast, though it retained responsibility for taxation, defense, and foreign policy, including relations with the rest of Ireland, and controlled over 80 percent of the devolved administration's revenue.[20] Westminster also reserved the powers to legislate itself on any devolved matters and to suspend the devolved administration. Stormont was expressly forbidden to make any laws that would interfere with religious equality.[21]

In Dublin, the Dáil rejected Britain's offer of partition and demanded full sovereign independence. Fighting between the IRA and British forces continued until July 1921, when both sides concluded that they could not achieve military victory at an acceptable price and commenced negotiations. The Anglo-Irish Treaty of December 1921 canceled the 1920 act in relation to the south and gave the Dáil considerably more autonomy than the new administration in Belfast. The Dáil acquired full responsibility for internal and external affairs and taxation in the twenty-six counties and took the name of the Irish Free State.

The 1921 treaty provided for a boundary commission to review the location of the north-south border so that as many people as possible could live in the state of their choice. Nationalist supporters of the treaty argued, and many Unionists believed, that the commission would award Dublin so much territory that Northern Ireland would become unworkable. Two of the six counties had Catholic majorities of 56 percent.[22] Unionist leaders announced that they would not yield an inch of territory, whatever the commission recommended. In the event, it never formally reported. In December 1925, Dublin and London amended the treaty so that the border would remain as it had been set, and the council was abandoned.

The defiant stands and bloody events of 1912 to 1925 put their marks on both new jurisdictions and their political systems. Many on both sides concluded that, in dealings with Britain, violence and the threat of violence paid off. Leaders and advocates of armed resistance became heads of government, paramilitary networks became official state security forces, and the political division initiated by the dispute over home rule became reified in two sets of governmental institutions in Dublin and Belfast. In the north, this political architecture meant in effect that an apparently unassailable Unionist majority would dominate a dissatisfied Nationalist minority with no effective outlet for its aspirations and grievances.

The authors of the partition settlement did not intend it to be permanent. Britain's primary objective was to disengage from a costly conflict that it could not win. But the creation of a perpetual Unionist government in Northern Ireland in practice blocked progress toward the solution that both the Liberal government and the new Free State government wanted: independence for the entire island as a single state. Partition gave Unionist leaders no incentive to cooperate in any process leading to unification and many reasons not to.

After partition, the republican leadership in the south divided into pro- and antitreaty factions. The latter fought a bitter civil war against their old colleagues in the state forces, which killed many more Irish people than the Anglo-Irish War had. It ended with the surrender of the antitreaty faction in May 1923. The two sides evolved into the two main political parties of today's Republic of Ireland: Fine Gael (pro-treaty) and Fianna Fáil (antitreaty).

In the north, the IRA continued to attack the forces of the new Northern Ireland regime, formed out of the RIC's northeastern units, and there was intense intercommunal violence. Collins approved a series of raids across the border that led to the kidnapping of forty-two prominent Unionists.[23] Unable to rely on Britain to ensure the security of the new state, the Unionist government incorporated a substantial element from the UVF into its new police service, the Royal Ulster Constabulary. From June 1920 to 1922, 428 people were killed and 1,766 wounded in civil disturbances. Even after the cessation of significant IRA activity, some senior figures in the Unionist Party continued to view all Catholics as potential rebels.[24]

Northern Ireland from 1925 to 1968 broadly fitted Lustick's control model as outlined in chapter 1. The minority was excluded from power and politically passive at the regional level. While the Unionists had equipped themselves with the legal powers required to deal with any anticipated challenge to their authority, they did not need to resort to extravagant displays of force or use the full range of powers at their disposal to retain their dominant position.

History has bequeathed three sociocultural divisions to the people of Northern Ireland: religion (Catholic versus Protestant), ethnicity (Irish versus British), and status (native versus settler). At least as important as any actual events are the narratives that both sides have woven around them. For Nationalists, the Easter Rising is the subject of annual commemorations, including events promoted by the Irish state. Many Unionists parade every July to commemorate the battle of the Boyne as the seminal event that paved the way for parliamentary democracy in Britain and confirmed the primacy of Protestantism. Both anniversaries even now retain the power to generate violence on the streets.

## Political Ideologies

Dixon has described how Northern Ireland's politicians exploit ideology in pursuit of popular support.[25] The battle over home rule established the ideologies that dominate political discourse in Northern Ireland to this day: Irish nationalism; the reaction to it, which is Ulster unionism; and their more militant cousins, Irish republicanism and Ulster loyalism.[26]

### Irish Nationalism

The traditional Irish nationalist view is that the people of Ireland form one nation, which has the right to self-determination. Nationalists aspire to incorporate Northern Ireland into the Irish state. They assume that unity is historically inevitable and blame Britain for keeping the nation divided. They depict partition as the cause of the conflict, an artificial settlement imposed by Britain to keep as much control over Ireland as possible. British oppression is a recurring theme in the nationalist narrative.[27]

Within the nationalist tradition, Irish republicanism traces its distinctive ideological history to the rebellion of the United Irishmen in 1789 and so claims a nonsectarian ancestry, although in practice it attracts almost no electoral support from Protestants. Gerry Adams, a leading proponent of the republican position, has argued that unionists do not have the same right as nationalists to self-determination since they are no more than a disaffected minority within the Irish nation.[28]

The most obvious difference between nationalism and republicanism for the purpose of this book is that republicans have been more willing to endorse violence as a means to achieve unification, more hostile to the pursuit of compromise within the established constitutional framework, and less inclined to recognize the legitimacy of the existing state in the Republic.

### Ulster Unionism

Unionism originally emerged during the home rule crisis of the 1880s as a reaction against nationalism and has ever since tended to define itself in terms of what it opposes. Originally Unionists resisted any form of separation from Britain for any part of Ireland. Since partition, they have accepted the secession of the southern state, but reject Nationalists' demands to extend its jurisdiction over the entire island. Many Unionists argue that there are two distinct communities in Ireland, British Protestant Unionists and Irish Catholic Nationalists; the conflict arises because nationalists refuse to recognize this right and would end if they genuinely accepted it.

Unionists have especially resented three elements in the Irish constitution of 1937: the territorial claim to Northern Ireland, the privileged position of the Catholic Church, and the adoption of Irish as the Republic's primary official language. Unionists maintain that both traditions in Northern Ireland benefit economically from the union, that they have a fundamental right to their British identity, and that the Irish state with its Catholic ethos has failed to protect the culture and rights of its Protestant citizens. Rose identifies a subset of unionists as loyalists, who are prepared to use force to defend the union.[29]

Bruce argues that the idealized Britain of conventional unionist thinking ceased to exist decades ago. Contemporary England offends many Protestants' religious and moral sensibilities, as they share the conservative views of their Catholic neighbors on, for example, legalizing abortion.[30] Bruce also distinguishes between the two traditions' relationships with the nations to which they consider themselves to belong. While nationalists depict themselves as part of the Irish nation, illegitimately sundered, unionists see themselves as a regional minority within the United Kingdom, a besieged group to which the majority in Britain are either indifferent or hostile. Thus the conflict is not between two national or ethnic groups of equal standing but between one group that considers itself part of a nation dismembered and another that sees itself as perched on the margin of a nation that accepts its membership in that nation only with reluctance.

### Parallels

Nationalism, unionism, republicanism, and loyalism have mirrored and sustained one another. They contain common values and expectations that have been especially tenacious because they have been mutually reinforcing. Both nationalism and unionism aspire to a model of democratic governance that emphasizes the rights of the majority rather than protecting the rights of the minority.[31] Both see politics as a zero-sum game, incorporate historical narratives that legitimize violence as a necessary means to protect fundamental political objectives, are suspicious of compromise, depict their own side as victimized by the other side, and idolize martyrs who gave up their lives rather than surrender cherished values. Each is predisposed to seeing the other in black-and-white terms and inclined to view those who do not fit into the prevailing duality, such as antisectarian socialists, as mutations of their traditional opponents, pursuing hostile goals by stealth.[32]

## Popular Political Attitudes

### National Identity

An extensive survey of popular political attitudes in 1968, just before the Troubles began, showed an unusually high level of congruence between religious affiliation and national allegiance, as the division between unionism and nationalism closely paralleled that between Protestants and Catholics.[33] When Protestants and Catholics were asked whether they usually thought of themselves as British, Irish, Ulster, or other, 71 percent of Protestants identified with Britain or Ulster while 76 percent of Catholics identified with Ireland, though not necessarily with the southern state. However, on the Catholic side, a significant minority was less concerned about the national question than about the need to improve the position of its own community within the union. Another survey, conducted in 1967, found that around 63 percent of nationalist voters supported a British connection of some sort and only 38 percent favored a fully independent all-Ireland republic.[34] Also, on the Protestant side, there was a significant division between those whose primary allegiance was to a Protestant Ulster and those who identified with a pluralist United Kingdom. The first group tended toward loyalist views and the values of evangelical Protestantism. The second cherished British ideals, perceived as liberal and democratic, and associated the first group with sectarianism and aggression.[35]

### The Border

The same 1968 survey as above found that 56 percent of Catholic respondents and 23 percent of Protestants would like to have seen the border abolished, while 45 percent of Protestants and 21 percent of Catholics wanted no change. Catholics' preference for a united Ireland apparently drew strength from their anger at discrimination: 74 percent agreed with the proposition that "in parts of Northern Ireland Catholics are treated unfairly," while 45 percent said they would approve if Nationalist Party leaders talked less about the border issue. Subsequent survey evidence consistently suggests that the Protestant community feels more strongly about the border than Catholics, revealing, on one hand, intense Protestant hostility toward any form of united Ireland, and on the other, only diffuse support among Catholics for a united Ireland even in the long term.[36]

### Violence

The 1968 survey also found that 52 percent of Protestants were "prepared to resort to any measures necessary" to keep Northern Ireland "a Protestant country," while 82 percent thought it had been right fifty years earlier to prepare to fight to keep Northern Ireland British. This was despite the obvious dissonance between support for subversion and the values of loyalty and respect for the law that unionist ideology asserts.[37] On the Catholic side, 83 percent disagreed with the proposition that it would be right to take any measures necessary to end partition and bring Ulster into the Irish republic, but 60 percent thought it had been right fifty years earlier for people in the south to fight for independence.

Each side was more willing to condemn the violence of the other than its own. There was sufficient ambivalence, particularly in the endorsement of historical violence, to allow openings for a new generation of republican rebels and their loyalist opponents to attract broad popular support. Participant observation studies undertaken in republican and loyalist districts illustrate this ambivalence. One implication for the leaders of a paramilitary organization is that they should use traditional religious and political narratives to legitimize their violent actions.[38] As Whyte concludes, "there are variations in the strength of feeling in both communities. While the moderates in both might be induced to compromise, the intransigent elements are sufficiently strong to make compromise difficult."[39]

## Political Organizations

Support for political parties in Northern Ireland broadly follows the cleavages in national allegiance, religious affiliation, and political ideology described above. So tight is the link between voting and religion that basic voting decisions may best be viewed as expressions of allegiance to a tradition rather than choices between competing candidates or policy packages.[40] For most of the electorate, identity has already determined whether they will vote Nationalist or Unionist. The conscious choice regards which candidate to vote for within each of those community designations.

The match between religion and party has been most marked on the Protestant side. In 1968, over 99 percent of Protestants who specified a party identified with a unionist party, and 86 percent with the Unionist Party.[41] Less than 1 percent said they supported Nationalist parties.[42] On the Catholic side, 58 percent supported a Nationalist candidate. The lower Catholic figure reflects the disorganization of the Nationalist Party at the time and that Nationalist candidates were not available in every constituency; in their absence, many Catholics voted for the Northern Ireland Labour Party (NILP), which supported the union but drew supporters from both traditions.

The two major parties were exclusive on religious grounds: 95 percent of Unionist Party supporters were Protestants and 99 percent of Nationalist Party supporters were Catholics. The internal unity of each depended on the existence of the threat posed by the other.[43]

### The Unionist Party

The Ulster Unionist Party dominated politics in Northern Ireland from 1920 until the mid-1970s, always winning a comfortable majority of votes and seats in elections both to the devolved parliament and to Westminster. It formed every government of Northern Ireland from 1920 until 1972. It was closely associated with the Orange Order, an exclusively Protestant cultural organization that provided Unionist Party leaders with a convenient vehicle to mobilize grassroots support. The order's core purpose was to oppose Catholicism, and within the party there was considerable resistance to the idea that Catholics should be encouraged to join at all, though the party's local constituency associations could decide for themselves whether or not to admit them.[44] The party had never nominated a Catholic candidate for election to Stormont.[45]

### Nationalists

On the Nationalist side, by 1968, forty-seven years of impotence had left what remained of the old Irish Nationalist Party in Northern Ireland disorganized and demoralized. Rose has described it as "a loose alliance of local notables" rather than a coherent political party.[46] These men had little incentive toward purposeful political activity since they had no prospect of extracting significant concessions from the Unionist monolith and no possibility of forming a government. Nationalists did, however, have some electoral representation at the local government level. Seven of the twenty-four urban district councils and four of the twenty-seven rural district councils were in Nationalist hands.

### Cross-Community Parties

Parties that tried to attract support from both communities enjoyed little electoral success. Before 1969, the largest of these was the NILP, with which 11 percent of Protestants and 27 percent of Catholics identified, and which the British Labour Party loosely supported.[47] Its best electoral performance came in 1958, when it won four of the fifty-two seats in the Northern Ireland parliament. The Unionist Party reacted by showing a renewed interest in the well-being of the Protestant working class, and after 1964 the NILP never presented a serious threat to the Unionists' hegemony.

### Paramilitary Organizations

The boundaries between mainstream political parties and paramilitary organizations have always tended to be porous in Northern Ireland, especially in times of crisis. The Unionist Party and the UVF were closely linked in the 1910s, with overlapping leaderships. Leaders of the Nationalist Party included former IRA men who had fought against Britain in the Anglo-Irish War.

Small loyalist groups were already in place and committing sectarian crimes in the few years immediately before the Troubles began. In 1966, a small group of loyalists assumed the name of the UVF—though any historical connections were tenuous at best—and conducted a series of violent attacks against Catholics in west Belfast. The Unionist government responded by outlawing membership in the organization.

On the republican side, the IRA had from 1956 to 1962 conducted sporadic attacks from bases in the south against customs installations and police stations in Northern Ireland. In 1966, on the eve of the anniversary of the Easter Rising, the IRA's ruling Army Council initiated planning for a new campaign that would combine acts of violence with political agitation. At the time, the IRA had around 1,000 members.[48] Although its leadership was predominantly southern, its weapons were few and obsolete, and its popular support was slight, the Stormont government took the threat seriously, mindful of the salience of the republican threat for its supporters.

## Organized Religion

There is not space here to examine all the organizations that contributed to the deep divisions in Northern Ireland's society in 1968. In addition to political parties, they included schools, newspapers, community cultural and social networks, labor and business federations, and sporting organizations. But the churches had a special significance. Although declining, church attendance was high relative to other regions of northern Europe.[49] Hickey has attributed this at least partially to the need to affirm group solidarity in a divided society.[50] Religious institutions, especially endogamous marriage and denominational education, have provided two of the strongest mechanisms that validate and sustain ethnonational differentiation.[51]

In 1968, both communities showed a high level of endorsement of fundamentalist religious values: 72 percent of Protestants and 77 percent of Catholics agreed with the proposition that miracles had happened just as described in the Bible.[52] Although the conflict is about national identity and political power rather than theological doctrine, religion is more than just a convenient label for two population segments with incompatible interests. There is a symbiotic relationship between political and religious institutions.[53] The terms *Catholic* and *Protestant* do not mean the same in Northern Ireland as elsewhere. They signify unique belief systems that each combine distinctive ideas about religion, politics, and community allegiance.[54] Thanks to largely segregated education systems, these belief systems are handed down with their religious labels from generation to generation.

## The Churches in Politics

The Catholic Church was the largest denomination in Northern Ireland, commanding the adherence of some 41 percent of the population. It was organized on an all-Ireland basis and had traditionally opposed British rule. During the home rule period, Catholic priests had actively campaigned on behalf of the Nationalist Party. The Church had condemned the leftist violence of the Easter Rising but supported the Irish side in the Anglo-Irish War. Since 1937 the constitution of Ireland had formally recognized it as "the guardian of the Faith professed by the great majority of the citizens," and as such it had a privileged position in the formulation of Irish social policies.[55] It was also important in providing education, health, and social services in the Republic as well as education in Northern Ireland.

Spokesmen for the Catholic Church made no secret of their support for a united Ireland. A survey conducted in 1968 in the border area found that all the priests interviewed opposed partition and considered themselves Irish rather than British. Many had been active in selecting and campaigning for Nationalist Party candidates.[56] While the Church condemned violence in principle, influential bishops and priests frequently argued that republican violence was a justifiable response to state repression and discrimination.

In contrast, the Protestant churches were highly fragmented. The 1961 census recognized fifty-five different denominations. The two largest were Presbyterians, accounting for some 47 percent of the Protestant population, and the Church of Ireland, accounting for 38 percent.[57] Both continued to be organized on an all-island basis as before partition, but their northern representatives strongly supported the Unionist administration at Stormont. Both condemned political violence, in particular when its source was republican.

Neither Protestant church has had an officially privileged status anywhere in Ireland since the disestablishment of the Church of Ireland in 1869. But Protestant clergy in the north enjoyed disproportionate political influence under the Stormont administration. They exercised a conservative influence over education and social policies comparable with that of the Catholic Church in the Republic. Partly as a consequence, Northern Ireland did not replicate legislation introduced to make divorce and abortion easier in England and Wales during the 1960s. Protestant clergy occupied senior positions in the Unionist Party and were well represented as members of parliament both at Stormont and at Westminster.

Protestant clergymen also exerted political influence through the Orange Order, which was important in creating and maintaining the Unionist Party. The order was formally entitled to 122 seats out of 760 on the Ulster Unionist Council, the party's governing body. Hunter has described it as "the cement in the Protestant political power structure and until recently the ladder to political success."[58] Rose estimated that in 1968, 32 percent of Protestant men were members.[59] Although it provided cohesion for unionism in times of crisis, it also contributed to schisms. Moderate Unionists tended to see it as intolerant and reactionary, and it drew support disproportionately from the lower socioeconomic classes.[60] To many Protestants the order's annual parades were harmless celebrations of their cultural heritage, but to many Catholics they were threatening displays of territorial domination that refreshed yearly the injustices of the past.

Although less than 1 percent of Protestants were members, the Free Presbyterian Church deserves special mention. Ian Paisley established it during the 1950s as a vehicle for opposition to the ecumenical movement in Protestantism. Building on a foundation of biblical fundamentalism, Paisley went on to construct a much larger political movement, which from 1964 forcefully challenged the Unionist Party's dominance within the Unionist community.[61]

### The Churches in Education

The main churches play a major part in the governance of education in Northern Ireland. In the 1920s, Protestant and Catholic clergy joined forces to defeat an effort by the Unionist minister for education to introduce a system of secular state schools.[62] By 1968 the Protestant churches no longer ran their own schools, though they had a right of representation on the governing bodies of state schools. The Catholic Church continued to run its own system of maintained schools with a distinctive Catholic ethos, funded predominantly by the state. Ninety-eight percent of children attended schools predominantly serving children from only one tradition; the exceptions were in sparsely populated rural districts served by a single school.

The curricula and ethos of state and Catholic schools differed dramatically. State schools promoted a British identity, taught British history, and introduced children to the same sports as their counterparts in Britain: rugby, football, cricket, and hockey. Catholic schools taught specifically Catholic religious values, including preparation for first communion; promoted an Irish identity; taught Irish history, including the narrative of

British oppression; and played Irish games, such as hurling and Gaelic football. Segregated education meant (and still means) that most children grew up with only limited experience of their peers across the communal frontier. As Hunter has observed, "In these circumstances it is hardly surprising that myths and prejudices flourish and the miasma of superstition and mistrust grows, unchecked by any knowledge of or contact with the other community."[63]

### Religious Beliefs and Political Ideas

The churches in Northern Ireland have preserved and promoted symbols and values that link political ideology with religious belief, underpinning the secular conflict with the intensity of devotional commitment. Ecclesiastical teachings and political messages are intertwined. One commentator has noted that the churches are important to "encouraging, exalting, and extending the kind of tribal-sectarian self-righteousness which forms a culture in which violence so easily multiplies."[64] A particularly striking illustration of this is in the work of Patrick Pearse, one of the instigators of the Easter Rising, who fantasized about redemption through gory sacrifice: "As the blood of the martyrs was the seed of saints," he wrote, "so the blood of the patriot will be the sacred seed from which alone can spring new forces and fresh life into a nation that is drifting into the putrescence of decay."[65]

Bowden writes of "the union of the rosary and the gun" that emerged during the Irish cultural revival from 1880 to 1914, a resurgence of national self-esteem that underpinned popular support for the republican cause.[66] This political renaissance was linked to a religious revival. The pious and nationalistic education offered to young men, by the Christian Brothers in particular, contributed substantially to reshaping republicanism as a popular ideology. Similarly, Bruce finds that while the Protestant churches reject violence in principle, evangelical Protestantism has been important in creating some Unionists' ethnic identities. Bruce also usefully reminds us that anti-Catholicism was not invented in Northern Ireland. Britain remained deliberately and self-consciously anti-Catholic well into the nineteenth century. Until the Catholic Emancipation Act of 1829, Catholics in Britain were excluded from most parts of civil society, and even after the act, Catholics continued to be excluded from many high offices, including the monarchy, simply by virtue of their religion. The justification for this was essentially that, because they professed a higher allegiance to Rome, Catholics could not be trusted to be loyal to a Protestant monarch.[67]

Finally, Russell has found a significant correlation between the strength of religious feeling in schoolchildren and their readiness to endorse the use of violence for political purposes. Strongly religious Protestant children were 20 percent more likely to endorse violence than their less religious counterparts; on the Catholic side, the corresponding difference was 30 percent.[68]

### Mutual Mistrust

Many Protestants saw the Catholic Church as authoritarian and oppressive, stifling debate and imposing hierarchical authority on its adherents. They resented the *ne temere* doctrine, requiring the children of mixed marriages to be raised as Catholics. They saw this as an important cause of the reduction in the southern Protestant population, which averaged 1 percent for every year after partition.[69] Catholics correspondingly resented the political influence of Protestant clergy and the Orange Order in the Unionist Party, identifying the order with a fanatical hatred of their church, its values, and its adherents.

## Geography and Demography

### Population Balance

The six counties of Northern Ireland have long been distinguished from the rest of Ireland by virtue of the proportion of Protestants living there, a legacy of the original colonization. Partition assigned to Northern Ireland all counties where Protestants constituted over 40 percent of the population. According to census returns, the Catholic proportion remained at between 33.5 percent and 35.2 percent from 1901 to 1961. Catholics had a higher birth rate, but this was offset by their higher emigration rate. During the 1960s the differential in birth rates increased and emigration fell, so that the Catholic proportion increased to 36.8 percent in the official 1971 census. The actual proportion was probably higher than this, however, as 41 percent of the respondents to Rose's 1968 unofficial survey described themselves as Catholics. The disparity probably reflects a reluctance among Catholics to describe themselves as such to government officials.

The reported shift in the population balance was significant both in itself and because it provided fuel for political agitation playing on Unionist fears and encouraging Nationalist aspirations. Popular belief in both communities has consistently overestimated the speed and probability of a transition to a Catholic majority and its presumed political implications.

### Population Distribution

A second material demographic factor is the distribution of the two communities within major towns and across the region. They are neither wholly segregated nor evenly mixed. Catholics outnumber Protestants in the west, along the border, and in west Belfast. Across the region, however, the two communities are patchworked together. In most large towns, there are well-defined Catholic and Protestant ghettos.[70] It was at the interfaces between Catholic and Protestant ghettos in Belfast and Londonderry— the two largest towns—that sectarian rioting erupted in 1968.[71]

### Territoriality

Geography matters not only because of the material facts of boundary, segregation, and propinquity but also because of the symbolic significance that the two communities attach to the integrity of their territories. Parades and demonstrations continue to have political resonance, maintain traditional identities, and affirm conflicting positions at the regional level as well as assert communal claims to territory at the local level. Provocateurs on either side can easily generate trouble by marching into or encroaching on territory occupied or claimed by the other.[72] An important precursor of the disorder in 1968 was a series of protest marches on behalf of the minority, which were ostensibly antisectarian but which, to many observers from both traditions, manifested Catholic claims against shared or Protestant territory.

## Socioeconomic Class

### Modernization Theory

It has been suggested that the process of economic modernization gives opposing cultural traditions a common interest in wealth creation, creating socioeconomic class divisions that cut across historical ethnic and cultural cleavages and so reduce their political salience.[73] The implication is that economic progress will, over time, inevitably displace communal identity as the primary source of political attitudes and electoral behavior.

This has not been Northern Ireland's experience. A socioeconomic class structure typical of Western industrial societies emerged in and around Belfast during the nineteenth century and, to some extent, this cut across the established ethnic and cultural cleavages. But though Catholics were disproportionately represented among lower-income groups at the start of the Troubles, the population of Northern Ireland has never consisted of a Protestant upper caste and a Catholic lower caste. At the outbreak of the Troubles there were more poor Protestants than poor Catholics.[74] Class cuts across the community divide, but its political salience has never been sufficient to displace cultural differentiation and national allegiance as the main axis of political debate and division.

## Marxian Theory

Traditional Marxian analysts have argued that aggravation between the two traditions was fomented by ruling-class interests to prevent the emergence of a united labor movement opposed to British imperialism and exploitation.[75] These writers identify two techniques Unionist leaders used to prolong their hegemony: sectarian rhetoric and differential discrimination. Empirical research suggests, however, that although both techniques were used, they did not fundamentally alter the attitudes of Protestant workers, and they were intended to undermine electoral rivals rather than to thwart the threat of class war.[76]

Some Marxian analyses have been more subtle. Writing in 1979, Bew, Gibbon, and Patterson accepted that the conflict was rooted in the deep division between the two traditions, but argued that the Troubles had been precipitated by specific developments in the political sphere. In their account, the Unionist leadership had pursued a populist strategy incorporating sectarian rhetoric and discrimination to strengthen and sustain its control over the Protestant working class. The Troubles had been precipitated by the failure of this strategy to withstand the pressures generated by Catholic mobilization.[77]

From a non-Marxian perspective, Whyte likewise contends that Northern Ireland's particular context, class cleavages within the two traditions, increased the intensity and salience of the conflict by encouraging elites to resort to sectarian rhetoric as a means to retain working-class support. Unionist politicians exaggerated the dangers of republican subversion in order to secure the allegiance of their working-class constituents; likewise, nationalist politicians persuaded their working-class constituents to attribute Catholic deprivation to Unionist discrimination.[78] The tendency of working-class voters on both sides of the divide to emphasize traditional cultural differences between them has been reinforced by the much greater probability that they live in ghetto areas adjacent to the opposing community. Such areas have suffered disproportionately from the violence.

## Relative Deprivation

Gurr has identified the perception of relative deprivation as a major cause of political disorder worldwide.[79] In deeply divided societies, this perception is likely to generate accusations of discrimination.[80] The evidence shows that Catholics in Northern Ireland have suffered both actual relative and objective discrimination.

Researching census and survey data for the period 1968 to 1971, Aunger concludes that Catholics were relatively disadvantaged in both public and

**Table 2.1    Share of Religious Groups in Occupational Class in Five English-Speaking Societies (percent)**

| Society | Year | Upper middle | | Manual working | |
|---------|------|------------|----------|------------|----------|
| | | Protestant | Catholic | Protestant | Catholic |
| Northern Ireland | 1968 | 16 | 9 | 48 | 58 |
| Great Britain | 1963 | 13 | 8 | 58 | 63 |
| United States | 1957 | 24 | 17 | 48 | 55 |
| Australia | 1971 | 21 | 16 | 54 | 62 |
| New Zealand | 1976 | 29 | 24 | 46 | 49 |

*Source:* Adapted from Christopher Hewitt, "Catholic Grievances, Catholic Nationalism, and Violence in Northern Ireland during the Civil Rights Period: A Reconsideration," *British Journal of Sociology,* vol. 32, no. 3 (1981), 369.

private sector employment.[81] He finds that 60 percent of Protestants but only 48 percent of Catholics fell into the top three occupational classes; 15 percent of Protestants but 25 percent of Catholics were unskilled or unemployed; Catholics in white-collar jobs were more likely to be employed in positions in which they came into contact primarily with other Catholics, such as teaching and retailing; and Catholics tended to have lower status jobs than Protestants in the same working environment—for example, 43 percent of nurses but only 21 percent of doctors were Catholic. Occupational inequalities were reflected in income stratification, but the differential was greatest in unemployment rates. In 1971 Catholic men were more than twice as likely as Protestant men to be unemployed. These findings measure relative deprivation, not discrimination. Cross-national research shows that a similar relationship between Catholics and Protestants existed at the time in other mixed but predominantly Protestant English-speaking societies in which discrimination has not been such a salient political issue, as table 2.1 shows.

Nationalist activists at the time compared the experience of Catholics in Northern Ireland with that of black Americans. In reality, black Americans were considerably worse off relatively: 23 percent of whites but only 6 percent of blacks were classified as upper middle class, while 75 percent of blacks and only 53 percent of whites were manual working class. The important difference between Northern Ireland and the other societies in the table is the social and cultural context in which the divergence occurred, and the political meanings attached to it.

In 1968, 74 percent of Catholics in Northern Ireland agreed with the proposition that in places Catholics were treated unfairly. This belief was itself divisive, in that the same proportion of Protestants disagreed with it.[82] In explaining the disparities between the two groups, Catholic respondents accused the Protestant establishment of discrimination, whereas

Protestants tended to blame Catholics' attitudes toward work and economic success. Commentators and researchers have offered other explanations. First, there was a higher concentration of Catholics in the three
western counties, where agricultural land is poorer, industry and infrastructure are less well developed, and the markets of Britain and Europe
are more expensive to access. Both Protestants and Catholics in the west
suffered from lower incomes and a greater risk of unemployment. Second,
Catholics were more likely to be unqualified or unskilled, reflecting differences in priorities between the Catholic and state school systems.[83] Third,
alienated from the Northern Ireland state, many Catholics were unwilling
to work for the police, the civil service, or other public sector employers.
Those who joined the police in particular ran the risk of ostracism and
violence from their own side. Some preferred to work for the public sector
in the Republic. Once a pattern of abstentionism was created, it was hard
to change. Fourth, Catholic families were larger on average, which could
make full-time employment less attractive as a result of the benefits system
and the need to devote time to childrearing.[84] Fifth, traditional Catholic
value systems place less emphasis than does Protestantism on business and
financial success relative to other values.[85] Sixth, informal networks for
filling vacancies tend to perpetuate past patterns of employment; once a
differential is established it tends to persist.

## Discrimination

Each of the above explanations may account for some of the economic
differentials between the two groups, but there is sufficient evidence to
conclude that deliberate discrimination was a significant contribution. This
worked both ways. For example, the chairman of the Nationalist Party was
a businessman who employed almost sixty people and not a single Protestant.[86] But because the Unionist Party ran the regional government and
most local councils, Nationalists suffered disproportionately as a result.

At the highest level, the Unionist government oversaw the system of
recruitment to the regional civil service. In 1959, only 6 percent of senior
civil servants were Catholic.[87] In the judiciary, Catholics in 1969 held only
6 of 68 senior appointments. Only 49 of 332 people appointed to statutory
bodies were Catholics.[88] Whatever the reasons behind these differences, it
is clear that the Catholic middle class did not participate on equal terms at
the top of the regional administration.

There is also clear evidence of deliberate discrimination in local government in the western counties of Londonderry, Tyrone, and Fermanagh.
This relates to elections, senior appointments, and the allocation of public

housing.[89] Until 1972, there were seventy-three councils across Northern Ireland, only eleven of which were controlled by Nationalists.[90] Partly as a result of Nationalists' boycotting the Local Government Boundaries Commission, ward boundaries had been drawn in 1922 so as effectively to deprive them of control of thirteen councils in the west that would otherwise have been theirs.[91] In Londonderry, an official report published in 1969 found that a population that was 60 percent Catholic elected twelve Unionist and eight Nationalist councillors because the ward boundaries had been drawn to reduce the value of each Catholic vote.

The Unionist Party's advantage in electoral boundaries was enhanced by allocating places in public housing projects. That Catholics were packed into a few constituencies reduced the power of their votes. Moreover, the franchise retained a property qualification that the Labour government had abolished in Britain in the 1940s. Aunger has calculated that this disenfranchised 30 percent of Catholic adults and 19 percent of Protestants, skewing election results in wards where the population was closely balanced.[92] This was no accident. The Unionist Party was well aware that if it removed this barrier, it would lose control over Londonderry, Tyrone, and Fermanagh.[93]

Both Nationalist and Unionist councils allocated patronage resources differentially between the two communities. In Londonderry, a Catholic held only one of the ten highest-paid posts, while 30 percent of the council's white-collar employees were Catholic.[94] Figures such as these do not prove that those who made the appointments were guilty of deliberate discrimination. Many Nationalists objected in principle to working for the state and its institutions, did not apply for such appointments, and would not have agreed to serve if invited. Political patronage applies in most democratic societies, and the Unionist Party was no less likely than any other political party to favor its friends. Nevertheless, a 1969 report concluded that a number of local councils in the west had systematically discriminated against minority applicants for jobs and houses.[95] The Unionist government was at fault to the extent that ministers knew about the problem and chose not to correct it.

Although the above provides no justification for discrimination, if the northern Unionists saw themselves as providing "a Protestant Parliament and a Protestant State,"[96] the southern parties once in government created a Catholic state in which the Catholic Church had a constitutionally privileged position, exercised substantial influence over social policies, and controlled the delivery of most educational, health, and social services. Until the 1990s that Church required the offspring of mixed marriages to be raised as Catholics.

## Law Enforcement

As Whyte has reported, "Protestants and Catholics have contrasting attitudes towards the security forces, to the courts, and to particular security policies. The gap between them on security policy is even larger than on constitutional issue."[97] Two principal allegations of discrimination against Catholics in law enforcement surfaced during the 1960s: that the police were sectarian in composition, outlook, and conduct, and that the Unionist regime was using law enforcement to suppress peaceful political protest on behalf of the minority.

Northern Ireland was born in a context of violent conflict, and the Unionist government perceived itself as having powerful opponents on and inside its borders as well as within the British political elite. The threat of republican subversion ebbed and flowed, but never went away entirely. From 1956 to 1962, the IRA resumed its cross-border campaign, attacking customs posts, police officers, and police stations.

The devolved administration inherited the former RIC in Northern Ireland. Unlike English police forces, the RIC had been organized and equipped on the European pattern, recognizing that its functions included preventing insurgency. Out of the RIC was formed the Royal Ulster Constabulary (RUC), which continued to combine the RIC's paramilitary role with conventional civil policing. The RUC had tackled IRA campaigns in every decade since 1921, and in the mid-1960s was alert to the possibility that it might have to do so again. The composition of the force was predominantly Protestant; it had tried from time to time to attract more Catholic recruits, but with limited success.[98] It was accountable to a Unionist minister upholding the laws of a jurisdiction that had come into being because of Protestant agitation. It would have been remarkable if the RUC had invariably acted with complete evenhandedness between Unionists and Nationalists.[99]

Upon taking control of the RUC, the Unionist government created a new auxiliary force, the Ulster Special Constabulary (USC). A majority of special constables were also Orangemen—members of the Orange Order—and many members of the original UVF were co-opted into the USC, partly with a view to restraining their sectarian enthusiasms. The USC was in practice exclusively Protestant.

The Stormont minister of home affairs held sweeping powers to suppress activities that he considered subversive. He could ban political organizations, prevent public meetings and parades, imprison suspects indefinitely without trial, and take virtually any steps that he considered necessary to quell political unrest. These emergency powers were used rigorously against republicans and less frequently against loyalists.[100] The 1969 report

concluded that their existence operated "in the circumstances as a continuing cause of irritation and friction within the body politic."[101] Thus, while
the machinery of law and order was designed to control insurrection, its
existence provided ammunition for the regime's opponents.

## The Government of Ireland

Northern Ireland did not (and does not) exist in isolation from the rest of
the world, and an important analytic perspective views the conflict as the
unresolved residue of an older series of battles between Catholicism and
Protestantism that extended across Europe. Partition restructured the relationship between Britain and Ireland and confined the malaise to the new
Northern Ireland, but did not fully resolve the historical conflict between
the two nations.[102]

Since partition, the leaders of Fianna Fáil and Fine Gael have resorted
to republican rhetoric to see off their rivals. At the onset of the Troubles,
the southern electorate was more nationalistic than the Catholic minority
in the north. A plurality of northern Catholics considered that the most
workable and acceptable solution to the conflict would leave them inside
the United Kingdom, whereas an overwhelming majority of southern respondents preferred unification outside the United Kingdom.[103]

Barrington has identified the republican rhetoric of the southern parties
as an important source of support and legitimacy for the IRA, which ran
as follows.

> For thirty-five years its leaders had been waging a cold war against the north, and if
> the cold war had now become a shooting war, those who started and carried on the
> cold war had to accept their share of the responsibility. The policy of its leaders had
> been to coerce the north through the intervention of England, the United States,
> or some outside power; the policy of the illegal organizations was to do the job
> themselves. One could call the former policy a constitutional policy and the latter a
> physical force policy, but both are basically policies of coercion.[104]

Fianna Fáil came to power under former IRA leader Eamon de Valera
in 1932, and in 1937 produced a new national constitution. Far from invit-
ing Unionists to consider the merits of unification, the document widened
the division in Ireland in several ways. It asserted Ireland's full sovereign
independence from Britain and claimed jurisdiction over the whole island, in defiance of the 1925 treaty; abandoned the republican ideal of a
secular pluralist state and formalized the special position of the Catholic
Church; and banned divorce. As one dissident Dáil minister has observed,
"It would be hard to think of a combination of propositions more likely
to sustain and stiffen the siege mentality of Protestant Ulster."[105] Unionists have noted that the Protestant population of the southern state fell by

almost a third between 1911 and 1926.[106] The division between the two parts of the island was widened even further when the Republic decided to remain neutral in the war against Nazi Germany, as de Valera turned down a request from Britain to make Irish ports available to ships protecting supply convoys from the United States.

One Northern Ireland senior civil servant has described the Irish government's contribution to the problem as follows:

> Despite its nominal adherence to the Treaty of 1925, every subsequent move by the South towards de jure as well as de facto independence ... strengthened the suspicions of the Unionists and undermined the political bona fides within the North of the minority qua minority. It is a paradox, but nevertheless true, that responsibility for the polarisation of politics in the North rests as much with the Republic as with the parties in Northern Ireland itself. In particular, the denial by the Republic even of the legitimacy of the constitution of Northern Ireland has been a factor of great potency.[107]

Despite Unionists' suspicions and Nationalists' continuing hostility to partition, the prime ministers of Ireland and Northern Ireland in 1965 began a dialogue about cross-border cooperation for economic development, the first meaningful discussions between the two governments for forty years. Although progress was slow, in early 1968 the prospects for a rapprochement between the two jurisdictions looked promising, until events intervened.

## The Government of the United Kingdom

### The Constitutional Guarantee

London has provided the Unionist tradition with a series of constitutional guarantees. The Ireland Act 1949, formalizing the Republic's departure from the Commonwealth, declared "that in no event will Northern Ireland or any part thereof cease to be part of His Majesty's dominions and of the United Kingdom without the consent of the Parliament of Northern Ireland."[108] Britain's experiences in the war against Nazi Germany briefly convinced Whitehall that it had a strategic interest in retaining control over the part of Ireland that could be used to protect the sea-lanes into Glasgow and Liverpool. As officials privately advised ministers, "So far as it can be foreseen, it will never be to Great Britain's advantage that Northern Ireland should form a territory outside His Majesty's jurisdiction. Indeed, it would seem unlikely that Great Britain would ever be able to agree to this even if the people of Northern Ireland desired it."[109]

On the other hand, the leaders of both traditions in Ireland have recognized that Westminster could as easily amend the 1949 act as it had made it. In contrast to the Irish state, with its constitutional claim to jurisdiction over the north, successive British governments have depicted themselves as having no particular interest in retaining Northern Ireland. The asymmetry between these two positions has led Unionists to distrust British guarantees and to rely instead on their own physical strength; it has also encouraged republicans to believe that sufficient pressure can tip the scales toward British withdrawal. Unionist leaders knew that, but for their threat of violent resistance, the British government would have persisted with home rule legislation in 1914. In 1968 a substantial faction in the ruling British Labour Party, including Prime Minister Harold Wilson, supported Irish unification as a long-term goal.

### The Parity Principle

As part of the United Kingdom, Northern Ireland shared in the development of the British welfare state from 1946. The UK government accepted that the devolved administration should enjoy parity in the provision of public services regardless of its ability to finance them from local revenue. By 1968, the UK Treasury was subsidizing public expenditure in Northern Ireland by some £100 million annually.[110] This parity principle had six marked effects. First, it widened the economic gap between the two parts of Ireland, and so reinforced the impacts of partition.[111] Second, it slowed down the rate of Catholic emigration and expanded Catholics' expectations of the state for education, employment, housing, and other public services.[112] Third, it divided the Unionist establishment during the 1960s, as central ministries committed to regional planning sought to prise power away from local councils. Fourth, it gave Catholic voters a personal stake in the union, moderating their support for the Nationalist cause. Pensions, social security payments, and public service standards were all visibly higher in the north. Fifth, it created a university-educated Catholic middle class with greater self-confidence, higher aspirations, and less conservative values. Finally, it rendered the Unionist government more dependent on the UK financial subvention, and hence susceptible to pressure from Westminster.

## Countervailing Conditions

With such a deep division, a history of violence, irreconcilable political objectives, and so little room for compromise, it might seem surprising that the level of violence was as low as it was in Northern Ireland from 1925 to 1968. A number of countervailing conditions help to explain why. Although there were two distinct communities, there was a broad spectrum of opinion within each, from moderate constitutionalists to militant hard-liners. A large majority of people in both communities was committed to the principles of representative democracy as practiced in the United Kingdom and Ireland. The Catholic and Protestant religious traditions were both opposed to violence in principle, and church leaders frequently condemned it. Although a majority of the urban working class lived in segregated districts, most middle-class residential areas were integrated, and many people had friends, neighbors, and coworkers on the other side of the divide. Higher-level education was integrated (except for teacher training), as were many large workforces. Although the communal division was based on the fundamental attributes of religion and national identity, it was not generally experienced as racial. Both communities spoke English.

Free elections and a free press allowed the public expression of diverse political views. Nationalists controlled eleven of the seventy-three local councils. This was fewer than their proportion of the electorate would have justified but permitted them control over a range of issues and services in those districts.[113] The partition settlement could be considered fair in that it gave each of the two major cultural traditions on the island a state and parliament. If people felt very strongly about the national question, they could always move to the other jurisdiction—indeed, during the process of partition many did. Both communities in the north benefited from the British welfare state. However deprived they might have felt compared with their Protestant neighbors, Catholics in the north were on average better off financially and in the availability of public services than their neighbors to the south. And ultimately, republicans who were tempted to resort to violence faced a substantial obstacle in the Stormont government, with its paramilitary police capability and comprehensive emergency legislation.

## Summary

The preconditions that made the Troubles possible did not make them inevitable. Partition enabled London to withdraw from Ireland, but it did not do so entirely. Westminster retained ultimate responsibility for the administration of Northern Ireland. It partially succeeded in meeting the competing demands of armed republicans and loyalists, giving each tradition a state with which it could identify and in which it had a clear majority, but it did so at the expense of northern Nationalists. They were a substantial minority, largely excluded from participation in the regional government and disadvantaged in local government. Electoral outcomes were determined by what Nationalists regarded as the unfinished business of partition at the expense of other issues. In this divided society, political behavior was grounded in loyalties to religious organizations, ideological traditions, and perceptions of national identity rather than class or policy preferences. As explained in the section above on popular attitudes toward political violence, both communities celebrated traditions of successful physical force. Once mobilized, there was sufficient disaffection on the Catholic side to sustain widespread support for disorderly protest, and there was enough paranoia on the Protestant side to destroy attempts by moderate Unionist leaders to create a more inclusive society.

The fundamental division between the two sides was exacerbated by the political power of the churches and the Orange Order; by educational and residential segregation; by Catholics' perceptions of injustice; and by actual discrimination in local government elections, housing, public and private sector employment, and the application of public order legislation. Paralleling the conflict at the national level, there was a string of latent territorial conflicts at town and village level, wherever Catholic and Protestant ghettos met. For some families, active engagement in political subversion had long been a way of life, transmitted down the generations.

The political positions taken by the governments of the Republic of Ireland and the United Kingdom complicated and reinforced the internal preconditions. As a minority on the island, Unionists felt threatened by the territorial claim in the Republic's constitution, the legitimacy it conferred on republican insurgency, and the IRA's ability to strike from across the border. They contrasted Dublin's commitment to a single all-Ireland state with London's apparent indifference to the union. Conversely, as a minority in Northern Ireland, Nationalists felt oppressed by Britain's guarantee to Unionism, implying the use of force if necessary, and by the legitimacy it conferred on the Unionist state. Nationalist activists felt abandoned and betrayed by the political parties in Dublin.

All this set the stage for the unrest to follow.

## Notes

1.    C. Townshend, *Political Violence in Ireland* (Oxford: Clarendon Press, 1983), 1.

2.    For a succinct history of Northern Ireland, see T. Hennessey, *A History of Northern Ireland 1920–1996* (Basingstoke: Macmillan, 1997). For critical assessments of some of the political scientific studies and political commentaries, see J. Whyte, *Interpreting Northern Ireland* (Oxford: Clarendon Press, 1990); J. McGarry and B. O'Leary, *Explaining Northern Ireland* (Oxford: Blackwell, 1995).

3.    D.A. Hibbs, *Mass Political Violence* (New York: Wiley, 1973).

4.    E. Nordlinger, *Conflict Regulation in Divided Societies* (Cambridge, MA: Harvard University Press, 1972).

5.    A. Lijphart, *Democracy in Plural Societies* (New Haven, CT: Yale University Press, 1977), 34.

6. "The Troubles" is the euphemism that people in Northern Ireland (and elsewhere) commonly use for the political violence.

7. R. Rose, *Governing without Consensus* (London: Faber, 1971).

8. H. Jackson, *The Two Irelands: A Dual Study of Intergroup Tensions*, Report no. 2 (London: Minority Rights Group, 1971).

9. Townshend, *Political Violence*, 5.

10. For fuller accounts of the historical background, see P. Bew, *Ireland: The Politics of Enmity 1789–2006* (Oxford: Oxford University Press, 2007); A. Jackson, *Home Rule: An Irish History 1800–2000* (London: Weidenfeld and Nicolson, 2003); and R. Foster, *Modern Ireland 1600–1972* (London: Allen Lane, 1988). For a full account of developments from 1963 to 1970, see T. Hennessey, *The Origins of the Troubles* (Dublin: Gill and Macmillan, 2005).

11. Rose, *Governing without Consensus*, 79.

12. P. Clayton, "Religion, Ethnicity, and Colonialism as Explanations of the Northern Ireland Conflict," in D. Miller, ed., *Rethinking Northern Ireland* (Harlow: Addison-Wesley Longman, 1998).

13. J.P. Darby, *Northern Ireland: The Background to the Conflict* (Syracuse, NY: Syracuse University Press, 1983), 15.

14. P. Gibbon, *The Origins of Ulster Unionism* (Manchester: Manchester University Press, 1975).

15. A.T.Q. Stewart, *The Narrow Ground* (London: Faber, 1977), 144.

16. Darby, *Northern Ireland*.

17. The full text of the Covenant is available through the Northern Ireland Public Record Office at www.proni.gov.uk (accessed October 27, 2010).

18. Townshend, *Political Violence*.

19. Sir James Craig, prime minister of Northern Ireland, cited in F.S.L. Lyons, *Ireland since the Famine* (London: Weidenfeld and Nicholson, 1971), 683.

20. P. Buckland, *The Factory of Grievances* (Dublin: Gill and Macmillan, 1979), 4.

21. Section 5 of the Government of Ireland Act 1920 prohibited the Northern Ireland Parliament from introducing any laws interfering with religious equality:
"In the exercise of their power to make laws under this Act neither the Parliament of Southern Ireland nor the Parliament of Northern Ireland shall make a law so as either directly or indirectly to establish or endow any religion, or prohibit or restrict the free exercise thereof, or give a preference, privilege, or advantage, or impose any disability or disadvantage, on account of religious belief or religious or ecclesiastical status, or make any religious belief or religious ceremony a condition of the validity of any marriage, or affect prejudicially the right of any child to attend a school receiving public money without attending the religious instruction at that school, or alter the constitution of any religious body except where the alteration is approved on behalf of the religious body by the governing body thereof."

22. Rose, *Governing without Consensus*, 90.

23. H. Patterson, *Ireland since 1939: The Persistence of Conflict* (Dublin: Penguin, 2006), 4.

24. Patterson, *Ireland since 1939*, 5.

25. P. Dixon, *Northern Ireland: The Politics of War and Peace* (New York: Palgrave, 2001).

26. For fuller accounts of the competing ideologies, see McGarry and O'Leary, *Explaining Northern Ireland*.

27.   During the 1970s, a new strand of Nationalist thinking emerged that retained Irish unification as its eventual goal, but identified the source of the problem not as British interference but as Protestant reluctance to join what they saw as an authoritarian Catholic state. See, e.g., G. Fitzgerald, *Towards a New Ireland* (Dublin: Gill and Macmillan, 1972).

28.   G. Adams, *A Pathway to Peace* (Cork: Mercier, 1988), 41.

29.   Rose, *Governing without Consensus*.

30.   S. Bruce, *God Save Ulster! The Religion and Politics of Paisleyism* (Oxford: Oxford University Press, 1989), 251.

31.   R. Bourke, *Peace in Ireland: The War of Ideas* (London: Pimlico, 2003).

32.   S. Nelson, *Ulster's Uncertain Defenders* (Belfast: Appletree Press, 1984), 36.

33.   Rose, *Governing without Consensus*.

34.   Hennessey, *Northern Ireland*, 17.

35.   Bruce, *God Save Ulster*.

36.   Whyte, *Interpreting Northern Ireland*, 80.

37.   Nelson, *Ulster's Uncertain Defenders*.

38.   See, e.g., F. Burton, *The Politics of Legitimacy* (London: Routledge Kegan Paul, 1978).

39.   Whyte, *Interpreting Northern Ireland*, 102.

40.   E.A. Aunger, *In Search of Political Stability: A Comparative Study of New Brunswick and Northern Ireland* (Montreal: McGill-Queen's University Press, 1981), 25.

41.   Rose, *Governing without Consensus*.

42.   Whyte, *Interpreting Northern Ireland*.

43.   Gibbon, *Origins of Ulster Unionism*, 25.

44.   Hennessey, *Origins of the Troubles*, 18.

45.   Rose, *Governing without Consensus*, 224.

46.   Ibid., 221.

47.   Ibid., 235.

48.   R. English, *Armed Struggle: The History of the IRA* (Oxford: Pan Macmillan, 2004), 84.

49.   E. Moxon-Browne, *Nation, Class, and Creed in Northern Ireland* (Aldershot: Gower, 1983), 125.

50.   J. Hickey, "Religion as a Variable in the Sociological Analysis of Northern Ireland," *Social Studies*, vol. 5, no. 3–4 (Winter 1976–77), 184.

51.   B. O'Leary and J. McGarry, *The Politics of Antagonism: Understanding Northern Ireland* (London: Athlone Press), 4.

52.   Rose, *Governing without Consensus*, 261.

53.   J. Hunter, "An Analysis of the Conflict in Northern Ireland," in D. Rea, ed., *Political Cooperation in Divided Societies* (Dublin: Gill and Macmillan, 1982), 32.

54.   C.C. O'Brien, *States of Ireland* (London: Granada, 1974), 287.

55.   J.H. Whyte, *Church and State in Modern Ireland, 1923–1970* (Dublin: Gill and Macmillan, 1980).

56.   Rose, *Governing without Consensus*, 251.

57.   Ibid., 253.

58.   Hunter, *Analysis of the Conflict*, 34.

59.   Rose, *Governing without Consensus*, 257.

60. D.P. Barritt and C.F. Carter, *The Northern Ireland Problem* (Oxford: Oxford University Press 1962), 62.

61. See, e.g., Hennessey, *Origins of the Troubles,* 54.

62. Buckland, *Factory of Grievances,* 247.

63. Hunter, *Analysis of the Conflict,* 36.

64. O'Brien, *States of Ireland,* 290.

65. Cited in F.S.L. Lyons, *Culture and Anarchy in Ireland 1890–1939* (Oxford: Clarendon Press, 1979), 90.

66. T. Bowden, *The Breakdown of Public Security: The Case of Ireland 1916–1921 and Palestine 1936–1939* (London: Sage, 1977).

67. Bruce, *God Save Ulster,* 13–14.

68. J. Russell, cited in Hunter, *Analysis of the Conflict.*

69. B. Walsh, *Religion and Demographic Behavior in Ireland* (Dublin: Economic and Social Research Institute, 1970).

70. A ghetto is defined as a neighborhood with 90 percent or more households belonging to the same community.

71. Unionists prefer this name for the city. Nationalists prefer the precolonial name, Derry. I use both terms interchangeably.

72. Jackson, *The Two Irelands,* 6.

73. For an influential interpretation of the Northern Ireland conflict in economic terms, see D.J. Smith and G. Chambers, *Inequality in Northern Ireland* (Oxford: Clarendon Press, 1991).

74. Rose, *Governing without Consensus,* 289

75. E.g., M. Farrell, *The Orange State* (London: Pluto Press, 1976); L. de Paor, *Divided Ulster* (London: Penguin, 1970).

76. Whyte, *Interpreting Northern Ireland,* 261.

77. P. Bew, P. Gibbon, and H. Patterson, *The State in Northern Ireland 1921–72* (Manchester: Manchester University Press, 1979).

78. J. Whyte, "An Interpretation of the Northern Ireland Problem," unpublished paper, Department of Politics, Queen's University Belfast, 1982

79. T.R. Gurr, *Why Men Rebel* (Princeton, NJ: Princeton University Press, 1970).

80. R. Harris, *Prejudice and Tolerance in Ulster* (Manchester: Manchester University Press, 1972), 219.

81. E.A. Aunger, "Religion and Occupational Class in Northern Ireland," *Economic and Social Review,* vol. 7, no. 1 (October 1975), 1–17.

82. Rose, *Governing without Consensus,* 272.

83. Barritt and Carter, *The Northern Ireland Problem,* 62.

84. C. Hewitt, "Catholic Grievances, Catholic Nationalism, and Violence in Northern Ireland during the Civil Rights Period: A Reconsideration," *British Journal of Sociology,* vol. 32, no. 3 (1981), 368.

85. For a comprehensive sociological history of this difference and its economic implications, see R.H. Tawney, *Religion and the Rise of Capitalism* (London: Penguin, 1940).

86. Hennessey, *Origins of the Troubles,* 72.

87. Barritt and Carter, *The Northern Ireland Problem,* 96.

88.　M. Wallace, *Northern Ireland: Fifty Years of Self-Government* (New York: Barnes and Noble, 1971), 117.

89.　Much of this evidence is contained in the Cameron Report, which the Unionist government commissioned: *Disturbances in Northern Ireland: Report of the Cameron Commission*, Cmd 532 (Belfast: HMSO, 1969). Cameron was particularly critical of the Londonderry City Council.

90.　W.D. Birrell, "Relative Deprivation as a Factor in the Conflict in Northern Ireland," *Sociological Review*, vol. 20, no. 3 (1972), 324.

91.　J. Whyte, "How Much Discrimination Was There under the Unionist Regime, 1921–1968?" in T. Gallagher and J. O'Connell, eds., *Contemporary Irish Studies* (Manchester: Manchester University Press, 1983), 6. This article is also available through the CAIN web service.

92.　Aunger, *In Search of Political Stability*, 100.

93.　H. Patterson and E. Kaufmann, *Unionism and Orangeism in Northern Ireland since 1945* (Manchester: Manchester University Press 2007), 57.

94.　Whyte, "How Much Discrimination?" 8.

95.　Government of Northern Ireland, *"Disturbances in Northern Ireland"*—Cmd 532, also known as the Cameron Report (Belfast: HMSO, September 1969)

96.　Sir James Craig, Northern Ireland's first prime minister, cited in T. Hennessey, *Northern Ireland: The Origins of the Troubles* (Dublin: Gill and Macamillan, 2005), xiii.

97.　Whyte, *Interpreting Northern Ireland*, 102.

98.　Hunt Report: *Report of the Advisory Committee on Police in Northern Ireland*, Cmd 535 (Belfast: HMSO, 1969).

99.　Whyte, "How Much Discrimination?" 24.

100.　Buckland, *Factory of Grievances*, 219.

101.　Cameron Report, paragraph 144.

102.　J. Ruane and J. Todd, *The Dynamics of Conflict in Northern Ireland* (Cambridge: Cambridge University Press, 1996), 7; O'Leary and McGarry, *Politics of Antagonism*, 3.

103.　E.E. Davis and R. Sinnott, *Attitudes in the Republic of Ireland Relevant to the Northern Ireland Problem* (Dublin: Economic and Social Research Institute, 1979), 55.

104.　Cited in P.J. Arthur, *Government and Politics of Northern Ireland* (Harlow: Longman, 1980), 71.

105.　O'Brien, *States of Ireland*, 116.

106.　Patterson, *Ireland since 1939*, 15.

107.　N. Dugdale, "The Essential Requirements of a Constitutional Settlement in Northern Ireland," CAB 130/561, October 3, 1972.

108.　UK Parliament, Ireland Act 1949, Section 1(2).

109.　Cited in P. Bew and H. Patterson, *The British State and the Ulster Crisis: From Wilson to Thatcher* (London: Verso, 1985), 9.

110.　Rose, *Governing without Consensus*, 119.

111.　F.S.L. Lyons, *Ireland since the Famine* (London: Weidenfeld and Nicholson, 1971), 731.

112.　Arthur, *Government and Politics*, 74.

113.　The Cameron Report found that Nationalist councillors were as likely as Unionists to use their positions to benefit their coreligionists at the expense of the other side.

# 3
# Reform, 1969

*Generally speaking, the most perilous moment for a bad gov-*
*ernment is one when it seeks to mend its ways. Only consum-*
*mate statecraft can enable a king to save his throne when after*
*a long spell of oppressive rule he sets to improving the lot of his*
*subjects.*                               —Alexis de Tocqueville[1]

In October 1968, a protest campaign originating in the Nationalist community in Northern Ireland hit the headlines. Under pressure from the
Labour government of Harold Wilson, Unionist prime minister Terence O'Neill offered a package of concessions to the Nationalists, but this
did not prevent further disorder as the protesters expanded their demands.
Increasing violence deepened longstanding divisions in the Unionist Party,
resulting in O'Neill's resignation. Following severe intercommunal rioting
in July and August 1969, which stretched the police service beyond its capability, Wilson sent 6,000 British soldiers to Northern Ireland to restore
order. This intervention gave Labour ministers direct responsibility for the
administration of Northern Ireland, and they induced O'Neill to bring in
a more radical package of reforms, which included restructuring and disarming the Royal Ulster Constabulary (RUC).

## The Problem

### The Protest Campaign

The Northern Ireland Civil Rights Association (NICRA) came into being
in January 1967. Its first steering committee comprised thirteen members
ranging from radical republicans to representatives from the Northern
Ireland Labour Party (NILP) and the trade union movement. Although
its constitution was explicitly antisectarian, its grassroots members were

predominantly Catholic. NICRA differed from traditional Nationalist organizations in calling for equal rights for everyone within the British state rather than Irish unification.

At first NICRA focused on individual cases of discrimination in the allocation of public housing in the three western counties. But in August 1968, inspired and energized by the U.S. civil rights movement and the antiwar demonstrations spreading across Europe, it began to organize marches against systemic discrimination. An ad hoc committee comprising radical elements from NICRA and other local groups arranged for a protest to be held in Londonderry on October 5. Loyalists responded by arranging a counterdemonstration at the same time and place. Concerned at the risk of a violent confrontation, the minister of home affairs, Bill Craig, banned both marches on the advice of local police. The loyalists complied, but some two thousand people turned out to support NICRA. To secure favorable publicity, some were determined to provoke the police into brutality.[2] There was a violent confrontation during which, according to a subsequent official report (the Cameron Report), the RUC used "unnecessary and ill controlled force in the dispersal of the demonstrators."[3] A two-day battle followed between the police and residents of the Catholic Bogside district, as a result of which eighty-eight people, including eleven police officers, received hospital attention.

The protest and police action secured international coverage for NICRA. Taking a close interest in Northern Ireland for the first time, British national television relayed dramatic pictures of police using batons and a water cannon against unarmed protesters. The front row of marchers confronting the RUC included three Labour members of parliament (MPs) from Westminster and the chairman of the NILP.

Over the next three months, the original NICRA coalition broke down. The movement became more radical, attracted new supporters, and added police violence to its list of grievances. A network of local associations was established that stretched across the region, formulating demands to remove the property qualification for voting in local government elections, outlaw discrimination in public service employment and in the allocation of public housing, create machinery for the redress of individuals' complaints against local councils, repeal the Special Powers Act, and disband the Ulster Special Constabulary (USC).

## O'Neill's Dilemma

Terence O'Neill had been prime minister of Northern Ireland since March 1963. Educated at Eton, a privileged school in England, he had no sympathy for parochial Unionism. For him, "being a Unionist meant being British or more exactly English, rather than being antinationalist and anti-Catholic. His values were those of cosmopolitan, highly educated, and cultured London society."[4] He tried to reshape his administration's priorities toward regional development, economic regeneration, and social transformation. He successfully persuaded the UK Treasury to include Northern Ireland in its national policy of support for lagging areas.[5] This modernization strategy was originally designed to see off an electoral challenge from the NILP; O'Neill sought to persuade the UK government that it would also reduce the political salience of partition over time.

However, O'Neill's policies generated new grievances within Northern Ireland, as significant decisions about the allocation of public money inevitably had potentially sectarian implications. As on the rest of the island, the eastern seaboard was the most attractive area for investment, and it was to the east that O'Neill's development plans offered the greatest rewards, including jobs, houses, and a new town that Unionists decided to name after their first prime minister, Lord Craigavon. Nationalists in the west interpreted this concentration of development in the east as further evidence of discrimination.

O'Neill's strategy also alienated his own party's local constituency associations, since it stripped them of power and patronage. In 1965 the Ulster Unionist Council, the party's governing body, passed a resolution condemning the "dictatorial manner" of recent government planning proposals.[6] O'Neill in response made little attempt to conceal his distaste for the bulk of his constituency activists.

O'Neill's approach thus both created a new mood of expectation among the minority and made it more difficult to sustain grassroots support among the majority. Recognizing the electoral risk, he reacted to the protest demonstrations with "a steely resolve to do nothing that would add to the strains that his anti-NILP strategy was placing on Unionist Party unity."[7]

But the international media coverage of October 1968 meant that he had to act. He shared the dilemma with his cabinet:

> Can any of us truthfully say . . . that the minority has no grievance calling for a remedy? Believe me, I realise the appalling political difficulties we face. The first reaction of our own people to the antics of Fitt and Currie [civil rights leaders] and the abuse of the world's press is to retreat into old hard-line attitudes. But if this is all we can offer we face a period when we govern Ulster by police power alone. . . . Concessions could well be the wisest course.[8]

Wisest because the Unionists came under intense pressure from Wilson. Since 1965, Wilson had sporadically tried to persuade O'Neill to move further and faster in addressing Nationalists' grievances. He had accepted O'Neill's presentation of himself as a moderate struggling to drag the Unionist establishment into line with mainstream Conservative thinking in Britain.[9] He had trusted O'Neill's assessment of the limits to which he could go without jeopardizing his leadership.

But the events of October 1968 jolted Wilson into action. He summoned O'Neill to London and demanded changes urgently. He informed Home Secretary James Callaghan that the status quo could not continue, for two reasons: "(i) Pressure in the House [of Commons] for the UK Government to take action in a situation where they had responsibility without power; (ii) The increasing difficulty of reconciling the situation in Northern Ireland with our International obligations on Human Rights."[10] In preparing the briefing notes that Wilson used for his meeting with O'Neill, the NILP argued that there was a real danger of violence escalating unless O'Neill made major concessions quickly. In particular, the NILP wanted Northern Ireland's voting qualifications brought into line with Britain's—a change that would improve NILP's own electoral prospects.[11]

The meeting was held on November 4. O'Neill brought his two most trenchant internal critics, Bill Craig and Brian Faulkner, to hear Wilson's message firsthand. Craig was minister of home affairs, responsible for policing and public order; in this capacity he had taken the controversial decision to ban the protest march in Derry on October 5. Faulkner was minister of commerce, and had a reputation for energy and ambition; O'Neill regarded him as a potential rival for the party leadership. Having expressed his concern at the disturbances in Derry and their causes, Wilson raised five areas for action that the NILP had identified for him, which closely reflected NICRA's agenda: the local government franchise, the allocation of public housing, the appointment of an ombudsman, a review of the Special Powers Act, and an official inquiry into the riots and their causes. O'Neill replied with a vague commitment to breaking down old animosities, but Craig was more specific. He rehearsed a series of arguments against significant reforms in each of these areas and for good measure described the role that Irish Republican Army (IRA) activists had played in the civil rights campaign.

Wilson was exasperated by what he viewed as Craig's sectarian intransigence, and warned of Labour backbenchers' determination "to establish human rights in Northern Ireland"; he threatened that, unless the Unionists acted quickly to meet the protesters' demands, Wilson would face "irresistible pressures for legislation at Westminster." Both sides of the meeting recognized that legislating for Northern Ireland in the national parliament would create a break with precedent that would seriously undermine Stormont's authority.[12]

Wilson repeated the threat in public the following day, telling the Commons that if Unionist hard-liners obstructed reform, he would "need to consider a fundamental appraisal of our relations with Northern Ireland."[13] He spelled out that this could mean revoking the financial relationship from which Northern Ireland gained an annual subvention of some £100 million. Other possible penalties included a review of Northern Ireland's constitutional status within the United Kingdom. In case any Unionists missed the message, Wilson also wrote O'Neill a personal letter that he invited him to show to his colleagues. In this he expressed "disappointment ... that you were not able to promise more immediate action on the matters we discussed" and asked for two specific pledges to be given within six months: to bring the local government franchise into line with Britain's and to ensure proper standards of housing allocation. He again threatened to legislate for reform at Westminster, adding, "I think we would both agree that it is infinitely more desirable that any legislation should proceed from Stormont."[14]

Wilson's threats achieved their immediate objective. Three days later O'Neill announced a package of reforms that included abolishing the business vote in local government elections; reviewing the property qualification for the local government franchise; replacing the elected but gerrymandered Londonderry Corporation with an unelected Development Commission; speeding up the restructuring of local government, a process he had already begun in 1967; introducing a points system for the allocation of public housing; appointing an ombudsman to investigate individuals' complaints of maladministration against local government; reviewing (but not repealing) the Special Powers Act; and commissioning an inquiry into the disorder and its causes. The British premier did not get all that he had demanded. O'Neill told him that it would be politically impossible for him to remove the property qualification for the local government franchise immediately, which the Labour leader reluctantly accepted. In the currency of the day it was nevertheless a substantial package.

The more accommodating leaders of the civil rights movement credited O'Neill for his positive response, recognized that it exposed him to serious political risks within his party, and calculated that it would harm their cause if Craig were to overthrow him. Following further clashes in December, they called a halt to the demonstrations. But others more radical argued that it was foolish to abandon the tactic when it was working so well. This faction had no interest in helping O'Neill, since their goal was not to reform but to overthrow Stormont. Under the banner of People's Democracy (PD), a group of student and republican leaders organized a parade across the region from Belfast to Derry, which they presented as having modeled on the 1966 Selma to Montgomery march. The marchers recognized that "we wouldn't finish the march without being molested."[15] Loyalists rose to the bait "with all the unthinking automatism of Pavlov's dog."[16] Attacks on the marchers—some 350 of them—stimulated fresh intercommunal rioting in Derry, during which police again entered the Bogside, where, according to the Cameron Report, they beat people, damaged property, and shouted sectarian abuse.[17]

The PD march ended any remaining prospect of creating cross-community support for the protest campaign. O'Neill's Unionist opponents seized the opportunity to attack him more vigorously. Fundamentalist preacher Ian Paisley called for O'Neill's resignation, and powerful figures inside his own party openly denounced him and his policies. Their motives were diverse. Some had always been uncomfortable with his conciliatory gestures toward the minority; some were determined to resist interference from London; some saw a chance to advance their own political careers; some disliked him personally; some saw the protest campaign as a façade for republican subversion; many saw the failure of the earlier reform package to end the disorder immediately as evidence that the protesters were insatiable, short of Stormont's destruction.

Within three months of Wilson's intervention, three ministers had left O'Neill's cabinet. O'Neill sacked Craig on December 11 for a speech publicly advocating defiance of Westminster. In January 1969, William Morgan— the minister of health and social services—and Brian Faulkner resigned in protest at O'Neill's decision to commission an inquiry into the disorder, which they depicted as a humiliating concession to Wilson. A substantial proportion of O'Neill's Stormont MPs concurred and publicly called for his resignation. O'Neill responded by calling a snap election for February 24. Appealing directly to the electorate, he presented them with a stark choice, whether "to go forward into a bright future within the United Kingdom as a united people" or "sink back into the bog of religious differences."[18]

O'Neill's televised appeal did not achieve the overwhelming victory he had hoped for. For the first time in its history the Unionist Party went into an election seriously divided. Where a local constituency association had nominated a candidate who had called for his resignation, O'Neill fielded an unofficial pro-O'Neill candidate. Although the party won thirty-nine of the fifty-two seats and subsequently confirmed O'Neill as leader, many of the associations split into factions for and against him. A determined group of dissidents—one-third of the incoming parliamentary party— openly opposed him and his policies.[19] They were now able to add to their litany of complaint that he had bypassed proper procedures and put himself before the party.

Wilson nevertheless kept up the pressure, with the result that O'Neill told his cabinet colleagues on April 22 that he intended to remove the remaining property qualifications for the local government franchise, and that he would resign if the parliamentary party opposed him. At this, more of his supporters defected. He resigned on April 28 rather than face a confidence vote at the UUC, which he would almost certainly have lost; he later explained that he had hoped to save his policies from "extremists."[20] He was replaced by Major James Chichester-Clark, another old Etonian, whose reputation was for decency rather than political acumen. Chichester-Clark announced that he would stand by O'Neill's commitments to reform.

O'Neill had been handicapped by his aloof personality, upper-class associations, and inability to understand the dynamics of the party that he led. But it is debatable whether a Unionist leader better endowed with social and political skills could have navigated his way successfully out of the maze in which he found himself. O'Neill's strategy of conciliatory gestures and modest reforms raised Nationalists' expectations without fulfilling them and gave his Unionist rivals powerful ammunition to use against him. An official report later described his problem as follows:

> If it [the Unionist government] stood firm it attracted violent opposition. Yet to promise reform under threats to law and order was a recipe to encourage further demonstrations and counter-demonstrations, and to increase rather than diminish the risk of confrontations between minority groups and the police.... The reform programme had left opposition activists dissatisfied but at the same time it had evoked hostility from some Protestants.... In these circumstances sectarian conflict was to be expected, unless the police were strong enough to prevent it. But the police were not strong enough.[21]

### The Collapse of Policing

Further contributing to O'Neill's downfall was a series of explosions at electricity and water installations during March and April 1969, which the RUC at first attributed to the IRA; they were in fact perpetrated by loyalist extremists attempting to discredit O'Neill.[22] Violent clashes continued. By July 1969, traditionally divisive issues—in particular the dispute over policing—had largely displaced discrimination as the driving force behind the disorder, and the locus of activity had shifted to republican neighborhoods in Derry and Belfast. There had been rioting after the Orange parades in July, and a further parade scheduled for August 12 was expected to cause more trouble. It was to pass close to the Bogside, where residents were determined to prevent a repetition of previous police and loyalist incursions. Republicans and other activists organized themselves as the Derry Citizens' Defence Association (DCDA) to prepare for battle, and IRA volunteers were keen to take on the RUC.[23] Over the four days before the march, a local dairy lost 43,000 glass bottles as petrol bombs were prepared.[24]

Despite reservations from Wilson and Callaghan, Chichester-Clark decided to let the parade proceed, taking the view that to ban it would be as dangerous as not, and politically more damaging for the Unionist Party. A riot duly occurred. The Bogsiders hurled missiles at the marchers, who then tried to break through the police lines separating them from their attackers. The RUC stood their ground for two hours but eventually, caught between two angry crowds, drew their batons and entered the Bogside, apparently unaware of the reception prepared for them. A prolonged battle followed, during which the DCDA organized an efficient assembly line for petrol bombs. Outnumbered and outmaneuvered, the police resorted to the use of tear gas. The Protestant crowd weighed in behind them.

The leaders of the protest then called for further demonstrations across Northern Ireland. Fueled by exaggerated accounts of police atrocities and encouraged by rumors that the Irish army was about to cross the border to support the republican resistance, the rioting spread to other towns. Stormont reacted to these developments by calling out the USC to support the regular police. The worst violence occurred in Belfast. Both sides feared that their darkest nightmares of ethnic violence were about to become real and acted accordingly. Protestant mobs invaded Catholic districts and arsonists destroyed hundreds of houses, leaving thousands of people homeless, predominantly Catholics. A local police commander in Belfast decided that he was facing a full-scale insurrection and, lacking more appropriate equipment, deployed light armored cars in the confined spaces of a Catholic residential area. Although republicans had made extensive preparations for the Battle of the Bogside, they had not anticipated having to defend republican communities in Belfast as well. Seven people were killed. After that, many Catholics in interface districts resolved never to be left defenseless again.

After two days' fighting, the police were exhausted. The chief constable conceded that the task was beyond them. Stormont ministers had little alternative but to ask London for troop reinforcements. Within a week, six thousand British soldiers had arrived—twice the number of regular police officers in the RUC. The rioting immediately ended. Many (although not all) of the radical protest leaders were delighted, recognizing that the intervention of the British army represented a major humiliation for Stormont. From now on, London would have to take responsibility for the proper administration of Northern Ireland. One young republican who participated in the fighting in Derry described the arrival of the soldiers as "an enormous event of great historical significance . . . it had a liberating effect on the people."[25]

## The Strategy

### The Downing Street Declaration

Three months earlier, UK home secretary James Callaghan, whose portfolio included Northern Ireland among a raft of miscellaneous issues, had briefed the British cabinet on the prospective deployment of the army to restore order in Northern Ireland. Echoing Wilson's earlier warnings to O'Neill, he told his colleagues that he had informed Stormont that the presence of British soldiers on the streets "would create a completely new situation and that we should be bound to look most carefully at the implications and indeed to re-examine our whole constitutional relationships."[26]

UK ministers had acquired a direct stake not only in resolving the conflict but also in tackling its causes. As Callaghan later wrote, "It was obvious that the Westminster Government would take a close interest both in the executive actions of the Northern Ireland Government and in their general policy if British troops were to be on the receiving end of disagreements on that policy."[27] They decided that they could not wait for Chichester-Clark to proceed at his own pace, slowed down by the resistance of the Unionist Party.

Two objectives required immediate attention: to make the RUC more effective and acceptable to the minority and to tackle Catholics' perceptions of discrimination.[28] Callaghan and Wilson met Chichester-Clark in London on August 19, 1969, and induced him to agree to a further package of reforms, this time including policing. The package was outlined in a statement that became known as the Downing Street Communiqué and Declaration.[29] On security, the communiqué summarized the new dispensation. The general officer commanding (GOC)—the top army officer in Northern Ireland—would take overall responsibility for security operations, including the deployment of the RUC for security tasks. He would be accountable to the Ministry of Defence (MoD) in London, not to the Northern Ireland government, and would assume full command and control of the USC for all purposes, including their organization and the custody of their weapons. The USC would be rapidly withdrawn from riot and crowd control duties. The army would be withdrawn as soon as order had been restored. The two governments would "discuss" the future of policing, while Stormont would commission an impartial investigation into the disorder. Finally, two senior officials from Whitehall would be stationed in Belfast to represent London's increased interest in Northern Ireland's affairs.

The document heralded a transformation in the relationship between London and Belfast. Henceforth Stormont would operate under constant supervision from Whitehall and Westminster; its survival would depend on London's goodwill. The Unionist government would no longer have any paramilitary capability and would have to implement the reforms Wilson required whether it wanted to or not. In the most controversial areas of public administration—policing and political reform—Stormont had become a puppet of the British Labour government. Wilson did not try to conceal the Unionists' humiliation.

Chichester-Clark bowed to the inevitable and over the next two months committed himself to additional reforms: redrawing local government electoral boundaries impartially; transferring responsibility for public housing to a new regional housing authority; creating a community relations commission, half of whose members would be Catholic; reviewing the law on incitement to religious hatred; and including an antidiscrimination clause in public contracts. This considerably extended the package that London had insisted on before the army intervened and introduced measures—such as the commission—that NICRA had never asked for.

### The Hunt Reforms

Callaghan's proposals for reforming the RUC generated the most serious challenge to Stormont's authority. To withdraw the army rapidly, London had to ensure that the RUC was properly organized, trained, and equipped to deal with any likely future disorders. Chichester-Clark agreed that the RUC should be strengthened; its failure to deal with the riots had shaken him. But Callaghan wanted it also to be restructured, reorganized, and placed under new (English) leadership. Chichester-Clark was in no position to argue. He was concerned that the force was under strength, that the proportion of Catholics in it was only 11 percent, and that its use by Craig against the NICRA demonstrations had reinforced Catholic alienation from it.

There was no doubting that the RUC's performance in dealing with the disorder had been inadequate. As mentioned above, the Cameron Report found that in 1968 the police had used "unnecessary and ill controlled force" against demonstrators, and that "there were instances of police indiscipline and violence towards persons unassociated with rioting or disorder" that "had provoked serious hostility to the police, particularly among the Catholic population of Londonderry, and an increasing disbelief in their impartiality towards non-Unionists."[30] This alienation of the minority was matched by a corresponding animosity on the part of many policemen.[31] Of the eleven people who died as a result of the unrest during July and August 1969, five were Catholics killed by the RUC and three Catholics probably killed by the RUC. There was no evidence that any of them had seriously threatened the police. One was a nine-year-old boy hit by indiscriminate fire from a police machine gun.

Although the regular RUC was responsible for most of the deaths and injuries, complaints focused on the USC, which the protesters depicted as a sectarian instrument of oppression. Its 8,285 members were all Protestants; in some locations, they used Orange halls for drilling and training; and some USC men had taken part in the loyalist counterdemonstrations. When the regular RUC came under serious pressure after the rioting, local police commanders had been authorized to deploy the USC for crowd control. During the August rioting they caused a number of casualties, including at least one death. Their practical contribution to the control of the disorder was slight, but their symbolic part in escalating it was considerable.

UK ministers singled the USC out for particular criticism.[32] They decided that it must be abolished, but were afraid to announce this immediately in case of a loyalist backlash. Instead they persuaded Stormont to agree to creating a small advisory committee on the future of the RUC. Callaghan selected as its chairman Lord Hunt, a former colonial governor who had impressed him in previous work for the Home Office. Callaghan wanted a quick win: "The first need was urgency: the first criterion by which to judge any reform proposal was the likely speed of its effects."[33] Police reform was attractive because it promised quick and visible changes, in contrast to the reforms already promised in housing and local government. Callaghan set Hunt a tight deadline, and he completed his report in under six weeks.

Hunt recommended a series of actions to strengthen and professionalize the RUC, including more officers, improved equipment and training, a new organizational structure, regular inspections by senior officers from England, new linkages with police forces and institutions in Britain, and a vigorous drive to recruit more Catholics. These were uncontroversial. But other recommendations undermined the capacity of the police to protect state security, and these provoked intense resistance from Unionists: Hunt called to abandon the RUC's paramilitary role; generally disarm the force; create an independent police authority in line with the English model, with representation from both communities; and replace the USC with a new force under the control of the GOC. UK ministers were determined that the USC's replacement should not be merely a rebranded USC. They accepted a suggestion from the Catholic primate of all Ireland, Cardinal Conway, that it should have about 250 British—meaning not Northern Irish—officers and noncommissioned officers (NCOs) in its command structure.[34]

Callaghan had already decided to disband the USC even before the Hunt Committee had been appointed.[35] Wilson was determined that the Unionists should not have access to "a private army." According to Irish diplomat Eamon Gallagher, the prime minister considered that the possession of such a force by the white minority administration had wrecked his Rhodesia policy, and he was determined not to repeat the mistake in dealing with the settlers of Northern Ireland.[36] Wilson and Callaghan had not at first intended to replace the USC with anything, but three considerations Hunt raised persuaded Callaghan to do so. First, it was clear that if the regular RUC assumed an exclusively civilian role, some force would be needed that could protect key installations and guard against the continuing threat of insurgency.[37] Hunt had in mind the possibility of a renewed IRA campaign along the lines of 1956–62 and the explosions of the previous spring. He assessed the probability of such attacks as "not great," but reasoned that public anxiety would not be allayed unless precautions were seen to be taken.[38] Without such a force, it would be difficult politically and practically to withdraw the regular army quickly.

Second, although London did not make this explicit, Unionist leaders had already reacted with hostility to suggestions that the USC should be disbanded. Following Wilson's remarks and press speculation in August, Chichester-Clark and his cabinet had threatened to resign.[39] If this had precipitated an election, it was likely that a less cooperative administration would have resulted. The creation of a new army regiment helped to avert this danger.

Third, London did not welcome the prospect of there falling outside its control a network of over eight thousand committed Protestants, trained, armed, disaffected, and with a sudden surplus of time and energy. Under army command, it was reasoned, the former USC members' commitment to public service could be channelled into harmless activities. This final consideration swayed doubting ministers.[40] From London's perspective, the Ulster Defence Regiment (UDR), which began operations in 1970, represented a substantial improvement on the USC. It would be only half as large; it would be under the command of the army; it could be used to free up regular soldiers, for example by taking on guard duty and manning checkpoints; and it could be stood down once it had served its purpose.[41]

Wilson later wrote that the Northern Ireland government had accepted the Hunt recommendations without question.[42] In fact, Chichester-Clark assented only under powerful pressure from Callaghan and with great reluctance. The Northern Ireland cabinet came close to resigning collectively over the disbanding of the USC. They saw it as stripping them of the means to secure the state and its borders just as a serious threat of renewed republican violence was emerging. Chichester-Clark later wrote that his acceptance of the Hunt recommendations had undermined his leadership of the Unionist Party more than any other single item in the successive reform packages.[43]

## The Options

The deployment of British troops in Northern Ireland added urgency to implementing the reform program. Callaghan reformulated his objectives as being to restore order and guarantee the civil rights of the minority. He attributed the disorder to Stormont's failure to respond quickly and effectively to grievances he considered justified. The previous year, he had told Unionist ministers that "the violence would inevitably grow if the Northern Ireland Government refused to meet legitimate political demands."[44] Wilson went further, describing the disorder as "the culmination of nearly fifty years of the unimaginative inertia and repression of successive unchallenged, and because of Ulster's history unchallengeable Ulster Unionist Governments."[45]

Recognizing that if they had to deploy troops for any length of time to maintain order in Northern Ireland, they would require a more coherent policy, the UK cabinet considered four broad options in the run-up to August 1969: using the army simply to reinforce Stormont, direct rule from Westminster, pressing Stormont for faster and further reforms, and complete withdrawal.

### Reinforcing Stormont

Discussions between Stormont and London about calling in troops to reinforce the RUC had taken place in 1966 and again in April 1969.[46] Northern Ireland ministers pointed out that the armed forces had a general duty to support the civil authorities as necessary to enforce law and order. This applied to the garrison routinely stationed in Northern Ireland, to the first tranche of reinforcements deployed in spring 1969 to guard public utilities, and to any additional soldiers who might be sent subsequently. Since they were acting in this capacity, Stormont should control them.[47] Chichester-Clark cited as a precedent the deployment of the army to reinforce the RUC during sectarian riots in Belfast in the 1930s. He argued that it would be both unconstitutional and politically dangerous for London to take back powers that had been devolved for almost fifty years. It would further undermine the authority of the Stormont administration, already under attack from both sides, weaken his leadership of the Unionist Party, and encourage disorder by rewarding it. Stormont's

enemies would redouble their efforts if they knew that the army deployment could result in direct rule or a reduction in Stormont's powers.[48] The
Stormont leader was willing to concede that UK ministers should set the
political parameters within which the soldiers would operate and retain
the power to veto specific actions.

Callaghan disagreed, arguing that the army must be openly and trans-
parently accountable to Westminster; the national government could not
permit its troops, or even reinforcements from police forces in Britain, to
take instructions from a subordinate administration. This was a political
decision rather than a clarification of the legal position. Whitehall officials'
advice to Callaghan had been unambiguous: the armed forces were required by law to assist in the maintenance of order throughout the United
Kingdom if called on to do so by the civil power, in this case the Stormont
minister of home affairs.[49]

### Direct Rule

Republicans had been calling for some time for Northern Ireland to be
governed directly from Westminster. Some saw this as a necessary first
step toward a united Ireland; others' primary interest was in stripping their
Unionist opponents of power, particularly control over security. Callaghan
had contingency plans for direct rule drawn up during winter 1968–69
for use if someone such as Craig—whom he described as "an extreme and
uncompromising right-winger"—replaced O'Neill and openly repudiated
the reform program, or if the sporadic disorders in specific locations deteriorated into a general breakdown of law and order.[50] These contingency
plans included draft legislation empowering the governor to take control
of the devolved administration.[51] It was thought that any period of direct
rule must be brief and might be followed by a revised constitution for
Northern Ireland, incorporating external safeguards for human rights; by
the full incorporation of Northern Ireland into Great Britain; or even by
its detachment from the United Kingdom altogether. In considering these
plans, ministers noted, "In the longer term, the most desirable solution
from the British point of view might be a union of Northern and Southern
Ireland."[52]

When O'Neill resigned in April 1969, UK ministers discussed whether
to implement their contingency plans. They satisfied themselves that
Chichester-Clark would adhere to O'Neill's policy of reform, and would
perhaps be better at winning grassroots support for it. To ensure that he
did his best, Callaghan told him on August 6 that Britain was prepared to
introduce direct rule if progress with the reforms was unsatisfactory, or if
it became necessary to use troops to control rioting on a continuous basis.

It would then be "a case of taking over all Northern Ireland's affairs or none."[53] Whitehall officials reinforced this warning, advising their Stormont counterparts that "in view of the serious constitutional consequences of the use of troops it would be advisable for Northern Ireland to endure a quite considerable degree of disorder before involving military assistance." When Stormont cabinet secretary Sir Harold Black queried what these consequences might be, his counterpart in the Home Office answered that Callaghan believed that "if he decided to put troops on the streets he might be committing the UK government to take over the government of Northern Ireland."[54]

Whatever value Wilson and Callaghan might have extracted from the threats, their intention was to introduce direct rule only as a last resort.[55] In discussing strategy with the cabinet, Callaghan advised that "it would be better to avoid direct intervention and to use the Northern Ireland Government as agents. . . . It was important to remember that the majority of the population of NI were Protestant; in seeking to allay the apprehensions of the Catholics, they must not drive the majority beyond endurance." His colleagues agreed that "Direct Rule . . . would pose a severe administrative problem and would impose the risk of armed conflict with the Protestant community." However, if Chichester-Clark failed to comply, "more drastic measures would be inevitable." Ministers explicitly identified the withdrawal and disarming of the USC as one of the core conditions that Stormont must accept.[56]

Direct rule implied a deeper and longer intervention than UK ministers wanted. Callaghan later wrote: "I had no confidence that if the Ulster Unionist Government were replaced British intervention in Irish affairs would make the situation better in the long run."[57] Callaghan feared in particular that direct rule would provoke a violent loyalist reaction, which might require the deployment of over 20,000 troops to keep the peace—more than could be made available for a protracted period.[58]

The anxiety was reinforced by advice from Black, who responded to the suggestion from Whitehall officials that Callaghan might impose direct rule with an angry memo to the Home Office portraying the likely consequence as "a frightening reaction from the Protestant community which could make anything that has happened up to now seem like child's play: a provisional government might be set up with extreme elements at its head."[59] This was not a hollow warning. Craig had been making belligerent speeches at public meetings for the previous four months. Black also advanced a moral argument: "The action proposed by HMG [Her Majesty's Government] was surely only proper in the case of a recalcitrant and intractable government which was resisting desirable reforms. The present

administration in Northern Ireland, far from being reactionary, had em-
barked upon every reform suggested to them by London and were completely committed to the implementation of reform."

Callaghan recognized that direct rule would not in itself end discrimination or restore order. It would leave him with the responsibility for
pushing through a program of reforms that many Unionists would resist,
especially without the Stormont parliament as a forum for the orderly expression of their grievances. There would be no intermediary to blame for
slow progress or failure. Moreover, he did not know whether the RUC and
the Northern Ireland Civil Service would cooperate, and without their
willing engagement, the prospects for direct rule would be poor.[60] Failure
was probable, and likely to exact a high political price. Whatever its faults,
Stormont served the useful purpose of insulating UK ministers from an
intractable problem and the political blame for failing to solve it.[61]

A primary demand of those calling for direct rule was that the Stormont minister of home affairs should surrender his control over the RUC
and the institutions of criminal justice, which he might otherwise misuse
to suppress the grassroots campaign for reform. The Downing Street Declaration, the Hunt reforms, and the review of the Special Powers Act went
a long way toward meeting this demand without incurring the political
risks associated with full direct rule.

### Reform

UK ministers believed that a policy of accelerated reform would meet all
their broad objectives at low cost and risk and minimize the depth and
length of their unwanted entanglement in Northern Irish affairs. It was
safely incremental, building on a foundation that had already been laid
while leaving the path open to other more radical options for the future,
including direct rule and complete withdrawal. Nationalists would welcome it warmly and Unionists would not resent it so bitterly as to provoke
violent protest or seriously undermine Chichester-Clark's leadership.[62]

At the same time, Callaghan recognized the danger that the reforms
would be interpreted on both sides as concessions to violence. Such an
interpretation would weaken Chichester-Clark's leadership and encourage
disorder. There was no guarantee that reforms would secure the minority's allegiance and a strong probability that they would stimulate other
demands that would be more difficult to meet, notably for the abolition of
Stormont. On the Protestant side, the perception that the authorities were
appeasing violence was likely to elicit counterviolence.[63] Callaghan had
anticipated a loyalist reaction against the policing reforms, although he
underestimated its intensity, optimistically believing that once Unionists

had let off steam, they would respect the authority of the state to which they had pledged their allegiance, as long as London could convince them that there was no serious threat to the union.[64] He was prepared to take this risk because the availability of the USC to Unionist leaders undermined London's control over developments.

The reform strategy was premised on the continuation of devolved government in Northern Ireland, qualified by the condition that Stormont should, in the future, govern under Westminster's direct political oversight and in the interest of both communities. Callaghan's commitment to the reform policy was diluted to the extent that he entertained strong reservations about Unionist ministers' competence. Reporting to the UK cabinet on September 4 after a visit to Northern Ireland, he described them as "bewildered and inert. It had been difficult to arouse them to a realization of the full gravity of the situation."[65] But there was nothing in the reform policy that precluded direct rule at a later stage if the Unionists failed to deliver; the reform package prepared the ground for direct rule by asserting Westminster's ultimate authority; taking control of security policies and operations; disbanding the USC, weakening the Unionist Party and its leadership; encouraging the minority to look to London for change; and injecting Whitehall officials into the heart of the Northern Ireland administration.

UK ministers did not intend eventually to introduce direct rule. All the evidence suggests that one of their priorities was to minimize the extent and duration of their involvement. During July, Callaghan wrote, "we were debating whether we should intervene, but hoping and praying that we would not have to. The advice that came to me from all sides was on no account to get sucked into the Irish bog."[66] The home secretary recognized that Stormont would be inhibited from asking for military support by the risk of greater political interference from London and would deploy the USC before asking for army reinforcements.[67] But he preferred to have the USC on the streets, with all the attending physical and political risks, rather than send in soldiers at an earlier stage, when their presence might have prevented low-level disorder from escalating out of control.

An indication of UK ministers' longer-term intentions lies in the proposal that Whitehall officials discussed at a meeting in April 1969. The mandarins noted that their masters had "envisaged the possibility of some form of round table conference to get to the root of the differences between the various factions and if possible to resolve them."[68] The officials were not enthusiastic, since the holding of a conference implied a willingness to intervene comprehensively and "would make it difficult to secure the willing attendance of representatives of the Northern Ireland Government and its supporters." This was especially the case if radical civil rights campaigners, Paisleyites, and the Irish government were included. Yet if they were not, this would surely defeat the object of the conference.

The civil servants concluded that a negotiation was unlikely to result in an agreement, given the depth and intensity of the differences between Unionist hard-liners and radical republicans. At the same time, they identified three potential benefits. Dialogue might in itself help to reduce tensions, and even if it failed, it would allow more time to prepare for direct rule. Finally, it would improve the government's presentational posture if it eventually had to introduce direct rule.

### Withdrawal

When the cabinet met on February 26, 1969, members aired a fourth and radical option: expelling Northern Ireland from the United Kingdom. They foresaw that this could lead either to an independent Northern Ireland or to absorption by the Republic. The five most influential ministers—the prime minister, home secretary, chancellor of the exchequer, foreign secretary, and defence secretary—each personally favored Irish unification as the best long-term solution.[69] They did not reveal this preference publicly, but others were less reticent. George Brown MP, who had until the previous year been deputy leader of the Labour Party and foreign secretary, openly endorsed the Nationalist argument that the minority could not expect equality in any foreseeable northern state, and consequently that the conflict could be resolved only by ending partition.[70]

The cabinet commissioned advice on the option from officials. When it arrived, it was to the effect that if Britain withdrew, "the regime would be likely to become more illiberal or no regime capable of maintaining law and order would exist." In these circumstances, "there seems a strong likelihood that political pressure would compel the Irish Republic to step in and annex the Six Counties."[71] Despite their personal preferences, ministers accepted their officials' conclusion that withdrawal might precipitate a bloody civil war. The fighting would likely spread to British cities with politically active Irish communities, such as Glasgow, Liverpool, Birmingham, and London, in which case the British Labour Party would pay a high price. Such a development would also present grave dangers to Britain's international diplomatic, defense, and economic interests.[72] Although this discussion laid the idea of immediate withdrawal to rest, it also led ministers to direct officials to explore ways of improving relations with the Republic for the longer term.[73]

## Uncertainties and Paradigms

### Managing Uncertainties

When the RUC collapsed in August 1969, UK ministers lacked accurate information about the principal actors and events in Northern Ireland.[74] Yet they had to act quickly. They also had to trade off four competing values in the face of substantial uncertainties: order on the streets, equity between the two communities, avoiding a loyalist backlash, and minimizing the depth and intensity of Britain's intervention.

Before 1969, Westminster had deliberately insulated itself from the region's affairs. Only one member of Wilson's cabinet had visited the region, a predecessor of Callaghan's who had spent a single afternoon there.[75] Callaghan had asked the security service MI5 to assess the prospect of IRA violence in November 1968—presumably to check the accuracy of Stormont's warnings—only to discover that they, like him, depended on the RUC for the information they had.[76] Thus, with little preparation, Whitehall had to tackle a major breakdown in order that had overwhelmed the local administration. Defense Secretary Denis Healey as late as May 1969 had told the cabinet during a discussion about possible intervention: "Frankly, Northern Ireland has completely different conditions from Britain and we shall be as blind men leading the blind if we go in there knowing nothing about the place."[77]

Healey accordingly suggested that something should be done to gather political intelligence, but Callaghan resisted this on the ground that it might damage his relationship with Chichester-Clark. In April, a single MI5 officer had been seconded at the RUC's request to support its Special Branch, and at the same time to report back on its objectivity and competence. In July, the army sent plainclothes soldiers to reconnoitre potential trouble spots. But before August, no senior UK officials had been located in Belfast. Lacking eyes and ears of its own in Northern Ireland, the cabinet relied heavily on four sources of information, each with its own agenda: Stormont ministers and their officials, proponents of reform in the British Labour Party, the London media, and the NILP. Until October 1968, Stormont's voice had prevailed. But the riots of that month initiated a period of intensive national media coverage of Northern Ireland's affairs and strengthened the influence of Labour backbenchers. UK ministers came increasingly to rely on these sources for an alternative view of events. Television in particular focused on the disorder in the streets at the expense of less visible and dramatic developments, such as the increasing tensions within unionism.

This information deficit was compounded by the need to respond urgently. UK ministers wanted to fix the problem and withdraw the troops within six months. They saw two substantive risks in failing to meet this deadline: that the army would itself come under attack and that loyalist leaders would mobilize effective opposition to reform, perhaps toppling Chichester-Clark.

In the circumstances, the cognitive process model would expect ministers not to plan strategically, to select and adhere to a single hypothesis as the basis for their policy decisions, and to rely heavily on understandings derived from previous experience. Ministers themselves have testified to the validity of these predictions. Making decisions quickly, they focused on immediate practical objectives that they believed could be achieved within two years, rather than tackling the preconditions underlying the disorder, in particular the conflict over national identity. Apart from direct rule as a last resort, they did not consider any substantive constitutional change in any depth. As Callaghan later wrote of the crisis weeks of August, "Although we had long discussions at the Home Office before leaving for that first visit to Belfast, there was not at that stage any real long-term planning: we were living from hand to mouth and making policy as we needed to."[78] Cabinet minister and diarist Richard Crossman noted: "It wasn't so much deciding what policy to have as being able to excuse it."[79]

### Causes of Disorder

O'Neill had commissioned an official inquiry into the causes of the violence in October 1968. The resulting Cameron Report argued that the determining factor was the emergence in the 1960s of a "much larger Catholic middle class . . . which is less ready to acquiesce in the situation of assumed (or established) inferiority and discrimination than was the case in the past."[80] UK ministers agreed with the finding that Catholic complaints about discrimination in local government and housing had substantial foundation in fact, and that Stormont's failure even to acknowledge this was "an immediate and operative cause of the demonstrations and consequent disorders."[81] Callaghan also identified a substantial economic factor, telling his cabinet colleagues that the high level of unemployment in Derry had led to extremism and subsequent disorder, which spread to Belfast.[82]

Cameron's hypothesis—let us call it the legitimate grievances theory—was convenient for Callaghan in that it allowed him to link causally the values of equity and order. It justified intellectually the hope that reforms and continued economic growth would solve the problem. But it also allowed UK ministers to ignore the risk that perceived concessions to the protesters—however morally justifiable—might encourage further violence. That risk was great because of the very visible schism that already existed between Westminster and Stormont, which the Downing Street Declaration deepened and widened. Finally, the legitimate grievances theory drew a politically convenient veil over deeper and less tractable divisions over national allegiance, political power, and Northern Ireland's constitutional status. It allowed Callaghan to depict both Unionists' fears of republican insurgency and republicans' demands for Stormont's abolition as the obsessions of unreasonable people on the margins, rather than the mainstream political opinions that in the Northern Irish context they were.

Perhaps most important, according to the theory, the British Labour Party could potentially solve the problem in Northern Ireland in a way that fitted its ethos and values. National identity and ethnic rivalry were beyond the reach of policy, but discrimination and poverty could be tackled through effective legislation and sufficient funding. As if to illustrate this point, the senior UK official assigned to Belfast in August 1969 accurately noted that disagreement over partition was the primary cause of the violence, but at once dismissed it as an issue for policymakers: "I am afraid that it is illusory to imagine that there is a short- or even medium-term solution to that problem. . . . The problem therefore is mainly one of jobs and housing."[83] He called for a substantial increase in public spending to enable Northern Ireland to catch up with Britain. Callaghan responded, "I agree this must be the next phase."

Neither of the two governments in Ireland, however, adopted the legitimate grievances hypothesis. Dublin publicly attributed the unrest to the inevitable failure of partition and called on the British government to start working toward Irish unification as the only viable long-term solution. Chichester-Clark agreed to the Downing Street Declaration only under severe pressure and as the price he had to pay for British military and financial support; he did not accept its underlying rationale. The Stormont government blamed the disorder on republican dissidents and called for a robust security response. Even with the benefit of hindsight, Callaghan dismissed this as a parochial view: "The Northern Ireland prime minister seemed to revert to the traditional historic attitude in the dispute about the border as though this were the only point at issue."[84]

Partition may not have been the only precondition for the violence, but in the minds of the parties to the conflict it was at least very salient. Accounting for the political effects of the NICRA campaign requires a fuller explanation than the legitimate grievances hypothesis. Such an explanation must cover a spectrum of attitudes across the Nationalist community, including the opportunistic Marxism of the republican leadership in Derry and Belfast, the fashionable international radicalism of the PD movement and its student followers, the moderate demands of the emerging Catholic professional class, and a deep-rooted feeling of ethnic humiliation running across the Catholic community.

An alternative hypothesis is that the people who directed the protest campaign sought not limited political reforms but the destabilization of Stormont and ultimately the end of partition. Ironically echoing the advice Bill Craig had given to Harold Wilson, Sinn Féin president Gerry Adams has since claimed that the entire campaign was "the creation of the republican leadership."[85] This may overstate the case, but there is no reason to doubt the finding of the Cameron Commission that

> There was early infiltration of the Civil Rights Association both centrally and locally by subversive left wing and revolutionary elements which were prepared to use the Civil Rights movement to further their own purposes, and were ready to exploit grievances in order to provoke and foment disorder and violence in the guise of supporting a non-violent movement.[86]

After the failure of the IRA's 1956–62 cross-border campaign, the republican movement acquired new leaders who developed a revolutionary Marxist political strategy hostile both to unionism and to traditional nationalism. IRA chief of staff Cathal Goulding argued that since sectarian discrimination was an essential prop for the unionist state, to campaign for civil rights reforms was in effect to campaign for the state's destruction. Goulding and others predicted that the turbulence would unite Catholic and Protestant workers in a class alliance that would ultimately overthrow both capitalism and partition. The campaign would

> force O'Neill to concede more than he wants to or than he can dare give without risking overthrow by the more reactionary elements among the Unionists. . . . Demand more than may be demanded by the compromising elements that exist among the Catholic leadership. Seek to associate as wide a section of the community as possible with these demands, in particular the well-intentioned people in the Protestant population and the trade union movement.[87]

The republican movement was highly fragmented and never directly controlled NICRA. Nevertheless, this outline strategy, published in 1966, describes quite well what the radicals actually did. But they unleashed powerful forces they could not control. Far from uniting Protestant and Catholic workers, the protests resulted in the creation of new sectarian paramilitary organizations, the members of which were to kill one another for the next three decades.[88]

## British Standards

UK ministers' emphasis on Catholic grievances was rooted in a conception of political life based on their own experience of politics in Britain. While recognizing that Northern Ireland's political culture was very different, they assumed that the main problem with the administration of Northern Ireland was that it was not British enough. If only it would behave even-handedly, they reasoned, the minority would give it their allegiance. As we saw in chapter 2, academic research into political attitudes at the time tends to refute this belief.

The concept of a segment of the population giving its allegiance to an-other nation was unfamiliar to UK ministers. They viewed the conflict as an anachronism that persisted because of discrimination, rather than a continuing struggle between the irreconcilable demands of two national identities. Crossman referred to O'Neill as "the man we were relying on in Northern Ireland to do our job of dragging Ulster out of its eighteenth-century Catholic-Protestant conflict."[89] Callaghan—formerly a shop stew-ard—shared the view of the socialist faction in the civil rights campaign that a durable resolution could be achieved by uniting the Protestant and Catholic working classes in the labor movement. He thought this could best be done through the NILP[90] and wanted the British Labour Party to support its smaller brother financially, organizationally, and morally in constructing a "normal" left-right division in Northern Irish politics.[91]

The tendency to look to British models for a solution to the problem extended to the scale and quality of the administration. Callaghan and Wilson questioned why such a small region needed its own parliament, with a full complement of officeholders and procedures modeled on West-minster. During his first visit to Northern Ireland, Callaghan wrote, "It was always in my mind that by British standards the Northern Ireland Cabinet and Parliament was little more than an enlarged county council, with rather greater powers for raising taxes and spending money and an unhealthy political control over the police."[92]

Callaghan also applied British norms to policing. The Hunt Committee comprised Hunt and two senior British police officers. Its recommenda-tions were based on the principle that the RUC should be brought into line with "the mainland." Callaghan's officials rejected the suggestion that the RUC should be reconstituted on a county basis, so that the community structure of each area would be more closely reflected in the force that served it, on the ground that this "would run counter to the trend in the UK towards larger police forces."[93] Even as Hunt was writing his report, Home Office officials were working on a proposal to draft British police-men into Northern Ireland to help establish "a 'normal' policing system—

i.e., one more like the system we are familiar with here rather than the RUC system."[94] Neither ministers nor senior officials showed any appreciation of the reasons why things had been ordered differently in Ireland, or of the possibility of using other models as the basis for change, such as the Republic's police service, the Garda Síochána.

### Reasonable People

Linked to the concept of British standards was that of reasonable people, meaning those political activists, commentators, and voters in Northern Ireland who sought to comply with the accepted norms of the British political establishment. As T.E. Utley, an English commentator sympathetic to the Unionist position, has observed, "British policy assumed the existence or at least the potential existence of a 'center'—an amorphous mass of responsible, tolerant, silent, and simple people ready to be mobilized in defense of compromise."[95] Without benefit of any evidence, Hunt expressed the opinion that his recommendations would "be widely accepted by reasonable men and women in Northern Ireland"[96]; presumably, not accepting his recommendations would be proof of their irrationality. Like Callaghan, Hunt discounted the significance of the conflict over national identity, arguing that the reformed RUC could "play a leading part, not only in enforcing law and order, but in helping to create a new climate of respect for the law, a new attitude of friendship between its members and the public, and a sense of obligation among all men of goodwill to cooperate with the police in fulfilling their civic duties."[97] This suggests a fundamental failure to appreciate that Nationalists rejected the RUC not merely because of instances of misconduct or discrimination but because it represented at street level a state apparatus the very existence of which they opposed, along with their enforced inclusion in its territory. Whether the RUC was armed or unarmed, hostile or friendly, this objection remained. Correspondingly, Unionists tended to support the RUC uncritically, seeing it as their most reliable line of defense against republican subversion, IRA terrorism, and the enforcement of Dublin's territorial claim.

### Britain's Role

Within the conceptual framework of the legitimate grievances hypothesis, the UK government positioned itself as a neutral mediator. This was politically more convenient than (as Stormont would have wished) the role of sovereign authority with ultimate responsibility for ensuring security and stability in Northern Ireland, or (as republicans saw it) as an occupying colonial power that should withdraw as soon as possible. Labour ministers defined their task as persuading the two sides to accept a fair (i.e., British) compromise. Wilson summarized this stance at one cabinet meeting: "we were not going to underwrite a reactionary government. We had agreed to put in troops to restore law and order but not to keep them there indefinitely to maintain it. We must keep firmly in the middle of the road."[98] This conception contributed to eliminating the options of reinforcing Stormont, direct rule, and immediate withdrawal, since none of these would have been evenhanded enough.

## Politics

Labour backbenchers at Westminster had since 1965 been raising concerns about discrimination in Northern Ireland. After deploying troops in August 1969, ministers could no longer reply that this was an internal matter for Stormont. Parliamentary pressure was amplified by national media coverage of the rioting and by the diplomatic activities of the Irish government.

### The Backbenches

Britain's Labour Party had traditionally seen itself and been seen by Unionists as anti-Unionist in outlook. In power, however, it has seldom acted on what it once called its "deeply held belief" in the cause of Irish unity, instead displaying what one researcher has called "ambivalence and ambiguity" over the issue.[99] When Labour came to office in 1964 for the first time since 1951, it was with a new generation of MPs who tended to support decolonization, and many depicted Northern Ireland as one of Britain's last colonies.[100] Some supported Irish unification; others were more concerned about anti-Catholic discrimination.[101] In June 1965, sixty of them came together to launch the Campaign for Democracy in Ulster (CDU) as a parliamentary pressure group to campaign for reform. The CDU gained momentum after the March 1966 general election, in which Labour increased its parliamentary majority.

The CDU asserted Westminster's supremacy over Stormont, arguing that the British government should intervene to ensure a positive response from the Unionist government to the protesters' demands. The group strongly influenced the Labour Party's thinking on Northern Ireland and encouraged NICRA to focus on the un-British nature of democracy there. It also generated tensions between the British Labour Party and the NILP, whose Unionist members were disturbed by the CDU's bias toward nationalism and concerned about protecting their support base in Protestant areas.[102]

In the 1966 election, Gerry Fitt was elected as Westminster MP for the predominantly Catholic constituency of West Belfast. Describing himself

as a republican socialist, Fitt was the only MP from the nationalist tradition to take his seat, as the Nationalist Party was boycotting the British
parliament. Fitt's biographer has depicted him as a nationalist in Belfast
and a socialist in Westminster. Like the CDU, Fitt came to see the potential of an effective street protest campaign to drive a wedge between
Westminster and Stormont and hence destabilize the Unionist regime.[103]
He used his Commons seat to press energetically for both British withdrawal and immediate reforms to improve his constituents' quality of life.
He worked closely with the CDU, voted with Labour on most issues (in
contrast to the Unionist MPs of the day), and guided Labour MPs toward
his own interpretation of events in Northern Ireland as they unfolded.

In April 1967, three CDU MPs visited Northern Ireland at Fitt's invitation to investigate allegations of discrimination. After meeting trade
unionists, civil rights campaigners, and representatives of nationalist political groups, they produced a report that foreshadowed Cameron's findings. They found evidence of discrimination in the allocation of public
housing and local government jobs, and highlighted the gerrymandering
of local government electoral boundaries in Londonderry. They called for
the establishment of a royal commission to investigate and the appointment of an ombudsman to handle complaints of maladministration.[104]
By 1968, over 100 Labour MPs had signed a petition supporting these
demands.

Having failed to make progress in lobbying Callaghan, Paul Rose, the
chair of the CDU, advised Stormont MP and NICRA activist Austin
Currie in January 1968 that "no British government—including this Labour government—will intervene to remedy injustice in Northern Ireland
unless you people there force it to do so." This prompted Currie to organize the first civil rights protest, a housing squat in the Tyrone village of
Caledon, on June 20, and to propose that NICRA organize a series of civil
rights marches.[105] To maximize the political impact at Westminster, Fitt
and four British Labour MPs walked in the front row of the Derry march
on October 5.

As we have seen, the MPs' presence succeeded in attracting international
publicity. There was widespread television coverage of RUC officers hitting
Fitt and others. Fitt later acknowledged that he had made the most of the
photo opportunity—or as Bernadette Devlin, another republican activist
who was present, put it, "Gerry stuck his head under a police baton."[106]
Street theater succeeded where lobbying had failed. The CDU produced a
report for Wilson asserting that the police had attacked unarmed demonstrators without provocation. They called on Wilson to take control of the
RUC, arguing that the House of Commons could not ignore an assault on

one of its members by the agents of a subordinate administration. Helped by the media coverage they had stimulated, the CDU had at last secured a place for Northern Ireland on the British national political agenda.[107]

The parliamentary Labour Party responded by setting up a special Northern Ireland Group, effectively formalizing the CDU. Its influence was at first constrained by a ruling that issues could not be raised at Westminster for which a minister of the Northern Ireland government was accountable to Stormont. Such issues included policing and the local government franchise.[108] But Fitt and his CDU allies broke through that procedural barrier when British soldiers were deployed onto the streets of Northern Ireland. With Westminster clearly responsible for security, they could raise any matters affecting security, including the need for reform, and bypass and undermine Stormont by appealing directly to the sovereign government. Callaghan could no longer hide behind the politically convenient doctrine of nonintervention. Taking full advantage of this new context, Fitt secured an audience with Wilson on September 9, presenting himself as spokesman for the entire Catholic community.

In forty-seven years of electoral politics, the old Nationalist Party had made no headway in confronting the Unionist monolith, but thanks to a combination of street politics, media coverage, and their success in cultivating Labour MPs, the protest movement had circumvented and encircled Stormont. In the future, the important decisions about political development in Northern Ireland would be made by UK ministers whose authority derived not from the unionist electorate but from their constituents in England, Scotland, and Wales.

Wilson and Callaghan knew they were vulnerable to the criticism that the unrest could have been avoided if they had acted sooner. They had foreseen this danger when they met Chichester-Clark in May 1969, citing "difficult political and Parliamentary problems" that the army's intervention would create for them.[109] They would have to account for their stewardship of Northern Ireland to the Labour Party conference in September and to the Commons when it reconvened in October. Callaghan rose to the challenge and later congratulated himself on his success. By forcing Stormont to accept further reforms, "we had forestalled the outburst that would otherwise have come when the Cameron Commission published its conclusions in fourteen days' time condemning inadequate and unfair allocation of houses in Catholic areas and discrimination in local government jobs, among other things."[110]

When Parliament reassembled on October 13, the main business was a debate on Northern Ireland led by Callaghan, who announced the government's acceptance of the Hunt recommendations. Thanks to the speed with which Callaghan had acted, the Labour backbenchers who spoke attacked not him but the Unionists, and they did so in terms designed to strengthen Callaghan's hand in dealing with them. There was no criticism of his previous record.[111] Whether the reforms would actually work was for another day.

### The Opposition

Although organizationally distinct, the Conservative and Unionist Parties at Westminster had traditionally been allies, and Unionist MPs normally voted with the Conservatives. Before April 1969, this arrangement had delivered eleven apparently secure votes for the Conservatives. Thus it was not in the interest of the Conservative Party to advocate withdrawal from Northern Ireland, support NICRA, or otherwise upset the Unionists. The Conservatives' general disposition was to oppose any further intervention in Northern Ireland than was strictly necessary. As long as Callaghan could present himself publicly as working with the Northern Ireland government, he could rely on the parliamentary opposition to support him.

Conservative leader Edward Heath endorsed O'Neill's policy of reaching out to the Catholic community and tried to strengthen O'Neill's hand in his struggle against Craig and Paisley. In November 1968, he wrote O'Neill an open letter refuting Craig's assertion that Stormont should resist pressure for change from Labour and wait for the Conservatives to come back into power; he insisted that he would not accept any reversal of the reforms already announced.[112] In September 1969, responding to media coverage of the disorder, Heath distanced himself from the Unionist government, depicting it as entirely independent of the Conservative Party.[113] During a visit to Northern Ireland the following month, Conservative spokesman Quentin Hogg reinforced the message: "I am backing Callaghan for all I am worth. Any Unionist who thinks he will get a better deal out of me than out of Jim is an ass."[114]

A handful of Conservative and Unionist MPs favored simply reinforcing Stormont without requiring further reforms. But the public compliance of successive Northern Irish prime ministers with Labour's demands limited this group's scope for opposing the reform strategy openly, and their ability to influence policy was insignificant relative to that of the CDU.

Callaghan was grateful for Heath's support and went out of his way to maintain the bipartisan consensus. He was concerned that if the Commons split over the issue, so would the country, and a difficult problem might then become insoluble: "I took very great care in the House not to inflame the Conservatives on the Northern Ireland issue," he wrote, "as I could justly have done, by referring to past history and their part in it."[115]

The need to retain the Conservatives' support suggested a policy of gradual reform rather than radical transformation.

## Media and Public Opinion

The CDU at Westminster was rooted in a broader network of republican and socialist activists in Irish immigrant populations in England.[116] The community CDU was launched in London in 1965. It grew out of the Connolly Association, a strongly antipartitionist body that around 1962 had published a pamphlet called "Our Plan to End Partition."[117] Its anonymous authors argued that a program of franchise and other reforms would liberate the political power of the Nationalist community and thereby enormously strengthen the effort to attain unity. Westminster had the power to impose reform, and it should be forced to do so.[118] The community CDU's effective leader, Paddy Byrne, was a local councillor and influential member of his Labour Party branch who corresponded with activists in Northern Ireland, including the Campaign for Social Justice, a precursor of NICRA.

At a more general level, British public opinion gave at best weak and qualified support for maintaining the union. A survey conducted in June 1967 found that 45 percent of respondents thought that the British government should encourage Northern Ireland to join up with the Republic; 19 percent were against the idea and 36 percent did not know.[119] Before October 1968, however, Northern Ireland had not been a salient issue. Media coverage was slight and intermittent. The *Sunday Times* had produced a report in 1966 and the BBC's news magazine *24 Hours* had covered allegations of gerrymandering in Derry in 1967, but as a media construct, the Northern Ireland problem did not yet exist. Perhaps the most important consequence of the events of October 1968 is that they initiated a transformation in the volume and depth of media coverage. As Wilson told one Unionist MP on October 22, "Up to now we have perhaps had to rely on the statements of himself and others on these matters. Since then we have had British television."[120]

There is no doubt that the British and international news media played an important part in NICRA's success. News editors largely accepted the protesters' accounts of the issues at stake and gave them sympathetic coverage. Journalists from London were warmly received in Catholic areas.[121] By November 1968, "the civil rights movement had won the media war in Britain. The bulk of the media saw the Unionists as bigoted and antediluvian. . . . The civil rights campaigners were in contrast bathed by the media in the white light of righteousness."[122] National newspaper editorials called for firm action to make Stormont introduce reforms quickly. Their message was echoed in television news coverage, which focused on police violence. A report from *The Times,* the newspaper favored by the British establishment, gives the flavor of the coverage at the height of the 1969 rioting:

INNOCENT PEOPLE AT RISK LIKE SITTING DUCKS

I saw the shooting last night. Today I saw the blood and the bullet holes and I will never believe that the police engaged in the Falls Road battle behaved correctly. The degree of mistakes can be disputed, but mistakes there must have been.[123]

The UK national media focused on the "hated" and "controversial" USC, implying that this force was responsible for most of the mistakes: "In dozens of riots this year no one had been killed by shooting until the day the B Specials (USC) moved in. The Specials are relatively ill-trained, exclusively Protestant, and disliked intensely by the Catholics."[124] An official inquiry subsequently refuted the notion that the USC had been responsible for most of the killings, but at the time it was widely believed. Lacking independent sources of street-level information—or perhaps because it suited their political purposes—British ministers accepted and acted on the media condemnation.[125] However, it should not be thought that Whitehall took the media coverage entirely at face value. As the Hunt Committee complained,

We feel bound to deplore the extent to which some press and television coverage of these events has resulted in magnifying, in the minds of readers and viewers, the actual extent of the disorders, in generalising the impression of misconduct by the police and of bad relations between police and public, while sometimes failing correspondingly to illustrate the calm which has prevailed in most parts of Ulster, or the degree of deliberate provocation, the danger and the strain under which the police, frequently and for long periods, tried to do their duty, as well as the fact that the great majority acted not only with courage but with restraint.[126]

## The International Dimension

During the early 1960s, the Irish government of Sean Lemass devised a new policy of constructive engagement toward Northern Ireland, which complemented O'Neill's strategy of modernization. Lemass was not impressed by complaints from northern Nationalists about discrimination and gerrymandering; he regarded the leaders of the Nationalist Party in Northern Ireland as sectarian and reactionary, no better than the regime they opposed.[127] In an interview after his retirement, he observed of northern Nationalists that "for them the day partition ended would be the day they would get their foot on the throat of the Orangemen."[128] As a gesture of reconciliation and in an attempt to open up an agenda for practical cross-border cooperation in areas such as trade and tourism, Lemass met

O'Neill at Stormont on January 12, 1965, the first meeting between leaders of the two jurisdictions since 1922.

Like O'Neill, however, Lemass was constrained by hard-liners within
his own party, Fianna Fáil, and in particular by his minister for external
affairs, Frank Aiken. Even as Lemass implicitly recognized the legitimacy
of partition by reaching out to O'Neill, the Irish government continued to
campaign internationally against Northern Ireland's very existence. This
made it politically difficult for O'Neill to realize the potential created by
his relationship with Lemass.[129] Jack Lynch replaced Lemass as taoiseach
in November 1966,[130] though he maintained Lemass's policy of incremental rapprochement. When one of his senior officials, T.K. Whitaker, went
north to meet Unionist ministers at Stormont, the agenda comprised such
routine issues as customs duties, a minor cross-border road, the control
of foot-and-mouth disease, and the sharing of museum exhibits. There
was no mention of discrimination, partition, or the status of northern
Nationalists.[131]

Lemass set up and after his replacement sat on a Dáil committee to
explore the possibility of amending the Irish constitution. When the committee reported in 1967 it proposed that Article 3, laying claim to Northern Ireland, should be rephrased in less polemical terms. Lynch was sympathetic, but the strength of republican sentiment in Fianna Fáil was so great
that nothing was done. Finance Minister Charlie Haughey condemned
the idea, emphasizing gratuitously as he did so that he saw no objection in
principle to using force to assert the Republic's territorial claim; the only
objections were of expediency.[132]

As in Britain, Ireland's political elite, mass media, and public opinion
discovered Northern Ireland as a salient issue only in October 1968. Even
then, Lemass hoped that "two or three wet days will finish these things."[133]
The Irish cabinet discussed the issue just once before the dramatic events
of July and August 1969, and the Irish civil service was completely unpre-
pared for what happened. Despite the constitutional claim and historical
importance of partition as an issue in Irish politics, there were in Dublin,
as in London, no senior officials assigned to cover Northern Ireland.

The collapse of public order in the north nevertheless prompted a sharp
change in Dublin's diplomatic posture. The unspoken policy of gentle rapprochement stopped and Fianna Fáil ministers reverted to a hard-line public stance reminiscent of the 1920s. Even for internal business purposes,
Irish civil servants dropped the term *Northern Ireland*, which Lemass had
introduced, and reverted to the traditional republican *six counties*. At a
meeting in London on August 1, Irish minister for external affairs Patrick
Hillery warned British foreign secretary Michael Stewart that if the dis-

order spilled across the border, the Republic would no longer treat it as a purely British issue. This was not an offer of help. The implicit threat was of raising the issue at the United Nations. For Callaghan, this would require London to demonstrate that it "was effectively able to intervene, control the situation, and introduce policies that would remove the causes of the revolt."[134] Like the pressure from the CDU, Dublin's stand influenced British ministers against unconditionally reinforcing Stormont; London had to be seen to respond to the protesters' demands.

At the height of the riots, on August 13, Lynch declared in a television broadcast that Stormont could no longer maintain order on the streets and that he did not regard the RUC as impartial. Northern Nationalist leaders, including Fitt, had called on Callaghan to send in soldiers to protect Nationalist neighborhoods; they understood the political consequences at Westminster. Lynch, however, with an eye to his own hard-line critics, announced that it would be unacceptable for the British army to intervene in the north. He declared that "The Irish government can no longer stand by and see innocent people injured and perhaps worse."[135] Reviving Ireland's territorial claim, he called on London to begin negotiations with him on how best to work toward Irish unification. He called up two thousand army reservists and moved soldiers to the border, where they posed for photographers before setting up field hospitals for refugees from the north.

The British recognized that the above were gestures intended to placate Fianna Fáil hard-liners and in particular Lynch's leadership rivals. But Callaghan privately described Lynch's broadcast as "putting the fat in the fire" and indicated that Irish ministers' statements and actions during August had contributed perversely to the breakdown in public order that had made it necessary for the British army to be deployed.[136] In the wake of Lynch's speech, rumors spread across republican communities in the north that the Irish army would shortly be crossing the border to support their defiance of the Unionists. It was in response to these developments that Chichester-Clark ordered the general mobilization of the USC.

Two days after Lynch's broadcast, UK ministers met Hillery at his request in London. The Irish minister criticized them for allowing the march in Derry to proceed, denounced the RUC, and proposed, as a threat, that the British soldiers in the north should be replaced by a joint British-Irish peacekeeping force under the aegis of the United Nations. Hillery indicated that the purpose of Dublin's public protests was not to embarrass the British but to outflank republican extremism.[137] UK ministers replied that Northern Ireland was an internal matter and gave Hillery "a courteous brush-off."[138]

The ministers were not too concerned about the threat of an Irish invasion; they simply did not believe it would happen. But the Irish had other weapons. Callaghan complained to his cabinet colleagues about Dublin's diplomatic offensive and about its failure—if it was serious about building a united Ireland—to make any effort to conciliate Protestant opinion.[139] The British were also anxious about the potential consequences of a republican resurgence for Lynch's leadership and, hence, for political and economic stability in Ireland, where there were substantial British investments. They knew that Lynch's rivals were looking for opportunities either to force him to take a tougher stand on the north or embarrass him for not having done so. Three influential ministers—Neil Blaney (agriculture), Kevin Boland (local government), and Charles Haughey (finance)—were trying to force Lynch to support the republican campaign against Stormont with more than just words. Evidence subsequently available shows that they wanted him to instruct the Irish army to cross the border and help man the barricades in the frontier towns of Derry and Newry. They did not imagine that the Irish army could defeat the British militarily, but saw the invasion as a tactic to trigger UN intervention.

British ministers accepted the advice of their ambassador in Dublin, Sir Andrew Gilchrist, that "Lynch had to be seen to be taking some action."[140] In a private conversation with Gilchrist, the taoiseach said he had done the minimum necessary to avert an IRA propaganda coup. He acknowledged that the south was quite incapable of "taking over" the north in the foreseeable future. All he aspired to for the moment was to be consulted during Britain's process of policy development. He accepted that substantial social and financial adjustments would be needed in the south to prepare for unity and estimated that these would take up to fifteen years to complete.[141] He proposed that the two governments should work together toward eventual unification in small steps; direct rule should not be introduced, since it would create new impediments to unification; and it would be preferable for future negotiations to be conducted through routine diplomatic channels, outside the spotlight. Gilchrist accordingly advised his masters to consult Lynch on the substance of any future reforms.[142]

While Irish ministers were not in a position to require London to include them in their decision-making process, agree to a joint peacekeeping force, or draw up plans for eventual unification, they could influence British policy to the extent that London wanted to keep Lynch securely in office to prevent further inflammatory statements and avoid diplomatic embarrassment. These considerations all favored a policy of urgent reform in the short term and closer cooperation, potentially leading toward unification, in the longer term. They counted against reinforcing Stormont, direct rule, and any actions that might give Lynch's rivals ammunition to use against him, such as permitting Chichester-Clark to backpedal on the reform program.

## Wilson

Wilson and Callaghan directed policy on Northern Ireland in consultation with Defence Secretary Denis Healey and Foreign Secretary Michael Stewart, to the virtual exclusion of the rest of the British cabinet.[143] Within this small group, there were substantial disagreements over the extent to which they should intervene and the speed with which they should move. Wilson was the most interventionist and impatient; Healey complained about his "crazy desire to go out there and take things over."[144]

Even before attaining the premiership, Wilson had made known that he personally sympathized with the Nationalist cause.[145] In 1964, he wrote to Patricia McCluskey, one of the founders of the Campaign for Social Justice (CSJ, the precursor of NICRA), deploring discrimination and promising that Labour would tackle it in part by "introducing new and impartial procedures for the allocation of houses and setting up joint tribunals to which particular cases of alleged discrimination in public appointments can be referred."[146] In a second letter he wrote that "a Labour Government would do everything in its power to see that the infringements of justice to which you are so rightly drawing attention are effectively dealt with." He encouraged the CSJ to vote for NILP candidates in the forthcoming Westminster election. Wilson's letters were published in the Northern Ireland press, stimulating the campaigners' expectations and Unionists' antipathy.[147]

Wilson's sympathies with the reform movement were matched by his distaste for the "reactionary" Orange Order. He has described the Orange parades that preceded the disorder in August 1969 as "processions in which grown men would feel it an obligation to march, wearing their obligatory sashes and decorations and carrying their inflammatory slogans, through a city that was as dry as tinder and explosive as a gunpowder charge."[148]

Wilson was also keen to engage with Dublin on the possibility of working toward eventual unification. In March 1965, during a visit to Dublin, he called for three-way talks on the future of Ireland.[149] Wilson's public statements encouraged civil rights campaigners and republicans to believe that if they could induce Westminster to take more responsibility for Northern Ireland, this would help them to achieve their aims, and correspondingly conditioned Unionists' hostile response to the protest movement.[150]

Once in office, however, Wilson proved reluctant to impinge on Stormont's jurisdiction, though he had an interest in curbing the powers of the Unionist MPs at Westminster, who generally voted with his Conservative opponents. This had especially irritated him during his first administration, from 1964 to 1966, when Labour's overall majority had been reduced to only three: He recorded that "every vote in Parliament was an agony for the whips. . . . Labour members were almost chained to the House."[151] At his first business meeting with O'Neill in May 1965, he complained that Labour had almost lost an important vote on the future of the British steel industry "because twelve Ulster members voted against the Government on a matter which did not concern Ulster." He suggested that "as a matter of good taste the Ulster members might like to consider whether it was right for them to vote" on such issues.[152] But there was little O'Neill could do to discipline the Unionists at Westminster MPs. Under the party rules they were accountable not to him but to their local constituency associations. They continued to vote with the Conservatives. Wilson returned to the attack during the general election campaign of March 1966, when he suggested to a group of journalists from Dublin that Northern Ireland's MPs might be removed from Westminster and their functions transferred to a joint north-south parliamentary committee under British chairmanship.[153] This threat was hardly a token of commitment to the union.

At his next meeting with Wilson, on August 5, 1966, O'Neill reported on his efforts to improve community and cross-border relations and described the difficulties he was facing as a consequence of opposition from what Wilson called "his atavistic grassroots supporters and many of his backbenchers, to say nothing of a black reactionary group in his Cabinet."[154] O'Neill asked for a breathing space of six months. Wilson concurred, but insisted that there should then be further reforms, including a review of the franchise and the appointment of an ombudsman. O'Neill did not refuse outright, but argued that the proposed reforms might prove counterproductive, exacerbating the problem without tackling its sectarian roots. Concluding the meeting, Wilson issued another of his thinly veiled threats; he "undertook to do his best to restrain those numerous members of the House of Commons who felt that action should be taken to end discrimination in Northern Ireland. He emphasized however that while he might succeed in doing this for a time he could not nor would he seek to restrain these Members throughout the whole of the present Parliament. . . . Progress must be made if the position was to be held."[155]

When O'Neill's six months were up, Wilson summoned him back to Downing Street. The discussion centred on what the official record called "allegations of discrimination between the two religious and political groups within the Six Counties." Wilson began by indicating that he and his cabinet colleagues were taking flak from the CDU. He repeated his complaint about Unionist MPs' voting behavior, contrasting the inability of his backbenchers even to question ministers about discrimination in

Northern Ireland with the power of Northern Ireland MPs to vote on issues that affected only England. He then turned up the heat: "He knew
that the minds of some of these [CDU] Members were turning towards
the possibility of action in the fields where the United Kingdom Parliament did have an effective voice in Northern Ireland particularly in the
matter of the provision of funds to the Northern Ireland Government.
In the circumstances there must be movement." He went on to make a
remarkable offer reinforced by another threat:

> As he saw it the pressures for reform could not be resisted within the framework of
> the present arrangements between Great Britain and Northern Ireland—nor indeed
> would he think that they should be resisted. His assessment was that within a period
> of about three years [i.e., within the expected lifetime of his administration] one of
> two things must happen. Either (1) the Westminster Parliament would insist on
> interfering more and more with the internal affairs of Northern Ireland with the
> inevitable erosion of the "division of powers" which formed the basis of the present
> arrangements or (2) an agreement would be reached whereby the British Parliament
> and Government would refrain from interfering at all in Northern Ireland affairs
> provided that Northern Irish members of the Westminster Parliament observed the
> same discretion on voting on matters appertaining to Britain.[156]

The implication is that however strongly Labour backbenchers felt about
civil rights in Northern Ireland, Wilson could and would restrain them if
the Unionists would agree not to vote at Westminster on issues that did
not concern Northern Ireland. We can only speculate about whether and
how the prime minister would have delivered on such a deal had it been
agreed, as the Westminster Unionists did not deliver the requested discretion. The consequences Wilson so presciently predicted duly followed. His
preoccupation with restricting the Unionists' voting powers continued. In
November 1968 he was again threatening to remove the Ulster MPs from
Westminster unless Stormont complied with his demands.[157]
    Apart from the Unionists' voting record in the Commons, Wilson
had other political motives for presenting himself as sympathetic to Irish
nationalism. As an MP he represented Huyton in Liverpool, which of all
English constituencies had, as he himself said, "pretty well the highest
proportion of Irish votes, albeit mostly of the second or third generation." He was fond of reminding ministers in Dublin that he represented
more Irish voters than they did.[158] And as party leader it suited him
to respond positively to the demands of the Labour left on this issue.
Many of his backbenchers had become disenchanted with his style of
government, including Paul Rose, chair of the CDU, who echoed a common complaint when he wrote that Wilson seemed obsessed with tactics
at the expense of principle.[159] Expressing concern for the minority in

Northern Ireland gave Wilson an opportunity to placate his left-wing critics at no personal cost.

Wilson was not unique among cabinet ministers in sympathizing with the minority—most believed that NICRA's demands were legitimate. His actions in government fell short of the promises he had made in opposition, and were constrained by the level of support he could command in the cabinet and Commons. Nevertheless, it is clear that he repeatedly took the initiative personally in pressing Stormont to reform and in threatening various forms of punishment if the Unionists failed to comply. Although on holiday for much of the crisis month of August 1969, he personally drafted the Downing Street Declaration, in effect blaming Stormont for the disorder and committing London to guarantee the minority's rights over its head.[160] The other ministers most directly involved, Callaghan and Healey, have clearly indicated that they would not have pressed Stormont so hard, fast, or publicly. In the context of Northern Ireland, Healey later noted, "Harold ballsed up everything he touched."[161] Of course, that is not how Wilson saw it. He later declared that his handling of the challenge had helped strengthen Labour's popular standing. They had been seen to act "with manifest firmness and authority in a demonstrably difficult situation."[162]

## Callaghan

Jim Callaghan became home secretary in November 1967. His relationship with Wilson had been strained throughout 1969 as a result of his determined public opposition to the government's industrial relations policy—opposition that eventually prevailed, to Wilson's annoyance. Wilson saw Callaghan as a potential leadership challenger, one with too much support in the party and trade union movement to be removed from the cabinet.[163] In April 1969 he set up an informal inner cabinet of seven ministers to plan and coordinate long-term policies, from which he explicitly excluded Callaghan.[164] But the home secretary's performance over Northern Ireland won him increased respect across the party, and Wilson readmitted him to the inner circle in September.[165]

Both men privately favored a united Ireland by mutual agreement between the two traditions as the best long-term solution.[166] Both sought to weaken the Unionist Party. Callaghan told a political journalist privately that he wanted "to do down the Unionists."[167] The most obvious difference between them concerned the pace and intensity of intervention. Callaghan tried to restrain Wilson because he and his Home Office officials were concerned about the political consequences for O'Neill of being seen to buckle under pressure from a Labour government in London, and because of the long-term constitutional implications of eroding the established division of powers. When Wilson threatened O'Neill in October 1968 that Westminster would legislate for local government franchise reform if Stormont failed to do so promptly, Callaghan wrote to the prime minister suggesting that "excessive pressure from here at the present moment would not we think bring about the best results."[168]

Callaghan followed the letter with a policy memorandum for the Cabinet, in which he argued for minimal interference with the constitutional settlement of 1920; taking care not to provoke loyalist hostility by moving too fast; and helping O'Neill to stay in office, as no other probable Unionist leader would be as likely to secure any significant support from the Catholic minority. In an implicit rebuke to Wilson, he suggested that early reform in the local government franchise should not be regarded as the only acceptable measure of progress, and warned that if Westminster overrode Stormont on this issue, more communal violence could result, for which London would have to take responsibility.[169] The result was a compromise. The cabinet agreed that O'Neill "should be given the best possible chance to consolidate his position. . . . But indefinite delay would be unacceptable. . . . The aim should be to keep Captain O'Neill as prime minister, but to keep him moving towards reform."[170] It was too late to apply the brakes, however. Two months later O'Neill resigned.

In the wake of the riots of August 1969, Wilson proposed that a UK minister should be appointed with exclusive responsibility for Northern Ireland. This would have levered Callaghan out of a star role in the public eye and expanded Wilson's own influence. *The Times* published a story that officials were reluctant to take responsibility for providing political intelligence on Northern Ireland unless covered by the authority of a resident minister.[171] Callaghan opposed the idea: "I wanted to keep the problem in my own hands. Also, I thought that a resident Minister might get us more involved in Northern Ireland than was necessary."[172] On this occasion Callaghan prevailed.

The two men also disagreed over how quickly they should move in disbanding the USC. Wilson saw this as an essential first step toward ending Unionist control.[173] He accordingly forced Callaghan's hand, announcing during a television interview on August 19 that the USC would be "phased out of their present role." This ambiguous phrase masked a difference over whether they should be disbanded immediately, as Wilson wanted, or only after the Hunt Committee had reported. Wilson's declaration preempted its recommendations, added urgency to the production of its report, and incensed loyalists.[174] Crossman, who elsewhere criticizes Callaghan's lack of imagination and loyalty, has described Callaghan in this context as "once again shrewd and sensible, keeping himself in charge of the situation, re-straining Harold and not letting him poke his nose in too far."[175]

Aside from restraining Wilson, Callaghan had two personal motives for keeping control of the issue. It enhanced his reputation, and he enjoyed his newfound role as crisis manager. He became so enthusiastic that he later wrote a book about Northern Ireland, in which he described the first weeks after the arrival of the troops on the streets as

> the most meaningful experience of my political life. . . . In August 1969, the situation required me to exercise real authority, to do it quickly or be swamped. We had to take the initiative to restore the situation and I was moving with tremendous speed all the time. It was a most enviable position for any politician to be in: the cabinet was on holiday, Harold Wilson was in the Scillies, Parliament was not in session, and there was I in charge, pulling levers here, pushing levers there, saying get this, fetch so-and-so, and the whole machine absolutely buzzed.[176]

Callaghan also wanted to help the NILP: "I believed that the British La-bour Party should pin its official support to the Northern Ireland Labour Party because of its close links with the trade union movement which has always been a non-sectarian force in the North."[177] This, of course, was another reason to break the power of the Unionist Party.

### Conclusion: The Pressure Balance

The protest campaign drew its strength from Irish nationalist networks in England, but the overwhelming demand at Westminster, in the La-bour movement, in the media, and internationally was for reforms rather than British withdrawal. Many of those whose ultimate objective was to overthrow Stormont—including Fitt—saw radical reform as a promising first step on the pathway to unification. In pushing the reform program through, Labour ministers hoped to appease their own backbenchers and activists without alienating the Conservative opposition. By retaining the Stormont administration they hoped to buy time and to insulate them-selves from the political costs of failure.

Political factors ruled out Stormont's preferred option of simply using the army to reinforce the RUC, since Wilson and Callaghan wanted to avoid the domestic and international criticism they would suffer if they were seen to be propping up a failed Unionist administration. Callaghan later wrote:

> We would have been placed in an impossible position if British troops were commit-ted to Northern Ireland for a substantial period while the Ulster Unionist Govern-ment sat behind British bayonets and failed to make the necessary changes. Such a position could never have endured and I do not believe that any of the parties in the British Parliament would have supported it.[178]

## Structure and Doctrine

### Overview

Three Whitehall departments were involved in forming Northern Ireland policy in 1969: the Home Office, responsible for liaison with the Stormont administration and oversight of the security service MI5; the MoD, responsible for the army and from August 1969 for all security policies and operations in Northern Ireland; and the Foreign Office, responsible for relations with the Republic and other countries.

The Cabinet Office performed a coordinating role, providing information and advice for the prime minister and cabinet. Its functions included servicing meetings of the cabinet and its committees, and taking forward discrete cross-departmental policy initiatives. Its senior official was the cabinet secretary, who was also the prime minister's personal adviser and head of the civil service. It serviced the standing cabinet committee on Northern Ireland, known as MISC 238, which met for the first time on February 26, 1969, two days after the Northern Ireland election.

The Northern Ireland government was responsible for all the local government, criminal justice, social policy, and human rights issues covered by the reform program. Major exclusions from its devolved powers were taxation, defense, and foreign affairs.

The key agencies on the ground were the army, over which UK ministers held direct political control, and the RUC, over which they assumed political control in August 1969 in respect of security operations and the USC.

In practice, especially after August 1969, London's reach extended much further than this description of the formal relationship suggests. UK ministers effectively controlled the substance and pace of reform. The span of their control was determined not by statute but their own political calculations, which required them to ensure the full and rapid implementation of reforms while propping up Stormont's dwindling authority. The most telling constraint was to avoid pushing the Northern Ireland prime minister so hard that he lost his leadership position.

### Home Office

Callaghan's desire to minimize Britain's entanglement—and his advice to Wilson before August 1969—reflected the advice he received from his officials in the Home Office. The department's priorities included the important and politically contentious fields of policing and criminal justice, immigration, race relations, and broadcasting. Northern Ireland affairs had until 1968 been the responsibility of a general division that also dealt with insignificant matters, such as the licensing of London taxicabs, British Summer Time, and the administration of state-owned pubs in Carlisle.[179] No senior officials worked exclusively on the issue, and the department relied heavily on the Northern Ireland Civil Service for such information and advice as it needed. Most of the dealings between officials of the two governments concerned the size of the national subvention toward public spending in the region.[180]

The Home Office had a reputation as the most conservative and least proactive of all Whitehall departments. Its structural insulation from Northern Ireland was reinforced and sustained by an official doctrine that depicted its role as representing Stormont's interests in Whitehall, rather than regulating or monitoring its activities. One senior official had described its functions as follows:

1. To act as the official channel of communication between the Governments of the United Kingdom and Northern Ireland.
2. To ensure that Northern Ireland's constitutional rights are not infringed and to watch Northern Ireland's interests generally.
3. To safeguard her interests with regard to schemes under the Agricultural Marketing Acts
4. To ensure that the views of the Government of Northern Ireland on matters affecting them are made known to the Government of the United Kingdom.
5. Questions of law and order are entirely for the Government of Northern Ireland.[181]

In a report on allegations of religious discrimination prepared during Wilson's first administration, civil servants advised that any attempt to impose reform legislation on Northern Ireland under the 1920 act would result in a disastrous rupture between the two governments. Allegations of discrimination and gerrymandering fell squarely within the area of peace, order, and good government, for which the Northern Ireland government had full responsibility.[182] The Home Office continued to oppose political intervention in Stormont's affairs until summer 1971. An influential member of the NILP has commented: "The Home Office officials were not only unhelpful, they were downright obstructive, and we had grounds for believing they were secretly furnishing Stormont with reports to Labour ministers."[183]

The Home Office's doctrine on Northern Ireland led it to oppose direct rule and any reforms that would endanger the future sustainability of the Northern Ireland government. Officials were particularly anxious about procedural innovations; in response to Wilson's proposals for intervention, the Home Office–led officials' committee on Northern Ireland decided in April 1969 that "ministers should be advised to deliberate most carefully before making any offer to Captain O'Neill to introduce legislation at Westminster on the franchise in Northern Ireland."[184] Callaghan evidently agreed.

The Home Office's reluctance to intervene was reinforced by its lack of preparations to do so. It had no program that it could take off the shelf to address ministers' objectives, only experience of policing and race relations in England, which is what it drew on when required rapidly to come up with reform proposals in August 1969. The creation of a community relations commission and the introduction of legislation to outlaw inflammatory rhetoric mirrored race relations initiatives which it had recently introduced in Britain.

### UK Representative

Ministers recognized in October 1968 that their ability to assess developments in Northern Ireland was hampered by their dependence on Stormont for information. They could access alternative perspectives through the NILP and the trade union movement, but these sources too had their own agendas. This lack of objective sources put them at a disadvantage relative to the news media. They identified a particular need for direct access to RUC intelligence to assess the strength of the republican threat that Craig and other Unionists asserted was at the root of the violence. This deficit was discussed at a meeting of Whitehall officials on April 25, 1969, when ministers tasked the MoD and MI5 to establish liaison arrangements with the RUC.[185] Ministers also tasked MI5 to explore what potential there might be for acquiring independent sources of information on "matters where Northern Ireland sources might be ineffective or unreliable."[186]

With the army on the streets in August, the need for good political and military intelligence became more pressing. Callaghan decided to establish an official Whitehall presence in Northern Ireland, independent of the Stormont machine. This became known as the UK Representative (UKREP). Officially its role was threefold: to represent the UK government in Northern Ireland, to oversee the joint Whitehall-Stormont committees set up to implement the reform program, and to maintain contact with representatives of all shades of opinion.[187] UKREP helped to improve London's political intelligence, and perhaps most important, as Callaghan later acknowledged, it was "able to bring very direct influence to bear on the policies of the Northern Ireland Government."[188]

To staff UKREP, a team of Whitehall civil servants was dispatched to Belfast under the direction of Wilson's former private secretary, diplomat

Oliver Wright. Wilson had previously used Wright to negotiate on his behalf with Ian Smith, the Rhodesian rebel leader, following Smith's unilateral declaration of independence in 1965. Callaghan thought that this experience would equip Wright well for dealing with Chichester-Clark and the Unionist Party.[189] Wright reported directly to Wilson and Callaghan, rather than through the regular Home Office channels.[190] He also stood outside the organizational structure of the Northern Ireland Civil Service, and made no attempt to integrate his role with theirs.

Callaghan asked Wright to keep influential Catholics in touch with the progress of the reforms, so that their views could be considered in formulating the necessary legislation.[191] One of Wright's first actions was to meet the Catholic primate of Ireland, Cardinal Conway, and to ask him to persuade the nationalist opposition at Stormont to participate in the legislative process.[192] The creation of UKREP gave the leaders of the Catholic community direct access to the highest level of UK policymaking.

In his first report to Callaghan, Wright traced the Northern Ireland problem back to the colonization of Ulster. Present fears and expectations had compounded a long history of conflict and mistrust between native and settler communities. The Protestant majority feared "the unimpeded progress to majority rule of an eventual Catholic majority caused by the higher Catholic birth rate. . . . in about two decades."[193] Wright apparently accepted the validity of this demographic prediction and believed that it would inevitably result in a united Ireland. He agreed that the government's policy was correct of promoting a more just society—he could hardly have asserted otherwise—but added the qualification that both sides saw the reform strategy as smoothing the way "to the inevitability of first Catholic rule in Ulster and then a united Ireland ruled from Dublin."

Wright's explanation was very different from that in the Cameron Report; Wright even criticized Cameron for neglecting Protestants' fears. He stressed the importance of protecting and reinforcing Stormont's authority: "Only Stormont has any real prospect of carrying its own people with it as it institutes the reforms to which both Governments are committed. If the authority of the Northern Ireland Government is undermined . . . the Northern Ireland Government will fall and HMG will be left without an instrument with which to put the reforms into effect." To this end—and to encourage Stormont ministers to sell the reform strategy to their constituents rather than merely tolerating it—he argued that the security forces must quickly remove the barricades that republicans had erected in Belfast and Londonderry during August 1969. He reasoned that the barricades both encouraged a culture of lawlessness and nourished Chichester-Clark's hard-line critics. Noting how vulnerable Chichester-Clark was, he added that "in the last resort it must suit the Catholics to be clobbered by us if that is the only way we can get justice for them."

Finally, Wright suggested that once the reforms had bedded down, London should initiate a dialogue with Dublin, not about long-term unification but about redressing Protestant grievances against the south, including the territorial claim in the Republic's constitution. Wright's assessment was a timely reminder, which strengthened Callaghan's position relative to Wilson's, that the success of the reform strategy depended on the survival of a cooperative Unionist administration. The probable alternative would be direct rule. This required Callaghan to achieve a fine political balance: "In your dealings with the Northern Ireland government you may wish to steer a difficult course between on the one hand making them look as if they are your puppets and on the other making it look as if you found them distasteful to deal with. For better or worse, they are the best Northern Ireland Government we've got."[194]

While the assessment came too late to influence the humiliating terms in which Wilson had drafted the Downing Street Declaration, it may have helped persuade other ministers of the case for replacing the USC rather than simply disbanding it.

### Defense

When the army moved onto the streets of Northern Ireland in August 1969, the MoD took its place alongside the Home Office in the Whitehall policymaking arena, an important development that had far-reaching consequences. The MoD was not bound by the doctrine of nonintervention but opposed direct rule for a reason of its own: the fear of a loyalist backlash, which would require a deeper and longer military intervention.[195] Healey told the first cabinet meeting after the deployment of troops that "they should aim to retain the Northern Ireland Government as an effective force, for in that way they stood more chance of being able to withdraw the troops."[196] He warned that the forces available for deployment to Northern Ireland would be "quite inadequate to cope with a major emergency such as would arise if the Protestant majority were stung into armed opposition." With eight battalions in Northern Ireland, Britain had reached the limit of availability of troops not already committed to the North Atlantic Treaty Organization.[197] Consequently, Healey argued that Wilson should push Chichester-Clark "only as far as he wanted to go."

Once the soldiers had gone onto the streets, the MoD's first priority was to withdraw them as quickly as possible. The army had learned from colonial peacekeeping missions that after a few months, it was likely to be rejected by at least one of the parties to a civil conflict. It wanted out of Northern Ireland before the honeymoon turned sour.[198] The MoD favored the reform strategy as the best option for limiting the scale and length of the army's involvement. In direct dealings with Chichester-Clark, Healey emphasized that the British forces could only buy the Northern Ireland government time. It was up to Stormont ministers to sell the reforms actively and face down their hard-line opponents.[199]

The MoD had a particular interest in creating an effective police force, acceptable to both sides, that would permit the soldiers to withdraw from the streets as quickly as possible.[200] Healey thus expressed reservations about disbanding the USC, proposing instead that they should be disarmed and their activities limited to guarding key installations, patrolling the border, and defending police stations.[201] Senior army commanders had a more immediate stake in policing reform arising from their day-to-day work. They wanted clear primacy over the RUC, and robustly opposed the suggestion that Stormont ministers and police commanders should retain any control over security operations. The MoD promoted this position in Whitehall. It did not want to share its resources and responsibilities with a subordinate administration with which—unlike their Home Office colleagues—it had no longstanding relationship, and which moreover was out of favor with its political masters.

There was a clear conflict between the MoD position and the doctrine the Northern Ireland government invoked, which was that the troops were operating in aid of civil power—that is, effectively as reinforcements for the RUC under the political direction of the Stormont minister of home affairs. That this doctrine properly reflected the legal position was confirmed in a briefing paper prepared by Whitehall lawyers for Wilson in December 1968; under common law, the military had a duty to aid the civil power if requested. In an emergency, there was nothing to prevent a local RUC inspector requesting assistance from a local military commander, who could be deemed to be in breach of the regulations if he delayed or refused.[202] As we have seen, however, it was not politically expedient for Wilson and Callaghan to act on this advice. That the army disliked it gave them further justification for ignoring it.

The Downing Street Declaration gave the MoD the primacy it wanted by distinguishing between security operations and civil policing, for which the chief constable would continue to be accountable to Stormont. There was no basis for this distinction in law. The Hunt recommendations were intended to clarify and strengthen it. By disarming the RUC, Callaghan gave the army a monopoly on the legitimate use of armed force as a response to protest. By replacing the USC with a locally recruited regiment of the British army, he transferred vital functions and an important resource from Stormont to Westminster. He hoped that these changes would allow the other regiments to be withdrawn quickly.[203] But difficult ambiguities persisted that blocked the realization of that objective. At what point, for example, did a rowdy demonstration overseen by unarmed police officers become a riot requiring a military response? Who was responsible for collecting and coordinating intelligence on potential insurgents? What if the police were threatened or attacked with guns or explosives?

### Foreign Office

The Foreign Office had three principal interests to protect: Britain's relationships with Ireland, Britain's relationships with the United States and other countries with influential Irish immigrant constituencies, and Britain's international image. The Foreign Office had traditionally treated the Republic of Ireland differently from other sovereign states. Until October 1968, the British embassy in Dublin had related not to the Foreign Office but to the Commonwealth Office, which dealt with former British colonies, even though Ireland had withdrawn from the Commonwealth in 1947.[204] It reflected a fundamental ambiguity at the core of the British state's view of its relationships with Ireland: that neither jurisdiction on the island was either wholly British or wholly foreign.

Whereas Home Office officials tended to define the problem as seen through the eyes of their informants at Stormont, British ambassadors to Ireland were inclined to adopt Dublin's perspective. Thus in September 1969 Sir Andrew Gilchrist told a meeting of senior officials in Whitehall that there was "no hope of Dublin accepting the continuation of the Stormont constitution in its present form," and consequently it was in Britain's interest "to explore means by which the Dublin Government could be associated with the creation of new arrangements for Ulster which would be acceptable to all the people living there . . . this would involve some constitutional device to overcome the built-in Protestant majority at Stormont."[205]

### Summary

Surveying the events in retrospect, it may appear surprising that the unification option was not explored in greater depth. The key policymakers personally favored it, and some saw it as the only viable solution. There was a strong faction in the ruling Labour Party that advocated it, and the party as a whole had an obvious political interest in removing Unionist MPs from Westminster. So why did Wilson's government not pursue unification more actively?

The short answer is that while ministers saw unification as the only sustainable solution in the long term, they also believed that it would be dangerous and counterproductive to let this be publicly known. It would have undermined progress toward their most pressing objectives of ending the disorder, implementing the reform program, sustaining the devolved administration, and preventing a violent loyalist backlash. They accepted the advice given by their civil servants, that precipitate withdrawal would stiffen Unionist resistance and cause a complete breakdown in order, leading potentially to violent protests by Irish communities in Britain and annexation by the Republic.[206]

Nonetheless Callaghan told the cabinet on September 4, 1969, that "the whole Irish problem was once more on the move and that there would be pressure for fundamental changes going far beyond what was at present contemplated . . . if there were to be any prospect of a final solution, relations between the North and South of Ireland, and between the South and the United Kingdom must be lifted to a different plane. As things stood at present, this was likely to take a long time." This statement reflected Wilson's broader project of improving relationships between the two states. At the end of this meeting, ministers instructed officials to explore what more might be done to reduce current obstacles to unification.[207]

Two weeks later the British ambassador in Dublin reported on a private conversation with Lynch. The taoiseach had acknowledged that the south was quite incapable of "taking over" the north in the foreseeable future. All that Lynch aspired to for the moment was to be included in the British policymaking process. He had accepted Callaghan's point that substantial social and financial adjustments would be required in the south to prepare for unity and had told the British ambassador that he estimated that these would take between seven and fifteen years to complete.[208]

British ministers had more immediate problems to address on the streets of Northern Ireland. The violence would be exacerbated if the substance of their dialogue with Lynch were to be widely known there. Recording a conversation with the tánaiste (Irish deputy prime minister), Erskine Childers, during a banquet on March 18, 1970, Wilson noted that "one had to consider against the undoubted long term advantages of what he [Childers] was suggesting [a dialogue between London and Dublin to pave the way for eventual unification], the danger of worsening the position in the short term."[209]

More urgently, in 1970 Wilson had a general election to fight.

## Notes

1.    A. de Tocqueville, *Alexis de Tocqueville on Democracy, Revolution, and Society*, ed. John Stone and Stephen Mennell (Chicago: University of Chicago Press, 1980), 230.

2.    As reported by one of the protest organizers, republican socialist Eamonn McCann. See L. Clarke, *Sunday Times*, October 5, 2008.

3.    Cameron Report: *Disturbances in Northern Ireland: Report of the Cameron Commission*, Cmd 532 (Belfast: HMSO, 1969), 93.

4.    S. Bruce, *God Save Ulster! The Religion and Politics of Paisleyism* (Oxford: Oxford University Press, 1989), 69.

5.    H. Patterson, *Ireland since 1939: The Persistence of Conflict* (Dublin: Penguin, 2006), 186.

6.    Ibid., 190.

7.    Ibid., 193.

8.    CAB 4/1406, October 14, 1968.

9.    H. Wilson, *The Labour Government 1964–1970: A Personal Record* (London: Weidenfeld and Nicholson, 1971), 270; J. Callaghan, *A House Divided* (London: Collins, 1973), 5.

10.   PREM 13/2847, October 7, 1968.

11.   PREM 13/2847, October 8, 1968.

12.   PREM 13/2841, note of November 8, 1968.

13.   Hansard v772, column 690, November 5, 1968. Hansard is the official record of Commons debates.

14.   PREM 13/2841, November 19, 1968.

15.   T. Hennessey, *A History of Northern Ireland 1920–1996* (Basingstoke: Macmillan, 1997), 151.

16.   K. Bloomfield, *Stormont in Crisis: A Memoir* (Belfast: Blackstaff, 1994), 102.

17.   Cameron Report, 73.

18.   Terence O'Neill, *Ulster at the Crossroads* (London: Faber, 1969), 68.

19.   Ibid., 69.

20.   J.F. Harbinson, *The Ulster Unionist Party* (Belfast: Blackstaff, 1974), 154.

21.   Scarman Report: *Violence and Disturbance in Northern Ireland in 1969*, Cmd 566 (Belfast: HMSO, 1972).

22.   Scarman Report, 24.

23.   Ibid., 66.

24.   Sunday Times Insight Team, *Ulster* (London: Penguin, 1972), 119.

25.   Martin McGuinness MP, interviewed on "Battle of the Bogside," BBC television, September 4, 2006. McGuinness went on to become deputy first minister of Northern Ireland.

26.   CAB 130/416, memorandum of May 1, 1969.

27.   J. Callaghan, *A House Divided: The Dilemma of Northern Ireland* (London: Collins, 1973), 46.

28.   Ibid., 54.

29.   Reprinted in Callaghan, *House Divided*, 191.

30.   Cameron Report, 93.

31.   Scarman Report, 15.

32. Wilson, *Labour Government*, 694.

33. Insight Team, *Ulster*, 144.

34. CJ 3/73, September 16, 1969.

35. Callaghan, *House Divided*, 63.

36. NAI 2002/8/508, briefing note for meeting with Wilson, November 16, 1971.

37. Hunt Report: *Report of the Advisory Committee on Police in Northern Ireland*, Cmd 535 (Belfast: HMSO, 1969), paragraph 167.

38. Hunt Report, paragraph 27.

39. Insight Team, *Ulster*, 147.

40. Barbara Castle, *The Castle Diaries* (London: Weidenfeld and Nicholson, 1984), 716.

41. CAB 128/46, October 7, 1969.

42. Wilson, *Labour Government*, 717.

43. *Belfast Newsletter* [daily newspaper], July 27, 1971.

44. Callaghan, *House Divided*, 10.

45. Wilson, *Labour Government*, 692.

46. Scarman Report, 130

47. Callaghan, *House Divided*, 20.

48. Chris Ryder, *The Fateful Split: Catholics and the Royal Ulster Constabulary* (London: Methuen, 2004), 118.

49. T. Hennessey, *The Origins of the Troubles* (Dublin: Gill and Macmillan, 2005), 167.

50. Callaghan, *House Divided*, 23. For further details of these plans, see G. Warner, "Putting Pressure on O'Neill," *Irish Studies Review*, vol. 13, no. 1 (2005), 13–31.

51. The post of governor of Northern Ireland, the monarch's representative, had hitherto been largely ceremonial.

52. PREM 13/2842, minutes of meeting, February 19, 1969.

53. PRONI, CAB4/1458/14.

54. E. Phoenix, *Irish Times*, January 1, 2000.

55. Castle, *Diaries*, 696.

56. CAB 128/46, August 19, 1969.

57. Callaghan, *House Divided*, 25.

58. Insight Team, *Ulster*, 103.

59. E. Phoenix, *Irish Times*, January 1, 1999.

60. Callaghan, *House Divided*, 22.

61. R. Rose, *Governing without Consensus* (London: Faber, 1971), 124.

62. Callaghan, *House Divided*, 24.

63. When the two governments announced their proposals for police reform, there was rioting in Protestant areas, during which a policeman was killed.

64. Insight Team, *Ulster*, 162.

65. CAB 128/46, September 4, 1969.

66. Callaghan, *House Divided*, 15.

67. CAB 130/416, memorandum from Callaghan to Cabinet, May 1, 1969.

68. CAB 130/422, April 28, 1969.

69. Insight Team, *Ulster*, 162.

70. Hansard, April 22, 1969.

71. Donnelly, *Irish Times*, January 1, 2000.

72. CAB 130/416, March 31, 1969.

73. CAB 130/422, minutes of meeting on September 19, 1969.

74. Callaghan, *House Divided*, 23; Castle, *Diaries*, 700.

75. Insight Team, *Ulster*, 81.

76. Security Service archives, cited in C. Andrew, *The Defence of the Realm* (London: Allen Lane, 2009), 602.

77. R.H.S. Crossman, *The Diaries of a Cabinet Minister*, vol. 3 (London: Cape, 1977), 478.

78. Callaghan, *House Divided*, 623.

79. Crossman, *Diaries*, 623.

80. Cameron Report, 15.

81. Ibid., 55.

82. CAB 128/46, September 4, 1969.

83. CJ 3/18, Wright to Callaghan, January 20, 1970.

84. Callaghan, *House Divided*, 46.

85. G. Adams, *Politics of Irish Freedom* (Dingle: Brandon, 1986), 17.

86. Cameron Report, 92.

87. Bulletin published by the Wolfe Tone Societies in August 1966, cited in Bob Purdie, *Politics in the Streets: The Origins of the Civil Rights Movement in Northern Ireland* (Belfast: Blackstaff Press, 1990), 128.

88. R. English, *Armed Struggle: The History of the IRA* (Oxford: Pan Macmillan, 2004), 92.

89. Crossman, *Diaries*, 381.

90. Callaghan, *House Divided*, 157.

91. P. Bew and H. Patterson, *The British State and the Ulster Crisis* (London: Verso, 1985), 24.

92. Callaghan, *House Divided*, 77.

93. CAB 130/422, note of meeting on August 22, 1969.

94. CJ 3/73, Waddell to Callaghan, September 10, 1969.

95. T.E. Utley, *Lessons of Ulster* (London: Dent, 1975), 25.

96. Hunt Report, paragraph 18.

97. Ibid., paragraph 10.

98. Castle, *Diaries*, 700.

99. W.P. McCarrick, "The British Labour Party, British Politics, and Ireland, 1886–1924," doctoral thesis, School of Politics, University of Ulster, Coleraine, 1992.

100. P. Dixon, *Northern Ireland: The Politics of War and Peace* (New York: Palgrave, 2001), 77. See also M.A. Murphy, *Gerry Fitt: Political Chameleon* (Cork: Mercia, 2007), chapter 3.

101. Wilson, *Labour Government*, 270.

102. Terry Cradden, "Labour and the NILP," in P. Catterall and S. McDougall, eds., *The Northern Ireland Question and British Politics* (London: Macmillan, 1996), 83–84.

103. See Murphy, *Gerry Fitt*, chapter 3, for a fuller account of Fitt's achievements in using civil rights issues at Westminster against the Unionist regime.

104. P. Rose, *Backbencher's Dilemma* (London: Muller, 1981), 195–98.

105. Austin Currie, *Irish News*, June 23, 2008.

106. Murphy, *Gerry Fitt*, 120.

107. Wilson, *The Labour Government*, 671.

108. H.G. Calvert, *Constitutional Law in Northern Ireland* (London: Stevens, 1968), 95.

109. PREM 13/2848, note of meeting, May 16, 1969.

110. Callaghan, *House Divided*, 96.

111. Wilson, *The Labour Government*, 719.

112. Callaghan, *House Divided*, 12.

113. *The Times*, September 11, 1969.

114. Callaghan, *House Divided*, 108.

115. Ibid., 64.

116. See Murphy, *Gerry Fitt*, chapter 3, for a more detailed account of the CDU's origins in the Connolly Association and in Irish immigrant networks in Britain.

117. "Our Plan to End Partition," Connolly Association, London, 1962.

118. Purdie, *Politics in the Streets*, 104.

119. P. Dixon, "Contemporary Unionism and the Tactics of Resistance," in M.J. Bric and J. Coakley, eds., *From Political Violence to Negotiated Settlement* (Dublin: UCD Press, 2004), 138.

120. Wilson, *The Labour Government*, 671. Note that "British" again: another example of UK ministers' tendency to separate Northern Ireland from Britain and assert the superiority of mainland standards.

121. E. McCann, *The British Press and Northern Ireland* (London: Socialist Research Centre, 1971), 3.

122. E. Moloney, "The Media: Asking the Right Questions?" in M. Farrell, ed., *Twenty Years On* (Dingle: Brandon, 1988).

123. "Innocent People at Risk like Sitting Ducks," *The Times*, August 15, 1969.

124. *The Times*, August 19, 1969.

125. Wilson, *The Labour Government*, 671, 693; Castle, *Diaries*, 699.

126. Hunt Report, paragraph 14.

127. Patterson, *Ireland since 1939*, 157.

128. J. Horgan, *Sean Lemass: The Enigmatic Patriot* (Dublin: Gill and Macmillan, 1997), 108.

129. Patterson, *Ireland since 1939*, 157.

130. The taoiseach is the Irish equivalent of the British prime minister.

131. NAI 99/1/82, note by T.K. Whitaker of a visit to Stormont on December 11, 1967.

132. Patterson, *Ireland since 1939*, 171.

133. Ibid., 170.

134. Callaghan, *House Divided*, 28.

135. Patterson, *Ireland since 1939*, 172.

136. Callaghan, *House Divided*, 28, 39.

137. R. Fanning, *Irish Times*, April 20, 2008.

138. Callaghan, *House Divided*, 51.

139. CAB 128/46, minutes of September 11, 1969.

140. Callaghan *House Divided*, 40.

141. CAB 130/422, "Interview with Taoiseach," 17 September 1969.

142. CAB 130/422, September 17 and 18, 1969.

143. Crossman, *Diaries,* 458.

144. Ibid., 478.

145. Dixon, *Northern Ireland,* 62. For a more detailed account of Wilson's steadily increasing efforts to pressure O'Neill, see Warner, "Putting Pressure on O'Neill."

146. B. Purdie, *Politics in the Streets,* 104.

147. P. Bew, P. Gibbon, and H Patterson, *The State in Northern Ireland 1921–72* (Manchester: Manchester University Press 1979), 191.

148. Wilson, *The Labour Government,* 692.

149. *Irish Times,* March 18, 1965.

150. Dixon, *Northern Ireland,* 64.

151. Wilson, *The Labour Government,* 99.

152. PREM 13/2266, note of May 19, 1965.

153. *Irish Times,* March 25 and 29, 1966.

154. Wilson, *The Labour Government,* 270.

155. PREM 13/2266, note of August 8, 1966.

156. PREM 13/2266, January 12, 1967.

157. Callaghan, *House Divided,* 10.

158. Ibid., 693; C.C. O'Brien, *States of Ireland* (London: Granada, 1974), 268.

159. Castle, *Diaries,* 648.

160. Wilson, *The Labour Government,* 695.

161. Cited in *Belfast Telegraph,* May 12, 2006.

162. Wilson, *The Labour Government,* 697.

163. A. Morgan, *Harold Wilson* (London: Pluto, 1997), 325.

164. Crossman, *Diaries,* 463.

165. Castle, *Diaries,* 706.

166. Callaghan, *House Divided,* 187.

167. Morgan, *Harold Wilson,* 352.

168. PREM 13/2841, note of December 20, 1968.

169. CAB 130/416, February 24, 1969.

170. CAB 130/416, February 26, 1969.

171. *The Times,* August 27, 1969.

172. Callaghan, *House Divided,* 66.

173. NAI 2002/8/508, secret "note on discussion at dinner" on November 18, 1971, signature illegible.

174. Callaghan, *House Divided,* 63.

175. Crossman, *Diaries,* 637.

176. Callaghan, *House Divided,* 70.

177. Ibid., 152.

178. Ibid., 21.

179. Ibid., 2.

180. W.D. Birrell, "The Stormont-Westminster Relationship," *Parliamentary Affairs*, vol. 26 (June 1973), 477.

181. F. Newsam, *The Home Office* (London: Allen and Unwin, 1954), 168–69.

182. Patterson, *Ireland since 1939*, 196.

183. C.E.B. Brett, *Long Shadows Cast Before* (Edinburgh: Bartholomew, 1978), 135. From the civil servants' perspective, the sharing of documents would simply have been good administrative practice. Home Office officials had established good working relationships with their Northern Irish counterparts over the years, and presumably saw no reason not to share information with them.

184. CAB 130/422, minutes of April 28, 1969.

185. CAB 130/422, note of April 28, 1969.

186. Ryder, *Fateful Split*, 107.

187. CJ 3/18, September 3, 1969.

188. Callaghan, *House Divided*, 61.

189. Ibid., 65.

190. Ibid., 66.

191. CJ 3/18, September 3, 1969.

192. CJ 3/18, August 30, 1969.

193. CJ 3/18, Wright to Callaghan, September 13, 1969.

194. CJ 3/18, October 3, 1969.

195. Crossman, *Diaries*, 622.

196. CAB 128/46, August 19, 1969.

197. CAB 128/46, September 4, 1969.

198. Callaghan, *House Divided*, 60.

199. CJ 3/18, September 19, 1969.

200. *The Times*, August 18, 1969.

201. Dixon, *Northern Ireland*, 111.

202. Ryder, *Fateful Split*, 103.

203. A.R. Hezlet, *The B Specials* (London: Stacey, 1972), 224.

204. P. Arthur, *Special Relationships: Britain, Ireland, and the Northern Ireland Problem* (Belfast: Blackstaff, 2000), 93.

205. CAB 130/422, record of September 18, 1969.

206. CAB 130/416, March 31, 1969.

207. CAB 128/46, minutes of meeting on September 4 1969.

208 CAB 130/422, "Interview with Taoiseach," note by the British Ambassador in Dublin, September 17, 1969.

209. PREM 13/3276, Note for the Record of March 18, 1970.

# 4

# Coercion and Internment, 1971

*Where troops have encamped, there will brambles grow: in the
wake of a mighty army bad harvests follow without fail.*

—Lao Tzu[1]

Wilson lost the election. In July 1970, a Conservative government took office in London that soon dropped its predecessor's pretense that continuing to micromanage the problem in Northern Ireland could solve the problem without undermining the Unionist government. The Northern Ireland election results demonstrated just how much damage the reforms had already done to the Unionist Party, London's chosen instrument for avoiding direct rule. The Conservatives accordingly delegated substantial political authority to Stormont and operational responsibility to army commanders on the ground.

On August 5, 1971, UK ministers acceded to a request from Northern Ireland's prime minister, Brian Faulkner, that suspected republican activists should be arrested and interned without trial under Stormont's Special Powers Act. Four days later, British soldiers arrested 340 people and interred them in makeshift prisons. These people were not charged with any offense and did not appear before any court. By December 14, 1,576 people had been detained and 934 of them had already been released after questioning.[2]

The introduction of internment was the most egregious instance of a coercive policy that first appeared in April 1970. Both Stormont and Dublin had used internment against earlier Irish Republican Army (IRA) campaigns. Army commanders, Westminster members of parliament (MPs), Nationalist leaders, and informed commentators all had predicted that it would lead to an intensely hostile reaction from the Catholic community. The ministers who introduced it were not convinced that it would achieve its stated goal of reducing violence. So why did they do it?

## The Problem

Part of the answer lies in the changing nature of the problem. On the Nationalist side, three new and very different organizations emerged out of the dissolution of the civil rights movement: the Social Democratic and Labour Party (SDLP), the Official IRA, and the Provisional IRA. On the Unionist side, the splits in the Unionist Party intensified and new loyalist paramilitary formations emerged at the neighborhood level. In terms of Tilly's classification, the nature of the violence evolved from collective protest and intercommunal rioting to internal war, even as reforms intended to reduce conflict were under way.[3]

By April 1971, Stormont had taken steps to honor most of its specific commitments. In line with the Hunt recommendations, the Royal Ulster Constabulary (RUC) had been restructured and disarmed, and was now overseen by a police authority on which Catholics were proportionately represented. The Ulster Special Constabulary (USC) had been disbanded and replaced by the Ulster Defence Regiment (UDR), a part-time unit of the British army. The property qualification had been removed from the local government franchise, bringing it into line with Britain's. An independent commission had begun redrawing local government electoral boundaries. An ombudsman had been appointed to investigate individuals' complaints against government agencies. The Community Relations Commission had been established with a Catholic chairman, accountable to a minister for community relations, who attended meetings of the Northern Ireland cabinet. Stormont had passed legislation to create the Housing Executive, a regional agency to oversee the building and allocation of public housing without partisan interference. And Whitehall officials, reporting directly to UK ministers, monitored Stormont's activities from vantage points at the heart of the devolved administration.

But the reforms by then made little practical difference to the working-class Catholics on whose behalf they had been claimed. More important, they failed to tackle the deeper preconditions for the violence. They did not address the underlying conflict over national identity, give security to those at risk of attack, or address Nationalists' fundamental complaints about social and economic equality and political exclusion.

### The IRA

In early 1969 the IRA was weak, divided, and without clear direction.[4] The events of August 1969 gave it a new purpose and popular legitimacy as the defender of Catholic neighborhoods under attack from loyalists.[5] But the pace of events took the leadership by surprise and opened up the major fault line in the organization, that between predominantly southern Marxist ideologues who favored a political strategy in partnership with radical leftist organizations throughout Ireland on one side, and traditionalists who rejected communism, favored a strategy of armed struggle, and sought to reconstruct the idealized republic of the 1916 uprising on the other. The latter strand included activists from the Catholic districts of inner Belfast and Derry, who were more immediately concerned with defending their local neighborhoods than with realizing a Marxist utopia.

In December 1969, the IRA's governing body, the Army Council, met in Dublin to review strategy. The leftist faction saw the British intervention as creating an opportunity to progress their objectives by constitutional means and decided to end their policy of abstaining from electoral politics. The traditionalists broke away to form the Provisional IRA,[6] or the Provisionals, the leaders of which maintained that the leftists' obsession with politics had undermined the IRA's core military role, resulting in its failure to defend the ghettos from loyalists' incursions. Over the coming months the Provisionals drew energy and new recruits from the fighting in the streets.[7] The leftists did not abandon paramilitarism. Their armed wing, which came to be known as the Official IRA—the Officials—was also active in many ghettos.

Whitehall observed the drift from civil rights to republican paramilitarism with concern, although officials did not yet appreciate the full significance of the IRA split. In January 1970 the Home Office submitted a memorandum to the Cabinet noting that "a movement that began by drawing attention to social grievances is now in danger of being more and more guided by its leaders towards the political aim of a united Irish Socialist republic, and some at least of those seeking control over the policies of the civil rights movements are developing attacks on the institutions of Government and the way of life both north and south of the border."[8]

Both IRA factions tried to present themselves as the legitimate heirs of the Easter Rising, but the Provisionals' greater capacity to organize at street level gave them a strong political advantage. For families living in immediate fear of attack, the rhetoric of class struggle seemed ridiculous, especially when it called for solidarity with working-class loyalists, the very people who recently had been burning down their homes.[9] The Provisionals set about securing funds, weapons, and political support from sympathizers in the south, the United States, and Britain. By July 1970, in the absence of any other effective vehicle for the mobilization, expression, and defense of their interests, the Provisionals had established themselves as the predominant faction in most republican communities in Northern Ireland.[10] At first, their priority was physically to protect the neighborhoods from which they drew their support, and they did not attack the army. But their leaders had already decided to take the fight to the British as soon as they could create the right political context.[11]

The Provisionals' progress can be traced through their tactical and technical innovations and measured by official statistics on violent incidents. In January 1970 they began a campaign of arson and bombing directed against shops, offices, and industrial premises across Northern Ireland. During the summer, they launched the newspaper *Republican News*; engaged for the first time in shooting battles with the army and loyalist paramilitaries; and deployed two new weapons, the car bomb and the nail bomb. In August 1970, the Provisionals began killing policemen. In January 1971, they killed their first alleged informer, J.J. Kavanagh.[12] On February 6, 1971, during a riot, they killed their first British soldier, gunner Robert Curtis. On March 10, they shot dead three young off-duty soldiers who had been drinking in Belfast. By July 1971, they had killed ten.

Each side's actions provoked an aggressive response from the other.[13] Every overtly coercive act by the army generated more popular support for the Provisionals, especially when innocent bystanders suffered. Some of the Provisional leaders were familiar with the British army and its operating methods from inside, having learned their soldiering on Her Majesty's service. They calculated from what they knew of Britain's campaigns in Aden and Cyprus that the British would start to negotiate for peace once the army's death toll had reached around thirty-six.

A second strand in Provisional strategy was to keep the Orange pot boiling. They saw in the angry Protestant reaction to their violence an opportunity to provoke sectarian confrontations, destabilize the Unionist government, and force Westminster to introduce direct rule, the essential next step on the path to an all-Ireland state. On April 13, 1971, gunmen fired on a crowd returning from an Orange parade in Belfast, leading to fierce intercommunal rioting. An intensification of the Provisionals' bombing campaign in July coincided with the traditional Orange parading season.

Although the Officials and various loyalist paramilitary organizations were also active at this time, the Provisionals were responsible for a majority of the 298 explosions, 320 shooting incidents, and 600 injuries that occurred from January to July 1971.[14] By July 1971 there were an estimated 200 active volunteers in the Officials and 500 in the Provisionals. Of the 700, about 130 were in Derry and 340 in Belfast.[15]

### The SDLP

Seven prominent Nationalist politicians came together in August 1970 to form a new political party, the SDLP, which rejected the conservative passivity of the old Nationalist Party. The SDLP's most prominent founding members were its nominal leader, Gerry Fitt MP, and chief strategist John Hume, a civil rights activist and Stormont MP for Londonderry since February 1969. The SDLP attracted support from hitherto independent elected representatives, the old Nationalist Party, the civil rights movement, and the Northern Ireland Labour Party (NILP). Like the Nationalist Party, it stood for Irish unification as a long-term goal, but unlike its predecessor it was willing in the interim to participate fully in the Stormont and Westminster parliaments and campaign for social reform within the United Kingdom. Unlike the IRA, it explicitly rejected violence.

UK ministers actively encouraged the establishment of the SDLP. Its combination of moderate nationalist with social democratic values appeared to them to open up the possibility of a sustainable compromise with unionism.[16] It provided a coherent minority leadership with which to negotiate and a nonviolent outlet for Catholic grievances. But it also presented the British Labour Party with a dilemma: whether to support the SDLP or the NILP, with which it had already established fraternal connections.

As home secretary, Callaghan had wanted the British Labour Party to agree to a request from the NILP for full affiliation, which, he argued, would help to put Northern Irish politics on a "normal" economic rather than a sectarian basis.[17] Now shadow home secretary, he told the Irish ambassador in London that he had been working hard to persuade the British Labour Party to support NILP candidates in every constituency in Northern Ireland.[18] However, the Irish government and the future leaders of the SDLP both lobbied hard against affiliation, arguing that it would damage their efforts to establish a new nonsectarian party of opposition.[19] The implication was that the NILP was sectarian because it was linked to a British national party, even though it attracted both Protestant and Catholic voters; the SDLP, which attracted almost exclusively Catholic voters, would somehow not be sectarian, even if the Irish government and Ireland's main political parties supported it. This lobbying succeeded. The British Labour Party turned down the NILP's request for affiliation in October 1970.

On the streets, the SDLP had to compete with the two IRA factions for popular support in republican communities. The balance of political advantage at any point depended to a large extent on their residents' perceptions of public agencies' capacity to protect them. The Provisionals' paramilitary capability gave them a substantial advantage in places at risk of loyalist attack, and wherever the forces of the state showed themselves unable or unwilling to guarantee residents' safety.

## Chichester-Clark

Westminster's reform strategy was originally constructed on the assumption that a Unionist prime minister could and would deliver the acquiescence of the Unionist population. By spring 1971, this assumption was no longer tenable.[20] Many Unionists saw the reform policy in general and the restructuring of the RUC in particular as irresponsible concessions to the threat of republican violence. While the Hunt reforms in themselves posed no immediate threat to Northern Ireland's constitutional status, they transferred responsibility for the security of the state to UK ministers, and unionists, not without cause, mistrusted the Labour Party's long-term intentions. Regardless of the substance of successive reform packages, many felt that O'Neill and Chichester-Clark should have more stoutly resisted Westminster's encroachments on Stormont's authority. Protestant districts had calmed down since the rioting that greeted the Hunt Report, but continuing anger over the changes in policing strengthened Chichester-Clark's hard-line challengers.

As early as October 1969, the newly appointed UK representative (UKREP) in Belfast was warning his masters in London that "the Chichester-Clark Government is clearly in danger of losing both the desire and the will to govern." Outside the Stormont cabinet, Craig was publicly questioning its durability, and inside it, Brian Faulkner was displaying a "barely repressible desire to take control."[21] In Unionist constituency associations across the country, hard-liners replaced moderates as office-bearers and potential election candidates.[22]

Three political developments in March and April 1970 damaged Chichester-Clark further. First, five prominent dissident Unionist MPs at Stormont voted against the Police Bill implementing the Hunt Report and were expelled from the parliamentary party for doing so.[23] Second, several leading moderates left the Unionist Party to set up Alliance, a new political party committed to the union but only as long as a majority of the population wanted it. Alliance dissociated itself from the Orange Order, proactively welcomed Catholic members, and enthusiastically endorsed the reform strategy. It drew active moderates away from the Unionist Party, where they could otherwise have supported Chichester-Clark in seeing off his hard-line opponents. Third, hard-liner Ian Paisley and a colleague, standing as "Protestant Unionists," inflicted a shattering defeat on the Unionist establishment by winning both of two Stormont by-elections, including one in O'Neill's former constituency.[24] Previously, the Unionist opposition at Stormont had consisted of two members of the NILP. Paisley's victory threatened the Unionists' presentation of themselves as staunch defenders of the union in a way that the NILP never could. Paisley notched up a second victory in the Westminster election of June 1970, winning the previously safe Unionist seat of North Antrim.

The explanation for the Unionists' poor electoral performances seemed clear to party leaders and activists alike. The reform policy was at best an electoral irrelevance and an embarrassment to those prepared to stand by it. Most Unionist candidates either ignored it in their election material or presented it as an unwelcome imposition from London. It was especially resented by the local constituency associations that were responsible for selecting candidates. There was a widespread perception that Labour ministers had deliberately humiliated the Unionists for party political reasons. The party at large wanted its leaders to stand up to Westminster, the Labour Party, and diktat from Whitehall.

The opposition inside the party was led by two former ministers, both sacked by O'Neill: Bill Craig and Harry West, an influential member of the Ulster Unionist Council. Beginning in August 1970, these two chipped away at Chichester-Clark's authority, repeatedly emphasizing the helplessness of unarmed RUC officers confronting republican gunmen and bombers and depicting every episode of IRA violence as validation of their warnings. As popular indignation grew, Chichester-Clark's grip on his party weakened, and it became more costly for him to pursue the implementation of Whitehall's reform agenda.

Following a series of increasingly provocative attacks, three young British soldiers were murdered on March 10, 1971. They were off duty and unarmed. Worse incidents were to become common, but a threshold had been crossed. The Provisionals had shown that they were not constrained by any chivalrous rules of war. This incident and the outrage it provoked helped Chichester-Clark's opponents to gain support for a confidence motion at the Ulster Unionist Council. The vote was scheduled for March 29, and Chichester-Clark calculated that he would lose unless he could quickly deliver a positive response to his challengers' demands.[25] These included the military occupation of republican neighborhoods, punitive raids and searches, curfews, closure of cross-border roads, economic sanctions against Dublin, rearming of the RUC, resurrection of the USC, and internment of republican activists.[26] Having surrendered control of security to London, Chichester-Clark could not meet any of them. He flew to London on March 16 to ask for five more battalions of troops to clamp down on republican districts, explaining that his position as party leader would otherwise be untenable.[27] UK ministers took advice from army commanders, who recommended that no military purpose would be served by any of the measures the Unionists proposed. Ministers were anxious to avoid a repetition of previous incidents, in which tough action by the army had alienated Catholic opinion. They accordingly agreed only to deploy troops already in Northern Ireland more visibly, so as to give the appearance of more intensive activity, and to provide 1,300 reinforcements. They offered this concession purely to prop up Chichester-Clark.

When Chichester-Clark reported his modest achievement to the Stormont Commons, Paisley and Craig attacked him for betraying Protestant interests, and no Unionist defended him.[28] On March 20 he resigned, declaring that his government was powerless to take the actions that its supporters were demanding.[29] The entire Unionist cabinet threatened to join him unless London introduced tougher security measures at once.[30]

For a few tense days, UK ministers faced the threat of the Northern Ireland government dissolving itself, thereby giving them direct responsibility for the administration of Northern Ireland under very unfavorable circumstances. They knew that Craig, now a candidate to succeed Chichester-Clark, was committed to reversing the policing reforms. They had prepared contingency plans to introduce direct rule to prevent this, but Craig—following the precedent set by Unionists during the home rule crisis in 1912—threatened that if they did so, he would set up an alternative government that would organize mass resistance.

### Loyalist Paramilitaries

UK ministers' fears of a loyalist rebellion were reinforced by the knowledge that loyalist paramilitary structures were already in place. In October 1969, Protestant paramilitaries had killed the first policeman to die as a result of the Troubles, Victor Arbuckle, ironically during rioting against the Hunt recommendations. When the army moved against loyalists during rioting in the Shankill area of west Belfast in June 1970, Ulster Volunteer Force (UVF) gunmen returned fire, and soldiers killed two of them.[31] In the same month, there were gun battles between IRA and UVF snipers around the Catholic Short Strand area in east Belfast, where two Protestants were shot dead. Like their republican counterparts, many of the people of the loyalist ghettos came to believe that the state was unwilling or unable to defend them and their homes, and so decided to organize their own defenses.

From February 1970, the UVF sporadically targeted moderate Unionists and Nationalists, exploding bombs at their homes and offices. They attacked Catholic businesses, churches, and schools. During 1970 they carried out an estimated 27 bomb attacks, mostly using pipe bombs; this was modest relative to the 130 land mines and bombs the IRA planted in the same year, but still lethal.

In March 1971, with the IRA campaign intensifying, Unionists at Westminster and Stormont demanded a third force under Stormont's control, in effect a replacement for the USC. In the loyalist estates of Belfast, gangs took to the streets, clashing with their Catholic counterparts and attacking property. They may have lacked political objectives, strategy, and organization, but their destructive behavior warned of what might happen if the British pushed loyalism too far.

## The Strategy

### Continuity

The Conservative government of Ted Heath came to power in June 1970. Reginald Maudling replaced James Callaghan as home secretary and Lord Peter Carrington became defence secretary. On June 23, Heath told his colleagues that the goal of the new administration should be to "calm Protestant apprehensions, reduce tensions, and make the most of their opportunity to make a fresh start."[32] Heath and Maudling were sensitive to the damage that Wilson's interventions and humiliating public statements had done to Stormont's authority, and were keen to sustain Chichester-Clark in office. Accordingly, they visibly delegated responsibility to Stormont ministers and army commanders while setting strategic goals and parameters, monitoring security policy and operations with a light touch. The new team agreed that they should "not only do all we can to maintain the momentum of reform but ... also take every opportunity of building up the authority and position of the Northern Ireland government."[33]

For their first nine months in office, the Conservatives publicly committed themselves to the policy lines established by their Labour predecessors, hoping that implementing the reform program would remove the causes of Catholic disaffection and so prevent future disorder. In the interim, the army was to maintain a visible presence to keep the peace. The Conservatives were reluctant to consider any further reforms until calm had been fully restored, as both sides might have interpreted this as a concession to violence. At the same time, in an echo of Wilson's threats to O'Neill, Maudling warned Unionist hard-liners that they would not be permitted to reverse the reform process: "To go back on what has been done or depart from the ideals of impartiality and reconciliation that lie at the heart of the policies of Her Majesty's Government and the Government of Northern Ireland would endanger the present constitutional arrangements under which Northern Ireland governs its own affairs."[34]

With Chichester-Clark's resignation in March 1971, Heath and Maudling faced a triple challenge: the accelerating campaign of terrorist violence, the failure of the reform strategy to prevent it, and the continuing disintegration of the Unionist regime. They could no longer credibly present the policy that they had inherited of hopeful muddling through as an effective response to a rapidly deteriorating situation.

## Faulkner

When Chichester-Clark resigned in March 1971, Heath and Maudling convinced themselves that the leading contender to succeed him, Brian Faulkner, would both maintain the momentum of reform and fend off the challenge from Craig. Although O'Neill continued from his new perch in the House of Lords to condemn Faulkner as a sectarian extremist, Maudling considered him both a pragmatist who would comply with London's directions and a more skillful and professional politician than any of his predecessors.[35] Carrington wrote that he was "a real politician, flexible, ambitious and unscrupulous." More important, he was the one Unionist leader who stood between the Conservatives and direct rule.[36]

Heath accordingly took steps to improve Faulkner's prospects. During a Westminster debate on Northern Ireland on March 22, he declared that the reform program was "very near completion" and that it had "removed grievances which may have existed before."[37] His message to the Unionist Party at Stormont as it chose its new leader was clear. The British government would not work with Craig, but if Faulkner won, it would not insist on any further reforms. When the votes were cast the following day, Faulkner beat Craig by twenty-six to four.

Over the next two weeks, London took steps to prop up Faulkner—which, had they been taken earlier and properly presented, might have prevented Chichester-Clark's resignation. The general officer commanding (GOC), General Harry Tuzo, issued instructions "encouraging more rapid and aggressive action" against rioters and troublemakers.[38] The cabinet commissioned work toward a more proactive security policy, including the creation of a full-time unit of the UDR, tighter control over border crossings, strengthening of the RUC's intelligence capability with reinforcements from Britain, and initiating contingency planning for internment.[39] Carrington also asked Tuzo to consider the scope for greater use of curfews.[40]

Faulkner acted swiftly to repair the fragmentation in his party. He sought to reconcile the main factions by including representatives of each in his cabinet, from the liberal Robin Bailie to the hard-line West. He later confirmed that West accepted the job "on the basis of what I was able to tell him about the more effective lines of action I intended to see pursued by the security forces."[41]

On April 1, Faulkner met Heath in London and came away convinced that they had achieved a meeting of minds. Heath agreed with him that in the new context created by the IRA campaign, security must take priority over further reform.[42] The two also agreed that internment should not be introduced except on the advice of the security forces, but that it would be prudent to make detailed contingency plans so that it could be introduced at short notice if necessary.

The circumstances in which Faulkner found himself were not promising. The loyalists and republicans who for their disparate reasons wanted to destroy Stormont had been encouraged by the fall of Chichester-Clark to redouble their efforts. Whatever Heath had said, the northern premier was caught between the demands of his party and the requirements of UK ministers. Attempting to reconcile these competing pressures, he adopted a two-pronged strategy, combining firm security measures with offers of influence at Stormont for Nationalist elected representatives. He also moved to defuse criticism from the British Labour Party by appointing NILP leader David Bleakley as his minister for community relations.

On June 22, 1971, Faulkner took the SDLP off guard by offering them a new deal in the Stormont Commons. Three new committees would be created to review and advise the government on health and social services, industrial development, and environment and local government issues. The SDLP would have proportionate representation on them and nominate chairmen to two of them. It was the first time a Unionist government had ever offered salaried posts in the administration to a Nationalist party. Although no executive powers were offered, it was a significant gesture in the political context of the time. Faulkner also indicated that other constitutional changes, such as the introduction of proportional representation for Stormont elections, could follow once a sufficient level of trust had been generated.

Hard-line republicans argued that the offer was a sham.[43] But some SDLP leaders—the intended beneficiaries—welcomed it. Paddy Devlin, a former IRA internee, described it as "Faulkner's finest hour." Bleakley called it "an important step forward."[44] On July 7, SDLP representatives sat down with their Unionist counterparts to thrash out the details. Before they could reach an agreement, however, British soldiers shot two Nationalists dead during rioting in Derry. The Provisionals exploited the resulting outrage in the community by accusing the SDLP of selling out their principles and their constituents for the baubles of office even as the occupying forces were murdering their constituents.

John Hume, the leader of the SDLP in Derry, mistrusted Faulkner and was less favorably disposed than Devlin to his offer of committee chairs. The UKREP reported when Faulkner acceded to the premiership that "Hume, in particular, smells blood and has been uncompromisingly hostile."[45] Without consulting Fitt, Hume now issued an important ultimatum. Unless London set up an independent public inquiry into the shootings, the SDLP would withdraw from Stormont. He calculated that this would hasten the confrontation, which he considered inevitable, between Westminster and the Unionists. This in turn would lead to the dissolution of Stormont and the introduction of direct rule. The British would have to discharge their proper responsibility themselves.

Maudling predictably refused to hold an inquiry. Despite Fitt's and Devlin's reservations, the SDLP closed ranks behind Hume and on July 16 withdrew from Stormont. Discussion of Faulkner's offer ended. The SDLP then further distanced itself from any possibility of reconciliation with the Unionists by announcing that it would boycott Stormont indefinitely and set up its own nonsectarian assembly.[46] Many Unionists saw the SDLP's withdrawal as confirmation of their long-held suspicions that Nationalists were not interested in reforming Stormont, only destroying it. Faulkner acknowledged the political predicament that the SDLP leaders faced, but thought their protest unreasonable, since their quarrel was with the British, not him. He later wrote that he regretted that they "were reduced to dragging along on the coat-tails of the IRA."[47]

*Faulkner's Predicament*

When Faulkner met Heath on April 1, he said that he would not agree to internment unless the army and police advised him that it "would bring IRA terrorism decisively to an end."[48] At that time both Tuzo and the chief constable were against it. What had changed three months later?

In his autobiography, Faulkner explained that by July, "the IRA had committed itself to total war against the State, and was demonstrating a capacity to carry it out on a more widespread and organised scale than ever before."[49] There were seventy-nine major explosions (as defined by the security forces) in July, compared with fifty-three in June, fifty-one in May, and thirty-nine in April. Particularly provocative for the Unionist establishment was a series of bombs that went off along Orange marching routes on July 12, accompanied by attacks on Orange halls. More broadly, attacks on commercial property were beginning to damage business confidence and deter capital investment. On July 17, the largest explosion of the Troubles to date wrecked the premises of the UK national newspaper, the *Daily Mirror.* The upsurge in violence ended Faulkner's honeymoon with his own party. The SDLP's withdrawal from Stormont blocked one of the two tracks in his dual strategy, that of rapprochement with constitutional nationalism. The possibility of enticing Nationalist representatives into government no longer existed as a restraint on tougher security measures, and the SDLP's action strengthened the hand of Unionists who maintained that Nationalists were not genuinely interested in accommodation.

Typical of the speeches at the Orange rallies on July 12 was that of Unionist grandee Sir Knox Cunningham, who called for the creation of a citizens' militia similar to the USC, the rearming of the RUC, and the introduction of internment. Cunningham added for good measure that if Stormont was not prepared to govern, it must be replaced.[50] Following the *Daily Mirror* explosion, junior minister John Taylor threatened publicly to resign unless the security forces took tougher measures against the IRA. His views were widely shared in the Northern Ireland cabinet, even by its more conciliatory members.[51] Six thousand shipyard workers marched through Belfast to demand internment.

All the above developments—the increased level of IRA violence coinciding with the Orange marching season, the SDLP's rejection of the offer of constitutional reform, the threats of his cabinet colleagues, and intense public pressure—did not persuade Faulkner that internment would be effective. But they did convince him that something must be done to shore up his government's flagging authority. As one of his civil service advisers has noted, "It would have been very difficult indeed for Faulkner to say in effect to his party and the wider public: 'I have a power to intern but I will not use it. I must in all honesty tell you that I can't think of any other way to bring the situation under control. We shall just have to grin and bear it.'"[52] Discussions with his police and army commanders convinced Faulkner that internment was the only major unused weapon in the government's arsenal that had any prospect of working.[53]

Faulkner could not have introduced such a profound change in security policy without the assent of UK ministers. Not only were they ultimately responsible for security policies but their soldiers were required to detain and guard the internees. They complied with Faulkner's request not so much because of the deteriorating security situation as because of the anticipated political consequences of inaction. After the upsurge in IRA bombing in July, Maudling reported to the cabinet that Faulkner was losing control of the Unionist Parliamentary Party. He warned "that we now had seriously to contemplate the possibility that we might be compelled to institute direct rule in Northern Ireland if Mr. Faulkner's administration was unable to retain its authority and was replaced by a regime whose policies we could not accept."[54]

Faulkner phoned Maudling on July 28 to report that all his cabinet colleagues believed that the time had come for internment. He did not ask for it, but warned that it might soon become politically necessary.[55] The next day, UK ministers noted the importance of sustaining Faulkner as the only credible candidate for prime minister of Northern Ireland with whom they could cooperate. If he were overthrown, "an extremist with unacceptable policies was likely to be chosen to succeed him." Internment was thus "the last action available to us short of direct rule."[56]

Maudling wrote to Faulkner on August 4, reminding him that the GOC was not recommending internment on military grounds and suggesting that a decision be deferred until after a potentially difficult Orange march scheduled for August 12.[57] But Faulkner calculated that he could not afford to wait any longer. He called Maudling and arranged to meet him in London the following day with Heath, Carrington, and Foreign Secretary Alec Douglas-Home. At the meeting Heath expressed concern about the impact of internment on moderate Catholic opinion and Britain's international reputation, and also suggested deferring a decision until after August 12.[58] He pointed out that if internment failed to improve matters, the only further option could be direct rule. Faulkner replied that direct rule would be a calamity, but if they could overcome the IRA, this would provide the necessary context for building on the reform program and improving community relations.

For the second part of the meeting, the ministers were joined by their security advisers: Chief of General Staff Michael Carver, GOC Tuzo, and Chief Constable Graham Shillington. Shillington said that the time for internment had arrived. The GOC gave a more nuanced response. He said that internment was not essential in strictly military terms, but qualified this by suggesting that it might help to speed the IRA's defeat; whether this was desirable was a matter for political judgment.

After a private consultation between UK ministers and their commanders, Heath announced "that if, as the responsible Minister, Mr. Faulkner informed them that it would be his intention to proceed to early internment, they would concur and ensure the necessary army support." This was to be accompanied by a ban on all parades. If there was any evidence of loyalists organizing subversion or terrorism, they too should be interned. Faulkner would get what he had asked for, but would carry the full political responsibility for any adverse consequences.[59]

## The Options

During the summer of 1971, UK ministers considered three main policy options: internment, direct rule, and in the long term, Irish unification. Once Faulkner had urgently requested internment, they had to act; doing nothing would have meant allowing him to go the way of Chichester-Clark, then having either to introduce direct rule or negotiate a better strategy with a successor who would probably be both less cooperative and less politically skillful.

*Internment*

Faulkner advanced a range of arguments to justify internment. First, he suggested, it would at least stop those interned from engaging in or organizing violence. Recent experience had shown that normal judicial processes were inadequate to cope with the IRA threat: witnesses had been killed, jury members had been intimidated, and sufficient evidence to convict was often impossible to obtain even when defendants openly admitted their crimes.[60] Second, Faulkner reflected on his use of internment as minister of home affairs during the last IRA campaign. Although the scale and intensity of the violence then had been relatively slight, that experience had convinced him that internment could demoralize the paramilitaries, break up their organization, exhaust their finances, and yield useful intelligence.[61] Third, he judged that internment was preferable to the other visibly tough measures being advocated by his Unionist critics. It would neither repudiate the reforms already introduced (as would recreating the USC or universally rearming the RUC), nor directly punish entire Catholic communities (as would block searches, reprisal raids, and curfews), nor expose soldiers to undue risk (as would the permanent military occupation of republican neighborhoods). Fourth, internment would demonstrate to his Unionist supporters and critics alike that he was determined to end the violence. Finally, he believed that SDLP leader Gerry Fitt privately supported it on the ground that the Catholic population of Belfast "would on the whole be vastly relieved by the removal of the IRA yoke on their necks."[62]

Before meeting Faulkner on August 5, UK ministers assembled to agree on what line to take. Weighing the arguments as outlined by their officials,[63] they identified three main benefits to internment: enabling Faulkner to demonstrate his determination to suppress IRA violence, disrupting IRA operations, and producing intelligence. Against internment were several other factors. Ministers had promised MPs that they would not introduce it except on the basis of professional military advice, and the GOC was not recommending it. There was no certainty that all the dangerous republican activists could be identified and lifted.[64] It would stimulate Nationalist support for and recruitment to the IRA. There would be a risk of reprisals, including kidnapping and assassination in Britain (bombing was not mentioned). It would be politically and diplomatically damaging. If it failed, no option other than direct rule would remain. Finally, to be fully effective it would need to be introduced simultaneously in the south, but the Irish government had indicated that it would not do so.

As the ministers discussed the pros and cons around the cabinet table, Maudling observed that "internment would have to be used at some time in the near future and the arguments in favour of using it sooner rather than later were strong." If it worked, it would avoid the necessity of introducing direct rule, but if direct rule could not be avoided, it would be preferable for internment already to be in place as a result of a Stormont decision.[65] The argument was also advanced that if Faulkner asked for internment when they met and it became known that they had refused, this would make Faulkner's position politically untenable, and thus, direct rule more likely.[66] Chichester-Clark's downfall had demonstrated the danger in allowing a supplicant Unionist prime minister to return to the Stormont bear pit empty-handed.

### Direct Rule

Maudling had updated Callaghan's contingency plans for direct rule for use if necessary to prevent Northern Ireland from falling into the hands of "an extremist leader," Craig being the obvious candidate.[67] But the Conservative home secretary was at least as keen as Callaghan had been to minimize Westminster's involvement. The arguments against direct rule remained as before: the threat of a loyalist backlash, further entanglement in "the Irish bog," and responsibility for a situation that London could not control. British ministers confirmed their predecessors' conclusions that direct rule should be a last resort. Before it was adopted, "the Northern Ireland Government should invoke their powers of internment."[68]

### Longer-Term Solutions

While publicly expressing confidence in the reform strategy and the Unionist leadership, Heath privately believed that neither further reforms nor tougher security measures alone would settle the problem in the longer term. On taking up office in July 1970, he had accordingly commissioned a small group of officials to examine possible political initiatives once peace had been restored or events had deteriorated to such an extent that direct rule had to be introduced. Officials from the Home Office set to work behind the scenes with colleagues from the Ministry of Defence (MoD), Foreign and Commonwealth Office (FCO), Treasury, Security Service, and Cabinet Office. This group did not include any representatives from the Northern Ireland Civil Service, and the Northern Ireland government learned about its deliberations only through informal contacts with sympathetic Home Office officials.[69] Like their ministerial counterparts, the group did not meet regularly until the crisis over Chichester-Clark's resignation stirred them to action in March 1971. Thereafter (holidays excluded) they met monthly. In May 1971 they considered a discussion paper prepared by the Home Office on what it called "the Irish Problem."[70] This identified a number of strategic options, including electoral law reforms, such as the introduction of proportional representation as a means to encourage "moderates and the minority"; independence; and redrawing the border with population transfers. In the short term, the mandarins agreed on the need to "sustain a moderate Government in power." In preparing for the longer term, they agreed that they "should examine how far the Irish Republic would be ready to adapt itself politically and socially to accommodate the Ulster Protestants." The minutes of their meetings record their view that direct rule "might not be consistent with our ultimate intention of promoting a united Ireland."[71] It is not precise about whose ultimate intention is meant, but the most plausible reading in the context is that it refers to the British government as a whole, including ministers.

In July 1971 the policy debate reached ministers, who ruled out the radical option of redrawing the border. They also decided against any process of negotiation with the IRA or the Irish government that might further weaken Faulkner's leadership. Instead, they opted to continue to grind down the IRA while pressing Faulkner to include moderate Nationalists in the Stormont administration.[72]

## Uncertainties and Paradigms

### Managing Uncertainties

In considering Faulkner's request for agreeing to introduce internment, UK ministers faced three major uncertainties. How severe were the party political pressures on Faulkner? How would the minority react? Could the security forces identify and catch enough key fighters to inflict a sufficiently decisive blow against the IRA? Internment would not be necessary if Faulkner's leadership were secure. It would not succeed if it provoked a violent reaction, if it did not seriously weaken the IRA, or if enough insurgent leaders escaped across the border to continue the campaign from there.[73]

To address the first question, Maudling asked UKREP Howard Smith to assess the pressures on Faulkner. Smith confirmed that Faulkner's ministers were strongly and unanimously pressing for internment. Smith had previously advised that Faulkner overemphasized security at the expense of reform and political progress; now, he reported, "If Faulkner does not get internment soon I think he will lose heart. He will cling to office as long as he can but his conversion to reform (which was largely a political calculation) may wear thin. He may also suffer defections from his cabinet which could make his position untenable." Noting that the army expected to achieve substantial benefits from internment, including intelligence information, Smith advised his masters to accede to Faulkner's request immediately. But he did so with the qualification that "unless internment is more dramatically and swiftly successful than we have a right to expect I do not rate it better than evens that Faulkner will be in office in say six months from now."[74]

On the likely minority reaction, Catholic leaders had made clear their intense opposition to internment and the emergency measures available under the Special Powers Act generally. The Northern Ireland Civil Rights Association (NICRA) had been demonstrating against the possibility for over a year, and Nationalist MP Frank McManus was warning that Nationalists would unite in resisting it "to the uttermost of their power."[75] In making his pitch to UK ministers, Faulkner had acknowledged that internment would block off such avenues to political reconciliation as remained and anticipated a bitter reaction from republicans. But he underestimated the scale and intensity of that reaction and the propaganda benefits that the IRA would derive from it.[76] Acting on the advice of a handful of senior security officials, he did not consult either his minister of community relations or others in tune with Nationalist thinking who might have given him a more accurate assessment.[77]

Faulkner made a serious miscalculation if he concluded that SDLP and other Catholic community leaders would accept internment. He later claimed to have been influenced by correspondence from people in republican districts urging him to "get these terrorists off our backs."[78] He apparently did not recognize or chose to deny that the sample of people who contacted him did not genuinely represent the communities they claimed to speak for, or that the IRA commanded substantial popular support without resort to intimidation. In reality the SDLP could not publicly have endorsed the policy, even had its leaders been personally inclined to do so. Many moderate Nationalists saw internment as an attack on the entire Catholic community, and as tending to legitimate the IRA's contention that republicans could never depend on a Unionist government to guarantee their security.

The mistake was not just Faulkner's. Army commanders too were over-optimistic in assessing the benefits of internment. The commander of land forces (CLF), Major-General Anthony Farrar-Hockley, argued that it would seriously disrupt IRA operations and yield a substantial intelligence dividend. For this the price would be worth paying, which he estimated as forty-eight hours or so of rioting, a propaganda attack by Nationalist politicians, and a few weeks of wild bombing and shooting from the residue of IRA men left with arms, which the army would eventually contain.[79] Nevertheless, the GOC's assessment of popular attitudes in republican communities, based on reports from army officers on the ground, proved more accurate than Faulkner's: "We've got to face the fact that perhaps as much as half of the Catholic community are in sympathy with Republican aims—and this is of course a perfectly legitimate aspiration."[80] This assessment was reflected in a report from the Home Office to Maudling: "The reaction of the Catholic community . . . is likely to be more marked than on previous occasions when internment has been used because of the close political connection between the current activity of the IRA and the actions of the minority community in claiming a larger share in the government of Northern Ireland."[81]

Attempting to reduce the intensity of the Nationalist reaction, Heath and Maudling made their agreement conditional on the banning of parades for the next six months, a measure directed primarily at the Orange institutions. Maudling also asked Faulkner "to lift some Protestants if you can."[82] Faulkner agreed to the ban on parades but not to the internment of loyalists. Both governments took advice from their security chiefs and UKREP, and both accepted the response, which was that there was no evidence of organized terrorism by Protestants on such a scale as to justify their detention. Faulkner later wrote, "The idea of arresting anyone as an exercise in political cosmetics was repugnant to me."

UK ministers' third uncertainty was whether the security forces could locate and capture a critical mass of the IRA's key leaders. The RUC had files on the older generation of IRA men from the 1950s and radical civil rights activists. But police officers had been withdrawn from republican areas since August 1969; the USC, which had been a rich source of low-grade local intelligence since 1969, had been disbanded; and the authorities had little useful information on the large majority of IRA members who had been recruited since then. This information deficit was compounded by republican residents' increasing hostility toward the army; the stringent punishments that both factions of the IRA meted out to informers; their fluid organizational structures; the army's practice of rotating regiments through Northern Ireland, so that each spent only four months there at a time; and the mutual hostility between the army and RUC Special Branch, which meant that each tended to keep the juiciest nuggets of information to itself.

A British military intelligence unit had been established in Northern Ireland in March 1970, primarily to collect information on loyalist paramilitaries. A year later, its database comprised an incoherent mixture of observations from soldiers in the streets, combined with information from two sources so close to the top of the IRA's command structure as to be useless except in defining that organization's broad strategic aims. On middle-grade issues, such as the identity of bombers and their planned targets, the unit's information was seriously lacking.[83] Nevertheless, military intelligence by February 1971 could assess the implications of internment more accurately than Faulkner managed six months later. Recommending that internment should be kept in reserve as a last resort, an anonymous agent wrote that the IRA was an elite organization, deliberately kept compact; that any gaps created by internment would be filled quickly from an established waiting list; and that "more martyrs will have been created; a new rallying point will have been provided for all the forces of dissent, and will bind them together."[84] In an attempt to remedy the information deficiency, 1,800 soldiers and policemen raided homes across Northern Ireland on July 23, 1971. They found that while the Provisionals and Officials were both careful not to keep written records about their own activities, each kept interesting files on the other. Material collected during these raids was used to prepare the final list of internees.

Recognizing that the uncertainties over internment could not be reduced to their satisfaction, UK ministers took pains to ensure that the political risks were transferred to Faulkner. Carrington in particular was determined that the Unionists should be seen to take full responsibility.[85] This suited Faulkner, whose critics had attacked him—as he had himself criticized O'Neill—for being London's puppet.

*Causes of Disorder*

As we have seen, the nature and intensity of the violence in Northern Ireland shifted dramatically in the eighteen months after September 1969. As the salience of the civil rights protests receded and IRA violence came to the fore, London came to see the cause of the problem as premeditated insurgency rather than deprivation and discrimination. Social and economic factors were still relevant, but primarily as issues that the IRA could exploit to secure popular support and media goodwill. Conservative ministers gradually dropped the legitimate grievances hypothesis in favor of an explanation that focused on the deliberate choices of IRA commanders. That paradigm shift helped make internment possible.

*Reasonable People*

The Conservatives continued to express the view that the solution lay in bringing Northern Ireland "up to British standards," depicting its elected representatives as largely devoid of reason. Carrington in his memoirs records "that an early visit impressed me most unfavourably with the bigotry—and insobriety—of a lot of the fairly senior people in Ulster politics whom I met."[86] The defence secretary told publisher Cecil King, ironically over lunch at the elite Turf Club, that he was "appalled by the bigotry, drunkenness, and stupidity of the Unionist Party in Ulster." He went on to depict Ian Paisley "as a man of such extreme views that no dickerings with him are possible."[87] Similarly, Carrington's army commanders in private expressed contempt for Chichester-Clark and his cabinet.[88]

Any Unionist leader who was deemed to be a hard-liner was excluded from serious dialogue and had no effective channel of communication with anyone in the British government.[89] This so concerned the speaker of the Commons that he wrote to Heath after a visit to Belfast in July 1971, arguing the case for building up a relationship with Ian Paisley instead of treating him as a pariah.[90] According to King, Maudling finally acted on this suggestion only in December 1971, when he offered Paisley a meeting. The encounter did not alter the home secretary's opinion of Paisley, whom he described as "a self-seeking thug."[91] Their hostility to hard-liners meant that the Conservatives could not countenance Faulkner's replacement by Craig, Paisley, or any other critic of the reform strategy. Thus, paradoxically, British ministers' determination to keep this tendency out of government strengthened the case for internment.

On the other side, the British depicted the IRA factions and their supporters as mere terrorists, hooligans, and extremists, an interpretation that made it easier for them to suspend the normal framework of legal rights and protections to which republicans were as much entitled as any other citizens, but also clouded their judgment about the consequences of internment.

### Britain's Role

The Conservatives differed from their Labour predecessors in their conception of the British government's proper relationship with the devolved administration. Like Labour, they presented themselves as neutral intermediaries. But at the same time they considered it right to uphold rather than undermine the Stormont government's authority. They did not see moderate Unionists as political rivals and had no electoral interest in building up the NILP.

## Politics

### General Election

We have seen that UK ministers shifted tack from reform to coercion primarily because they wanted to sustain the Stormont administration. There was strong continuity in British objectives from 1969 to 1971 to the extent that the desire to avoid direct rule was an overwhelming priority. Yet internment could not have been introduced if the political context at Westminster had not changed dramatically.

The most obvious changes came with the general election of June 18, 1970, which the Conservatives won with an overall majority of fifteen. The same election returned fewer Unionists than before at eight; three Irish republicans, each with a different party affiliation (Bernadette Devlin, independent republican; Frank McManus, Nationalist Unity; and Gerry Fitt, Republican Labour); and one Protestant Unionist (Ian Paisley). The Conservatives did not share Labour's electoral interest in weakening the Unionist Party, traditionally their allies at Westminster. Nationalists predicted that the Conservatives would reverse or slow down implementation of the reforms, reject proposals for further reform, and prop up Stormont at the expense of the Catholic community.

It would be wrong to attribute the policy shift that took place primarily to the change of governing party. Even before the election, British ministers had begun to question whether the reforms would be sufficient to prevent further disorder. The GOC had announced the government's new get-tough approach to rioting in April 1970, with Labour still in office. In the same month Callaghan at Westminster criticized the continuing complaints of civil rights leaders and blamed "a small minority of extremists" for the worsening violence.[92] However, in February 1971, with the first IRA shooting of British soldiers, Maudling began to talk as if all Catholic grievances had been removed, and even to attribute the violence to the success of the reforms.[93]

### Backbenchers

Parliamentary pressures reinforced Maudling's personal disposition to use Stormont to shield himself from the unpleasantness of Northern Ireland. In the Commons, the government was caught between a desire to maintain bipartisan consensus and pressure from a small but vocal group of its own backbenchers, who became increasingly angry about the failure to stem the upsurge in violence. This dilemma became especially uncomfortable after February 1971. In contrast to Labour, Conservative backbench pressure pushed ministers toward coercion rather than reform or withdrawal.

With a slim majority, the Conservative leadership in the Commons also was anxious to retain the support of the nine Unionist MPs.[94] During the crisis over Chichester-Clark's resignation in March, the Unionists threatened to end their custom of voting with the Conservatives in protest at London's refusal to introduce tougher security measures. By July, Maudling had become concerned that they were persuading a number of Conservative backbenchers to their way of thinking.[95]

In this the Unionists had the support of Enoch Powell, a former minister sacked by Heath from the shadow cabinet in 1968, who retained substantial personal influence among Conservative party activists and voters.

Powell had aspired to the leadership of the party; he and Heath personally detested each other.[96] Powell saw the Northern Ireland conflict in uncompromising terms as a war between two nations. From this perspective, the reform policy was irrelevant and detrimental to the United Kingdom's national interest: "To imagine that the fixed and settled intent of those whose purpose it is to use violence and terror to annex Northern Ireland could be deflected or appeased by 'reforms' was from the start a belief so patently childish as to raise doubts whether those who professed it could really be in earnest," he argued.[97]

Others on the right claimed that the IRA was linked to an international communist conspiracy. John Biggs-Davison MP warned that Britain's strategic interests would be seriously damaged if radical republicans established an all-Ireland socialist republic, which could become "Britain's Cuba."[98]

Demands for tougher action spread from the right to mainstream Conservative MPs when the IRA started shooting soldiers. Ministers were made painfully aware of their critics' strength at a heated meeting of the party's parliamentary Home Affairs Committee on March 22, 1971, which over 160 backbenchers attended.[99] This meeting had been arranged at the Unionists' request, and it was devoted to Northern Ireland. It took place in an atmosphere of great uncertainty. The Stormont Unionists were to meet the following morning to choose Chichester-Clark's successor, and Unionist MPs' continuing support for the government hung in the balance. The meeting was particularly uncomfortable for Maudling, in that the right-wing Monday Club, chaired by Biggs-Davison and including thirty Conservative MPs, was calling for him to resign over the issue.[100] The meeting was private, and no concessions to the Unionists were announced. But Maudling and Carrington received what observers described as "a nasty shock," a "grilling," and a "pasting."[101] Even normally compliant backbenchers were critical, and one report claimed that those who attended were unanimous in their support for the Unionists.[102]

The meeting was on the same day that Heath announced that the reform program had remedied "such minority grievances as there may have been,"[103] signaling an end to concessions; he also initiated action on a range of tougher security measures for implementation within the next two weeks, a concession to Unionist hard-liners that he had denied to Chichester-Clark only a few days earlier. Faulkner was aware of the advantage that the Conservative backbenchers' unrest gave him: "I knew that these pressures would strengthen my hand," he wrote.[104]

The impact of Conservative MPs' dissatisfaction was reinforced by government whips' concern over a potentially more dangerous revolt on an issue that Heath had made a personal priority: UK entry into the European Economic Community (EEC).[105] Over thirty Conservative MPs, led by Powell, were intensely against it, and the whips took seriously the possibility that this group would form an alliance with the Unionists to defeat the government on both issues.

Ministers found themselves in a similar predicament on July 28, when Conservative MPs again met to discuss Northern Ireland against a background of escalating violence. As before, Maudling faced demands for tougher action.[106] Amid talk of a loyalist backlash, his backbenchers called for internment, the imposition of martial law, curfews, and trade sanctions against the Republic unless it stopped the IRA operating from its territory. Unless effective measures were taken promptly, they argued, there was a real risk of Faulkner's being overthrown by extremists and full-scale civil war, which might then spread to Britain.[107] Some Unionist MPs again threatened to withhold their votes from the government. This time the threat was more immediate, since a vote on entry to the EEC was imminent.

### The Opposition

Callaghan has since written that if Labour had won the 1970 election, it was his intention to have convened a round-table conference to devise a new constitutional settlement, recognizing that the reform program would not solve all his problems.[108] Labour's manifesto did not include any proposals for constitutional change, although it did display partisan hostility toward the Unionist Party: "Fifty years of one-party Tory rule has led to social tensions and lack of opportunities which erupted into major disorders last summer."[109] But by 1971 the rift had grown between himself and Wilson, who believed that there could be no lasting solution short of unification.

Heath was as keen as Callaghan had been to retain the bipartisan consensus. He met Wilson for a confidential discussion on March 21, 1971, to discuss how to handle the crisis over Chichester-Clark's resignation. Wilson assured the prime minister that Labour would accept Faulkner as prime minister of Northern Ireland and state publicly that policy on the conflict was not a matter of dispute between the Westminster parties.[110]

As Labour's official spokesman, Callaghan expressed impatience with Nationalists "stringing the British government along, making fresh demands as soon as old ones were met."[111] He did not oppose internment in principle;[112] Maudling believed that his predecessor privately favored it, but had been dissuaded by his colleagues from saying so publicly.[113] According to Faulkner, Callaghan thought that internment should be accompanied by an offer to minority elected representatives of a stake in power at Stormont but recognized that the SDLP had just rejected such an offer, and that the atmosphere immediately after introducing internment would be unlikely to favor its acceptance.[114]

## Media and Public Opinion

In 1969, the general tenor of national news coverage had depicted a Catholic minority struggling for its rights against a Protestant regime led by a moderate but weak prime minister. By mid-1970, this had changed dramatically. The prevailing perspective had shifted from one of "reasonable Catholic grievance versus unreasonable Protestant discrimination" to "a dispute between warring tribes," one as bad as the other, with British peacekeepers caught in the middle.[115] The coverage broadly was for the British army, against republicans, and equivocal about Unionists.[116] The shift reflected the change in the nature of the violence, but also that it was directed against British soldiers rather than Northern Irish police officers. Where previously the dominant image had been of the RUC charging civil rights marchers, now it was of British troops retreating impotently before republican mobs throwing rocks, bottles, and petrol bombs—especially when the IRA began to kill soldiers.

Three other factors also influenced UK media coverage in the army's favor. First, British journalists identified with their army, men from similar backgrounds with familiar dialects sharing an uncomfortable and dangerous assignment in hostile territory. Second, they depended on army sources for inside stories. Working on tight deadlines, they often relied exclusively on information officers for up-to-date news about recent incidents. Third, ministers pressured the proprietors and senior editors of news organizations that criticized government policy, resulting in some self-censorship.[117] Of the serious national papers spanning mainstream political opinion in Britain, only the *Daily Telegraph*—traditionally closest to the Conservatives—opposed the imposition of further reforms on Stormont, on the grounds that London should not further undermine the authority of the devolved administration.[118] As the IRA campaign grew, the *Telegraph* argued that the slide toward civil war could be reversed only by restoring the power of the Northern Ireland government. Its editorials called for internment as a symbol of the UK government's determination to defeat terrorism. The *Telegraph* backed the Monday Club's demand for Maudling's resignation and held him personally responsible for blocking the policy.[119]

When the SDLP walked out of Stormont, it lost the sympathy of other serious national papers. Editorial coverage in *The Guardian* (often characterized as the voice of the soft left) and *The Times* (then reputedly the voice of the establishment) shifted towards the *Telegraph*'s position. As an editorialist in *The Times* argued, "It has often been said that violence cannot be brought to an end without conciliation. But it may now be more accurate to say that political conciliation cannot succeed until terrorism has been stamped out."[120] *The Spectator*, generally viewed as sympathetic to the Conservative Party, accused Maudling of muddling through without any clear sense of direction: "Northern Ireland is not being properly governed at present.... The Government of the United Kingdom of Great Britain and Northern Ireland must now act swiftly and decisively to restore peace and order within the confines of its direct authority and responsibility, however such peace and order is to be found."[121] The demands were not for internment as such, but as in Belfast, media pressure reinforced those inside the political system who were demanding more coercive action.

### The International Dimension

British ministers were concerned at the possible impact of internment on elite opinion in the Republic and further afield. Like their predecessors, they wanted to avoid any actions that might stimulate republican sentiment in the south. But as their attention shifted toward coercion, they necessarily drifted farther from Dublin's position. To be really effective, any policy that put security first required Dublin's cooperation, primarily in preventing its territory from being used as a base for insurgency.[122] But UK ministers did not trust their counterparts in Dublin either to cooperate wholeheartedly or to keep the content of any discussions about cooperation confidential. During the early part of 1971 they tended to depict the Irish as part of the problem rather than as a potential partner in crafting a solution.

The ministers' perception was not without foundation. On May 6, 1970, Taoiseach Jack Lynch had sacked two of his ministers, Charles Haughey and Neil Blaney, after a senior official in the Irish Justice Department had informed opposition leader Liam Cosgrave that the two ministers—both known for their republican sympathies—had attempted to import guns illegally for the IRA. Cosgrave raised the matter with Lynch, who then issued a statement announcing that he had already been informed of the conspiracy.[123] Evidence later emerged that the two ministers' activities had been funded with money allocated by the Irish cabinet in August 1969 "to provide aid for the victims of the current unrest in the Six Counties."[124] The money was to be administered by a committee of four, including Haughey and Blaney.

Material presented at Haughey's subsequent trial revealed that republicans from Derry had been given military training at Irish army camps;

that the Irish cabinet had allocated £100,000 to the aid fund, of which over £75,000 had been spent on purposes other than aid, including weapons for the Provisionals; that an undisclosed sum had been earmarked to pay for secret arms shipments from Europe; that some of the money had been used to pay for anti-Unionist propaganda; that Irish intelligence officers had tried to buy arms in Germany for the Provisionals; that Haughey had instructed customs officials to authorize entry of the weapons shipments without inspecting them; and that the intelligence officers involved in the weapons procurement understood that the purchases had been authorized at cabinet level. The weapons sought included 334 machine guns and 250,000 rounds of ammunition. Other evidence indicates that Haughey and Blaney personally authorized the arms shipments; that Fitt and Devlin had asked the Irish government for arms; and that the head of the Irish army's intelligence section had briefed the minister of defense, James Gibbons, about a meeting with republicans in October 1969 at which the illegal importations were planned.[125] The Irish ministers' support for republicans in the north had been offered on condition that they cut their links with the "communists" who controlled the IRA, which they did in December 1969.[126] The court dismissed the charges against Blaney. As for Haughey, the two intelligence officers, and the arms dealer accused with him, the jury concluded that the alleged arms importation could not have been illegal since the minister of defense had authorized it.[127] In short, members of the Irish cabinet had used or colluded in the use of government funds to help create and arm republican activists for a campaign of violence against the authorities in the north. By providing political and financial support and trying to provide arms, they and their intelligence officials helped to start an internal war against an ostensible ally and prospective partner in the EEC.[128] The Irish courts had exculpated them, and their careers in politics had continued.

Moreover, in September 1969—and this was not revealed until state papers were opened to the public decades later—the Irish army had prepared detailed plans for incursions into Northern Ireland. There would be no declaration of war. Covert operations would be directed at key infrastructure targets, such as television studios, harbors, and airports, and combined with conventional attacks on the towns of Newry and Derry. The intention was not to win a military victory but to establish that there was an international conflict under way that would justify calls for intervention by a UN peacekeeping force in place of the British army. The Irish army's plans also warned of the dangers: high casualties as the British struck back, destabilization in the north, and potentially widespread sectarian violence and ethnic cleansing.[129] Even further, the Irish cabinet instructed Defense

Minister Gibbons on February 6, 1970, to prepare the Irish army for incursions into Northern Ireland in the event of a breakdown of order there, and also to have rifles, machine guns, respirators, and ammunition ready for distribution at short notice to local "citizens' defence committees." The cabinet also decided they would not tell the British before sending their soldiers in.[130]

Although the full extent of the Irish government's preparations for intervention may not have been known at the time, the arms trial revelations strengthened the case of Conservatives and Unionists who believed that Stormont faced a republican conspiracy tacitly supported by Dublin. Lynch's firing of Blaney and Haughey and their subsequent prosecution provided some evidence of the Irish state's willingness to prevent such collusion, but the affair fueled Unionist hostility and British suspicions. As they saw it, Lynch had acted against the conspirators only under threat of public disclosure.

The arms trials posed a serious threat to Lynch's authority, but he handled it with some skill. Many Fianna Fáil activists and a substantial portion of public opinion supported the defendants, who were widely seen as helping patriotic Irishmen in the north to resist Unionist oppression. In this context, Lynch adopted the tactic of criticizing British policy in public while assuring the British ambassador behind the arras that he was doing no more than the exigencies of politics demanded. The taoiseach also set up an interdepartmental committee on the north. Comprising officials from his own department and the departments of finance and external affairs, it met regularly to oversee and advise him on developments in the "Six Counties." It was tasked with keeping in touch with all relevant aspects of Anglo-Irish relations, arranging for the in-depth study of possible long-term solutions, advising on contacts with friends in the north and in Britain, guiding and directing information activity abroad, and acting as a clearinghouse for the activities of other departments. Patrick Hillery, as minister for external affairs, addressed the committee's first meeting on June 18, 1970, when he made plain that "reunification" was the only long-term solution, that it could be achieved "at most within a generation, and that the main purpose of the Committee was to speed up the process, identify and remove obstacles."[131] The chair of the committee, S.G. Ronan of External Affairs, outlined a three-phase strategy comprising the formulation and implementation of genuine reforms and the protection of the minority against attack; reconciliation, with the objective of intensifying north-south contacts and cooperation and eliminating existing barriers; and negotiation of a constitutional settlement. In pursuit of this strategy, the Irish government supported the formation of the SDLP, kept regularly in touch with its leaders, and sought to maximize its influence with the British.

By January 1971, Ronan declared himself "reasonably happy" with progress, since most of the required reforms had either been introduced or were in the final stages of formulation. As they entered the second phase of the strategy, Irish ministers' public statements were likely to emphasize reconciliation more than reform. Their aim, Ronan said, "should be to keep the position fluid and not allow the situation in the North to solidify when all the reforms are legislated." It might also be necessary to review elements of the Irish constitution—such as Article 3 and the provisions relating to religion and family law—that were obstacles to reunification.[132]

By August, when UK ministers made the final decision on internment, they anticipated that it would generate widespread public condemnation in the Republic, which Lynch would join in, but they calculated that he would not raise the matter at the United Nations, a risk they were keen to avoid.[133] Alongside their occasional high-profile statements and gestures, Irish ministers continued to follow the approach Lynch had initiated of influencing British policy behind the scenes through the ambassador in Dublin and their own diplomats in London, the United States, and Europe. Their message was that British coercive policies would help the IRA to gain recruits and popular support, that a political initiative was needed that would give the minority a share in the north's administration, and that the British should indicate publicly that they would welcome unification in the longer term.[134]

Although they were at times irritated by Dublin's international lobbying, British ministers wanted to keep Lynch in power. They also tried to persuade him to encourage the SDLP to consider seriously Faulkner's proposal of June 1971 for an enhanced committee system at Stormont. But they were not especially receptive to his arguments against internment. Regarding security policy, they resented that both wings of the IRA operated with virtual impunity in the south; when known IRA members were brought to trial, the cases against them were almost invariably dismissed, and requests for their extradition to stand trial in the north were refused on the ground that their offences were "political."[135]

It was unduly optimistic for Faulkner to believe that Dublin might cooperate with his plans for internment, but it was not wholly groundless. The Irish government had introduced internment during the IRA campaign of the 1950s. In December 1970, Justice Minister Des O'Malley had announced that the policy was again under consideration. The *Irish Times* had reported that if internment were introduced in the north, it would follow in the Republic almost at once.[136] In preparing for a meeting of the cabinet on July 21, 1971, Maudling asked Douglas-Home to explore the possibility of cooperating with Dublin on internment. FCO officials responded that Lynch would cooperate only if there were a direct threat to human lives from the IRA in the Republic. British ambassador John Peck sounded out Lynch in hypothetical terms on July 30 with the draft of an agreed-upon text, which the British hoped the Irish would endorse if internment were introduced. This did not require that internment be introduced simultaneously in both jurisdictions. Lynch responded in unambiguous terms that he had no grounds for introducing internment and that if he tried to introduce it, his government would fall. He then argued that Britain should reflect very seriously on the likely consequences: an upsurge in recruitment to the IRA, and even moderate Nationalists identifying themselves with the internees.[137]

Peck spoke to Lynch again on August 9 after the internment operation had begun. He passed on a message from Heath asking Lynch to tell the northern minority that they should not interpret internment as directed against them but only at individuals who were deliberately using violence to create disorder. Peck later recorded Lynch's response: "He not only stated most emphatically that there was not the remotest possibility of internment being introduced in the Republic, but he gave me the most serious and solemn warning that the consequences in the North would be catastrophic: for every man put behind wire a hundred would volunteer."[138]

The British did not seriously expect Lynch to introduce internment, and made little serious attempt to induce him to do so. If they had offered something in return, they might have received a more positive response. Two days after the first arrests, Hillery told Maudling that Dublin had not ruled internment out entirely, but would introduce it only if it could be presented as part of a move toward a united Ireland.[139]

On the broader international front, introducing internment required Britain to enter a partial derogation from the European Convention on Human Rights. Although acceptance of the convention was not a condition of entry to the EEC, Heath was concerned not to give existing members who opposed Britain's membership—notably France—any grounds to exclude it. British diplomats were anxious also about negative press coverage in Europe, with its wartime memories of internment, and in countries with substantial populations of Irish descent, such as the United States and Australia.[140] Heath considered all these factors but set them aside on the ground that the situation in Northern Ireland required decisive action urgently.[141] Again they highlighted the importance of ensuring that Faulkner shouldered the responsibility.

### Heath

Heath did not share Wilson's enthusiasm for intervention in Northern Ireland. He was not at first particularly attentive to the issue and unwilling to intrude on the territory of his home secretary.[142] He deliberately reversed Wilson's tactic of summoning Northern Ireland's leaders to Downing Street for meetings, as this "gave the false impression that they were puppets of the Westminster government, which they were certainly not." Instead he would send a reluctant Maudling to Belfast.[143] He told Faulkner at their first meeting as premiers that he would not push Stormont around in public, preferring a two-way partnership.[144] Aside from official channels, he kept personally in touch with developments in Northern Ireland through his friend Robin Chichester-Clark, brother of the Northern Ireland prime minister, who was a Unionist MP at Westminster and also a junior minister (for employment) in Heath's government. Chichester-Clark was foremost among the Unionist MPs who successfully pressed Heath to introduce tougher security measures after his brother's resignation.

Until March 1971, Heath left it to Maudling and Carrington to handle London's relationships with Stormont, expecting Chichester-Clark to take day-to-day political responsibility for implementing the policies to which the two governments had agreed. However, he took a personal interest in ensuring that Faulkner rather than Craig replaced Chichester-Clark, and that the transition passed smoothly. He met Faulkner shortly afterward, forming a positive impression of him as "a brisk, hard-working, and dynamic politician who realized that Northern Ireland had to modernise or it was doomed."[145] On this basis, for the next five months, he was content to let the Stormont premier do his job.

It is nevertheless clear from Heath's autobiography that he privately accepted the prevailing view of the British political elite that explained the violence primarily in terms of Unionists' historical mistreatment of Catholics. He envisaged a political solution in which "the decent, moderate majority" would unite across the sectarian divide as the power of the polar extremes—represented by Paisleyism and the IRA, respectively—was gradually eroded by the irresistible forces of reason and modernization: "I had come to the view years before that there was only one way of achieving any permanent solution for Northern Ireland; some form of power sharing between the two communities. I also believed that the Republic of Ireland had to be brought into the relationship once more."[146]

### Maudling

Where Callaghan had engaged energetically with the Northern Ireland issue as a personal challenge and the means to renew a faltering political career, Maudling adopted a much more reserved approach, avoiding emotional rhetoric and grand public gestures. Chichester-Clark told his parliamentary party after meeting the new home secretary that "where there has been suspicion in the past there was now relationship and trust."[147] Faulkner subsequently compared Maudling favorably with Callaghan for not setting up "superficial circuses and messianic visits" and appreciated his "style of quietly efficient politics."[148]

Less favorably, Maudling's many critics have described him as clever but idle and distracted by personal issues, blaming him for losing the momentum his predecessor had generated.[149] Callaghan describes him as a lethargic character with a reputation for allowing important matters to drift.[150] One senior army commander complained: "Reggie Maudling had no idea. He would never go out. . . . After his first visit here he sat in my office with his head in his hands and said 'Oh these bloody people! How are you going to deal with them?' 'Well,' I said, 'Secretary of State, we are not going to deal with them. It's you—your lot who have to deal with them. We have got to have a policy.' But we never did have a policy. That was the problem."[151] Heath later acknowledged Maudling's limitations: "Reggie had a brilliant brain and a complete grasp of the complexities . . . but he was not at his most effective in dealing with people less intrinsically reasonable than himself."[152] This was not just a matter of a relaxed personal operating style. Maudling at first adopted the Home Office's strict view of Westminster's constitutional relationship with Stormont: that within its areas of competence, the devolved administration should as far as possible be left alone.[153] He accordingly delegated more authority to Stormont ministers and army commanders than Callaghan had done, and did not monitor security operations so closely.

### Conclusion

Each step in the restoration of Stormont's authority for security after August 1969 was immediately preceded by a significant development in the UK political system. The June 1970 election result changed the key decision makers, their approach to tackling the problem, their political incentives, and networks of influence. Chichester-Clark's resignation and a hostile political reaction to the killings of the first British soldiers gave impetus to the process of planning for internment. A similar reaction to increased IRA violence in July 1971 immediately preceded the decision actually to introduce internment. In both cases, Unionist MPs threatened to withdraw their support for the Conservatives, and influential media demanded firm action from Maudling without further delay. Ministers calculated that whatever the risks and uncertainties, internment would be politically preferable to inaction as long as it was clear that the responsibility for introducing it lay with Stormont. If it succeeded, they would get the credit and the bipartisan consensus would be restored; if it failed, they could blame Faulkner.

## Structure and Doctrine

The shifts in the political context were accompanied by a transformation in the structural relationship between Belfast and London. The period from August 1969 to August 1971 saw four important developments: a stepped delegation of authority from London to Stormont, increasing influence of the MoD in Whitehall, the army's assumption of responsibility for maintaining order in republican areas, and the emergence of UKREP as a key source of advice to UK ministers.

### Delegation

Formally the Conservatives retained the division of political responsibility set out in the Downing Street Declaration. UK ministers were accountable to Westminster for security policies and operations, while Unionist ministers answered to Stormont for civil policing and criminal justice matters. In practice, however, Stormont's influence over military operations increased as soon as the Conservatives came to power, and grew in steps over the following year. Maudling's light touch fitted well with the traditional doctrine and practice of the Home Office, which Wilson's aggressive interventionism and Callaghan's micromanagerial activism had rudely interrupted. The ministerial committee on Northern Ireland met only twice during 1970 and not again until March 1971, when it had to tackle the crisis over Chichester-Clark's resignation.

Under Labour, a joint security committee (JSC) had been created at Stormont to coordinate the actions of the army and RUC. It consisted of the GOC, the chief constable, and the Stormont minister for home affairs as chair. Other Stormont ministers and UKREP also attended. In theory, UK ministers' approval was needed for any change in security policy that had substantial resource implications or political consequences at Westminster. In practice, Maudling and Carrington allowed a great deal of political discretion to pass to the JSC, especially after Faulkner replaced Chichester-Clark. As minister for home affairs, Faulkner chaired the JSC himself.

Under Labour, UK ministers had closely supervised the JSC's decisions, which covered such details as whether water cannons should be deployed in specific crowd control situations. This close political monitoring had greatly irritated army commanders.[154] Immediately on taking office, Maudling renounced this degree of supervision.[155] Conservative ministers reportedly never vetoed a JSC decision.[156] Maudling told a radio interviewer that it was not for him to tell soldiers how to do their jobs; the GOC had full authority to do what he wanted.[157] The contrast with the previous administration is reflected in Callaghan's criticism: "However good the men on the spot were at executive action, they needed continuous political guidance. . . . These matters are small in themselves, but they can have very large political consequences."[158]

Under Chichester-Clark's premiership, senior army commanders had resisted taking political direction from the Unionists. One of the GOC's arguments for denying Chichester-Clark the tougher military actions he demanded in March 1971 was that "if we once allow Stormont to lay down detailed instructions for military action the future freedom of action of the security forces will be seriously prejudiced."[159] But they were more responsive to Faulkner, who enthusiastically filled the vacuum created by Maudling's absence.[160] This effectively meant that the army was required increasingly—and reluctantly—to respond to the political needs of the Unionist leader. Faulkner set up a small security unit at Stormont, the functions of which included preparing contingency plans for internment.[161] To head it he appointed Bill Stout, a Northern Ireland civil servant with whom he had previously worked as minister for home affairs; Stout had helped plan for internment during the IRA campaign of the 1950s.[162] He was a wholehearted proponent of the policy, and he had a difficult relationship with his Whitehall counterparts.[163] At the same time, a joint working party drawn from RUC Special Branch and military intelligence was set up to prepare a list of people to intern.[164]

However, Whitehall did not withdraw from engagement with the problem. The Home Office regularly updated its contingency plans for direct rule, monitored developments on the security front and their political implications, and advised ministers on the various security measures that Conservative and Unionist MPs demanded. Home Office officials and army commanders started seriously examining the feasibility of internment soon after the Provisionals began to kill British soldiers, exploring such practical issues as the accommodation required and the availability of prison guards[165] and reporting to ministers on the likely political and military implications, tactics, and timing.[166]

On March 18, two days before Chichester-Clark's resignation, Maudling and Carrington instructed the GOC to start planning for internment, including finding suitable accommodation.[167] By March 31, the GOC had identified Long Kesh, a former army base, as the most suitable site. On April 27 the cabinet tasked Maudling and Carrington to find the finance to build the camp. With Stormont and the Home Office unwilling to contribute, Carrington stumped up on May 21, agreeing that the defense vote would pay.[168]

That UK ministers commissioned contingency planning for internment does not mean that they intended to introduce it; as with contingency planning for direct rule, they wanted to be prepared to move quickly if they had to. But that the organizations concerned had already prepared their contingency plans made it much more likely that internment would be introduced. It was the only tough option available when in August political developments required a swift dramatic gesture.

### Defense

In February 1970 the MoD felt sufficiently confident to withdraw three of the eight extra army units that had been deployed to deal with the original emergency. Their confidence was misplaced. One consequence of the escalation of republican violence from spring 1970 was that the ministry assigned more people to work on the problem on a longer-term basis. In Whitehall, a new unit was created—Military Operations Branch 4, or MOB4—the responsibilities of which included preparing for internment. The ministry's influence rapidly expanded to match that of the Home Office. While Maudling's department retained formal responsibility for relations with Stormont, the MoD derived its influence from the substantial presence of British forces on the ground. Defense ministers and mandarins fed army commanders' concerns and preferences directly into the policy-making process in Whitehall. Sir James Dunnett, the permanent under secretary (highest-ranking official) at the MoD, was an influential participant in the officials' group that Heath tasked to work up options for a long-term solution.[169]

There was a parallel strengthening in the army's command structure in Northern Ireland. Intelligence available by June 1970 indicated that the IRA was planning a protracted period of sectarian confrontations, sabotage of businesses, and attacks on security forces across the region. Abandoning hope of early withdrawal, the army dug in. A third brigade headquarters was set up to cover the southern border area and a new senior post was created, that of CLF, to support the GOC by taking responsibility for the day-to-day conduct of operations.

Ironically in view of Unionist hard-liners' professed admiration for the army, it was Carrington who refused Chichester-Clark's request for tougher measures against republicans in spring 1971 and senior army commanders, who until July 1971 mounted the most effective opposition to internment. They argued that there was no military justification for it—that it would raise tensions, strengthen the IRA, and increase violence. They were equally skeptical about the other tough measures Unionist ministers advocated. When the GOC eventually agreed to internment on August 2, he did so only with great reluctance, arguing that an alternative policy of repeatedly arresting and interrogating known IRA activists would be more effective in both disrupting IRA operations and gathering intelligence.[170] The army did, however, want Faulkner to ban the loyalist parade in Derry on August 12. Faulkner contended that he could not politically afford to ban the march unless some firm measures were taken at the same time against the IRA.[171] This offer of a tradeoff reduced Tuzo's opposition, as did the fact that a number of his colleagues had revised their calculations in response to the deteriorating security situation.[172] Looking ahead, the CLF, Farrar-Hockley, argued that if direct rule were introduced before internment—which might prove to be the only alternative if Faulkner resigned—the Unionists would argue that they had been denied an important weapon in the battle against terrorism that would add to their sense of grievance.[173]

Another factor in the army's eventual compliance with Faulkner's request was the sheer momentum of the internment project. It had a name: Operation Demetrius. Planning had proceeded apace since the spring with the engagement of Faulkner's security unit, RUC Special Branch, military intelligence, MOB4, and the army headquarters in Northern Ireland. Their plans covered the arrest operation itself, accommodation and security for the internees, the threat of increased IRA cross-border attacks, and the likelihood of widespread disorder in Belfast and Londonderry. Accommodation for 150 internees would be available by September 11, and places for a further 450 internees and staff by November 13. The army also had contingency plans for the possible introduction of direct rule, in place by the end of November. If internment failed, they were prepared for that also.

The projected timetable for internment was accelerated in response to Faulkner's representations in July. Carrington told Tuzo on July 20 that unless he could come up with an alternative to relieve the political pressures for action, internment would have to be introduced ahead of schedule.[174] Carver and Tuzo believed that the "double act" of a ban on marches and internment was the only appropriate military measure still untried. They also came around to the view that if it were not introduced, Faulkner would be replaced by someone less competent and harder to work with.[175]

While some senior commanders acquiesced, others made no secret of their anxieties. Word of their doubts reached opposition defence spokesman Roy Hattersley, who attacked Heath for breaking his undertaking to introduce internment only on the advice of his military commanders. The best the prime minister could do in reply was to assert: "Those who say that this action was taken against the advice of the Services are wrong and cannot substantiate the accusation."[176] The broad fact is that they accepted it for political reasons, but did not advocate it militarily.

No explanation of internment would be complete that neglected the contribution to the escalation of violence of the army's actions in Catholic working-class neighborhoods, especially in Belfast and Derry. In many instances, soldiers and their officers displayed great tolerance and sensitivity, and did their best to promote good relations with local residents. But in other cases their actions blatantly contradicted UK ministers' pledges to evenhanded law enforcement and socioeconomic improvement. Routines and procedures focused on suppressing disorder; for convenience I refer to these collectively as the military security approach to policing, which Byman (see chapter 1) would identify as brute force.

In stark contrast to the civil policing approach Hunt prescribed, the military security approach included a readiness to punish rioters collectively and without concern for normal police procedures of arrest and trial; the indiscriminate use of tear gas, rubber bullets, and water cannons; measures that effectively made entire communities pay for the crimes of a few, such as widespread curfews; and a willingness to detain people and search property indiscriminately to obtain intelligence.[177] As eminent sociologist Paddy Hillyard has observed, "It has not been simply a matter of the widespread curtailment of basic rights through the widespread abuse of powers of stop, arrest and search, but the constant and systematic harassment of thousands of people within clearly defined areas."[178]

Throughout 1969 and 1970, Chief Constable Young had tried to establish a civil police presence in republican districts. Young argued that the army's high profile and aggressive behavior were generating tension on the streets and making his task impossible. He repeatedly tried to persuade army commanders to adopt gentler methods. In November 1969, he proposed joint army-RUC riot squads armed only with batons. The GOC rejected this proposal, insisting that soldiers must carry guns "to show that they mean business."[179] This argument might equally well have been advanced against the Hunt reforms in relation to the RUC. But Callaghan did not intervene.

Full-time RUC patrols began in parts of Catholic west Belfast in January 1970. In September, the GOC announced that the RUC, although still unarmed, would assume complete responsibility for law and order, including dealing with riots. As had been the case before August 1969, the army would intervene only in exceptional circumstances where the police could not cope.[180] In practice this proved to be optimistic and unworkable. The army continued to carry the responsibility for such order as there was in republican districts, as well as for security operations generally. Demoralized, hamstrung, and inadequately resourced, the RUC simply could not take over the task. In part this was because of Young's insistence that the force should follow the English model. Even the officers assigned to deal with street disturbances were not permitted to use batons, carry shields, or wear protective gear. More aggressive measures, such as using tear gas or returning sniper fire, were left to the army.

The GOC disagreed with the division of labor. As far as he was concerned, the army had no policing function; the RUC needed to be expanded and its newly formed special patrol groups given all the equipment they needed to deal with rioters "who do not hesitate to use any weapon at hand."[181] The GOC acknowledged that it would take at least until April 1975 before the RUC could be fully expanded to its full complement of 4,940, the number considered necessary to prevent a recurrence of the 1969 breakdown.[182] But there were no plans to equip them with effective riot control gear. Clearly, there was a divergence of views between ministers and their military commanders.

Under pressure to restore order in the absence of effective policing and confronted with snipers intent on killing, army officers on the ground adopted a series of tactics in republican areas that further alienated their residents, provoked retaliatory violence, and steadily narrowed their own scope for maneuver. Since the RUC continued to police the Protestant areas, in which their presence was generally accepted, the obvious disparity in approach between the two communities further reinforced Catholics' sense of injustice.

The difficulty had surfaced by January 1970, and republican activists did little to discourage confrontations between patrolling soldiers and local residents. In April 1970—still under Labour—the army used tear gas for the first time against Catholic rioters in west Belfast.[183] The gas affected bystanders as well as rioters, including people still in their houses, creating solidarity where there had been none. It immediately boosted IRA recruitment. Residents saw it as an inappropriate reaction to adolescent gang behavior, which in any other part of the UK would have been tackled through normal civilian policing. Worse, Scottish (Protestant) soldiers taunted residents with sectarian songs and abuse.[184] Despite this, Hattersley, then a junior defence minister, blamed the violence on "sinister elements" encouraging people to attack the soldiers.[185] A local priest reported that he could find no evidence of misconduct by the army, but that "there are people in this area who apparently do not want normal conditions to prevail and are out to create trouble at all costs."[186]

Labour ministers had long recognized the danger that the army would be sucked into the conflict but hoped, without any supporting evidence, that Nationalists would accept the restructured RUC before this happened. When Labour was defeated, many Catholics expected the incoming Conservative administration to side with its Unionist allies. They were particularly sensitive to any sign of a shift in policy during the Orange marching season, from June to August.

The Falls curfew of July 1971 amply confirmed their expectations. Without the close political oversight imposed by Callaghan, commanders resorted to standard operating procedures derived from their recent colonial experiences in Aden, Cyprus, Kenya, and Malaya. This was graphically illustrated when soldiers newly arrived in Northern Ireland unfurled a banner ordering rioters to disperse in Arabic.[187] Two weeks after the election, and after days and nights of violent sectarian rioting and shooting in Derry and Belfast, the JSC decided that the army should respond to the next outbreak of disorder with an overwhelming display of force, a decision Whitehall defense minister Lord Balniel endorsed.[188] Two days later, on July 3, a patrol discovered a modest cache of weapons in a house in the Catholic Falls area of west Belfast. The resulting arrests initiated a heavy and well-orchestrated riot. Overwhelmed, the patrol withdrew. Residents put up barricades to prevent them returning. Previously, the army's practice had been to talk down such barricades, but this time soldiers invaded the area in force. During the next two days the army imposed a curfew over an area of some five thousand houses and conducted block searches—that is, searching an entire neighborhood for arms and intelligence without having grounds for believing that anything would be found in any specific house. By the time the curfew was lifted, four people had been killed and some three hundred arrested.[189] Eighteen soldiers were wounded.

A senior UK civil servant told a reporter that the curfew marked "the turning point in our policy in Ulster. It was then that the Army began to be viewed in a different light. Before they had been regarded by the bulk of the Catholic population as protectors. That operation turned things absolutely upside down."[190] The army said that the searches had uncovered 106 weapons, 20,000 rounds of ammunition, 100 homemade bombs, and 250 pounds of explosives—an arsenal beyond the requirements of local community defense, even if some of the guns were antiquated souvenirs of earlier campaigns. But the political cost was great. The indiscriminate use of tear gas, the destruction of homes and sacred objects, and acts of abuse and intimidation all confirmed many Catholics' belief that the army was now dancing to the Unionists' tune, and led residents to conclude that they must look elsewhere for their defense.

The military security approach thus played into the hands of the IRA, and it seized the opportunity.[191] As one commentator has noted, "Attrition with the British Army was vital in producing the atmosphere in which the new IRA grew and in which their violence gradually became acceptable to people who would not otherwise have condoned or supported it."[192] British ministers and senior officials recognized the political damage inflicted by the Falls curfew. UKREP later wrote to Maudling that it was "regarded by the Catholic population as punitive and partial. . . . [It] gave new life to traditional Irish nationalism and created an atmosphere in which the resurgent militancy of the IRA could flourish."[193] The cabinet belatedly decided on July 13, 1970, that "the political implications of searches or other security operations in the Bogside, or in any Roman Catholic area, were potentially so serious that no action of this kind should be taken without previous reference to Ministers in London."[194] It was too late. The damage had been done and hostile preconceptions reinforced. British ministers recognized that it was the Provisionals' strategy to "contrive confrontations between security forces and civilian crowds in order to discredit government and security forces."[195] They adjusted their tactics accordingly; Carrington identified a need for improving the collection and use of intelligence. But by acting on the mistaken assumption that the republican districts supported the IRA en masse, the soldiers concerned largely made it true.

An English sociologist who spent nine months living in west Belfast shortly after the curfew noted the inconsistency in the army's methods: "The absurdity reached its height when the paratroopers were running amok one day and posting cards through residents' doors offering their assistance in any way they could help the next."[196] The same observer attributed the IRA's political success to its close identification with the cultural, social, and political traditions of the communities in which it was rooted.[197] The ideology of republicanism promoted the solidarity that enabled the ghettos to resist the attacks directed at them by loyalist gangs and state security forces.

The military security approach also undermined constitutional nationalist leaders. As Paddy Devlin later recalled, "Gerry Fitt and I witnessed voters and workers . . . turn against us to join the Provisionals. Even some of our most dedicated workers and supporters . . . turned against us."[198] Army commanders made matters worse for the moderates at street level by negotiating directly with republican activists over issues such as the removal of barricades and access for military foot patrols. Republican activists thereby acquired a reputation for influence and delivery that their more peaceable rivals did not have.

Although the GOC did not consider internment a military necessity, it was a logical extension of the military security approach, and the manner in which the operation was conducted displayed the worst features of that approach, in particular the routine use of excessive force.[199] With hindsight, four aspects stand out as especially counterproductive:[200] first, the inclusion of people not presently active in the IRA, whether because Special Branch intelligence was out of date or because the net was widened to include the radical wing of the civil rights movement; second, the arresting soldiers' casual brutality; third, the intensive interrogation techniques used on some of the internees; and finally, the conditions in some of the internment camps, in particular the Maidstone prison ship in Belfast, used because the planned long-term accommodation at Long Kesh was not yet ready.

Still, toward the end of 1970, an influential group of army commanders argued in favor of the military security approach, not just as a necessary fallback but as a more effective way of tackling the insurgency. They denied the popularity of republicanism as a solidarity-building ideology and asserted that the IRA had intimidated the ghettos into acquiescence. They also highlighted the importance of demonstrating a clear determination to prevail. Any concessions would be taken as a sign of weakness and encourage the Provisionals to intensify their efforts. One of the most visible of these counterinsurgency theorists was Brigadier Frank Kitson, who commanded the Parachute Brigade in west Belfast from September 1970 to April 1972. Kitson personified the army's experience of colonial insurgency, having served in Kenya, Malaya, and Aden. Before going to Belfast, he had written an influential manual on counterinsurgency tactics.[201] He emphasized the importance of good coordination among government agencies, of propaganda and intelligence gathering, and of striking the right balance between maintaining constitutional safeguards and tackling immediate threats to people's physical security. But he also advocated pressuring entire communities to reduce their support for insurgents: "Although with an eye to world opinion and the need to retain the allegiance of the people, no more force than is necessary for containing the situation should be used, conditions can be made reasonably uncomfortable for the population as a whole, in order to provide an incentive for a return to normal life and to act as a deterrent towards a resumption of the campaign."[202]

It is unclear how much impact Kitson's thinking had. Some commentators have suggested that he was sent to Belfast to test his theories.[203] Others maintain that his superiors thought them too unconventional.[204] Whatever the reality, this controversial commander was responsible for the conduct of military operations in Belfast at a crucial time—even if the army did not officially apply his approach or mechanistically follow any single predetermined strategy. Senior commanders and defense officials did take steps to learn from their experiences in Northern Ireland. In the wake of the Falls curfew, the MoD set up a working party on internal security tactical doctrine to review its procedures.

In a paper prepared for the group's first meeting, officials noted that the army's colonial experience had been gained against unsophisticated and poorly equipped opponents and outside the scrutiny of a critical national press; events in Northern Ireland pointed to a new kind of challenge, to which the army would have to adapt.[205] Unfortunately, instead of pressing ahead to produce the required alternative approach, members of the working party set off on a study tour of the United States and other places more attractive than Belfast and Derry.

In Northern Ireland, many commanders were acutely aware of the dangers of the military security approach.[206] Knowing that blanket actions were likely to be counterproductive, officers frequently withdrew their men from tense situations. Until January 1971, local commanders commonly discussed potential threats to the peace with local republican activists in an attempt to negotiate agreed solutions. But when the Provisionals began killing soldiers, even conciliatory commanders took a tougher line, and the spiral of violence accelerated. On March 24, 1971, coinciding with Faulkner's arrival as chair of the JSC, army headquarters issued a directive requiring field commanders to pursue more aggressive tactics. There were to be no more no-go areas for the army. The battle had become self-sustaining, independent of its original causes.

## UKREP

Rather than strengthening the Northern Ireland departments to which they had been attached, the Whitehall civil servants posted to Northern Ireland in August 1969 set about developing their own independent contacts and agendas. One consequence was that an alternative and more receptive path opened up for Nationalist representatives to air their views, with the result that Stormont's authority was further undermined and an opportunity to create a more responsive devolved administration was lost.[207]

By March 1971, the UKREP—now Ronald Burroughs—had established himself as a third source of official advice to UK ministers, independent of the army and Stormont. They looked to him for alternative guidance on Catholic opinion and political issues, particularly the performance and prospects of the Stormont government. Burroughs routinely undermined Chichester-Clark's authority. When the Northern Irish prime minister called for troop reinforcements, Burroughs advised the Home Office that only "military window-dressing" should be given, which UK ministers followed.[208] On quitting the post in April 1971, Burroughs reported that implementation of the reform program was well advanced, but that this still left "a highly unstable situation in which an impatient Catholic minority confronts a nervous Protestant majority, and where the British army maintains, with some difficulty, an extremely fragile peace." "Extremist Protestants" were flourishing, a sign "that the Protestant community were putting their faith once more in a policy not of social reform, but of keeping the Papishes in their proper places."[209]

Burroughs' successor Howard Smith also was generally critical of the Unionist position and skeptical about whether internment would work. In his first dispatch to Maudling, he criticized Faulkner for overemphasizing security at the expense of social and political reform, and for failing to recognize that "if there is a solution to the problems of Northern Ireland it is not, at bottom, a military one."[210] Smith contributed to the Cabinet's final decision on internment, advising ministers that its immediate introduction was essential to keep Faulkner in office.

### Foreign Office

As well as providing most of the senior staff at UKREP, the FCO was able to influence policy through its ambassador in Dublin and directly in Whitehall. Sir John Peck was sympathetic to the Irish government's position and fed Lynch's arguments into the Whitehall machine, where they were widely circulated.[211] The ambassador's accounts of Dublin's representations were not confined to strategic issues. On the eve of the Unionist Party's election to replace Chichester-Clark, he relayed Patrick Hillery's assessment—reflecting the consensus of the Nationalist political establishment—that Faulkner was not to be trusted and more dangerous than Craig since "he was plausible enough and could convey an impression of moderation which might bamboozle Westminster and the moderate Unionists in Stormont."[212]

In Whitehall, the FCO briefed ministers that "any decision to intern must be taken on security grounds and not to alleviate Unionist pressures on Faulkner." If it appeared that Faulkner was about to be toppled in favor of Craig, direct rule must be introduced immediately, so that Craig could not present himself as leading a legitimate government in exile.[213] This advice did not prevail, but it was not discarded.

### Summary

The Northern Ireland election results of June 1970 demonstrated just how much damage the reforms had already done to the Unionist Party,

London's chosen instrument for avoiding direct rule. The Conservatives accordingly delegated substantial political authority to Stormont and operational responsibility to army commanders. Meanwhile, by March 1971, two IRA factions had emerged that could initiate and sustain concerted campaigns of insurgent violence directed against the British army, the RUC, and commercial interests. Their intention was to overthrow Stormont. Further reforms would not appease them.

Within unionism, Alliance had removed a substantial voice for moderation from the Unionist Party, while the intensification of IRA violence had strengthened support for hard-liners inside and outside the party. Chichester-Clark had resigned, and the Unionist cabinet was in open revolt. This crisis required UK ministers to act decisively. They viewed Faulkner as a more competent operator than his predecessor and their last hope of avoiding direct rule, and as the violence intensified, they accepted Faulkner's assessment that no further political initiative could succeed until order had been restored. The new paradigm they developed to explain the violence attributed it to the machinations of the IRA.

While the broad shift in policy direction occurred under the Conservatives, it would be wrong to conclude that they had decided before they came to power to replace reform with coercion. Like their Labour predecessors, they believed that a political initiative was needed to give the minority some stake in the government of Northern Ireland. They also shared Labour ministers' view that this would help pave the way for the long-term objective of Irish unification, which collectively they did not oppose. But their delegation of political responsibility to Stormont and army commanders facilitated the shifts in policy from reform to coercion that followed. Three moments in the drift of power back to Stormont stand out: the decision to delegate responsibility for operational decisions to the JSC in June 1970, the decision to adopt a tougher approach to security in response to Chichester-Clark's resignation in March 1971, and the decision to relax the requirement that internment should be introduced only on the professional recommendation of army commanders in August 1971.

British ministers acceded to Faulkner's request to introduce internment prematurely because they calculated that otherwise he would be overthrown imminently by his restive cabinet and parliamentary party, forcing them to introduce direct rule in highly unfavorable conditions. Deciding to try the less painful option first would give them more time to plan for direct rule, should it be necessary; silence criticisms from Conservative and Unionist backbenchers and an angry press; and save them the political costs of having to introduce internment themselves. In weighing the pros and cons of internment, ministers accepted Faulkner's unduly optimistic assessment. Partly because the official planning process for internment had not been completed, they failed to minimize the adverse publicity and political criticism which ensued, and in particular to secure even the acquiescence of the Irish government. From a political perspective, UK ministers could justify allowing Faulkner internment by arguing that it was the only available means to protect the reform program from the imminent threat of a takeover by Unionist hard-liners, thus preserving bipartisan consensus even as many Labour backbenchers strongly opposed the policy. Heath was more concerned about the international criticism but willing to take a diplomatic hit to secure Faulkner's survival.

In organizational terms, the army was increasingly important in shaping policy through adoption of the military security approach to policing and through its influence in Whitehall. Like their counterparts in the RUC, most army commanders opposed internment, considering that the IRA would welcome and exploit it. But they also calculated that it was the least harmful visibly tough measure not yet applied, and recognized the value of keeping Faulkner in office even as they resented having to skew their security operations for political reasons. If Faulkner fell, they might have to tackle loyalist and republican paramilitaries simultaneously.

As it turned out, internment provided Faulkner only with a brief stay of execution. Its consequences, anticipated by Lynch and Hume but not by him, yielded ample ammunition for his political enemies, for the diplomats who mistrusted him and the commanders who resented his interference in military decision-making.

## Notes

1.    Lao Tzu, *Tao Te Ching*, trans. D.C. Lau (London: Penguin, 1963), 88.
2.    K. Boyle, T. Hadden, and P. Hillyard, *Law and State: The Case of Northern Ireland* (London: Martin Robertson, 1975), 57.
3.    C. Tilly, "Revolutions and Collective Violence," in F. Greenstein and N. Polsby, eds., *Handbook of Political Science*, vol. 3 (Reading, MA: Addison-Wesley, 1975).
4.    G. Adams, *Politics of Irish Freedom* (Dingle: Brandon, 1986), 52.
5.    R. English, *Armed Struggle: The History of the IRA* (Oxford: Pan Macmillan, 2004), 104.
6.    The Provisionals' name included a patriotic reference to the provisional Irish government declared during the 1916 rising.
7.    English, *Armed Struggle*, 108.
8.    CAB 130/444, January 19, 1970.
9.    C.C. O'Brien, *States of Ireland* (London: Granada, 1974), 177.
10.   Lord Chalfont, "The Balance of Military Forces," in B. Crozier, ed., *The Ulster Debate* (London: Institute for the Study of Conflict, 1972), 53.
11.   English, *Armed Struggle*, 125.

12.   M. Dillon and P. Lehane, *Political Murder in Northern Ireland* (London: Penguin, 1973).

13.   Curtis's killer was himself shot dead by the British on May 15.

14.   *Sunday Times*, November 7, 1971.

15.   Ministry of Defence (MoD), "Operation Banner: An Analysis of Military Operations in Northern Ireland," Ministry of Defence paper, July 2006. The paper was made available for a period through the website of the Pat Finucane Centre (www.serve.com/pfc), but subsequently withdrawn by the ministry in response to complaints from the center.

16.   I. McAllister, *The Northern Ireland Social Democratic and Labour Party* (London: Macmillan, 1977).

17.   CAB 130/433, March 19, 1970.

18.   *Irish Times*, January 1, 2001.

19.   CJ 3/18, Wright to Home Office, February 19, 1970. See also NAI 20028/415, minutes of the ninth meeting of the Inter-Departmental Committee on the North, at which DEA officials expressed the view that the main political parties in the south should provide funds for the SDLP.

20.   R. Rose, "Is the United Kingdom a State? Northern Ireland as a Test Case," in P.J. Madgwick and R. Rose, eds., *The Territorial Dimension in UK Politics* (London: Macmillan, 1982), 182.

21.   CJ 3/18, Wright to Cairncross, October 15, 1969.

22.   CJ 3/18, Wright to Callaghan, March 6, 1970. I have used the terms *moderate* and *hard-liner* throughout to describe how political activists and the positions they took were depicted, mainly by British policymakers and commentators, without endorsing that assessment myself.

23.   H. Patterson and E. Kaufmann, *Unionism and Orangeism in Northern Ireland since 1945* (Manchester: Manchester University Press 2007), 103.

24.   W.D. Flackes, *Northern Ireland: A Political Directory, 1968–1979* (Dublin: Gill and Macmillan, 1983), 264.

25.   *Belfast Telegraph*, March 17, 1971.

26.   *Irish Times*, March 22, 1971.

27.   CAB 134/3011, note of meeting on March 17, 1971.

28.   *Belfast Telegraph*, March 19, 1971.

29.   K. Bloomfield, *Stormont in Crisis: A Memoir* (Belfast: Blackstaff, 1994), 136.

30.   *Belfast Telegraph*, March 20, 1971.

31.   The UVF is the longest-established loyalist paramilitary organization. Like the IRA, it likes to trace its origins back to the period before partition.

32.   *Irish Times*, January 1, 2001.

33.   PREM 15/100, minutes of cabinet meeting on June 22, 1970.

34.   Statement by Maudling reported in *Financial Times*, August 11, 1970.

35.   R. Maudling, *Memoirs* (London: Sidgwick and Jackson, 1978), 179.

36.   C. King, *Diary 1970–74* (London: Cape, 1975), 99.

37.   Hansard, March 22, 1971, col. 41.

38.   PREM 15/476, March 24, 1971.

39.   CAB 134/3011, minutes of meeting on March 31, 1971.

40.   PREM 15/477, Trend to Heath, April 8, 1971.

41.   B. Faulkner, *Memoirs of a Statesman* (London: Weidenfeld and Nicholson 1978), 84.

42.   Ibid., 93.

43.   M. Farrell, *Northern Ireland: The Orange State* (London: Pluto, 1976), 280.

44.   D. Bleakley, *Faulkner: Conflict and Consent in Irish Politics* (London: Mowbray's, 1974), 81.

45.   PREM 15/476, telegrams of March 22 and 23, 1971.

46.   Robert Ramsay, Faulkner's principal private secretary, has argued that the SDLP's withdrawal from Stormont was engineered by the Department of Foreign Affairs in Dublin. He adduces as evidence for this, first, a conversation with John Hume in 1999, and second, similarities in style and substance between other DFA documents and the SDLP's public statement announcing the withdrawal, issued on July 16, 1971. See R. Ramsay, *Ringside Seats* (Dublin: Irish Academic Press, 2009), 83.

47.   Faulkner, *Memoirs*, 108.

48.   PREM 15/477, minutes dated April 5, 1971.

49.   Faulkner, *Memoirs*, 115.

50.   *Belfast Newsletter*, July 13, 1971.

51.   *Belfast Newsletter*, July 19, 1971.

52.   Bloomfield, *Stormont in Crisis*, 149.

53.   Faulkner, *Memoirs*, 116.

54.   CAB 128/48, meeting of July 22, 1971.

55.   CJ 4/462, note of July 28, 1971.

56.   CAB 134/3011, minutes of July 29, 1971.

57.   CJ 4/56, Maudling to Faulkner, August 4, 1971.

58.   CAB 130/522, minutes of meeting on August 5, 1971.

59.   Faulkner, *Memoirs*, 120.

60.   Ibid., 119.

61.   Ibid., 117.

62.   PREM 15/475, Burroughs to Maudling, March 2, 1971.

63.   CJ 4/56, August 5, 1971.

64.   Carrington had told a confidant in April that "the number of IRA in Northern Ireland is about two thousand, of whom eight hundred are in Belfast. They [the security services] have the names and addresses of less than half, and think that any attempt to round up the men they do know would be only 50 percent successful. He [Carrington] seemed to think that an internment policy that was only about 25 percent successful would be worse than nothing." See King, *Diary*, 99.

65.   FCO 33/1465, Smith to Maudling, July 20, 1971.

66.   CAB 130/522, meeting on August 5, 1971.

67.   CAB 134/3012, March 15, 1971.

68.   CAB 128/48, minutes of meeting on July 22, 1971.

69.   Personal interview.

70.   CAB 134/3012, May 3, 1971.

71.   CAB 134/3012, minutes of meeting on May 19, 1971.

72.   PREM 14/1010, "Northern Ireland: Contingency Planning," July 22, 1971.

73.   Faulkner, *Memoirs*, 117.

74. CJ 4/56, Smith to Maudling, August 5, 1971.

75. Hansard, August 5, 1971, col. 1883.

76. Faulkner, *Memoirs*, 119, 123.

77. Bleakley, *Faulkner,* 95.

78. Faulkner, *Memoirs,* 119.

79. CJ 4/56, White to Crawford, August 3, 1971.

80. *The Listener,* June 17, 1971, 772.

81. CJ 4/56, report by officials, August 5, 1971.

82. Faulkner, *Memoirs,* 119.

83. Sunday Times Insight Team, *Ulster* (London: Penguin, 1972), 262.

84. CJ 4/462, unsigned and undated note filed between January 20 and February 8.

85. CJ 4/56, White to Crawford, August 3, 1971.

86. Cited in K Bloomfield, *A Tragedy of Errors* (Liverpool: Liverpool University Press, 2007), 26.

87. King, *Diary,* 99. In 2007, as the result of the peace strategy pursued by the Blair government, Ian Paisley became first minister of Northern Ireland.

88. D. Hamill, *Pig in the Middle: The Army in Northern Ireland, 1969–1985* (London: Methuen, 1985), 50.

89. King, *Diary,* 137–38.

90. CJ 4/132, letter from Heath's office to Maudling's of July 22, 1971.

91. King, *Diary*, 158.

92. Hansard, April 7, 1970, cols. 318, 321.

93. Hansard, February 15, 1971, col. 1321.

94. *The Times,* March 20, 1971.

95. CAB 128/48, minutes of meeting on July 22, 1971.

96. King, *Diary,* 58, 87.

97. J. Enoch Powell, *Still to Decide* (London: Batsford, 1972), 180.

98. J.A. Biggs-Davison, *The Hand is Red* (London: Johnson, 1974).

99. P. Norton, *Conservative Dissidents* (London: Temple Smith, 1978), 50.

100. *Irish Times,* March 23, 1971.

101. Ibid.; *New Statesman,* March 26, 1971; *Spectator,* March 27, 1971.

102. *Belfast Telegraph,* March 26, 1971.

103. Hansard, vol. 814, col. 41, March 22, 1971.

104. Faulkner, *Memoirs*, 91.

105. D. Hurd, *An End to Promises* (London: Collins, 1979), 57.

106. *The Times,* July 29, 1971.

107. See, e.g., comments by Angus Maude, Hansard, August 5, 1971, col. 1897.

108. Callaghan, *House Divided*, 137

109. Citation dated May 28, 1970, in NIO Press Clippings file on the Labour Party, held at the Linenhall Library Irish Political Collection, Belfast.

110. PREM 15/476, note for the record, March 24, 1971.

111. Insight Team, *Ulster,* 222.

112. Callaghan, *House Divided*, 165.

113. CAB 130/522, minutes of meeting on August 5, 1971.

114. Faulkner, *Memoirs*, 121.

115. D. Butler, *The Trouble with Reporting Northern Ireland* (Aldershot: Avebury, 1995), 62.

116. See, e.g., L. Curtis, *Ireland: The Propaganda War* (London: Pluto, 1984), 25.

117. Curtis, *Ireland*.

118. Callaghan, *House Divided*, 26.

119. *Daily Telegraph*, July 15 and 21, 1971.

120. *The Times*, July 19, 1971.

121. *The Spectator*, July 17, 1971, 84.

122. J. Peck, *Dublin from Downing Street* (Dublin: Gill and Macmillan, 1978), 114.

123. T. Hennessey, *The Origins of the Troubles* (Dublin: Gill and Macmillan, 2005), 374.

124. Cabinet minutes cited in *Irish Times*, January 1, 2003.

125. R. Rose, *Governing without Consensus* (London: Faber, 1971), 168; Insight Team, *Ulster*, 188–90; de Breadun, *Irish Times*, January 1, 2003; M.A. Murphy, *Gerry Fitt: Political Chameleon* (Cork: Mercia, 2007), 140.

126. H. Patterson, *Ireland since 1939: The Persistence of Conflict* (Dublin: Penguin, 2006), 174.

127. PREM 15/476, note of meeting between prime minister and taoiseach, October 21, 1970.

128. Hennessey, *Origins of the Troubles*, 367.

129. *Irish Times*, August 31, 2009.

130. *Irish Times*, January 1, 2001.

131. NAI 2002/8/415, minutes of June 18, 1970

132. NAI 2002/8/415, minutes of January 14, 1971.

133. CJ4/56, report by officials of August 5, 1971.

134. Peck, *Dublin from Downing Street*, 114.

135. Ibid., 125.

136. *Irish Times*, July 15, 1971.

137. PREM 15/478, July 30, 1971. Peck in his memoirs neglects to mention this hypothetical discussion with the taoiseach and claims to have been kept in the dark about the development of plans for internment. This omission perhaps reflects the concern he expressed in a telegram to London (FCO 33/1465, August 8, 1971) that Lynch should be able to deny publicly that he had been consulted before the decision to intern was made.

138. Peck, *Dublin from Downing Street*, 128.

139. *Irish Times*, January 1, 2002.

140. CJ 4/56, August 5, 1971.

141. E. Heath, *The Course of My Life* (London: Hodder and Stoughton, 1998), 428.

142. M. Laing, *Edward Heath* (London: Sidgwick and Jackson, 1972), 219; Faulkner, *Memoirs*, 90.

143. Heath, *My Life*, 425.

144. Faulkner, *Memoirs*, 92.

145. Heath, *My Life*, 426.

146. Ibid., 423.

147. PRONI D/1327/22/4.

148. Faulkner, *Memoirs*, 91.

149. See, e.g., King, *Diary*, 15.

150. Callaghan, *House Divided*, 144–46, 155.

151. Hamill, *Pig in the Middle*, 35.

152. Heath, *My Life*, 425.

153. Insight Team, *Ulster*, 232.

154. Bloomfield, *Stormont in Crisis*, 133; personal interviews.

155. Callaghan, *House Divided*, 144.

156. *Fortnight*, February 9, 1972.

157. *The Times*, March 22, 1971.

158. Callaghan, *House Divided*, 144.

159. DEFE 25/303, March 2, 1971.

160. W.D. Birrell, "The Stormont-Westminster Relationship," in *Parliamentary Affairs*, vol. 26 (June 1973), 489.

161. Hamill, *Pig in the Middle*, 53.

162. *Belfast Telegraph*, March 26, 1971.

163. Personal interview, 2006.

164. Insight Team, *Ulster*, 261.

165. CJ 4/462, Woodfield to Allen, February 11, 1971.

166. CAB 134/3011, minutes of March 11, 1971.

167. CAB 134/3011, minutes of March 18, 1971.

168. PREM 15/477, Carrington to Heath, May 21, 1971.

169. CAB 134/3012, minutes of May 19, 1971.

170. *Irish Times*, January 1, 2002.

171. Hamill, *Pig in the Middle*, 56.

172. Faulkner, *Memoirs*, 117. As commander of land forces, Farrar-Hockley was the second most senior commander in the region.

173. CJ 4/56, White to Crawford, August 3, 1971.

174. Insight Team, *Ulster*, 263.

175. Hamill, *Pig in the Middle*, 57.

176. Hansard, September 23, 1971, col. 324.

177. Boyle, Hadden, and Hillyard, *Law and State*, 41.

178. Paddy Hillyard, *The Coercive State* (London: Fontana, 1988), 169.

179. Insight Team, *Ulster*, 172.

180. Hamill, *Pig in the Middle*, 39.

181. DEFE 24/980, relations between the army and the RUC, July 29, 1970.

182. Ryder, *Fateful Split*, 171.

183. Hamill, *Pig in the Middle*, 31.

184. S. Murphy and V. Burke, "Rioting in the Upper Springfield Road, Easter 1970," *Newman Review*, vol. 3, no. 1 (1970), 26.

185. *The Times*, April 4, 1970.

186. *Irish News,* May 19, 1970.

187. P. Taylor, *Brits: The War against the IRA* (London: Bloomsbury, 2002), 31–32.

188. Insight Team, *Ulster,* 215.

189. A subsequent ruling of the Northern Ireland High Court declared in effect that army commanders did not have the legal authority to impose or enforce a curfew—or to take any action ostensibly authorized under Stormont's Special Powers legislation. See next chapter.

190. Insight Team, *Ulster,* 205.

191. Adams, *Irish Freedom,* 52.

192. English, *Armed Struggle,* 134.

193. CJ 4/56, Burroughs to Maudling, April 14, 1971.

194. DEFE 24/980, Hockaday to Woodfield, November 9, 1970.

195. FCO 33/1076, Burroughs to Home Office, July 31, 1970.

196. F. Burton, *The Politics of Legitimacy* (London: Routledge and Kegan Paul, 1978), 87.

197. Ibid., 128.

198. P. Devlin, *Straight Left: An Autobiography* (Devlin: Belfast, 1993), 134.

199. Boyle, Hadden, and Hillyard, *Law and State.*

200. The Compton Report: *Report of the Enquiry into the Allegations against the Security Forces of Physical Brutality in Northern Ireland Arising out of Events on 9th August 1971* (London: HMSO, 1971).

201. F. Kitson, *Low Intensity Operations: Subversion, Insurgency, and Peacekeeping* (London: Faber, 1971).

202. Kitson, *Low Intensity Operations,* 87.

203. E.g., M. Dillon and D. Lehane, *Political Murder in Northern Ireland* (London: Penguin, 1973); R. Faligot, "Special War in Northern Ireland," in *Crane Bag,* vol. 4, no. 2 (1980).

204. Hamill, *Pig in the Middle,* 41.

205. HO 325/132, Ministry of Defence paper of July 31, 1970.

206. See, e.g., R. Evelegh, *Peace-keeping in a Democratic Society* (London: Hurst, 1978).

207. J.A. Oliver, *Working at Stormont* (Dublin: Institute of Public Administration, 1978), 99.

208. PREM 15/476.

209. CJ 4/56, Burroughs to Maudling, April 14, 1971.

210. CJ 3/98, Smith to Maudling, June 10, 1971.

211. It is a measure of the extent to which Peck had gone native, in FCO parlance, that he decided, contrary to precedent, to spend his retirement in Ireland.

212. PREM 15/476, telegram of March 13, 1971.

213. FCO 33/1465, briefing note of July 28, 1971.

# 5
# Imposing Direct Rule, 1972

*We cannot continue as at present.* —Ted Heath[1]

From June 1970 to August 1971, London had increasingly delegated responsibility for security policy and political development to Stormont. After internment, in the face of intense and sustained protests from Nationalist Ireland, UK ministers increasingly felt that a different approach was needed. On March 24, 1972, Heath told the Commons he had proposed to Faulkner that, first, control over security and criminal justice should be transferred from Stormont to Westminster, and second, that the constitution of Northern Ireland should be reformed to guarantee Nationalist elected representatives cabinet seats. Unable to agree to either proposal, Faulkner and his cabinet resigned. Heath then suspended Stormont and introduced direct rule—the policy that Labour and Conservative ministers had been trying to avoid since 1968. It gave them immediate responsibility for all aspects of government in Northern Ireland, including day-to-day administration, policing, and political development, at a time of increasingly violent conflict in the face of huge dangers and uncertainties.

## The Problem

By January 1972, internment had not achieved its stated objective of reducing the violence. Deaths, injuries, and property damage all rose dramatically in the weeks after August 9. There was fierce rioting in republican districts. Over the first four days, twenty-three people were killed and there were more than a hundred explosions. In a six-week period, more than 2,000 families abandoned their homes as a result of violence, intimidation, and fear.[2] Over four months, the death toll rose to 114, up from 8 during the previous four months. For the first time, Irish Republican Army (IRA) bombs killed civilians.

165

Nor did internment break the IRA's command structure as Faulkner had hoped. Many republican activists had foreseen the sweep—tipped off by an informer in the Stormont Ministry of Home Affairs—and had left home. On August 13, Belfast IRA commander Joe Cahill told a clandestine press conference that only thirty Provisional IRA members had been interned and that the leadership had barely been touched.[3] Even allowing for some bravado, the Provisionals showed that they could still run an effective propaganda campaign and create mayhem on the streets.

### The Nationalist Side

Many Catholics, including middle-class moderates, saw internment as a punitive measure directed against their entire community. Few accepted British ministers' depiction of it as a carefully executed military operation aimed at the IRA.[4] In the weeks following the initial arrests, new recruits flowed into the IRA faster than they could be assimilated, and popular support swelled.[5] Reports of casual brutality by the soldiers making the arrests and guarding the internees widened and deepened the outrage, creating solidarity across the Nationalist community. Worse, stories circulated and were widely believed that the internees were being tortured.[6]

In response, Maudling set up an official inquiry under the chairmanship of a retired civil servant, Sir Edmund Compton, who was asked to investigate all allegations of physical brutality. When he reported in November 1971, and despite an emollient preface from Maudling, Compton went some way toward confirming the allegations. During interrogation at least twelve internees had been singled out for systematic deprivation of food, sleep, and drink; kept isolated and hooded; forced to stand in stressful postures for long periods; and subjected to continuous white noise.[7] The British army routinely used these methods in training soldiers to resist the techniques that might be used against them if they were captured.[8] Compton described them as "ill treatment" rather than brutality. But that did not render them any more acceptable to Nationalist and international opinion.

Catholic leaders complained that no loyalists had been interned,[9] rejecting Faulkner's justification that the IRA was the only subversive organization actively engaged in terrorism. They pointed out that loyalists had blown up water and electricity installations, killed policemen and civilians, and organized violent rioting. They interpreted the fact that many internees were released within a few days as evidence not of the system's leniency but of their innocence. Oliver Napier, leader of the Alliance Party, complained: "Every Northern Ireland Catholic sees the introduction of internment as the abandonment of the reform programme and the end of the principle of equal citizenship."[10]

Social Democratic and Labour Party (SDLP) leaders Hume and Fitt flew to London to put their case to Maudling. They demanded the release of the internees and assurances about the conditions in which they were to be kept, and complained about the aggressive methods soldiers used during arrests. Hume argued that coercion could not succeed against the IRA because the Catholic community did not trust the security forces. To restore their confidence, a new system of government was required, in which Nationalists shared power as of right. He proposed an assembly elected by the proportional representation (PR) method and an executive elected by the assembly. Nationalists would be guaranteed a share in decision-making across all agencies of government. The SDLP would be willing and able to sell such a system to its constituents. This was the only credible way to reduce support for the IRA. Maudling should announce immediately that he would be prepared to discuss wide-reaching changes in Northern Ireland's constitution as soon as the violence stopped. In return, the SDLP would publicly emphasize that it had no intention of imposing a single all-island state against the wishes of the Unionist community. But if Maudling did not concede, the SDLP would initiate a campaign of civil disobedience, including a rent and rates strike.

Maudling undertook only to consider Hume's ideas carefully.[11] The campaign of civil disobedience accordingly began on August 16. Prominent Catholics, including 130 local councillors, withdrew from membership of public bodies. Some 200 Catholics resigned from the Ulster Defence Regiment, weakening the government's claim to have replaced the Ulster Special Constabulary (USC) with a nonsectarian body. The minister of community relations, David Bleakley, also resigned, saying: "Internment is not, as some see it, an isolated security issue; it is a test of policy direction. More than any single issue, it separates Protestant and Roman Catholic and tragically it has alienated the Roman Catholic community at the very moment when community cooperation is most vital."[12] Four hundred twenty-five Catholic priests—four out of five in the north—signed a petition condemning internment as "immoral and unjust."[13] Over 20,000 households withheld rental payments to public authorities and private landlords. All this was intended "to demonstrate clearly that a large section of this community has withdrawn its consent from the system of government. . . . No system of government can survive if a significant section of the population is determined that it will not be governed."[14]

Even before internment, Hume had been calling for Stormont's abolition. The popular Catholic reaction against internment strengthened the collective resolve of the SDLP leadership, which raised the stakes by setting five minimum conditions to be met before it would engage in talks with Maudling:[15] an end to internment, the suspension of Stormont, the appointment of a commission representing Unionists and Nationalists to run the devolved administration pending the outcome of talks on future constitutional arrangements, the participation of Dublin in the talks, and the inclusion of Irish unification on the agenda. The SDLP also announced its intention to develop an "alternative assembly,"[16] constructed around the Nationalist MPs who had withdrawn from Stormont. This was a powerful declaration of Nationalists' alienation from the constitutional order.

Both IRA factions took advantage of the shift in public sentiment to escalate violence and discredit the British. The Provisionals began a more widespread bombing campaign aimed at "economic targets," forcing security forces to spread themselves more thinly. IRA tactics included informing against the most obviously harmless people in republican districts, prompting the army to raid their homes and arrest them.[17] In Derry, republican activists built and manned barricades as they had done in August 1969, although they were now excluding the British rather than the Royal Ulster Constabulary (RUC). That the army tolerated these no-go areas enabled the IRA over the coming weeks to consolidate its hold over life inside the barricades, create localized microcultures of rebellion, and launch their attacks from secure bases.

The army subsequently described the period as the onset of a classic insurgency, after which "both the official and provisional wings of the Irish Republican Army fought the security forces in more-or-less formed bodies. Both had a structure of companies, battalions, and brigades, with a recognisable structure and headquarters staff. Protracted firefights were common."[18] By the end of the year the IRA comprised some 2,000 volunteers—about 1,300 Provisionals and 750 Official IRA—of whom about 880 were active. A further 400 had been interned.

UK Representative (UKREP) Howard Smith reported on August 17 that while internment had significantly disrupted the IRA, the political costs had been higher than anticipated. Most serious was "an almost complete polarisation between the communities." The SDLP leadership had rallied around Hume's view that it was no longer enough to be included in the Stormont administration; they now wanted it to be dismantled. Smith added that Hume apparently did not realize that "the consequence of maintaining their present attitudes could well be the disappearance of all politicians from places of power: that is to say, they and equally unenlightened Unionists may be forcing the country into direct rule."[19]

The massive Catholic reaction against internment led UK ministers to mistrust Faulkner, his advice, and what they now saw as his intransigence.[20] Heath had accepted that internment would create problems, but he had trusted Faulkner's assessment of their size, and this had proved disastrously wrong.[21] There followed a significant shift of emphasis in London, away from propping up Faulkner and toward negotiating with the SDLP.[22] The SDLP's leaders recognized the opportunity that the new conditions had given them. According to a senior official of the Irish Department of External Affairs, who spoke to them in October 1971, "even the most pacific of them have now begun to say that they have a vested interest in the continuance of violence as long as Stormont exists."[23]

### The Unionist Side

Internment's failure to reduce the violence meant that it failed also in its undeclared objective of shoring up Faulkner as the leader of Unionism. The intensity of the republican reaction stimulated new activity on the loyalist side, especially where Protestant neighborhoods bordered on Catholic ones. In September 1971 the loyalist vigilante groups that had emerged since 1969 to confront the IRA at street level came together under the umbrella of the Ulster Defence Association (UDA). By December, loyalists were displaying new rifles and ammunition to journalists and showing some evidence of military training. In the same month, loyalist bombers killed fifteen people in the most deadly single explosion to date, at a Catholic bar in Belfast.

Inside the Unionist Party, Craig endorsed a register of volunteers prepared to defend the union by force if necessary. In October 1971 he tabled a censure motion against Faulkner at Stormont. When this failed to attract sufficient support, he set up a steering committee including members from forty-three of the party's fifty-two constituency associations. Their stated intention was to reverse the Hunt reforms, resist further interference from London, and oppose any changes in Northern Ireland's constitutional status. Craig openly defied party policy by arguing for independence as preferable to any further reforms that might take Northern Ireland in the direction of Dublin rule. Faulkner also faced external challengers. In September Paisley joined a group of Unionist defectors to create the Democratic Unionist Party (DUP). In February 1972, with the SDLP still boycotting Stormont, the DUP became the official opposition. Paisley announced his intention of becoming the next prime minister of Northern Ireland. Terence O'Neill warned Heath that if elections were permitted to run their course, this was a real possibility.

Recognizing the ever-widening gap between the rank and file of the Unionist Party and its leadership, Maudling in September submitted a secret paper for discussion at the cabinet's defence and overseas policy committee. The issue was what to do if the next Northern Ireland general election (to be held at any time before February 1974) seemed likely to result in the return of an extremist majority.[24]

Two options were identified. First, Westminster could allow the election to go ahead, but introduce direct rule if the extremist government refused to sign up for or tried to reverse the reform program. Second, it could introduce direct rule before the election if an extremist victory was anticipated, to prevent the new government from assuming the legitimacy an electoral victory would give it. The paper indicated that Maudling's object of concern was "Mr. Paisley or other extremists." It assumed that there could be no serious prospect of an accommodation with such people. At a cabinet meeting the following day, ministers noted that direct rule might be "forced on us unless we were prepared to accept an extreme Protestant Government in place of the present Administration."[25]

Faulkner also had to contend with disaffection among the party's moderates. After internment a new strain of thinking emerged to public prominence, represented by the New Ulster Movement (NUM). This group had come together upon O'Neill's resignation in April 1969 with the intention of protecting and developing his policy of reconciliation. Faulkner dismissed it as "an associated organization of liberals and do-gooders," complaining that it had more influence with UK ministers than it deserved.[26] The NUM now began lobbying for a cross-community government that would bring Catholic and Protestant elected representatives together at least for the period of the emergency. This echoed the Northern Ireland Labour Party (NILP) proposal for an interim "community government"[27] headed by Faulkner but including Catholic ministers, and the SDLP's demand for an interim cross-community commission.

## The Options

The intense and widespread Catholic reaction against internment led UK ministers to conclude that the political initiative Faulkner had offered in June must be renewed and, since the SDLP would not work with Faulkner, must be guaranteed by Westminster. But what form should it take and how radical should it be? Maudling at first favored the incremental option his officials proposed: modest constitutional reforms, similar to those already rejected by the SDLP, to help and encourage moderates on both sides who were advancing proposals for compromise solutions. A few days after internment, the home secretary told his cabinet colleagues that he planned to convene talks with Faulkner and Nationalist elected representatives, through which to develop "further means of giving representatives of the minority an active and prominent role in the processes of government and administration."[28] The resulting settlement might be based on Faulkner's June offer to the SDLP, but Westminster would underwrite it.[29] Faulkner agreed to engage, but the SDLP did not.

Maudling wrote to assure Faulkner that he accepted that "coalition government was not a practical proposition."[30] But a few days later he told the Commons that he was unhappy that the party in power at Stormont never changed.[31] During a Labour-initiated debate, he identified only two obstacles to a coalition government, both of which the SDLP could easily have overcome: "that anyone serving in such a government should reject the use of violence and that they should also accept that reunification should come about only with the consent of a majority of the people of Northern Ireland."[32] Although he offered no concrete commitment to constitutional reform, Maudling publicly pressed Faulkner to work toward providing "a permanent and guaranteed role for the minority community as well as the majority in the life and public affairs of the Province."[33]

Faulkner responded in October with a green (consultative) paper setting out further proposals as a basis for discussion with the SDLP.[34] He offered, first, a return to PR voting for Stormont elections, as originally required by the 1920 act, using the single transferable vote (STV) system with multi-member constituencies, as in the Republic; second, more Stormont seats to allow for more minority representatives; and third, places for non-Unionists in the cabinet at his discretion. The green paper suggested (without any supporting evidence) that introducing STV would encourage moderation and promote the emergence of new politics based on social and economic issues. But it explicitly rejected the idea of a "PR Government, where the parties in Parliament would be represented in the executive in proportion to their strength," as "fundamentally unrealistic . . . given the deep divisions of opinion which exist on quite fundamental issues."[35] Since Nationalists by definition sought to dissolve the union, Faulkner argued, they could not be expected to serve the state in Northern Ireland in good faith. Equally, to create an entrenched position in the cabinet for Catholics (rather than Nationalists) would "strengthen sectarian divisions and eliminate attempts to create nonsectarian political alignments."[36] Maudling again offered to discuss these proposals with SDLP leaders, but again they refused.

Faced with a renewed explosion of violence, an impasse over political negotiations, and the prospect of Faulkner's impending demise at the hands of what he later called "hardline incorrigibles," Heath commissioned a comprehensive policy review from his Whitehall officials.[37] From August 1971 until February 1972 he and his ministers examined an array of possible initiatives. They swiftly dismissed most as unworkable. But the British prime minister was no longer leaving it to Faulkner to set the pace. For the first time he was now leading the process himself, actively exploring and assessing options for radical transformation, including those proposed by factions in Northern Ireland other than the Stormont government.

The first product of the new approach was a short report from the central policy review staff, which Heath received from cabinet secretary Burke Trend on September 3. It reflected Hume's argument that it would be insufficient merely to achieve the "negative aim" of defeating the IRA, imposing order, and returning to the status quo. More radical options such as withdrawal should also be examined: "The fact that Northern Ireland is constitutionally part of the United Kingdom is no more or less relevant in terms of political realism than the fact that Algeria was part of metropolitan France." The report also drew attention to an important potential gain from withdrawal: "the net saving to public expenditure would be considerable."[38]

In a more guarded covering note, Trend—the head of the UK civil service—accepted the thrust of the argument that the existing reactive policy offered neither a permanent solution nor any immediate prospect of defeating the IRA. The situation was deteriorating, and eventually "the elastic must snap." Ministers should anticipate when this would happen and ensure that they at least received some credit for trying to avert the calamity by developing a political initiative while there was still time to do so.[39] As a first step, they should decide whether the union itself was open to negotiation. If not, the only radical departure immediately available was direct rule. This might create the possibility of an honest dialogue with Dublin, unhampered by the need to cater to the vulnerabilities of the Unionist leadership. Trend continued:

> It might then be feasible to think in terms of a settlement whereby, on the one hand, the restoration of some form of genuinely representative Government of Ulster would be dependent on the institution of new safeguards for the rights and interests of Roman Catholics in the Six Counties . . . and, on the other hand, the Dublin Government themselves would enter into a new undertaking to respect the sanctity of the Border and to cooperate actively with the Government of the United Kingdom in repressing any attempts to overthrow or to undermine the settlement.

Trend then invited Heath to consider three broad options for progress within the constitutional framework of a continuing union: repartition, or defining Protestant and Catholic areas and permitting those that chose to do so to transfer to the Republic; coalition, guaranteeing Catholics seats in the Stormont cabinet; and condominium, that is, joint government of Northern Ireland by Britain and Ireland. Heath decided that the first was unworkable in view of the distribution of the two populations and the last infeasible in view of the need for clear lines of command and control, especially in the current emergency. He accordingly opted for coalition. He later wrote in his memoirs that "power sharing was essential, at least as an interim measure"; he did not spell out what might follow after the interim period.[40]

Having clarified his own thinking, Heath next convened a small group (GEN 47) comprising the ministers directly responsible for Northern Ireland policy—Reginald Maudling (Home Office), Peter Carrington (Defence), Alec Douglas-Home (Foreign and Commonwealth Office), and Willie Whitelaw (Leader of the Commons)—to consider the options with him. Chairing their first meeting on October 6, 1971, he tasked them to produce "a concerted Northern Ireland policy, with its objects clearly defined in an order of priority . . . based on the best reconciliation that could be made between conflicting considerations."[41] He continued to maintain that Faulkner embodied their last prospect of avoiding direct rule, and that "the first priority should be the defeat of the gunmen using military means." But, as Trend had advised, he wanted to be ready to launch a new political initiative once this security activity had created a sufficiently favorable context for it to succeed.

On November 12, Maudling put before GEN 47 a proposal for "a government of national defence and reconstruction" in which "men of goodwill," including Nationalist elected representatives, would take part. Although this proposal demonstrated a willingness to advance toward the position the NUM and NILP favored, it fell far short of permanent coalition government and did not give Heath the "root and branch" review he had asked for. The prime minister was adamant that he wanted to rethink policy from scratch, and sent Maudling off to produce "a comprehensive analysis of all possible courses . . . no option should be omitted merely because it did not show immediate promise of success."[42]

The next time Maudling's team was obsessively thorough. They responded with a discussion paper identifying sixteen "possible courses of action," including some that Heath had already rejected.[43] One possibility was no change—continuing with "the present policy . . . to try to reach an agreement in discussion with representatives of the communities in Northern Ireland on ways in which both the majority and the minority can have an active, permanent, and guaranteed role in the life and public affairs of the Province." Another option built on Faulkner's green paper proposals, reforming Stormont, but pressing Faulkner also to take further steps, such as creating an advisory council to represent the interests of the minority and a parliamentary committee on public appointments. Third, a voluntary coalition could apply economic and political pressure on the leaders of both sides to induce them to form a coalition government voluntarily. Fourth, transferring the contentious policy area of security from Stormont to Westminster might open the door to cooperation between the two sides on social and economic issues. Fifth, and linked to the security transfer, Stormont could be reduced to the equivalent of a county council in England, stripped of its legislative status and security powers. Sixth, a commission government—a new nonelected body comprising Protestant and Catholic members appointed by the British—could be introduced as an interim measure, pending agreement on new political structures or a political realignment. Officials drew an analogy with the Londonderry Development Commission, which had replaced the discredited city council and was said to command the respect of both sides. Seventh, there could be a reversion to the 1920 act by setting up a Council of Ireland to promote north-south cooperation. Eighth involved condominium, whereby residents of Northern Ireland would choose either British or Irish citizenship and would be registered to vote accordingly. They would all be eligible to vote for an executive council that would administer the region under the guidance of a British and an Irish commissioner. Ninth involved a policy of deliberate hostility toward the Republic—that is, aggressive political and economic pressure on Dublin to bear down on the IRA. Measures could include suspending trade agreements, introducing immigration and customs controls, and treating Irish citizens living in Britain the same as other foreign nationals, effectively disenfranchising them. Finally there was direct rule, even though ministers had already indicated that they would not willingly adopt it as a permanent solution.

Maudling's paper also identified obstacles to the political transformation that Heath wanted. The SDLP had so far refused to take part in negotiations, what was acceptable to one side was likely to be rejected by the other, and London had little control over the political development process. Faulkner had already made plain that he would not serve in a government with Nationalists; SDLP leaders had likewise indicated that they would not serve under him. In the unlikely event that the parties successfully formed a voluntary coalition, the paper argued that it was doubtful whether the resulting administration could hold together before the challenges it inevitably would face.

The outcome of the discussions was that early in December ministers decided in favor of the green-paper-plus option, to be combined with pressure for voluntary coalition. If that could not be achieved, commission government would be an acceptable fallback. They also identified the possibility of requiring the majority to work with the minority, in effect mandating some form of coalition. Hostility toward the Republic was explicitly rejected on the ground that it would damage Britain's wider diplomatic and economic interests and impair the preparations then under way for the two countries' accession to the European Economic Community (EEC).[44]

*Reunification*

Maudling's paper identified reunification as a theoretical option but immediately dismissed it on the grounds that Dublin would not agree to take on the north's problems. As we have seen, however, senior officials had already distinguished between short- and long-term objectives, including unification. On November 8, the *Guardian* reported that "ministers would like nothing better than to be shot of the problems of Northern Ireland. Some privately conceded that probably the only permanent long-term solution to the problem of Ireland is its reunification. They would be happy in the meantime to see Stormont cut down to size as the Belfast Urban District Council. These views are even more prevalent and more strongly held within the civil service."[45]

On November 25, Heath offered the minority a substantial symbolic concession when he announced that "if at some future date the majority of the people of Northern Ireland want unification and express that desire in the appropriate constitutional manner, I do not believe any British government would stand in the way."[46] Although technically this did not depart from the 1949 act, it went some way toward meeting Nationalists' requests for a public statement of British neutrality. It also caught his officials off guard. When GEN 47 met the following week, the permanent under secretary (PUS) at the Home Office asked ministers for a steer on their long-term thinking: "Was a united Ireland inevitable, or should any new moves be regarded as steps on the path to an improved Stormont?" According to the official record, the ministers wanted to keep their options open, saying that "although there was no possibility that unification would become a practical possibility for many years, we should not resist and should indeed where appropriate welcome any measures which had the effect of reducing the gulf between North and South."[47]

*Coalition*

Heath next tasked his officials to work on two of the radical options that had survived the winnowing process: coalition and commission government. Both reflected proposals from the SDLP and moderate Unionism. They were to examine the experience of other countries with politically problematic community divisions and identify constitutional devices that could guarantee a role for the minority. The resulting report, which owed more to advice gathered from Britain's embassies than to serious cross-national research in political science, recommended that this could be done by, first, appointing minority elected representatives to cabinet seats in proportion to the parliamentary seats held by their party; second, guaranteeing them specific portfolios (such as health or community relations);

third, guaranteeing them a given number of portfolios, with the details to be negotiated; and fourth, appointing for each department a minister from one community to work alongside a minister from the other. Blocking devices could be incorporated to ensure that minority views on important issues could not be overridden. The report cited the example of Belgium, where a two-thirds majority of either main language group could stop any legislation considered harmful to community relations.

Ministers concluded that the coalition option was at least workable and that whatever devices might be used, minority elected representatives should be included by right in the Northern Ireland cabinet. The Home Office had advised that Faulkner was unlikely willingly to accept this, but also that "there are circumstances in which such a scheme might be tolerated as a solution imposed from Westminster."[48]

### Commission

Officials also produced a more detailed assessment of the commission government option. This included a list of functions to be transferred from Stormont to administrative agencies, such as the recently established Housing Executive, which could be structured to give Catholics a guaranteed level of representation.[49] Having considered the list, Heath briskly rejected the option on the grounds that it could interfere with the legislative process for reforming local government, which was already under way as part of Labour's original reform package.[50]

### Security Transfer

GEN 47 also considered in December a paper on responsibility for law and order that set out a range of options, including no change; a return to the arrangement set out in the Downing Street Declaration, whereby the general officer commanding (GOC) would have full control over the RUC in relation to all security operations; and full transfer to Westminster of responsibility for all security, policing, and criminal justice matters.

At the group's meeting on December 13, Heath summarized the case against the full transfer option, which he argued would leave UK ministers directly accountable to Westminster for matters too remote to control; make them directly responsible for law and order within a wider constitutional framework that remained unacceptable to the Nationalist minority; and give Whitehall no effective power over other important functions of government, such as housing and planning, that directly affected law and order.

### Direct Rule

On January 10, 1972, Trend summarized progress with the comprehensive policy review. He continued to advise that a political initiative from

London would be needed at some stage, but also that it must be carefully timed. He argued against stripping away any of Stormont's functions or transferring security to Westminster, since either of these would so weaken Faulkner's government that it could fall. The consequence would be that "we should find that we had merely precipitated the situation which we were trying to avoid"—direct rule.[51]

Trend advised that officials' analysis of constitutional devices in other countries indicated a more promising approach: "legislation at Westminster guaranteeing the Catholic minority a reasonable share in representation not only in Parliament but in the government, and incorporating blocking devices to prevent its purposes from being frustrated by the majority." These devices could be supplemented by new statutory safeguards against discrimination, for example in public appointments. Implementing these reforms could be made conditional on ending IRA violence; the Catholic community would have to be convinced that if the violence ended, the reforms would definitely follow.

In a top-secret paper for GEN 47 dated January 18, Maudling uncharacteristically argued for a much more aggressive approach.[52] It would include reassurance for Unionists supported by regular plebiscites, but, as he observed, these would in practice be meaningless, since "no Parliament has the ability to bind its successors." He declared that if the UK government could not negotiate an agreed-upon solution with the Northern Ireland parties, it should impose one. Elements in such a solution would include a guarantee of participation in government for Nationalists, drawing on the analysis of constitutional devices in other countries (he cited Lebanon as an example of successful power sharing!), and a reduction in Stormont's powers, primarily by transferring responsibility for law and order to Westminster. If the Northern Ireland parties refused to negotiate or work the new arrangements, commission government would be introduced as an interim measure. This would be very different from the concept Hume proposed, in that the commission would be an advisory rather than an executive body. In effect, there would be a period of direct rule with input from representatives (not necessarily elected) from both traditions.

Maudling's surprisingly radical package brought together ideas derived from discussions on the November options paper—mandatory coalition, security transfer, and commission government—with recommendations emerging from the officials' analysis of constitutional devices in other divided societies, and an idea that had recently emerged from discussions with certain Unionists, that of a border referendum. But it also contained three very substantial shifts from the cabinet's previous thinking. Responsibility for security would be transferred, a solution would be imposed if the regional parties could not agree, and a commission government would take the form of direct rule with an advisory council. It is not entirely clear what influenced Maudling to make these shifts, but they reflected high-level thinking in the Ministry of Defence (MoD) and advice from UKREP.

When GEN 47 discussed Maudling's proposals on January 20, his fellow ministers identified four serious objections. First, the proposed form of commission government could saddle London with responsibility for running Northern Ireland indefinitely. Second, the changes would alienate Protestants without winning over Catholics. Third, they would be read as a concession to violence and republican propaganda, dismaying Unionists and stimulating the IRA to further aggression. Finally, they were unnecessary since the security forces were already beating the IRA.

On the other hand, at least one argued that "the successes of the Army against the terrorists might make it desirable to seize the opportunity for an initiative before the Catholics on the one hand became irrevocably alienated, or the Protestants on the other hand reverted to an unyielding attitude against what they would regard as a beaten minority."[53]

GEN 47 was still debating the issues on January 27. Maudling had by then committed himself to the goal of bringing minority elected representatives into government as an objective in its own right, irrespective of whether it would weaken the IRA's popular support. He argued that the time had come "to begin persuading Mr. Faulkner in private that it was unrealistic to expect that, even after the terrorist campaign had been broken, the structure of politics in Northern Ireland could revert to its former shape, subject only to those changes which had already been implemented or which were envisaged in the NI government's green paper."[54]

## Events

### "Bloody Sunday"

A series of dramatic events burst into ministers' reflections during the next two months, pushing them toward accepting the radical proposals in Maudling's paper. The most explosive has become known as Bloody Sunday. Anti-internment protesters arranged a demonstration against internment in Derry on January 30. An estimated 4,000 people took part. Soldiers blocked their path. Some of the marchers threw stones and bottles; the soldiers first replied with rubber bullets and CS gas, then opened fire in disputed circumstances. They killed thirteen people and injured a further fourteen in four distinct locations. The army initially claimed that all those killed had either been shooting or throwing petrol bombs. Maudling reflected this in a statement to the Commons the following day. But local people and journalists who were present said otherwise. A local coroner's inquest concluded that some soldiers had run amok and murdered innocent people.[55] No soldiers were injured, no guns or bombs retrieved.

Heath responded to the resulting outcry by setting up an official inquiry chaired by Lord Widgery, the lord chief justice of England. Widgery in due course reported that, but for the soldiers' intervention, the day might have passed off without serious incident; that at most four of those killed might have been firing weapons or throwing nail bombs; and that the other nine had certainly been unarmed.[56] Whatever Widgery said, Nationalist opinion across Ireland had already determined that all thirteen victims had been wholly innocent. The incident renewed, intensified, and extended the solidarity that internment had created across the minority community: "Every single last remaining vestige of Catholic trust, confidence, and reluctant support that the Stormont or Westminster governments might have had on 29 January went out the door."[57] Twenty-five thousand people attended the funerals of the dead. Recruitment to the IRA soared, making up for the attrition caused by internment, and there was a fundamental shift in Catholic attitudes: "Up to this, mass support in the Northern Catholic population had been for civil rights and reform within the Northern state, with Irish unity following gradually. Now most Northern Catholics felt that the Northern state was unreformable, and that they would only get civil rights in a united Ireland. Their objective was no longer to reform Northern Ireland but to destroy it."[58] The mood shift extended across the island, and was summed up for the British ambassador in the declaration, "We are all IRA now."[59]

On the Protestant side, the incident accelerated the fragmentation in Unionism. Liberal Unionists denounced the shootings; hard-liners reacted against the mobilization of Nationalist protest. On February 18, former Unionist minister Phelim O'Neill shifted his allegiance to the Alliance Party at Stormont. Alliance leader Oliver Napier called on Heath to transfer responsibility for security away from Stormont, anticipating that this would precipitate Faulkner's resignation.[60]

The shootings and the intensity of the protests gave Heath a sharp jolt. According to his biographer, this "was the shock which convinced Heath and his senior colleagues that they must take an urgent grip of Northern Ireland before it slid uncontrollably into civil war."[61] The prime minister later wrote of this period: "I feared that we might, for the first time, be on the threshold of complete anarchy."[62]

### IRA Resurgence

In the wake of the shootings the Officials extended their bombing campaign to England. On February 22, declaring retaliation, they exploded a bomb at the headquarters of the Parachute Regiment at Aldershot, killing five cleaning women, a chaplain, and a gardener. On March 8, four car bombs were parked in Whitehall. Two exploded, killing 1 person and injuring 180. With these attacks the Officials crossed an important threshold. They reasoned that the British establishment was less likely to be sanguine about Ireland if they and their electorate in England felt personally at risk. Extra measures were taken to protect ministers, and Downing Street was closed to the public.

Both wings of the IRA escalated their activities in Northern Ireland. On February 25, the Officials attacked the Stormont junior minister for home affairs, John Taylor, hitting him with machine gun bullets in the face, throat, and jaw as he got into his car. On March 4, the Provisionals exploded a bomb in a crowded restaurant in Belfast, killing 2 young women and injuring 136 other people. No warning was given. On March 20, the same group used car bombs in the city for the first time, killing 6 people and injuring over 100.

Some observers interpreted the upsurge in violence as a sign that factions in the IRA were jostling for position in the expectation that the British would shortly suspend Stormont and offer political negotiations.[63] Ministers knew from intelligence sources that a struggle for power was under way between political and military factions in the Provisionals' Army Council.[64] Thus, although security measures had to be taken to tackle the violence, there was also a credible argument that a well-timed and carefully presented conciliatory offer might drive a wedge between Britain's republican adversaries.

### Legal Challenge

The third significant although less visible event was a ruling of the Northern Ireland High Court on February 23. In response to an appeal by John Hume, the court found that the army had exceeded its authority in arresting him for refusing to obey an order from an army officer. The judgment was based on the fact that the Government of Ireland Act 1920 explicitly withheld from Stormont the authority to legislate for the UK armed forces, whence, the court argued, the Special Powers Act could not be taken to cover any of the army's actions. This ruling raised doubts about the legality of the entire military security approach, including curfews, internment, and generalized searching.

Maudling responded to the court's decision by rushing a bill through Westminster. The Northern Ireland Act 1972 retrospectively empowered Stormont to confer powers and immunities on the army. Maudling told MPs that this was merely a technical measure confirming that the law was as everyone had previously assumed. But legal experts disagreed. Constitutional lawyer Claire Palley argued that the act legitimated Stormont's usurpation of security powers that properly belonged to the national government, when the opportunity should instead have been taken to transfer those powers unambiguously to Westminster.[65]

The cabinet had anticipated an adverse court ruling, noting that it "might reinforce the widely held feeling that the present division of powers between Westminster and Stormont was unsatisfactory and that the United Kingdom Government and Parliament should assume the whole of the responsibility for matters of law and order in Northern Ireland."[66] And so it did, drawing political attention to Stormont's exceptional security powers and the potential consequences of their exercise: "Sensitive political issues could be introduced by a subordinate Parliament creating powers in respect of the army, when in fact the real power lay with the Parliament at Westminster."[67] The ruling also highlighted that the Conservatives had permitted political control over security policy to drift back to Stormont, as described in chapter 4. It has been argued that in the political context of the time, the court's decision made direct rule inevitable.[68]

### Parker Report

The fourth significant event was the publication on March 2 of the report of the Parker Inquiry on the use of interrogation procedures during the initial internment operation. The report cleared the interrogating officers of torture and concluded that the information obtained had saved innocent lives. However, one of the tribunal members, Lord Gardiner, in a minority report condemned the methods used as illegal, morally unjustifiable, and alien to the traditions of British democracy. Responding to the report, Heath publicly undertook that techniques such as hooding, wall standing, and sleep deprivation would not be used in the future. Faulkner later said that he had not authorized the use of these techniques and had been unaware of the interrogators' intention to use them. But this did not stop the Parker Report occurring to Heath as yet another embarrassment arising from his efforts to keep Faulkner in office.

## The Final Weeks

### A New Calculus

As one Downing Street insider later noted, "For the next two months [after Bloody Sunday] . . . Irish affairs were in the melting pot. Ministers went back to first principles on Ireland. A completely new policy had to be devised and new people found to run it."[69] This implies that Bloody

Sunday was the most important factor in introducing direct rule. In fact, Heath had already committed himself to creating a coalition government of some kind, and Maudling had already concluded that a political settlement should, if necessary, be imposed, which would include the transfer of responsibility for security from Stormont to Westminster and the mandatory participation of Nationalists in government.

Bloody Sunday and the other three events, however, shifted the balance sharply among Heath's three priorities of keeping Faulkner in power, defeating the IRA militarily, and securing a permanent role for Nationalist representatives at Stormont. The Derry killings effectively terminated the strategy of using military force to uphold the Unionist administration. They reversed what little progress Faulkner had made toward attracting Catholics into public life, tended to validate across the Nationalist community the republican ideology of armed resistance, raised the price of bringing the SDLP to the negotiating table, and intensified the polarization between the two traditions. Assessing the damage at a crisis meeting on February 2, ministers had expressed concern that if responsibility for security were transferred to London, this might lead the IRA to attack targets in Britain.[70] When the Officials started bombing England three weeks later, that objection no longer held.

On February 3, Heath authorized the Cabinet Office to circulate a memorandum on political reform that assumed that "we cannot continue as at present."[71] This endorsed and built on elements in Maudling's January package: a plebiscite on the border, mandatory coalition (now rebranded as community government in deference to the SDLP), and the full transfer of security responsibilities to London.[72] It defined community government for the first time as "constitutional devices that will produce a coalition government with a fixed minimum of Ministerial posts in the Northern Ireland Government guaranteed to representatives in parliament of the minority." This fell well short of full power sharing; the memorandum did not propose proportionality in allocating ministerial posts.

Another of the immediate consequences of the Derry shootings was to dissolve London's inhibitions about direct rule. The memorandum reasoned that Faulkner was unlikely to accept the transfer of security or mandatory coalition. Since reform was now deemed more important than his survival, he would be permitted to resign, and because—as ministers had already decided the previous September—it was unlikely that any acceptable Unionist leader would be prepared to replace him, direct rule would almost certainly follow. But direct rule was reframed as a potential step forward. The memorandum contended that there was "a strong argument for a period of purgation from the present politics of Northern Ireland."[73]

An interregnum would allow time to repair Catholic alienation, consult with the parties on proposals for political reform, and open up the alternatives for fuller consideration. Heath later wrote: "I was resolved all along that we should now devote all our energies towards working for a lasting cross-community settlement—and only direct rule could offer us the breathing space necessary for building it."[74]

It took seven more weeks for Heath to bring his cabinet colleagues around to the same conclusion. His first step was to try to gauge Faulkner's likely reaction. He summoned the Unionist leader to London on February 4, when they discussed the option (which the cabinet had already dismissed) of redrawing the border to exclude problematic republican areas; a referendum on the border; Nationalist participation in the Northern Ireland cabinet; and his real concern, the security transfer. The Unionist leader concluded from this discussion that Heath was determined to launch a significant political initiative, had not yet decided what it should comprise, and would be willing to negotiate a package that Faulkner could sell to his backbenchers. Heath assured Faulkner that he was not contemplating direct rule: "I've told you Brian, we are in this together and we'll support you all the way, however long it takes."[75] Any initiative would be taken by agreement between them. So Faulkner set to thinking about "what would be necessary in order to get the SDLP back to the conference table in spite of all the hooks they had got themselves caught on, how far the London Government would press us to go as a result of the new pressures it was coming under, and how far we could afford to go ourselves without sacrificing some fundamental principle and without losing our political base in the community."[76]

Concluding from the meeting that Faulkner would resign rather than lose control over security, Trend suggested to Heath that it might be worth considering whether to claw back only responsibility for those security matters related to the emergency, including the operation of internment. This would leave Stormont in control of civic policing and everyday criminal justice, as agreed with Wilson in August 1969, and would probably prevent Faulkner from resigning.[77] Briskly abandoning his assurance to Faulkner and the stand he had himself taken only a few weeks previously, Heath dismissed this proposal on the ground that the two facets of policing were too interconnected.

When GEN 47 met again on February 9, Heath invited his colleagues to address three questions. Had the time come for a new political initiative? If so, what form should it take? How should it be put into effect? On timing, he gave a clear steer that, in his view, the time had come; there was no immediate possibility of a solution emerging from discussions with Nationalist political leaders, and in the worsening situation, the continuing demonstrations of the Northern Ireland Civil Rights Association (NICRA) against internment might soon provoke loyalists into violent counterdemonstrations.[78] On the form of the initiative, the discussion raised a series of further questions. Should the guarantee of participation in government extend to Protestant minority parties, such as the DUP, and intercommunal parties, such as Alliance? If not, how could their exclusion be justified? If the composition of the Stormont cabinet was to be determined by the proportion of seats each party held in the parliament, would the minority not continue to complain that their views would always be overridden? How would the Unionist community react to the transfer of security? If it retained responsibility for security, could a community government agree on the controversial issues involved, such as whether to end internment? Heath concluded the meeting by recording a consensus that the time had come for a political initiative and tasked officials to work up detailed proposals for it and its public presentation, including the extent to which the Northern Ireland parties should be consulted before it was announced.

At their next meeting, on February 16, GEN 47 agreed that the policy package should include a progressive reduction in the number of internees as a concession to induce the SDLP to engage in constructive dialogue. If Faulkner would not accede to this, Westminster should legislate to transfer responsibility for the operation of internment to London.[79] This was still substantially less than the full transfer of security powers proposed by Maudling in January. But when the discussion continued the following day, the committee reversed its position of the previous month by accepting Maudling's contention that a period of direct rule could be desirable. The arguments advanced in its favor were that it would allow London to control the political development process, help secure the confidence of the SDLP, reduce the Unionists' capacity to obstruct progress, and improve prospects for reaching an agreed outcome. Under direct rule the home secretary would hand over his Northern Ireland responsibilities to the holder of a new cabinet post, that of secretary of state for Northern Ireland, who would "have executive responsibility for Irish services" and would "be advised by a commission of responsible Northern Ireland citizens."[80] The direct-rule interregnum was expected to last from twelve to eighteen months, after which power would be transferred back to the new community government.[81]

On February 25—two days after the court ruling in the Hume case—Maudling told GEN 47 that there should be no further delay. He asserted that it was "essential for responsibility for the maintenance of law and order, which was in any case effectively in the hands of the Army, formally to be transferred to Westminster." However, if Faulkner were prepared to co-operate on this basis until the political reforms could be implemented, an interim period of direct rule might not be necessary. Trend—also reversing his position of six weeks earlier—maintained that the minority would not tolerate a further two years of Unionist rule, the period considered neces-sary to produce a reformed constitution: "a continuance of Unionist Gov-ernment in its present form deferred any hope of a peaceful solution."[82]

Summing up the discussion, and in deference to some of his ministers' continuing reservations, Heath agreed to sound Faulkner out again about the transfer of security. He also instructed that contingency planning for direct rule should press ahead, including drawing up a timetable for action; preparing two draft bills, one to introduce direct rule and an alternative to transfer responsibility for security to London; consulting UKREP on possible members for the proposed advisory commission; planning for a new Whitehall department to service the secretary of state and identifying key personnel for it; and emergency planning for a breakdown of public administration as a result of the Protestant reaction against direct rule.

## Faulkner's Offer

Unaware of the developments in London, Faulkner submitted his own ideas for reform to Heath on March 1. To his green paper proposals of October 1971 he added a review of the Special Powers Act, restricting the power of internment; legislative strengthening of safeguards against religious discrimination, including a comprehensive bill of rights; and a reconstruction program for republican districts damaged in the violence. On Nationalist participation in government, he extended his earlier offer of committee places to cover all government functions, including security, and to give the committees the power to initiate policy proposals. He also offered to share official posts in the Stormont Commons (such as speaker) with the opposition and to consult the minister of community relations on appointments to public bodies.

He addressed Nationalists' desires for closer north-south cooperation by proposing the creation of an intergovernmental council. To reduce Union-ist opposition to this, there would also be a binding international agree-ment, whereby Dublin would effectively renounce the territorial claim to Northern Ireland embodied in articles 2 and 3 of the Irish constitution, and a second agreement with Dublin on collaboration in the security arena, including the creation of a common law enforcement area, to en-sure that IRA members could be extradited for trial in the United King-dom. Faulkner later indicated that if pressed, he would also have agreed to a gradual increase in Catholic (but not Nationalist) membership of the Northern Ireland parliament and cabinet, as well as a progressive reduction in the number of internees and a return to the formal division of responsibility for security set out in the Downing Street Declaration, with its distinction between normal civic policing and security operations.[83]

On the same day, GEN 47 met to discuss the two draft bills covering direct rule and the security transfer. Members were still not convinced that the package would work. But they accepted Maudling's dismissive assessment of Faulkner's offer, which was that his proposals for minority participation were too little, too late. In the chair, Heath steered the discussion toward tactics—in particular whether to tell Faulkner that they intended to introduce direct rule immediately, or that they intended to take over responsibility for law and order, thereby causing him to resign. They decided on the latter, on the basis that Faulkner's resignation would give them a tangible public justification for direct rule that they would not otherwise have.

Heath finished the meeting by declaring that the only course available was a temporary period of direct rule.[84] The ministers' decision was not merely to transfer security powers—which is what Heath later told the Commons—but positively to introduce direct rule. Just as he had previously had to shoulder the political responsibility for the failings of internment, so Faulkner was made publicly responsible for the dissolution of his own administration. He was made an offer he could not accept.

### Cabinet Deliberations

Having cleared the GEN 47 committee, Heath next had to convince the full cabinet. When it met on March 3, Maudling summarized the case for direct rule. There were two communities in Northern Ireland that were "poles apart." The army had made "good progress" against the IRA, but military action alone could not bring lasting peace and stability. Faulkner's proposals for reform were insufficient, since the Catholic minority "were entitled to claim the just share in government which the present political system denied them"—a substantial shift of view since the previous August. A "decisive political initiative" by the UK government was therefore required. For this to succeed, London would have to assume full control over security and exercise direct responsibility for the administration of Northern Ireland for a period of up to two years.[85] Maudling justified the transfer of security on the grounds that it would bring the constitutional position into line with the everyday reality; the minority would not otherwise accept the administration of law and order as impartial. Moreover, Stormont lacked the resources to handle matters of this size and complexity properly. He contended that the introduction of border plebiscites, one to be held as soon as practicable and others at intervals of at least fifteen years, would "put the problem of the Border into cold storage." In the new climate of generosity thus created, moderate leaders, for the first time, would be able to make coalition government work. It had succeeded in other divided societies, so why not Northern Ireland?

Maudling finished by telling his colleagues: "I have come to the conclusion that the dangers of continuing with the present policy are now greater than the dangers of trying to make a new start."[86] A clean break was required "to establish constructive consultations with all political elements in Northern Ireland." Success could not be guaranteed, but if the initiative failed they would "at least in the long term draw the benefit for having proposed a solution that is just and equitable between the differing factions."[87]

The cabinet returned to the discussion on March 7. Carrington enthusiastically supported Maudling's proposals. He noted that the army had moved successfully against the Provisional IRA in Belfast, but that this "had led to an intensification of IRA activity in Border areas, where terrorists could find a ready refuge within the Republic." He believed that a political initiative would weaken the IRA campaign; "if it could contain elements capable of winning a measure of support among moderate Catholics, the IRA might forfeit much of the benevolent neutrality which they enjoyed at the hands of individuals who sympathised with their political aims even while abhorring their methods."[88]

Other ministers were not convinced, notably the Lord Chancellor Lord Hailsham. They objected that "community government . . . could not be reconciled with the democratic concept of responsibility to a Parliamentary majority." They doubted "whether participation in government as of right by the minority was practicable as a long term objective, and whether the imposition of United Kingdom rule was politically feasible as a short-term measure." They feared that the initiative "would fail to gain significant support from the minority and would at the same time alienate not only a large mass of majority opinion in Northern Ireland but also a considerable number of the Government's supporters in the United Kingdom Parliament." Any apparent concessions would encourage the IRA to intensify their campaign and extend it to Great Britain. There were other objections as well. It was uncertain whether the RUC, judiciary, and civil service in Northern Ireland would collaborate. There was no reason to suppose that relaxing the internment regime would reduce the level of violence. And finally, if—as seemed probable—community government proved unworkable, London would be burdened with direct rule indefinitely. Faced with these objections, the meeting did not reach a conclusion on either direct rule or community government, but Heath at least secured agreement to the transfer of responsibility for security, albeit with Hailsham continuing to insist that it could unleash a Protestant backlash.[89] Members felt that it was unsatisfactory that "they had publicly to defend the policy of internment while having neither the power to influence the detention orders which were made in particular instances nor proper access to the information upon which these decisions were made." They also agreed to a policy of releasing internees gradually, appointing a secretary of state for Northern Ireland, and holding a border plebiscite.[90]

### Heath Completes

When the cabinet returned to the issue two days later, Heath invited his colleagues to consider whether the measures already agreed would be sufficient to persuade the SDLP to participate in talks, or to persuade Lynch to take more effective action against the IRA. It was not a neutral question. Ministers again rehearsed their positions for and against the security transfer, community government, and direct rule. Attempting to secure consensus, Trend proposed "an initial step going no further than the transfer to Westminster of responsibility for all aspects of internment policy, leaving other questions of law and order with the Stormont Government." Heath quashed this, again arguing that internment could not sensibly be handled in isolation from other aspects of security. But the cabinet still failed to reach agreement.[91]

Heath was running out of patience. He believed that urgent action was needed to reverse a slide toward civil war. On March 13, Trend offered the prime minister tactical guidance on clinching the cabinet's compliance, advising him to argue three points. First, the cabinet had already agreed to transfer security to Westminster, but it would be wrong to separate this arbitrarily from the other functions of government. Second, neither the SDLP nor Dublin would cooperate as required if Stormont were left intact. Third, the longer the cabinet delayed, the greater the risk that they would be accused of doing too little too late. Trend also reminded Heath of two additional sources of time pressure: Parliament's Easter recess and the start of the Orange marching season in Northern Ireland.[92]

At the cabinet meeting the following day Heath piled on the pressure, asserting that "failure to act now would mean acquiescence in a situation in which terrorism could never completely be eradicated from Northern Ireland."[93] But the dissenting ministers continued to argue that community government would not work and that, once direct rule was imposed, London would not be able to extricate itself. They wanted Faulkner to remain in office after the security transfer. The upshot was that Heath again promised to sound out Faulkner and report back. Next time, he warned them, they would have to reach final decisions.

Heath had no intention of yielding any ground to the dissenters. He had made up his mind. He wrote the agenda for and set the tone of his conversation with Faulkner and defined the direction it would take. He was not in a mood to negotiate or compromise. When he called Faulkner on March 15 to set up a meeting, he would not tell him what the agenda was and did not indicate that he intended to announce his decisions immediately afterward.[94]

The meeting was held in London on March 22. Faulkner was accompanied by his deputy, Senator John Andrews, and three senior officials: Cabinet Secretary Sir Harold Black, Ken Bloomfield, and Robert Ramsay. Heath was accompanied by Maudling, Carrington, Douglas-Home, and Whitelaw. The meeting lasted over several sessions totaling nine hours. Sometimes the politicians met without their officials; sometimes each side met alone.

Heath opened the session by explaining "that an assessment of the military situation in Northern Ireland led to the conclusion that the successes achieved by the security forces against the terrorist campaign could be effectively consolidated only if an improvement in the political situation could be secured by political means." But he did not invite Faulkner to explain or improve on his proposals for a political initiative of March 1, or to discuss any of the changes that he had decided to introduce.[95] He simply declared that his cabinet had "unanimously" agreed on a far-reaching package, comprising periodic referenda on the border, a progressive reduction in the number of internees, the appointment of a secretary of state for Northern Ireland, formal transfer of control over all security matters, and open-ended talks with the SDLP, with a view to reaching agreement on a community government. He did not try to persuade Faulkner to remain in office. The record of the meeting suggests that he overstated his colleagues' unanimity and strayed beyond the remit they had given him; as we have seen, at least two cabinet ministers still had serious reservations about the proposals.

Faulkner at first thought Heath was bluffing, realizing only as the meeting progressed that he was being presented with a fait accompli. When he had had an opportunity to recover his equilibrium, he indicated that he could agree to the first three items, but not the security transfer or community government. He argued that to relinquish control over law and order in the current context would leave Stormont "bereft of any real influence and authority"; it would not really be a government at all.[96]

Heath broke off to consult his colleagues. They accepted Faulkner's contention that his government could not survive politically if it handed over its security responsibilities. At least one of those present suggested reverting to the compromise proposed by Trend: negotiating toward UK control over internment and a review of the Special Powers Act, but letting Stormont keep civil policing and criminal justice. Faulkner has since indicated that he would have accepted this. But Heath would not have it, arguing that it would not secure the necessary cooperation of Nationalist Ireland; it would be better to do nothing.

When the discussions resumed, Faulkner offered more concessions: to release 100 internees immediately; to share decisions on future internee releases with the home secretary; to share the chair of the JSC with a UK minister, each having a right of veto; to bring Northern Ireland's emergency legislation into line with Britain's; and to have a bill of rights for Northern Ireland enacted at Westminster. When the UK ministers convened during a second break, they decided that these concessions too fell short of what the cabinet had already agreed, in that they would not give London full control over security.

At the final session, Faulkner confirmed that he viewed direct rule as politically less damaging than the surrender of responsibility for security. He returned to Belfast to share the bombshell with his cabinet colleagues. They agreed that they could not give up security altogether and survive in office. Faulkner later wrote: "There was no negotiable exit from the cul-de-sac into which we had been led, and no attempt was made to disguise this."[97] Ramsay later wrote that Heath "hoped his first proposal would bring the game to an end; and had that not been the case he would simply have moved down a list of further, and increasingly unattractive, proposals until he succeeded in getting Faulkner and his colleagues to throw in their hand." Two Whitehall officials confirmed that this was Heath's intention.[98]

Heath had told Faulkner—which was not entirely the case—that the cabinet had already made up its mind and would reaffirm this decision when it met on March 23. When that meeting convened, the prime minister reminded his colleagues of the objectives they had already signed up for: to deprive the IRA of popular support, draw Nationalist elected representatives into political dialogue, and remove the inhibitions that, he said, had prevented Lynch from acting firmly against the IRA. He dismissed Faulkner's latest offer, including the further concessions offered during the previous day's meeting, as insufficient to achieve these objectives. He also complained that "Mr. Faulkner had not seemed fully to realise the nature of the problem either of persuading the representatives of the minority to resume active participation in the political life of the Province or of reestablishing law and order in areas such as the Bogside and Creggan districts of Londonderry. This attitude on his part . . . confronted the Cabinet with the need to take the final decision." Having dismissed Faulkner as intransigent and uncomprehending, he questioned his colleagues as to whether they were prepared to insist on the full transfer of security, knowing that this would almost certainly mean introducing direct rule immediately.[99]

Douglas-Home spoke first. He supported the prime minister, pointing out that Dublin would "almost certainly regard as unacceptable" Faulkner's proposal for "joint control over security in the Six Counties," would welcome the security transfer, and would endorse an interim period of direct rule. The dissenters rehearsed their previous arguments. This time Heath insisted on a decision. His clinching argument seems to have been an appeal to the cabinet's collective ego. They could all agree that "it would be politically intolerable for the Government to retreat so far from the requirements which the prime minister had indicated to Mr. Faulkner that it would be clear that they had no greater freedom of political initiative than the Northern Ireland Government were prepared to allow them." Having finally maneuvered and ground the dissenters down, Heath concluded the meeting: "There was no doubt that [the agreed initiative] entailed great risks; but even greater dangers would attend any alternative policy."[100]

## Uncertainties and Paradigms

### Managing Uncertainties

Introducing direct rule overturned over fifty years of constitutional convention and practice. It also reversed a firm policy position that both Labour and Conservative administrations had adopted since the Troubles began, a position Heath had confirmed in cabinet only three months earlier. Heath subsequently described direct rule as "one of the most difficult and painful decisions we ever had to take."[101] It was done in the face of great risks and uncertainties under substantial political and time pressures. The prolonged cabinet debate occurred in three major areas of concern: whether the Unionist reaction to the imposition of direct rule could be contained, whether the package would be sufficient to induce the SDLP to negotiate and Dublin to help in the fight against the IRA, and whether the Northern Ireland Civil Service (NICS) and RUC would collaborate. To address these issues, Heath brought senior officials from Belfast (UKREP Howard Smith) and Dublin (Ambassador John Peck) to London to speak to his colleagues in person. Smith indicated that there would be an adverse Protestant reaction, but it could be contained; the SDLP would not engage

in serious negotiation unless Stormont was suspended; and the civil service
and RUC would collaborate, although RUC Special Branch would have to
be handled with care. Peck added that in return for his cooperation, Lynch
would want a relaxation in the internment regime, "some alleviation of
what he saw as the inferior citizenship of the minority," a formulation that
fell well short of community government, and public recognition of the
possibility of unification in the long term.

### The Unionist Reaction

Heath had already taken advice on the likely scale of the loyalist reaction
from security officials. In January, the Joint Intelligence Committee (JIC)
had produced a report entitled "The Probable Reactions to the Introduction of Direct Rule in Northern Ireland."[102] The author, JIC chairman
Stewart Crawford, noted that both sides would see direct rule as "the first
step towards reunification." When Heath asked the GOC on March 1
about the danger of a Protestant backlash, the reply was that any reaction
was likely to develop slowly, enabling the army to send in reinforcements
gradually as they became necessary.[103]

But behind the advice lay some harsher realities. Poll results suggested
that only 25 percent of Protestants would accept "a new kind of government involving the abolition of Stormont and the introduction of direct
rule," while 72 percent would not.[104] Under direct rule, they would no longer have a legitimate outlet for their political aspirations and anxieties.
Loyalists also might consider that republican violence had achieved results
and launch violence of their own to halt what they would see as a slide
toward Dublin rule. The army might find itself at war with both communities simultaneously.

Craig had already begun to make preparations for mass resistance. On
February 9, he launched Vanguard, an umbrella body for loyalist political, trade union, and paramilitary groups. Vanguard's governing council
included Unionist MPs from Westminster and Stormont. It organized a
series of demonstrations; an estimated 70,000 people attended the largest,
on March 18, at which Craig inspected rows of men drilling in paramilitary uniform. He threatened chaos if UK ministers tampered with Northern Ireland's constitution.[105] Vanguard's activities, perversely, may have
counted against Faulkner, signaling to Heath, first, that the reforms he
considered necessary could not be made except under direct rule; second,
that it would be better to introduce direct rule immediately rather than
allowing the loyalist opposition to build momentum; and third, that loyalism was essentially defensive. Vanguard's protests showed that what Protestants feared was not direct rule but Dublin rule; they could be managed

as long as most Unionists could be persuaded that they were not going to be forced into the Republic.[106] The planned plebiscite would address this last point.[107]

The argument that it would be better to introduce direct rule sooner rather than later was reinforced by the hard line taken by Unionist backbenchers at Stormont. On March 15, they passed a resolution rejecting any move toward a united Ireland, any reduction in Stormont's powers, and any proposal for power sharing at cabinet level.[108] Faulkner probably hoped that this vote would strengthen his hand in negotiating with Heath, but again it may have had the opposite effect. UK ministers were not prepared to be seen to tolerate a junior partner who openly rejected their authority and policies. As long as the Unionists remained at Stormont, they would be able to use the authority of elected office as a resource to resist changes which Heath now considered both essential and urgent.

Divisions within Unionism gave the British confidence. Before internment, there had been speculation that Paisley and Craig might join forces. But after it, Paisley (who spoke out against internment) let it be known that he would rather have direct rule than the alternative Craig advocated, a unilateral declaration of independence. Paisley shared the view of some Unionist ministers and MPs that direct rule might actually strengthen the union by committing London more wholeheartedly to robust action against the IRA.[109] He also calculated that driving Faulkner out of office and further fragmenting the Unionist Party would benefit the DUP electorally.

## The Nationalist Reaction

Ministers did not doubt that Nationalists and their elected representatives would welcome the suspension of Stormont, the phasing out of internment, and the commitment to include them in government. But there were two major uncertainties on the Nationalist side: whether the package would be sufficient to bring the SDLP to the negotiating table and whether it would encourage the IRA to intensify its violence.

Even if London eventually achieved a constitutional settlement between the two sides, there was no reason to suppose that the experience of participating in a Stormont cabinet would induce the SDLP to drop their aspiration to a united Ireland. The Irish government and some SDLP members were lukewarm about community government, partly because it could give partition a new lease of life. And including some SDLP ministers in a Stormont administration would not placate the IRA. The best that could be hoped for was that it would strip away some of their public support.

On September 8, Fitt—recovering from a slipped disc in a Dublin nursing home—had told the British ambassador that he could persuade his colleagues to strike a deal with Faulkner if most of the internees were freed and the "real bad men" charged with specific offenses. He wanted Peck to persuade Irish ministers to support this initiative. In practice, however, Fitt proved unable to persuade Hume and the rest of the leadership to fall into line. Smith reported that none of the other SDLP leaders had much regard for Fitt and that some cordially disliked him.[110] Hume subsequently told an interviewer, "Gerry never made any contribution to debate within the party, to philosophy, to policy documents, to strategy. They were all written by me. Gerry was a figurehead."[111]

More characteristic of the SDLP position at the time was the message given by another of its founder members, civil rights activist Austin Currie, who told a public protest rally a month before Bloody Sunday that "within the next six or seven months, Faulkner and his rotten Unionist system will have been smashed. . . . I say to Maudling: 'Why the hell should we talk to you? We are winning and you are not.' . . . Even if Maudling got down on his bended knees and kissed all our backsides we would not be prepared to talk."[112]

Having convinced himself of the need for a radical initiative, Heath handled the cabinet's uncertainties and reservations by insisting that the package must be sufficiently radical to engage Nationalist Ireland. If the IRA campaign did not collapse quickly, exceptional security measures, including internment, would still be in place to deal with it. Difficult political negotiations would undoubtedly be required, but at least under the new dispensation they would take place under the control of the UK government, and they would no longer be constrained by the need to prop up a failing Unionist leader.

### The Public Services' Reaction

Ministers were particularly concerned that the task of the army and security services would become more difficult if RUC Special Branch withheld cooperation more than it had already been doing.[113] But there was less uncertainty than in 1969, when Callaghan had faced a similar dilemma. The USC had ceased to exist and had been replaced by the Ulster Defence Regiment (UDR), a regiment of the British army, accountable to Westminster. Maudling took advice from UKREP, which was to the effect that most of the civil service, the judiciary, and RUC would cooperate with direct rule.[114] The RUC and NICS would obey their new political masters so long as there was no immediate threat to the union or their livelihoods.[115] Having agreed on the action to take at their conclusive meeting on March 23, ministers instructed senior officials to visit Northern Ireland to remind RUC chiefs and senior civil servants of their allegiance to the Crown and to identify any individuals in potentially significant positions, such as Bill Stout, who might prove obstructive.

## Causes of Disorder

The decision to introduce direct rule cannot adequately be explained as a rational response to events, or even to the accumulation of negative events from Bloody Sunday to the publication of the Parker Report. It required a substantial intellectual shift from the patterns of understanding and belief that had made internment possible.

Before internment Heath and Maudling had broadly endorsed Faulkner's definition of the problem in terms primarily of the IRA's assault on the state. After internment, however, their dominant pattern of understanding came variously from Nationalist Ireland, moderate Unionists, and army commanders. It was essentially that the IRA insurgency drew its legitimacy and energy from Nationalists' exclusion from political decision-making at the regional level. Their general alienation was reinforced but not caused by discrete issues, such as discrimination in employment and bias in the operation of internment. Any long-term solution must therefore end that exclusion. As a distinctive and substantial political and cultural minority, Nationalists were entitled to a guaranteed share in government.

Fine Gael, the principal opposition party in the Republic, had proposed the idea of a coalition government as early as August 1969.[116] But at that time most Nationalist politicians in Northern Ireland had no interest in joining a regime they wanted to overthrow. Hume was apparently the first Nationalist elected representative in the north to take up the idea. It had become a matter of public discussion in Northern Ireland by spring 1971.[117]

Moderate unionism was another source of the new paradigm. It found articulation in a pamphlet written by political scientist John Whyte and published by the NUM in July 1971.[118] Whyte argued that the Westminster model was not suited to Northern Ireland's distinctive political circumstances, since it could never provide an outlet for Nationalist aspirations. It gave the Unionist Party a permanent monopoly on power, "with consequent tendencies to complacency, arrogance, and at times injustice," and excluded Nationalists, "with consequent tendencies to frustration, irresponsibility, and at times a hankering after violent solutions." Although he did not use the term "consociational democracy," Whyte took as his models the states that Lijphart had used a few years earlier to develop the concept—Switzerland and Austria—and thus recommended changing

Northern Ireland's constitution to include PR voting at parliamentary elections, all-party specialist committees at Stormont to oversee departments, a 50 percent increase in the number of Stormont MPs, a new method of selecting members for the senate, and an executive in which all major parties were represented in proportion to their strength in the parliament. He recognized the dangers of deadlock and complacency arising from the absence of a parliamentary opposition, but argued that these would be more than offset by the opportunities his proposals would create for opening up the administration to new talent and developing collaboration across the community divide. He did not attempt to conceal that his proposals were intended to advantage moderates (notably Alliance) in their struggle against "extremism." Whyte's first four proposals were reflected in Faulkner's green paper of October 1971.

The NUM put their case directly to Maudling on November 30, 1971.[119] By then they had lost faith in the possibility of transforming Stormont from within. Since the SDLP was pursuing a policy of abstention and Faulkner was unwilling to allow Nationalists into his cabinet, they argued that the only way forward was for Westminster to suspend Stormont and impose a cross-community commission made up of nine "eminent Ulstermen"—specifically not elected politicians—who would demonstrate that leadership could be given effectively across the social divide. The commission would oversee the transformation to a new dispensation in which power would be shared among elected representatives.

Whyte was not the only moderate Unionist advocating the sharing of power. In January 1972, the United Nations Association published a pamphlet written by Professor Harry Calvert, a specialist in public law who had previously served as an adviser to the Northern Ireland government. Calvert likewise identified the central issue as the effective exclusion of the Catholic community from the institutions of government, rather than discrimination, civil rights, or the national question.[120] It is unclear to what extent Maudling was influenced by the thinking of Whyte, Calvert, and other moderate Unionists, but the radical prescription he proposed to the cabinet in January 1972 reflected their proposals more closely than anything his Home Office officials had conceived before internment.

### British Standards

Given the emphasis UK ministers repeatedly placed on bringing British standards of fair play to Northern Ireland, it is ironic that British army personnel introduced and endorsed the interrogation procedures used against internees. Carrington and Maudling had both been told in advance of the intention to use them.[121] Bloody Sunday was the most egregious example of a military approach to security that was the antithesis of the civilian policing principles underpinning the Hunt report.

Yet just as Hunt had maintained that the RUC should be brought into line with an ideal English model, so ministers declared that the solution to the political problem lay in bringing Northern Ireland's political system into line with Britain's. Maudling later wrote: "Northern Ireland will never be at peace until . . . the political struggles of the Province are based, as they are in the rest of the United Kingdom, not on communal issues, but on the fundamental political issues which divide the Right wing from the Left over the whole range of our public life."[122] He told his cabinet colleagues that Unionists would have to accept that "Northern Ireland institutions must in future conform to the standards prevailing in the remainder of the United Kingdom."[123] The home secretary apparently saw no inconsistency in the assertion that a mandatory coalition along Lebanese lines was consistent with the principles and procedures of majoritarian democracy as practiced at Westminster.

There is another irony in the application of "British standards." The military security approach described in chapter 4 used tactics in Northern Ireland that were derived from the army's experiences in overseas colonial settings. Presented with dramatic and politically painful evidence of the failure of coercion, London changed its approach from coercion to conciliation but did not discard the colonial analogies. Ministers clearly intended to disregard inconvenient electoral outcomes and engineer more favorable ones. They envisaged the new secretary of state as a colonial governor, who would take advice from a carefully selected committee of safe and amenable natives. UK ministers did not really view Northern Ireland as a full component of the United Kingdom but as a place apart.

### Reasonable People

Related to their conception of British standards, UK ministers saw Northern Ireland's sectarian politics, and the politics of the Unionist Party in particular, as the dangerous legacy of a primitive past standing in the way of a sensible, just, and durable settlement.[124] In his memoirs Heath describes the conflict as a historical relic that challenged his administration's overarching ideological commitment to social and economic modernization. He attributes it to "the bitter, tribal loathing between the hard-line elements in the two communities, springing from an atavism which most of Europe discarded long ago." This had "inspired the Protestant majority to discriminate shamelessly against their fellow citizens for almost half a century."[125]

A central goal of Heath's modernizing strategy was to depoliticize the Northern Ireland administration by removing the big contentious issues from its agenda, in the belief that this would allow elected representatives from the two traditions to work harmoniously together on bread-and-butter issues. Thus, divisive matters such as the allocation of public housing would be handled by apolitical bureaucratic agencies, and regular border plebiscites would "take the Border out of the day-to-day political scene."[126] One of the arguments supporting the security transfer was that it would defuse conflict over such things as internment and interrogation procedures.

Thus freed at last from the primitive legacy of quarreling over partition, Northern Ireland's political leaders would regroup. Moderate parties of the center—by which UK ministers meant Alliance, Labour, and the SDLP—would grow and prosper, drawing support from communities newly liberated from their archaic obsessions. The emerging progressive leaders would first agree across the community divide on fair and modern constitutional arrangements, and in the longer term thrive as they were seen to address together the everyday tasks of public administration. In place of the old one-party parliament, a new regional assembly would include Protestant and Catholic elected representatives addressing common social and economic concerns. In their meetings with the British, the perceived representatives of moderation from both traditions naturally encouraged these hopeful and unsubstantiated beliefs.

## Politics

### The Backbenches

Even as the cabinet decided on direct rule, Heath freely acknowledged that he had no idea whether the proposed political initiative would succeed. Key ministers continued to have serious reservations about it weeks after it had been introduced, and months later UK ministers and officials were still debating not only whether coalition government was attainable but also whether it was preferable to other options such as complete legislative and administrative integration with the United Kingdom. It is simply not credible to argue that the British were at last driven exclusively by a coherent strategy grounded in rational analysis.

Heath told the cabinet that they could not continue as they were in Northern Ireland. But the reasons were political and to a large extent independent of events in the region. Heath's biographer has indicated that January and February 1972 "must rate as the most dreadful short period of concentrated stress ever endured by a British government in peacetime."[127]

As well as Northern Ireland, the prime minister had to contend with the threat of a national miners' strike, the worst unemployment figures since 1947, and a fierce parliamentary contest over membership in the EEC. Amid this turbulence, dissidents in the cabinet were concerned that the direct-rule package would erode support for the government among Conservative backbenchers.

Heath's critics vigorously opposed any reforms that could be interpreted as concessions to IRA violence. Enoch Powell argued fiercely against any constitutional reform, apart from full integration with the United Kingdom:

> The very notion that by one alteration or another, however arguable in itself, of the constitution in Northern Ireland the realities of this situation can be influenced is false and dangerous. Those who are conducting the war and those whom they hold in terror will not be in the least affected by any constitutional change in Northern Ireland. When they see the Government of the United Kingdom engaging eagerly in this kind of discussion, as though that held the clue and the secret, they say: "So we have come a long way. Violence has already pushed the Ulster Government and the British Government a good way already. We will exercise this power further. We will string them along. We are winning."[128]

Powell called for practical measures to convince republicans that the government was determined that they should not succeed: effective border controls, requiring citizens to carry proof of their identity, and rearming the RUC to enable them to discharge the full range of policing functions. Powell's arguments tempered some Conservative MPs' support for a political initiative. Others believed that internment would eventually deliver results. Having paid the price in disorder and political criticism, they held that the government should stand firm and reap the benefits.

While Powell and his allies opposed any real or apparent concession to republican violence in principle, they could not be described as friends of Faulkner. As early as January 1971, Powell had been calling for Stormont's permanent abolition. He held that it had originally been conceived as a vehicle to move Northern Ireland along the road to a united Ireland, and that its very existence tended to detach Northern Ireland from the rest of the United Kingdom. Coming at the issue from another angle, constituency activists at the Conservatives' annual conference in October attacked Maudling for risking soldiers' lives to protect Faulkner, arguing that Westminster would govern Northern Ireland better than Stormont had.[129] Finally, Ian Paisley used his position as a Westminster MP to lobby for Stormont's suspension.[130]

There was also a middle-of-the road lobby at Westminster for direct rule, echoing the NUM and Alliance in Northern Ireland. From the House of Lords, Terence O'Neill wrote to Heath on February 10, 1972, to complain about Maudling's inertia and Faulkner's duplicity. He argued that Faulkner had cleverly exploited the "empty threat" of a Protestant backlash; that internment had been a disaster, when its only purpose had been to save Faulkner's skin; and that direct rule could no longer be avoided.[131] Heath understood that some of the Unionist MPs at Westminster were privately disillusioned with Faulkner and his policies, and had already accepted that direct rule was imminent.[132] Some shared Powell's view that direct rule would strengthen the union, some that it would lead Heath to tackle the IRA more aggressively.

Having at last agreed on the action to take at their meeting on March 23, the cabinet decided to forestall criticism from their backbenchers by presenting direct rule as a necessary consequence of Faulkner's intransigent refusal to hand over security. To placate the right wing in the Conservative Party, they decided also to announce that they were examining more effective means to act against the IRA in Britain.[133]

One political factor that might have been expected to prevent a radical policy shift was the continuing cross-party opposition to the European Bill, providing for the United Kingdom to join the EEC. Powell and his supporters had voted against it at second reading on February 17, reducing the government's majority to eight. The support of Unionist MPs had been critical. If every other MP voted the same way and the Unionists all voted against the bill at third reading in protest against direct rule, the bill would be lost. Heath could have avoided this danger by deferring his ultimatum to Faulkner, and some commentators have complimented him for his courage in not doing so.[134] Perhaps it helped that he gave the leader of the Unionist MPs a job as an employment minister in the British government. Whatever the reason, the Unionists did not collectively oppose the European Bill, which passed with a safe majority on May 2.

### The Opposition

The Labour Party retained its interest in weakening the Unionist Party at Westminster and in Northern Ireland. Within a month of leaving office in June 1970, Callaghan noted in a letter to the general secretary of the British Labour Party: "If we are to succeed [in building up a Labour Party organization in Northern Ireland] it will be necessary to break the domination of the Ulster Unionist Party. This may be historically the moment to do it for their grip is feebler than it has been at any time since 1921."[135] Labour nevertheless formally adhered to the bipartisan consensus on the subject at Westminster until August 1971.

Internment and its consequences changed the context dramatically. On the Labour backbenches, the Campaign for Democracy in Ulster (CDU) had from the start been unhappy with Maudling's laissez-faire approach, and on occasion had voted against their own front bench on Northern Ireland issues. Until internment, Wilson had stuck to the position that Conservative policy was broadly the same as Labour's had been, albeit less well managed. Shortly after internment, one hundred Labour MPs wrote to ask Wilson to demand the recall of the Commons for an emergency debate. Wilson obliged, taking the opportunity also to attack the Conservatives for siding with the Unionists and to call for a new political initiative, to be taken in consultation with the Irish government.[136] Ministers reluctantly agreed, and the debate was held on September 22.

Gerry Fitt used the debate to demand that Stormont be replaced by "a new system of Government which will allow both the majority and minority communities in Northern Ireland to participate at all levels in the administration of that country."[137] During this exchange, Maudling first indicated publicly that the government wished to find "agreed means whereby an active, permanent and guaranteed place in the life and public affairs of Northern Ireland shall be available both to the minority and to the majority community."[138] The first result of this commitment was that Maudling pressed Faulkner to publish proposals for reform, which emerged as the green paper of October 1971. At the same time, in deference to Faulkner's concerns, Maudling told the Commons that it would be difficult to include Nationalists in the Northern Ireland cabinet since "one cannot create a cohesive Government if people do not denounce violence or if people are not prepared to accept the will of the majority on the fundamental point about the Border which succeeding Governments have always accepted in this country."[139] Defending himself against criticism for inaction, he pointed to two political processes already under way. At the international level, Heath would be meeting Lynch and Faulkner shortly to discuss how their three governments might work together more effectively. At the regional level, he was trying to arrange talks with the political parties and other community leaders in Northern Ireland—talks that the SDLP was boycotting.

Another strand in Maudling's self-defense was to distance himself from Faulkner. He declared that the Northern Ireland government had decided to introduce internment, which was technically true but—as Wilson immediately pointed out—disingenuous, in that it had been clearly established in August 1969 that UK ministers were accountable to Westminster for security policies and operations in Northern Ireland. If this was no longer the case, that was so only because the Conservatives had passed back to the Unionists the authority that Labour had taken from them.

As well as forcing the government to commit to a political strategy, Wilson used the September debate to attack internment as a gamble that had not paid off. He embarrassed Maudling with a series of probing questions. How many Unionists had been interned? Had the army called for internment? Who drew up the list of internees? Had Maudling approved the listing criteria? Wilson cited newspaper reports criticizing the government for "acting as the tool of a discredited Stormont administration." He also attacked Maudling for failing to take any effective steps to mollify the Nationalist community after internment, or to promote political progress. The opposition leader then set out his own proposals for a radical political initiative, including a review of Stormont's Special Powers Act, to be conducted by a joint parliamentary commission representing Westminster and Stormont and including Nationalist elected representatives; a new post of secretary of state for Northern Ireland, who would have no executive functions but would raise the level of UK engagement in Northern Ireland and liaise with the leaders of both traditions; and a formal structure to promote cross-border cooperation.

One of Wilson's motives in advancing his proposals at this time was to prevent his parliamentary party from splitting on the issue. The main factions were the CDU, which shared the SDLP's hostility toward internment; pragmatists such as Callaghan, who favored a gradual approach to reform and cross-border cooperation; and a group led by Kevin McNamara MP, which favored early British withdrawal as a first step toward unification.[140] Seeking the support of the first two groups, Wilson took a sideswipe at the third, rejecting "the facile so-called solution that Britain should withdraw and leave the two embattled factions to fight it out."[141]

Wilson attached particular importance to avoiding a split over Northern Ireland in part because a more serious division had opened up during the summer over Britain's entry into the EEC. Labour advocates of entry were moving toward open rebellion, and both sides were criticizing Wilson for allowing the fissure to develop. He could ill afford another challenge to his authority on one of the most salient issues of the day. He also feared that Callaghan, a potential leadership rival, might outflank him as he had earlier done on two important issues, prices and incomes policy and entry into the EEC.[142]

The September debate revealed considerable differences between the two men. Whereas Wilson concentrated on Nationalists' concerns, including relationships with Dublin, Callaghan focused on the SDLP's willingness to engage in government at Stormont once internment had ended. Unlike Wilson, Callaghan endorsed the NILP's proposals for an interim executive comprising Catholics and Protestants under Faulkner.[143] This foreshadowed Maudling's November 12 proposal for an emergency government comprising "men of goodwill" from both sides. Callaghan appealed for the maintenance of bipartisanship, dismissing Faulkner's arguments against PR government. In private conversation he was equally dismissive of Wilson's proposals for reunification.

Despite Wilson's efforts to maintain unity, Labour dissidents forced a division in which sixty-eight voted against the government. *The Economist* correctly predicted that Wilson would react to this opportunistically by moving closer to the positions Fitt and McNamara advocated.[144] He shifted Callaghan from the Northern Ireland portfolio, replacing him with a relatively inexperienced newcomer, Merlyn Rees. The peeling veneer of bipartisan consensus finally dissolved in November 1971, when the two main parties divided in a Commons vote.

From then until March 1972, Wilson personally led the development and expression of opposition policy. His busy public profile contrasted with the impression Maudling gave of plodding complacency. Wilson traveled to Dublin and Belfast for three days in November, accompanied by Rees. Keen to reconstruct the bipartisan consensus, Heath gave Wilson administrative support for this visit, and received a written report on his meetings with over forty delegations from across the spectrum of Irish political opinion, including the Dublin government and opposition. One contemporary observer commented that this trip represented "a genuine attempt by both leaders [Heath and Wilson] to find a bipartisan solution."[145]

The fruits of Wilson's travels did not immediately restore bipartisanship. Indeed, the fifteen-point plan he produced sent the two front benches for the first time through opposing lobbies. He presented it during a Commons debate, again initiated by Labour, on November 25,[146] outlining six main proposals. First, responsibility for all aspects of security should be transferred to Westminster. Second, elected representatives of the Nationalist minority should be included in the Stormont cabinet by right. Third, the main parties in the Dáil should be represented alongside their counterparts at Westminster and Stormont on a parliamentary commission that would examine what would be involved in agreeing on the constitution of a united Ireland, to be introduced within fifteen years. Fourth, if the commission made good progress, the Republic should join the British Commonwealth, undertake to cooperate actively in combating republican terrorism, and amend its constitution to remove its Catholic ethos. Fifth, to ease the process of unification, Britain would help finance improvements in the Irish welfare system. Finally, and as a first step, interparty talks should be held at Westminster, to be followed by further talks among the parties at Westminster and Stormont.

Wilson's statement attracted favorable attention in the press and at Westminster. This reflected a widespread feeling among MPs and commentators that something had to be done to halt the drift in Northern Ireland, combined with a pervasive lack of solid ideas as to what it should be. CDU leader Paul Rose MP hailed the occasion of Wilson's speech as "a historic day in the history of Northern Ireland. . . . [F]or the first time this century a Front Bench spokesman . . . has talked of a transitional period towards the reunification of an Ireland that was artificially divided because of the threat of force" by Unionists.[147] Wilson gained political credit for his visible activism, and when the Commons voted, Labour MPs of all factions united behind him in voting against the government.

Behind Wilson's rhetoric, which the SDLP welcomed and Faulkner denounced, Wilson's statement was noteworthy for what it did not say. He did not call for an immediate end to internment and conceded that the operation had yielded useful intelligence. He did not say that the army should be withdrawn within a fixed period and argued that a new "permanent military town" should be built in Northern Ireland to emphasize Britain's determination to remain until well after the violence had subsided.[148] While calling for talks, he explicitly dismissed the idea of implementing a constitutional initiative while the violence persisted. He rejected unification except by consent of the majority, which he recognized was unlikely to be given for the foreseeable future. Finally, he rejected both direct rule and the SDLP's proposal for a commission government.

Although no longer Labour's Northern Ireland spokesman, Callaghan continued to discuss the way forward with Maudling. Reporting to Heath in December, the home secretary said that his predecessor was arguing that "the Ulster Unionist Party was finished and the best hope of progress was in cooperation between the SDLP and Mr. Paisley." Callaghan had also made clear that his own position "differed from Mr. Wilson's in that Mr. Wilson regarded a united Ireland as the best solution, whereas Mr. Callaghan considered that a Paisley-Fitt alliance would take the pressure off the Border as an issue for some time."[149]

Heath very much wanted to restore bipartisanship.[150] Ministers recognized that divisions in parliament undermined the work of the army in Northern Ireland and threatened to reduce public support in Britain for its engagement there. Any political initiative—particularly one focusing on longer-term objectives—would have a greater chance of success if the opposition supported it.[151] Heath was concerned, too, that the existence of Wilson's plan exposed his government to criticism for having no new ideas of its own.[152]

The situation gave Wilson considerable influence over policy.[153] Heath had in November 1971 accepted in principle Wilson's invitation to negotiate on the substance and timing of an initiative, but wanted to agree on the way forward with his own ministers before actually doing so. He was concerned about the implications for Faulkner and for stability in Northern Ireland of starting a process that Wilson had already presented as potentially leading to a united Ireland. Commenting on the official record of Maudling's meeting with Callaghan, he noted "that the Labour Party are all set to do in the Unionist Government and would not be greatly concerned if Direct Rule was the consequence of doing so."[154]

Heath was slow to arrange the meeting he had promised with Wilson. He raised a series of obstacles, querying the agenda, who should attend, and whether the substance of their talks should be kept confidential. He finally engaged only after Bloody Sunday, and after Wilson had publicly denounced him for procrastination.[155] At the critical cabinet discussion on February 9, when ministers first seriously debated their proposed initiative after the shootings, they noted that "it would be necessary to secure the support of the Opposition at Westminster. Hostility on their part to the plan would seriously jeopardise the Bill that would be needed to give it effect."[156]

Having restored unity within his own party and provided a seemingly coherent alternative to what was widely perceived as government drift, Wilson was well placed to take advantage of ministers' increasing political discomfort during February 1972. His initial reaction to Bloody Sunday was to support the SDLP's contention that the event had changed the political context so dramatically that a united Ireland was now the only sustainable long-term solution. In a Commons debate on February 1, he and Rees attacked Heath and Maudling for delaying in setting up the promised interparty talks, again called for the full transfer of responsibility for security to Westminster as a matter of urgency, and demanded an early political initiative.

Heath finally met Wilson on the afternoon of February 16, between two intensive sessions of debate with his ministerial colleagues. The upshot was that Wilson agreed to work with the prime minister toward a mutually acceptable initiative on the understanding that he would be free to revive his own proposals if they could not reach agreement, or if the initiative failed. He assured the prime minister that the opposition would not seek to gain political advantage if direct rule proved necessary after Faulkner's refusal to accept the security transfer.[157] The following day Heath's cabinet committee reversed its earlier stand and agreed that direct rule would be desirable. Heath also spoke privately to Wilson about the possibility of an adverse High Court ruling on February 22; here again Wilson signaled a willingness to cooperate in having the necessary legislation rushed through the parliamentary process, but only on the condition that an agreed political initiative would quickly follow.[158]

Wilson kept up the pressure, aligning himself with the Irish government's position. He visited Dublin on March 13–14, when he met not only Lynch and leaders of the Irish opposition parties but also—to the taoiseach's dismay—spokesmen for the Provisionals. He then outraged Unionists by suggesting that the Provisionals' demands should be included on the agenda for the planned political talks: immediate withdrawal of the army from the streets, a declaration of intent to withdraw from Northern Ireland completely, the abolition of Stormont, and an amnesty for IRA members convicted of criminal offenses.

On March 20, Wilson arranged a further Commons debate, this time on "the failure of the Government to announce the long-promised political initiative on Northern Ireland" and its consequences. He argued that while the government procrastinated, loyalists—in particular Craig—were organizing to resist change by force if necessary. He raised the specter of the violence spreading to Britain, and again called for responsibility for security to be transferred to Westminster so that the army, and not Stormont, could be seen as protecting both communities. He argued that there was a "law of diminishing acceptability,"[159] meaning that reforms that would have reduced Catholic disaffection six months earlier would no longer be sufficient. Further procrastination might make still more radical measures necessary, thereby increasing the risk of a loyalist backlash. During the same debate, Callaghan blamed the delay on cabinet divisions and argued that the "able, ambitious and energetic" Faulkner had filled the vacuum that the home secretary had left.[160]

Once again, the House divided on party lines. Two days later Heath issued his uncompromising ultimatum to Faulkner. The direct-rule package included two of Wilson's three most important policy proposals from November 25: the security transfer and the commitment to work toward including elected minority representatives in the devolved administration. Faulkner had stoutly resisted both.

Wilson's press secretary has written of the distrust that soured the relationship between Heath and Wilson.[161] However, Wilson himself writes of his "close and continuous consultation" with the prime minister over direct rule. Whatever personal animosities there may have been, the two leaders shared an interest in restoring bipartisan consensus on Northern Ireland. Through Wilson the SDLP could feed into the process of policy development at the highest level without sacrificing the leverage it gained from boycotting Stormont and rejecting Maudling's offer of talks.

## Media and Public Opinion

Internment increased the salience of Northern Ireland as a popular political issue in Britain. Even immediately after the riots of August 1969, opinion surveys had found that it rated least important of ten major issues, but by November 1971, 20 percent of respondents thought it was the single most important problem facing the government, more than any other issue except unemployment.

Coverage in serious periodicals provides a second measure of salience. For the last six months of 1971, the British Humanities Index lists ninety-four articles on Northern Ireland, compared with forty-two and twenty-three respectively for the previous two half-years. With Wilson presenting himself as the proponent of statesmanlike initiatives and growing disquiet in their own party, Conservative ministers could ill afford to appear complacent or lacking in fresh ideas.

Pressure to do something must be distinguished from pressure to do any particular thing. In July 1971, pressure for action had contributed to the decision to introduce internment. One option in February 1972 would have been to introduce other coercive measures, such as the death penalty for lethal terrorist offenses, sustained curfews, restrictions on press coverage and political activity, sealing the border, or the selective assassination of IRA leaders. However, the broad tenor of the national press coverage at this period was against coercion, especially after Bloody Sunday.

The ill treatment of internees was an important news story from mid-September 1971, when allegations were first published in the *Sunday Times*. Although some editors at first held back the story in response to official pressure, once the *Sunday Times* had published, others followed. This coverage encouraged Labour backbenchers to vote against the government in the September emergency debate. The allegations continued and were partially confirmed in the Compton Report.[162] One commentator declared: "Britain has become steadily more ashamed of internment, stories of British atrocities have built up in the press and on television the deaths and injuries among British troops in such a thankless cause are increasingly questioned."[163]

After these revelations, the public lost faith in the merits of the army's intervention. A poll published in September 1971 indicated that 59 percent of people in Britain wanted their soldiers to be withdrawn immediately.[164] More disturbing for ministers, 48 percent of respondents in December 1971 said they disapproved of the government's handling of the problem, against 34 percent who approved. After internment, a majority of survey respondents said they thought Labour could handle the problem better than the Conservatives.

Internment, the interrogation techniques, and Nationalists' protests received intensive media coverage in Britain, much of it directed against the Unionist government. Characteristic of the liberal media view at this period is a full-length book published in January 1972 by a team of journalists from the *Sunday Times*. They concluded that Stormont could not survive because the state of Northern Ireland was itself was sectarian: "Protestant supremacy was the only reason why the State existed. As such the State itself was an immoral concept." The British army was defending "a morally indefensible entity."[165]

This was the media context for Bloody Sunday, which received extensive coverage and added greatly to the British public's dissatisfaction. *The Times* quoted a photographer for a national newspaper: "I was appalled. [The soldiers] opened up into a dense crowd of people. As far as I could see, they did not fire over people's heads at all. There appeared to be no warning."[166] Despite such eyewitness reports, many editors tried to justify the soldiers' behavior, shifting the blame onto the organizers of the march by pointing out that it was illegal. Even the reputedly liberal *Guardian* spoke of the army's "intolerably difficult task" and held that "neither side can escape condemnation."[167]

Associated with the exculpation of the army, the press tended to depict the conflict as one between two factions of irrational Irish extremists and essentially none of Britain's concern. As in 1969 there was little sympathy for the Unionists, who were now depicted as letting British soldiers fight their battles for them while refusing to offer even modest concessions to reasonable minority demands. During a cabinet discussion on the implications of Bloody Sunday on February 3, ministers noted that in Britain, "a growing section of public opinion wished to see British troops withdrawn." They concluded that "in order to retain a broad measure of public support for the maintenance of large military forces in Northern Ireland, it was desirable that movement towards some political solution of the conflict should be seen to be in prospect."[168] A bipartisan consensus would help to take the heat out of the public debate, and in this instance, Heath's strategy was aimed in part at reducing the popular appeal of the growing Troops Out movement in Britain.[169]

During February and March 1972, newspapers that were generally well disposed to the Conservative government trailed the direct-rule package in a series of inspired leaks apparently intended to test key players' reactions.[170] An editorial in *The Spectator*, which in July 1971 had called for tougher measures against the IRA, called for direct rule on the ground that Stormont could not satisfy the fundamental requirement of guaranteeing the minority a genuine role in the regional administration.[171] On

February 13, the *Sunday Times* reported that the government was considering important changes in the structure of the Stormont institutions: to bring in a Catholic as deputy prime minister, appoint three or four Catholics to the cabinet, and hold periodic referenda on the border. Faulkner complained to Heath that such reports were "distinctly unhelpful."[172] Heath replied that the articles were "pure speculation," a form of words that, while possibly true, did not deny the articles' accuracy.

Briefed by government mandarins, the establishment press bought into Heath's wishful thinking. *The Times* maintained that if Stormont's powers were reduced to match those of local government in England and border plebiscites were arranged, then "all logical and legislative if not all psychological obstacles to full Republican participation in government would be removed, as would the validity of Protestant fears and objections to mixed Unionist and Republican parties ... as the question of the border would be irrelevant to the issues with which Parliament was competent to deal, the political parties would be forced to campaign on the basis of their social and economic policies."[173] In a lengthy article, which Terence O'Neill commended in a private letter to Heath, commentator John Graham argued that the military security approach had not reduced the IRA's effectiveness, since the terrorists were able to strike without fear from across the border. The prospects for an internally negotiated political settlement were no better, since the gap between Unionists and Nationalists was too great. Consequently, any political solution must be imposed from outside.[174] On the eve of direct rule, an editorial in *The Spectator* encapsulated the media criticism of Maudling: "For months now the policy of doing nothing has been a failed policy ... the Government has been failing in its imperative duty. It has been transfixed in inactivity."[175]

## The International Dimension

The Irish government shared the Conservatives' interest in securing a peaceful settlement in Northern Ireland and weakening the IRA, if only to prevent the violence from spreading south. But they differed from London in that they had a direct interest in demonstrating to their constituents that their policies were producing improvements for the Nationalist minority and promoting—or at least not obstructing progress toward—unification. From the outset of the Troubles in 1969, they had sought to use the situation in Northern Ireland to advance their constitutional imperative of unification. Radical political reform favoring the Nationalist side would at least be a useful first step in that direction, since it would destroy the Unionist hegemony and admit Nationalists to positions of power and influence. This was particularly important if Dublin was at the same time seen to be cooperating with the British by tackling the IRA.

Britain's military security policy had exacerbated tensions between London and Dublin by July 1971; internment and its consequences made matters much worse. Paddy Hillery, the Irish minister for external affairs, visited Maudling in London on August 9 to protest and to demand "a political solution which would give the minority a proper opportunity to participate in the government of the Province."[176] He indicated that it would be politically impossible for the Irish government to take any action against the IRA that appeared to sustain "Orange rule" in Northern Ireland. As a first step, he proposed a commission government with 50-50 representation for the minority.

Lynch telephoned Heath on August 10, when he dismissed Faulkner's offer to the SDLP of a committee system at Stormont as too little, too late, and indicated that it had been overtaken by the reaction to internment. He then issued a public statement denouncing internment and (as in 1969) set up army camps along the border for Catholics who had abandoned their homes. He threatened that unless London abandoned its policy—which he depicted as attempting a military solution—he would publicly endorse the SDLP's protest campaign, including the rent and rates strike. Echoing Hume, he demanded that Stormont should "be replaced by an administration in which power and decision-making will be equally shared between Unionist and non-Unionist."[177] This was a significant new departure for the Irish government. In place of reunification, it sought (albeit only as a first step) to replace Stormont with a new form of shared devolved administration.

Heath at first replied with a curt telegram telling Lynch that it was unacceptable for Dublin to interfere in the affairs of the United Kingdom. He deplored "the fact that you should have publicly taken up a position so calculated not only to increase the tension in Northern Ireland but also to impair our effort to maintain good relations between the United Kingdom and the Irish Republic." This firm riposte delighted Faulkner but alarmed Whitehall. Ambassador Peck described the exchanges between the two premiers at this period as "a dialogue of the deaf."[178]

In the following days, the Foreign and Commonwealth Office (FCO) persuaded Heath that humiliating the taoiseach would make it more difficult for Lynch to cooperate in fighting the IRA and ending northern nationalists' disaffection. Lynch had not asserted Dublin's constitutional claim to the north but was instead calling for Nationalist participation at Stormont, a stance that implicitly recognized the fact of partition.[179] The diplomats convinced Heath that Lynch was "the best Irish Prime Minister

we are likely to have" and that if he fell from office, "the likeliest replacement for him was a government led by the likes of Charles Haughey."[180]

Thereafter Heath was noticeably more conciliatory. He invited Lynch
for a two-day summit at Chequers, his official country residence, on September 6–7. It was the two premiers' first meeting devoted to Northern Ireland. Heath not only initiated it but moved it up from the date originally
planned, October 20. Heath was accompanied by Trend, Lynch by Irish
ambassador O'Sullivan. The taoiseach began by rehearsing his contention
that partition was the root cause of the violence, and asked Heath to commit himself to working toward unification as the only effective long-term
solution. In the meantime, Stormont should be replaced by an administration that shared power between elected representatives from the two
communities. It would be politically impossible for the SDLP to return to
Stormont on any other basis. This was the same message that Hume had
given Maudling.

In reply, Heath indicated that the United Kingdom would not stand in
the way if a majority of the Northern Ireland electorate wanted to change
its constitutional status. He believed that in time, the accession of the UK
and Ireland to the EEC would lead to a solution. In the meantime, it did
not make sense for the SDLP to boycott Stormont, and a power-sharing
arrangement was undemocratic and hence unacceptable: 50-50 representation would be unfair to the majority. He agreed, however, that the
minority should have a guarantee of full and fair participation in government until such time as a majority favored unification. If minority elected
representatives wanted this, they should join in talks about the modalities
for bringing it about; it would be difficult to engineer participation in the
government of Northern Ireland for those who refused to negotiate and
were openly trying to destroy it.

Lynch replied that he was not prepared to encourage the SDLP's leaders to participate in dialogue with Maudling on that basis. They had indicated that they would talk on certain conditions, one of which was that
the Irish government should also be included. Irritated, Heath replied that
neither Faulkner nor the Conservative Party would accept four-way talks
on the internal business of Northern Ireland: "everybody recognized" that
the taoiseach and the SDLP were operating in tandem. On the second day
of the talks Heath offered to convene a joint meeting between the two of
them and Faulkner, without the SDLP. Lynch countered that if Heath
brought Faulkner as a Unionist representative, he should be entitled to
bring an SDLP representative. Heath again urged Lynch to press the SDLP
to cooperate. He said that there was never sympathy in Britain for abolishing an established institution, so there could be no question of replacing

Stormont with an unelected commission. Lynch persisted, referring to Switzerland and Belgium as possible models for a future constitution.

The meeting ended without any specific agreement. Yet Garret Fitzgerald, minister for external affairs in the next Irish government, later wrote that the two days "marked a significant advance on the British side since it recognised the Irish Government's legitimate interest in a situation threatening the security of both parts of the island."[181] The encounter also gave both leaders a better appreciation of each other's position. Previously, Heath had accepted Faulkner's contention that the solution to the problem lay in defeating the IRA militarily. Subsequently, he maintained that there could be no lasting solution without the cooperation of the Irish government and that the northern minority should have full and fair participation in the regional government. Heath also came to regard Irish Nationalism and Northern Irish Unionism as equally legitimate perspectives requiring institutional reconciliation. The British state would no longer act as a protagonist for the union. It would be a neutral umpire, seeking to ensure fair play between two equally valid (albeit in his view unenlightened and reactionary) political traditions. Whether Northern Ireland was British or not was a matter of indifference to the British state. It was for the people of the region to decide.

The immediate upshot of the meeting was that Heath persuaded Lynch and Faulkner, despite their reservations, to attend another extended meeting at Chequers on September 27–28. Faulkner was unwilling to be seen as accepting Dublin's right to interfere in Stormont's affairs, but agreed to attend on the understanding that he would not be discussing Northern Ireland's constitutional status.[182] Lynch agreed to attend on the basis that there should be no restrictions on the agenda. Clearly, both did not get what they wanted, though both told their supporters they had.

Lynch's officials prepared a series of briefs summarizing Dublin's thinking. Among the salient elements were[183] that Britain should withdraw its constitutional guarantee for the Unionists and indicate publicly that it favored Irish unity, and that "the North is in fact a dual State and should be organised accordingly." The British army should not be shoring up the Unionist regime; the IRA could be beaten only by moderate anti-Unionist leaders who could separate the Catholic community from them. To strengthen the moderates' position, there must be immediate and radical changes to break the Unionists' monopoly of power and open up new political options. The participation of minority representatives should be in a form that could bring about Irish unity rather than maintaining the union—that is, it should be for Nationalists as such rather than Catholics. An all-Ireland council should be established to work toward bringing the

two jurisdictions "into harmony," and as a first step, control over the administration of justice should be transferred temporarily from Stormont
to Westminster.

Heath's memoirs record the tripartite meeting as "one of the historic
events of my premiership." It was the first time that the leaders of the three
jurisdictions had met together since 1925. Lynch began by reiterating the
position he had previously outlined to Heath. Faulkner responded by rehearsing the reforms already implemented since 1969 and under way, and
emphasizing his willingness to do more once the IRA had been defeated.
As a matter of practical politics, he did not see how it would be possible for
Nationalists to participate in good faith in the Northern Ireland cabinet,
since their avowed intention was to abolish the Stormont system.

The following day, Heath and Lynch met without Faulkner. Heath indicated that he was not prepared to concede to the SDLP's demand for an
end to internment to bring them to the talks table, yet discussion offered
the only real hope of progress. Lynch replied that the great bulk of minority opinion supported the SDLP's stance, and warned that if the route to
political progress were obstructed, the Nationalist community would fall
increasingly under IRA influence. The talks then ended, again with no announcement of substantive agreement. In a final exchange with Maudling
and Heath, Faulkner expressed the view that the SDLP was more basically
republican "than they would like us to believe," and not really interested in
pursuing an agreement with Unionism: "What they really wanted was the
end of Stormont."[184]

Although the two September meetings did not produce any formal or
public agreement, they marked a turning point in British policy. Lynch
privately told his party colleagues that he had secured Heath's agreement
to include Nationalists by right in the Northern Ireland cabinet.[185] Heath
followed up swiftly, summoning Faulkner to Downing Street for a further
meeting on October 7, at which he pressed to include Nationalist elected
representatives at least in an interim emergency government. Faulkner refused, although he did agree to explore ways of including more "constitu-
tionalist" Catholics in decision-making, perhaps through a council composed of interest group representatives whose chair could sit in the cabinet.
Heath expressed disappointment at the limited scope of this concession
but encouraged Faulkner to proceed with the appointment of a minister who would at least be seen as representative of "responsible" minority
opinion.[186] Heath later wrote in his memoirs that he had come to believe
both that Catholics had to be given a positive role in governing the country in which they lived and that the Republic had to be brought into the
equation.[187] Lynch had successfully persuaded him to accept that the Irish

government had a legitimate role to play in developing a solution, and to consider seriously his proposals for the sharing of power.

Notwithstanding the improvements in relations at the highest level, the Irish government—still under pressure to prove its patriotic credentials—moved ahead with such measures as supporting the SDLP's alternative assembly rhetorically and financially, and preparing a case against Britain before the European Court in Strasbourg on the ground that the mistreatment of internees revealed in the Compton Report breached the European Convention on Human Rights.[188] The Irish rightly calculated that this would incense Heath. Hugh McCann, a senior Irish official, noted the tactical advantage this would give Dublin. Action in Strasbourg "would inevitably make the British much more careful in their handling of detainees and internees in the North. To the extent that this would slow down their gathering of intelligence information it would make it more difficult for them to make progress in the direction of a military solution. If they succeeded in containing the situation from a military point of view there would be less incentive for them to take unpalatable political action."[189] The obvious implications were that, first, Dublin recognized Britain's success in acquiring intelligence from internees and the value of that intelligence, and second, Dublin had a stake in impeding efforts to defeat the IRA, at least until Britain had agreed to introduce reforms that would open up the path to unification.

At a meeting on November 29, 1971, the Interdepartmental Committee on the North outlined the position to be taken in negotiation with the British in the new (and more favorable) context that Wilson's departure from bipartisanship created at Westminster:

> We should . . . inform the British that we have amassed an enormous amount of convincing material on allegations of torture, brutality, etc., in Northern Ireland; that the pressures on the government to take action in Strasbourg are almost irresistible; that the Irish government would prefer to see the matter settled amicably between the two countries; that we could only refrain from referring the matter to Strasbourg if internal security, law, and order were removed from Stormont's control; that it would be in Britain's interest that Stormont be given no further opportunity to blacken Britain's international image; that any realistic assessment of the situation in Northern Ireland could only lead to the conclusion that security matters will have to be removed from the Northern Ireland government at some stage.[190]

The British correspondingly recognized that hostility toward the Republic would not only kill off any prospect of cooperation in tackling the IRA but also damage Britain's wider diplomatic and economic interests and impair the preparations then under way for the two countries' accession to the EEC.[191]

As well as applying diplomatic pressure through Europe and negoti-ating directly with British ministers, Dublin sought to influence British policy through Wilson. The Irish contributed to developing Wilson's fif-teen-point plan, and before presenting it in the Commons, he outlined it to a select group of Irish ministers and officials at an off-the-record dinner the taoiseach held in his honor in Dublin.

In briefing the taoiseach for Wilson's visit, Eamon Gallagher of the Irish Department of External Affairs (DEA) noted the advantages National-ism would gain if Wilson ended the bipartisan approach at Westminster: "Principally it would serve notice on Unionism that a new order of things will be enforced on them sooner or later by a British Labour Government." Wilson could advance the Irish cause by showing Unionists that it was not necessarily in their interest to remain British at all costs. The Unionists' monopoly of authority in the north had to be broken: "John Hume is par-ticularly clear on this subject and the SDLP are adamant about it. Wilson should therefore be invited to support the idea of a bipolar government. . . . Support for the idea by the British Labour Party would make it ineluctable sooner rather than later." To guard against republican accusations that the sharing of power would perpetuate partition, there would also have to be a strong all-Ireland link, such as the Council of Ireland that Wilson had already proposed. In the long term, the council's purpose would be "to prepare for the transfer of sovereignty in the North from London to an all-Ireland Parliament in progressive steps." Tactically, Gallagher suggested that the taoiseach should flatter Wilson on his accomplishment in elimi-nating the USC, then point out that the logical next step was to elimi-nate the Unionist government, since it could no longer assert its authority without British support. The threat of a Unionist backlash should not be allowed to paralyze progress. As regards Maudling's planned round table conference, there was no point in trying to negotiate a solution. It would have to be imposed. "Stormont should be suspended: only when Unionism is reduced to being an equal partner with the minority in discussions will it become realistic about its position."[192]

According to the Irish official note of their ministers' "off-the-record" dinner conversation, Wilson said that the conflict could be ended only by "the production of a new magic formula designed to effect a political solu-tion to present difficulties." It "would have to be produced not at a meeting between Governments but at a special conference representing all politi-cal parties in Great Britain, Northern Ireland, and Southern Ireland—and indeed possibly taking account of political opinion not represented at the moment in the three parliaments (a euphemistic reference to the IRA)." Each of the interests represented would have to make sacrifices. In return for unification the parties in Dublin would have to agree to return to membership in the British Commonwealth. In a sideswipe at Heath, he "dismissed with acerbity the suggestion that the entry of the two islands into the EEC would have any bearing on the political solution to the partition question."[193]

Lynch had other levers to use against Heath. One was of particular importance to the British army: cooperation in controlling republican violence. First, in discussions with Peck, Lynch had made much of the political risks he would be taking if he moved against the IRA, and of the impossibility of doing so without visible evidence of progress toward unification. Second, he could influence the SDLP to act for or against British interests. He had promoted their alternative assembly and supported the rent and rates strike. In October, notwithstanding the gains he claimed to have made at earlier meetings, he instituted a partial boycott of his own, refusing to meet Heath again until and unless Britain first declared its interest in a united Ireland to be achieved by agreement and accepted the principle that minority elected representatives should be included in the government of the north by right.[194]

With the publication of Wilson's fifteen-point plan, their three-stage strategy for unification seemed to officials in Dublin to be working well.[195] On November 26, the secretary to the Interdepartmental Committee reported to the taoiseach that in light of Wilson's proposals, "the circumstances have sufficiently advanced to suggest that the [interdepartmental] unit should now consider in detail the possible shape of a long-term solution to Irish unity in a measurable time."[196] Despite his declared refusal to engage with Heath again until the British had something tangible to offer, Lynch kept his lines of communication open. He met Heath informally in London on December 6, after giving a speech to a gathering of British MPs and political journalists, using the occasion to stress the urgent need for a radical political initiative.[197] The two met again in Brussels on January 24, when the taoiseach argued that the time was ripe; the IRA had suffered a serious setback, but Protestants still remained "sufficiently alarmed to contemplate change."[198] He told Heath that "he was prepared to say to his own people that they could not expect a million Protestants to change their views on eventual unification unless they in the South made some changes of their own." When Heath signaled a reluctance to impose power sharing, Lynch threatened that if the British continued to let matters drift, he would take an initiative himself; he then indicated that he would shortly be meeting Wilson again. Thus, on a highly salient issue that he had made a personal priority, Heath faced the prospect of a potentially damaging challenge from an alliance between the Westminster opposition and a neighboring state, without the cooperation of which he could achieve neither his military nor his political objectives.

Bloody Sunday set back Lynch's plan to present himself as the leader of a new pluralist nationalism throughout Ireland. An estimated 30,000 people took part in a protest demonstration in Dublin, during which the British embassy was burned down. British stores were firebombed and workers closed Irish airports to British airlines. Lynch recalled the Irish ambassador from London and declared a day of national mourning. He demanded that the British army be withdrawn from Nationalist areas, internment ended, and a conference of all parties, including the Irish government, convened to seek agreement on new constitutional arrangements. He publicly endorsed the SDLP's withdrawal from Stormont by announcing that he would fund the "Assembly of the Northern Irish People," which it had created.[199] The British ambassador in Dublin lost no time in reporting to London that the shift in popular sentiment as a result of Bloody Sunday had made Lynch's already shaky position "extremely precarious."[200] Just as Faulkner had done in requesting the introduction of internment, so Lynch with Peck's help turned his weakness to advantage. His vulnerability strengthened his hand in dealing with Heath.

The breakdown in diplomatic relations with Dublin was highly unwelcome to Heath.[201] The *Observer* reported that Heath had been "astonished and disconcerted by the virulence of the Irish reactions to Derry" and in his gloomier moments envisaged Ireland as Britain's Cuba.[202] At a cabinet meeting on February 3, he argued that "it was desirable to lower the political tension in the Republic, if possible, particularly in view of Mr. Lynch's precarious position and the absence of any successor who could exert a moderating influence."[203]

Behind his public expressions of anger, Lynch was anxious to make progress. He was concerned about the costs of the conflict to the Irish economy. Republicans were raiding banks to raise funds, business confidence was sagging, inward investment was declining, and the tourist trade was suffering. He also faced political and security risks associated with the escalation in violence and its possible spread south. His own armed forces had advised him that Ireland's military strength was critically inadequate to meet a number of scenarios potentially arising out of the violence: armed insurgency in the Republic; incursions by the British or loyalists across the border; and any requirement to intervene in the north, such as to defend Catholic communities from loyalist attacks in the event of a sudden British withdrawal.[204]

Reassured by Peck that Heath was about to take a radical initiative, Lynch won support at Fianna Fáil's annual conference on February 20,

1972, for the proposal that minority elected representatives should participate in a new northern administration, a development that must have encouraged London to proceed. For if Lynch could take Fianna Fáil with him to support a policy that appeared to some to undermine Ireland's constitutional claim to the north, the prospects for success looked much more promising. If this was the official position of the state to which they aspired to belong, SDLP leaders would be under pressure at least to engage seriously in talks. A survey of public opinion in the Republic on the eve of direct rule showed that 68 percent of respondents would "support a political settlement which maintained the status of Northern Ireland as part of the United Kingdom but gave the Catholic minority equal civil rights and proportionate representation in the Stormont government."[205]

The taoiseach's willingness to compromise did not, of course, extend to sustaining Stormont. Lynch made no serious attempt to engage Faulkner in dialogue or to sell the benefits of a united Ireland to the Unionist community. Irish ministers did not trust Faulkner and did not believe that he would ever introduce the radical changes they wanted unless London forced him to. Lynch and Faulkner grandstanded to their respective parties by attacking one another in the media. Faulkner accused Lynch of interfering in Northern Ireland's affairs and of harboring terrorists for his own political ends, while Lynch condemned Faulkner for repressing Catholics and violating their human rights under the pretext of eradicating terrorism.[206] Faulkner's attacks on Lynch—consistent though they were with Heath's brusque telegram of August 1971—irritated British diplomats who were working to repair relations with Dublin. Unfortunately for Faulkner, Heath shared his officials' irritation.[207]

It is clear that having helped the SDLP into being, the Irish government continued to coordinate strategy and tactics with them. At a meeting between Irish ministers and SDLP notables on February 11, 1972, they exchanged intelligence and ideas on the expected British political initiative.[208] The SDLP indicated that in the adverse political context created by Bloody Sunday, they would have to reject any package that fell short of abolishing Stormont, setting up an interim commission to administer the north, four-way talks covering the process of unification, and an end to internment. They opposed "community government because it would be a permanent elected system." Presentationally, the Nationalist side should let the "diehard" Unionists reject the proposals first; the SDLP could then point to their unreasonableness. Once the commission had come into being, "Protestants would start to rethink their position." The SDLP pressed the ministers to move in the direction of accepting Protestant opinion on such family policy issues as divorce and contraception, where the Irish state appeared to be subject to the direction of the Catholic Church.

Knowing that Heath was greatly concerned about Britain's relations with America and Europe, Dublin further amplified its voice by lobbying friendly governments for the changes that it wanted in British policy.[209] Gerry Fitt had already conducted a speaking tour of Irish-American communities after internment began; he had also spoken to the secretary-general of the United Nations.[210] A report from the British embassy in Washington in December 1971 noted that, in pursuit of his bid for the Democratic Party's presidential nomination, U.S. senator Hubert Humphrey had called to end internment and unify Ireland, and that there was speculation that Senator Ted Kennedy intended to press to include a proposal for unification in the Democrats' platform for the 1972 presidential election.[211]

Dublin's diplomatic campaign intensified after Bloody Sunday. Patrick Hillery toured the United Nations, Washington, and the major capital cities of the EEC, calling on other states to press the United Kingdom for a radical initiative. Heath congratulated himself that "my cordial relationship with President Nixon ensured that the U.S. did not intervene, despite the pressure to which Nixon was subjected by his large Irish-American contingent."[212] The State Department may have rejected the lobbyists' demand for an official condemnation of Britain, but influential congressmen were less reticent. At a House Foreign Affairs Committee hearing on Northern Ireland, Senator Kennedy and Congressman Tip O'Neill called to abolish Stormont and substitute a United Nations peacekeeping force for the British army. British diplomats were concerned that republicans would exploit these developments to increase the flow of weapons and funds from the United States to the IRA.

Hillery's European visits were even more successful. As early as April 1971, Peck had advised Irish ministers to "play the EEC card for all it was worth" in negotiating with Heath, which they duly did.[213] Heath was particularly anxious that events in Ireland should not prejudice Britain's entry into the EEC.[214] He and Lynch both signed the treaty of accession in Brussels on January 29, 1972, and their two countries were scheduled to become full members in January 1973. As a leading Irish politician noted, "informed opinion in Dublin looks to pressure from EEC sources on the UK government as potentially the most hopeful external source of assistance towards a solution."[215] Robert Ramsay—who as Faulkner's principal private secretary had a ringside seat during the events of the period—suggests that "the threat from the French was decisive: the Stormont government was sacrificed on the altar of [Heath's] European ambitions."[216] Ramsay points to Hillery's February 8 visit to Paris and to a briefing paper prepared in the Quai d'Orsay for French foreign minister Maurice Schumann. This notes that while France had been reluctant to intervene in a British internal matter—in part because of France's own previous position on other nations' attempts to intervene in Algeria—it was for consideration whether France could simply stand back as the situation deteriorated: "As Great Britain and Ireland prepare to join the Common Market, the deterioration in Northern Ireland, if it continues, will be likely to weigh heavily on the good functioning of the Community and, consequently, will affect ourselves, even if only indirectly. Moreover, we cannot easily show ourselves to be disinterested in a matter which brings into conflict two friendly neighboring countries."[217] Schumann met British ambassador Christopher Soames in Paris on February 4.[218]

### Key Ministers

### Maudling

Until internment, Heath had been content to delegate responsibility for Northern Ireland to Maudling, Faulkner, and army commanders. After internment, he listened more attentively to Maudling's critics. Those who worked closely with the home secretary describe him as an intelligent and sophisticated political operator,[219] but Maudling's critics attacked him for failing to impose political direction, and many spoke of his disengagement from the issue. Heath's biographer suggests that Maudling did not pull his weight in cabinet—that he was too easygoing for the Home Office and distracted by the looming personal scandal that would lead to his resignation later in 1972.[220] Maurice Hayes, who met Maudling in London with a delegation from the Community Relations Commission, described how "the visit left my colleagues totally depressed at the apparent lack of information, poor understanding of the problem, and lack of strategic policy direction at the centre of the British government."[221] Publisher Cecil King, who made a habit of keeping in contact with both British and Irish ministers, told an Irish diplomat in January 1972 that he had told Heath to find another job for the home secretary because "Mr Maudling and the Irish are incapable of understanding each other."[222]

Some of Maudling's public statements do suggest a simplistic, overly optimistic, and passive view of the problem. In one Commons debate he said: "I look forward, as I am sure we all do, to the time when the political battles of Northern Ireland are fought between Conservative and Labour and not between Catholic and Protestant; there will not be a lasting solution in Northern Ireland until that is so."[223] This seems a rather extraordinary aspiration, especially since neither national party showed any intention of organizing in Northern Ireland; the leaderships of both were in fact moving in the opposite direction. He seems to have had difficulty empathizing with Northern Ireland and its people; he is best remembered there for his heartfelt complaint on the plane back from his first visit: "For God's sake bring me a large Scotch, what a bloody awful country."[224] The preamble to the cabinet paper in which he presented his strategic political initiative included this dismissive observation: "Sometimes it seems as if the people of Northern Ireland, or at any rate their political leaders, are possessed of a death wish."[225]

Moderate Unionists, such as O'Neill, were among Maudling's sternest critics. Michael Wolff—one of Heath's closest political advisers—wrote to the prime minister on February 5 to report on his contacts with the NUM: "They said that their 'disillusion with the lack of Westminster Government policy and leadership had brought them close to despair.' . . . They claim that the assault by Miss Devlin [Bernadette Devlin, the republican MP who physically attacked Maudling in the Commons after Bloody Sunday] has the widespread support of Protestants as well as Catholics because it 'seemed to be the only way to wake up the Home Secretary.'"[226] Maudling had a personal stake in the outcome of the cabinet's deliberations. By February 1972, he had by his own account become overwhelmed by the pressures of the job and wanted a Northern Ireland secretary appointed who would take the burden off his shoulders.[227]

## Heath

Neither cabinet records nor participants' memoirs reveal how much Heath held Maudling responsible for the deteriorating climate. He did not publicly criticize his home secretary. But he clearly concluded that more concentrated political attention needed to be devoted to the issue than Maudling—who bore other substantial official responsibilities—could give it. After internment Heath assumed direct responsibility for "the Irish problem," which he ranked as one of three priorities for his personal attention.[228] He set the parameters and forced the pace, requiring Maudling to take successively larger steps as the political pressures increased, from obliging Faulkner to come up with reform proposals in September, to voluntary coalition in November, the transfer of security powers, and mandatory coalition in January, and finally, direct rule. He did not spare Maudling's dignity. Faulkner noted that during one meeting with Heath and the taoiseach he had "felt sorry for Reggie Maudling, who was kept waiting at Chequers during the talks and had to ask various civil servants if they knew what was going on."[229]

Heath's memoirs note that Maudling was initially reluctant to introduce direct rule because he believed that Stormont was useful in insulating Westminster from an intractable and controversial problem.[230] Heath also confirms that all the other ministers directly involved at first opposed important elements in the direct-rule package. He claims that the cabinet eventually agreed unanimously on the package, but as we have seen, a close reading of the minutes suggests that they were not so much persuaded by the quality of the prime minister's arguments as ground into acquiescence by his repeated insistence on a dramatic move, sufficiently radical to secure the cooperation of Nationalist Ireland. He would not accept any decision other than acceptance.

Paul Arthur has commended Heath for "his sense of history, awareness of interdependence, and constructive imagination" in addressing the issue, while faulting his skills in conciliation and communication.[231] Peck describes a similar dichotomy: "Mr Heath has a penetrating mind and having discovered what he considers to be the right objective displays great tenacity and courage, without overmuch finesse or flexibility, in attaining it."[232] Others have described him as cold and aloof. Bloomfield, who met the prime minister while working for Faulkner, recalls "a lonely implacable arrogance at the heart of his nature, particularly when he assumed that grim, square-faced demeanour sometimes described as his 'Easter Island face.'"[233] He wore this face for his meeting with Faulkner on March 22, 1972, which he "brought to an unexpected and brutal crunch" by delivering his blunt ultimatum.[234] Heath himself subsequently conceded that he had "always found the Irish, all of them, extremely difficult to understand."[235]

*Carrington*

Defence Secretary Carrington was skeptical about the prospects for coalition government.[236] But he was also the first cabinet minister to argue the case for a radical change of direction. Within a few days of internment, he was lobbying for security to be transferred to Westminster and a political initiative to break the impasse.[237] This position reflected the views of senior military commanders, who resented having been bounced into internment against their professional judgment to save Faulkner's leadership. At a cabinet meeting on September 21, Carrington relayed the commanders' complaints. Internment had boosted IRA recruitment and led to the creation of no-go areas in Derry from which the army was excluded. If the security situation declined further, direct rule might become the only alternative to "an extreme Protestant Government."[238]

Carrington argued that military and policing operations should be integrated and that this could be done effectively only under full UK control.[239] The transfer was essential also to win the cooperation of the Nationalist minority and the Dublin government, without both of which the IRA could not be defeated. The other ministers at GEN 47—Douglas-Home,

Whitelaw, and Maudling—at first resisted Carrington's arguments for change.[240] But he stood his course until events and political pressures combined to help him to turn his colleagues around.

### Douglas-Home

During the critical cabinet debate on the direct-rule package, the foreign secretary wrote in a personal note to Heath: "I really dislike direct rule for Northern Ireland because I do not believe they are like the Scots or the Welsh and doubt if they ever will be."[241] He personally favored pushing the Unionists toward a united Ireland, although he did not spell out how. Like Carrington, he anticipated that the proposed discussions with the parties in Northern Ireland would fail to reach agreement. Unlike Carrington, he argued that direct rule would be seen as a concession to violence, which would encourage the IRA and divide the Conservative Party.[242]

### The Pressure Balance

From August 1971 to March 1972, Heath endured heavy political and diplomatic pressure to take a radical initiative. Against a backdrop of escalating death and destruction, his critics argued that the previous policies of reform and coercion had both demonstrably failed. Almost all the pressure—at Westminster, in the national media, and internationally—favored concessions to Nationalist Ireland, and even some in the Unionist Party agreed with this consensus. Apart from others in the Unionist Party, a handful of Conservative backbenchers, and one significant national newspaper, no serious player advocated either a predominantly coercive approach or merely incremental adjustments in the status quo. Outside the Protestant community in Northern Ireland, the Unionist Party was depicted as reactionary and sectarian, a view that UK ministers privately shared. Apart from a handful of Unionists and Conservative mavericks, detested by Heath and his senior ministers, Faulkner had no support in the Commons.

## Structure and Doctrine

The final strand of explanation focuses on the organizational dimension, particularly the prior decision to transfer responsibility for security from Belfast to Westminster. Organization theory would have predicted in 1969 that once Whitehall's bureaucracies had gained a foothold in Northern Ireland, they would seek gradually to extend their power and influence there. It is axiomatic that public sector agencies do not like competing for authority and resources within their areas of responsibility. Once Stormont had ceased to be a partner, it became a rival. When did the shift occur, and how did Whitehall respond?

## Home Office

The Home Office's constructionist doctrine had underpinned Maudling's initial hands-off approach to Northern Ireland. But it was thoroughly transformed by the political crises of March and August 1971, when Maudling had to justify his stewardship to the Commons. The Home Office by default assumed a role in developing policies for constitutional reform that took its senior officials well beyond their familiar territory of criminal justice, immigration, and race relations. From two staff members in October 1969, the Home Office had by June 1971 increased its Northern Ireland complement to twenty, including one under secretary—the third tier in the Whitehall hierarchy—and two assistant secretaries.

Advice for ministers was coordinated during this period by a committee of senior officials chaired by the PUS, the top official at the Home Office, and including the director general of the security service MI5. Originally activated by the crisis over Chichester-Clark's resignation, ministers tasked this group, dubbed the NI Officials, with addressing the imminent possibility of an administration at Stormont that openly defied their authority and refused to carry forward the reforms already agreed to. The group met at least monthly. They looked at draft legislation to replace Stormont and reviewed the military preparations for dealing with a possible loyalist reaction against direct rule. Naturally they considered the administrative implications. Inter alia, the Northern Ireland section at the Home Office would have to be expanded from two to six divisions.[243]

The group was actively exploring possibilities for radical constitutional reform as early as May 1971, long before Maudling pressed Faulkner into producing his green paper. They seconded an official named Pemberton to UKREP for ten days. Pemberton, who specialized in electoral reform, reportedly told John Hume in May 1971 that the Home Office intended "to bring about participation by the minority in the administration of the North. They are looking at multi-seat PR in local government and for Stormont itself with this in mind."[244] On May 19, NI Officials considered a memorandum prepared by the Home Office on "the Irish Problem." This outlined options for an initiative to be taken if the situation changed dramatically for the worse or, interestingly, for the better, "in which case there might be an opportunity to attempt to break out of the recurring cycles of tension and disorder." The options included electoral law reform, which, it was believed, would encourage moderates and the minority, for example by introducing PR voting for Stormont elections and remodeling the senate; direct rule; persuading Northern Ireland to become independent; and adjusting the border.

In discussing these proposals, the PUS noted that Britain's long-term objectives (not options) "must include the creation of a united Ireland. . . . In preparation for the longer term, we should examine how far the Irish Republic would be ready to adapt itself politically and socially to accommodate the Ulster Protestants." The mandarins also observed that "direct rule on a Scottish or Welsh pattern might not be consistent with our ultimate intention of promoting a united Ireland." One member—probably the Treasury representative—registered a financial interest in expelling Northern Ireland from the union, in that the province "was given a disproportionate amount of support from the Exchequer."[245]

When the Nationalist backlash against internment prompted Heath to give personal priority to the planned initiative, the Home Office created a high-level political development unit to focus exclusively on Northern Ireland. This moved beyond contingency planning to proactive thinking about Britain's long-term strategic objectives.[246] The officials who staffed the new unit saw their role not as stabilizing the Unionist government but as transforming the Northern Ireland constitution. Northern Ireland was no longer a routine issue for maintenance by junior staff at the bottom of the administrative hierarchy but an issue of high and continuing political salience through which ambitious officials could display creativity and advance their careers.

One of the new unit's first products was a top-secret paper summarizing the conditions under which direct rule might be imposed:[247] if a deliberate strategy was needed to break the political deadlock, if the IRA campaign rendered normal life impossible, if Protestants took up arms against the minority, if Faulkner resigned leaving no credible alternative, and if after a general election there was the possibility that "an extreme Protestant" might form an administration.[248] From this perspective direct rule looked increasingly attractive—Faulkner's position as Unionist Party leader was already precarious and crumbling—and the new doctrine recognized that it might be beneficial even if Stormont was in safe hands and the violence under control. This was a paradigm shift in official thinking, and ministers collectively followed suit three months later, in February 1972.

As Home Office resources and attention devoted to the problem grew, the capacity of the Stormont administration to influence UK policies correspondingly fell. After internment, relations between the NICS and the Home Office deteriorated sharply. One Northern Ireland permanent secretary noted with regret that the Home Office about this time "suddenly began for some unknown reason to be difficult with us. Anything we put

to them was regarded with suspicion and handled with tongs."[249] Whitehall had created its own internal capability to develop political plans and
constitutional proposals; it no longer needed Stormont. When Faulkner's
officials learned that the Home Office was preparing contingency plans
for transferring powers to Westminster, they began to draw up defensive
tactics of their own.[250]

Despite their newfound activism, Home Office mandarins remained
skeptical about the prospects for coalition government. As late as March 8,
1972, the PUS was advising Maudling to proceed with direct rule as an
end in itself, but to drop the community government element as "question-
able in principle and unworkable in practice."[251]

### Cabinet Office

It has been suggested that the impetus for direct rule came from the Central Policy Review Staff (CPRS), a think tank Heath created inside the
Cabinet Office to advise him on complex cross-departmental issues.[252] It
is certainly true that Heath received a preliminary options paper from the
CPRS on September 3, which persuaded him that some form of power
sharing was essential "at least as an interim measure."[253] However, other
material provided subsequently by the head of the CPRS, Lord Victor
Rothschild, includes superficial analysis and unworkable prescriptions,
suggesting that Rothschild was not being kept in the picture as policy
evolved. For instance, he submitted a paper written by one staff member
to Heath on March 2 arguing that the border question should be settled
through a free vote at Westminster, "which both sides would be bound to
accept." Failing that, a compromise over sovereignty would be necessary,
ideally in the form of joint authority (an option which Heath had already
dismissed). Northern Ireland would be divided into Protestant and Catholic zones. A new Catholic police force would be created to keep order in
the latter, with support as necessary from the Irish army. In the interest
of local democracy, each zone would have its own local government, and
the region would elect representatives to the national parliaments in both
London and Dublin.[254]

By commissioning a comprehensive policy review, however, Heath
opened the issue for consideration by the Cabinet Office, and particularly
Cabinet Secretary Trend. Heath's quest for innovative solutions encouraged officials across all the departments to come up with radical proposals. These newcomers to the issue had no reason to identify or work in
partnership with the Northern Ireland government; defining the Northern
Ireland government as part of the problem helped them to wrest control
from the old guard at the Home Office.

## UKREP

Since Wilson created UKREP in 1969, Faulkner had resented it as "an embassy to part of one's own country" that reported secretly to London and sympathetically received representations from all manner of disaffected groups, "who quickly came to see that they could thus bypass and undermine the devolved government structures."[255] The official papers now available confirm this assessment. Roland Burroughs, the second holder of the office, outlined his views on the problem and its likely progress in a report to the home secretary dated April 1971. According to Burroughs, the army's military security approach had "created an atmosphere in which the resurgent militancy of the IRA could flourish" and the Unionist Party might well "break up under the pressure of clamant demands for repressive measures which Mr. Faulkner's Government could not meet." However, this might open up the way for "electoral choice between potential governments" and "the emergence of a moderate centre party with a hope of exercising power." If Stormont had to be replaced, this "would surely mean finding ways in which the Catholic minority could by some means or another have an active voice in the decision-making processes here."[256] This prescription was startlingly different from UK ministers' public statements at the time, which continued to support a security-oriented policy intended to sustain the Unionist government, but it signaled the direction in which Whitehall's thinking was moving. Even as Faulkner was settling into office and five months before Maudling announced it as government policy, the idea of an active role for Catholic representatives in the Stormont cabinet was gestating in British officials' minds.

In September 1971, as one element in Heath's comprehensive search for a solution, Burroughs' successor, Howard Smith, set about harvesting ideas for a political initiative from "men of goodwill." He opened UK ministers up to a range of opinions on the Nationalist side. These confidants and UKREP—as the medium through which their views were conveyed—were disproportionately influential in the policy development process. Other political players regarded as extremists were largely ignored, whether elected representatives like Craig and Paisley or loyalist and republican paramilitaries. Having lost confidence in Faulkner, British ministers increasingly depended on Smith and his contacts for advice on the political mood in Northern Ireland.

The emphasis in Smith's work shifted from overseeing the implementation of the reform package and ironing out difficulties between Stormont and the army to seeking an accommodation with the SDLP and preparing the ground for a political initiative.[257] Smith's overtures to Fitt and Hume on Maudling's behalf reflected a significant shift in the balance of power.

It seems probable that UKREP actually influenced SDLP leaders to reject Faulkner's June offer of committee seats at Stormont—why would they accept a few committee places in a parliament controlled by Unionists if, as they learned from Pemberton and Smith, they could hold out and possibly in time secure full ministerial jobs?[258]

The idea of direct rule as a break with the past that would open up new avenues in the search for a lasting settlement surfaced in Smith's consultations with "moderate" Catholics. Maurice Hayes, chair of the Community Relations Commission, suggested a "caesura" in a paper he presented to Smith a few weeks after internment.[259] This argued that there had been such a loss of faith in government by so many in the community that it would be impossible to restore stability unless the current arrangements for government and policing were drastically revised. An interregnum would create space to negotiate alternative forms of government that would attract support from both communities. Smith submitted the proposal to Maudling, who invited Hayes to London to discuss it. Although Hayes came away from that meeting with the impression that Maudling did not understand the problem and was not seriously engaged, by January 1972 the home secretary was using the same argument himself.

Another visitor to UKREP was Ken Bloomfield, one of Faulkner's closest advisers and deputy secretary to the Northern Ireland cabinet. Bloomfield had been working with Faulkner on how best to respond to whatever initiative Heath might come up with, including the imposition of direct rule. He visited UKREP on December 17, 1971. Smith's note of the meeting indicates that Bloomfield was anxious that nobody in Faulkner's office should know about the visit.[260] As recorded by Smith, Bloomfield's views were, first, that "the situation was very bad and only strong remedies would have any chance of success." Second, "there would be no settlement and no breaking out of the cycle of violence unless policies were applied which not only met adequately the demands of the Catholics, but were also acceptable to the south." Third, Bloomfield "saw no hope of Stormont evolving by its own efforts into a parliamentary and governmental system acceptable to the Catholics. The green paper proposals would certainly not be enough. Faulkner's hopes that when (or if) violence was put down the Catholics would come round to cooperation were quite unrealistic." Fourth, since the Northern Ireland parties would not be able to agree on a constitutional solution, the British government should impose one. This should take the form of community government, with safeguards for the minority. The STV system could be used to elect an enlarged assembly. Although community government would open up the issue of eventual unification, Bloomfield maintained that Protestants would accept it if London imposed it. Smith concluded that these proposals should be given a good deal of weight in light of Bloomfield's ability, knowledge, and experience. We cannot be certain how influential they actually were, but Trend passed them on to Heath with the comment that "it is interesting that Bloomfield discounts all-party talks and seems now convinced that only an imposed settlement will meet the needs of the situation."[261] Bloomfield's ideas were reflected in the radical policy paper that Maudling presented to the cabinet on January 18, the first occasion when the idea of imposing a solution on Faulkner was seriously discussed at ministerial level.

Why did Bloomfield go to UKREP behind Faulkner's back? Ramsay identifies a number of possible motives: that he had remained loyal to Terence O'Neill, who resented Faulkner's success and was lobbying Heath to have him brought down; that he saw which way events were moving and made a shrewd career calculation; or simply that he thought this was the morally right thing to do.[262] Whatever the answer, his intervention clearly strengthened the hand of those in the Whitehall machine who were arguing for a dramatic initiative, firm action, acceptability to Dublin, and community government.

### Defence

Carrington's stand at cabinet reflected the interests of the MoD and army commanders in the region. The general strategic direction given by the ministry to the GOC changed in late 1971.[263] The Irish government knew by January 1972 that the British army was pressing for the transfer of security to Westminster.[264] Until then senior defense officials' priority had been "to resolve matters in Northern Ireland at reasonable cost and without undue distraction to the normal conduct of business," and to that end, "to keep Stormont in business if possible." After internment, Carrington and the MoD pressed for both security transfer and a political initiative, and were no longer interested in propping up Stormont. On the substance of constitutional change, the GOC told ministers that "from the military point of view the main objective of such an initiative should be to wean the mass of the Roman Catholic population from their sympathy with the aims of the IRA and thus isolate the terrorists from their base of support within the community."[265]

Army commanders had maintained since 1969 that military action alone would not end the violence or prevent a recurrence; the best the army could do was to maintain a reasonable level of order to enable local political leaders to hammer out a political settlement for the long term. They now argued that the Unionists had missed their opportunity to negotiate a settlement.[266] As a result, soldiers were being killed and the army was suffering from the hostility of republican communities for implementing policies—notably internment—that it had opposed and that had set back progress toward the day when it could withdraw. The army had gone into Northern Ireland with some 7,000 troops believing that they would be able to leave within two years at most. With twice as many troops committed, the problem was continuing to worsen. The Troops Out movement had been growing, and the army's involvement in Northern Ireland was damaging both its reputation and soldiers' morale. Moreover, the casualty rate for soldiers in Northern Ireland was generating protests from soldiers' families in Britain and impairing recruitment, which fell from 31,298 in 1971–72 to 26,484 in 1972–73. Senior commanders attributed this drop primarily to Northern Ireland.[267] The MoD wanted to maintain and (after November) restore bipartisanship at Westminster, believing that an overarching political consensus was essential to sustain public support in Britain for the Northern Ireland campaign.[268]

Army commanders in Northern Ireland also had a particular stake in the security transfer. This was partly a matter of bureaucratic competition, partly because the army's established counterinsurgency doctrine called for an integrated strategic response across all government agencies, which was clearly missing. The only way to secure such a response, they argued, was to centralize control in British hands. Colonel Robin Evelegh later wrote of his experience as a battalion commander in Belfast in 1972:

> To counter terrorism successfully, the Government must conduct a coordinated campaign bringing into harmony its economic, political, social, legal, military, police and public relations efforts against terrorism and insurrection so that each reinforces the others. No one aspect of society can itself be the area in which terrorism is defeated, because terrorism and rebellion is a malaise of the whole of society. Thus, while there is no purely military solution to such a problem, there is equally no purely political or purely economic or purely propaganda solution.[269]

Frank Kitson wrote a paper in December 1971 that reached the Home Office through UKREP. Kitson argued that the army had weakened the IRA in Belfast, but that future military successes would be increasingly hard to achieve. The army was trying to secure the support of local residents by working on community relations and neighborhood regeneration, but was "handicapped by lack of government policy relating to the way in which the community in Belfast should develop." Instead, the army needed strategic direction "beyond our immediate mission of destroying the IRA,"[270] the implication being that ministers had failed to give the necessary strategic leadership, coordinating activity across all government agencies and departments. If Unionist ministers would not lead, British ministers should.

The failure of coordination was especially problematic in the relation-ship between the army (controlled by London) and the RUC (controlled by Stormont). As another observer noted,

> The lessons learned in Kenya, Aden, Malaysia and even in the campaign in Ireland between 1919 and 1922 had been forgotten or ignored. There was no coordination between the various services such as MI5, MI6, the RUC, the Army, and other smaller units which had been set up. . . . The differing rivalries and loyalties did noth-ing to help the situation. Both MI6 and the RUC for instance would mark papers to ensure the other did not have access to them.[271]

At an institutional level, relationships between RUC officers and army commanders had never been cordial.[272] The police were demoralized af-ter Hunt and the army often viewed them as biased and ineffective. Al-though the GOC already had the authority to coordinate army and RUC operations, and although both were represented on Faulkner's JSC, both sides tended not to share intelligence, which permitted some republi-can informers to receive payment twice for the same items of informa-tion.[273] There were divisions over tactics and operating procedures, with the army tending to be tougher and less concerned about the niceties of legal procedure.

Bloody Sunday illustrated the difference starkly. Local RUC chief su-perintendent Frank Lagan had asked the army to allow the protest to take place without any military intervention. But the commander of land forces (CLF)—Major-General Robert Ford—impatient with rising levels of disorder in Derry, decided instead to detain anyone who tried to break through from the Bogside to the city's business center. British ministers endorsed this decision.[274] Ford deployed members of the Parachute Regi-ment, among the army's toughest, to snatch what their operating instruc-tions for the day called "hooligans and rioters."[275] Ford reasoned that since internment, a hard core of some 450 troublemakers had emerged in Derry who were bent on destroying the commercial life of the city. It was time to stop them.[276] In a paper to GOC Tuzo, he contended that the army had been failing in its duty to restore order in the area and went on: "I am coming to the conclusion that the minimum force necessary to achieve a restoration of law and order is to shoot selected ring leaders amongst the DYH [Derry Young Hooligans], after clear warnings have been issued."[277] Tuzo's response is not recorded.

Another illustration of the difference in approach is in the ill treatment of internees during interrogation. Five weeks after the Compton Report had criticized the practice, one Brigadier Lewis, having reviewed the state of intelligence in Northern Ireland, reported to his superiors in London that he was "very concerned about lack of interrogation in depth" by the

RUC, and that "some Special Branch out-station heads are NOT attempting to screw down arrested men and extract intelligence from them"; his colleagues "were due to do a quick visit by helicopter to these out-stations . . . to read the riot act."[278]

UK ministers did not share intelligence information with Faulkner, despite his role as chair of the JSC. In discussion among themselves, they noted that the RUC Special Branch's "techniques and leadership fell short of what we might be able to provide were the intelligence arrangements wholly in the hands of the UK Government."[279] It is unclear precisely what this meant, but in their eyes it clearly provided an argument for direct rule. Lord Carver, chief of the general staff in the mid-1970s, later wrote that the army found Special Branch inefficient and unreliable, and suspected that "some of its members had close links with Protestant extremists."[280]

Counterinsurgency doctrine held that the police should have primacy, since they were more effective in gathering intelligence, more able to secure popular support, cheaper, better trained for a policing role, and less vulnerable to criticism as an occupying force. Police primacy also reduced the chances of British soldiers being killed, leading to agitation in Britain for the troops to be brought home.[281] But the MoD would not accept police primacy if the RUC were controlled by Stormont. As far as they were concerned, the only way to integrate security policy and operations properly was to transfer responsibility for the RUC, internment, and criminal justice to Westminster. With full direct rule a British secretary of state could also pursue the fully integrated strategy outlined by Kitson. Thus, by December 1971, "At the MoD there appeared to be no alternative to Direct Rule. It seemed to be a logical step to centralise control of the police, the Army and political development. It remained only to decide when this should be done."[282]

The MoD also believed that a transfer would relieve army commanders of the need to take account of Stormont ministers' political agenda, removing the pressure to take measures—internment was the obvious example—that were counterproductive in security terms but necessary to sustain a Unionist leader in office.[283] Although the army had been responsible for the killings and the RUC had explicitly cautioned against the tactics that led to them, the political turbulence generated by Bloody Sunday opened up an opportunity to argue the army's case, which Carrington was more than willing to seize.[284]

There was also a wider strategic dimension to the MoD's interest. In May 1971 the PUS had undertaken an assessment of the defense implications of reunification. This eventually emerged in February 1972 in the form of a report from the chief of the defense staff, the head of Britain's armed services. It said that the use of defense and other facilities in Ireland by a hostile power could seriously threaten Britain's national security. Under reunification the danger would extend to British maritime and aircraft movements off the west coast of Scotland, including the submarine nuclear deterrent fleet based in the Holy Loch. The report concluded that in strategic defense terms, Britain's best option would be a friendly united Ireland. This would deny the military advantages of Irish facilities to any hostile power, potentially make them available to Britain, and free up 14,500 soldiers from Northern Ireland for service elsewhere. This conclusion was reflected in Carrington's contribution to the ministerial debate, that it was too much to expect Nationalists to wait twenty years for a united Ireland.[285]

The army also had a more immediate strategic interest in securing the cooperation of the Irish government. Commanders recognized that the border could not be closed effectively without incurring politically unacceptable costs, and that until Dublin acted resolutely the IRA would continue to operate from the south with relative impunity. Faulkner had argued the case for forcing Dublin to act, but there was another, less diplomatically costly and potentially more rewarding way of meeting the army's objectives: to secure Dublin's cooperation by offering concessions for which the Unionist Party, rather than British soldiers, would pay the price.

After a visit to Northern Ireland in December 1971, CGS Sir Michael Carver advised Carrington that there would shortly be a window of opportunity for a political initiative. Foreshadowing the argument Lynch put to Heath in January 1972, Carver said that it should be launched before Protestant opinion hardened against further reform in the knowledge that the IRA had been beaten.[286] It should not be delayed beyond mid-February. Carver proposed a transfer of law and order to Westminster, with the GOC assuming full responsibility for army and police operations "until terrorism is finally eliminated"; transferring as many areas of public administration as possible to nonelected boards on which the minority would be fully represented, and accountable to Stormont; and a commission to review the method of representation and election to the Stormont parliament. Carrington ensured that these proposals were reflected in Maudling's pivotal paper of January 18, in which the home secretary for the first time proposed the full transfer of security.

### Foreign and Commonwealth Office

The sustained Nationalist reaction against internment created a political crisis for the Conservative government, which Bloody Sunday exacerbated. The resulting shift in policy, from coercion to direct rule, was accompanied

by a transformation in the balance of power in Whitehall. By commissioning a fundamental policy review, Heath brought the FCO into the debate
on equal terms, introducing a range of new perspectives and interests into
the policymaking process. From September 1971 he enhanced the office's
role and influence by stressing the importance of an accommodation with
Dublin. The FCO alone of the Whitehall departments involved had a
presence in London, Dublin, and Belfast.

The foreign secretary personally favored unification as the best long-
term solution, and his stand was consistent with the FCO's organizational
interests. By June 1971, Irish diplomats were speculating that the department was systematically encouraging articles in the serious British media
about Irish unity as a realistic policy option.[287] The FCO certainly wanted
a political initiative that would improve relations with Dublin. The MoD's
arguments were strengthened to the extent that they were supported by
Britain's diplomats, who were especially concerned about the implications
of events in Northern Ireland for Britain's relations with the Republic and
by the threat of international criticism, particularly at the United Nations
and before the European Court.

During 1971, the FCO expanded the staffing which it devoted to the
Northern Ireland problem to match that of the Home Office. By the summer, it had an under secretary for the first time almost exclusively concerned with Ireland.[288] With the necessary capacity and Heath's approval,
the department could expand its role in the policy process substantially.
By December, its planning staff informed their counterparts in the MoD
that they had decided to prepare a detailed assessment for ministers of the
international implications of possible developments in Northern Ireland.
The factors they cited to justify this foray onto the Home Office's territory
were, first, the forthcoming presidential election campaign in the United
States, where "Senator Edward Kennedy was trying to exploit the situation
in Northern Ireland" to secure the Irish vote; second, pro-Irish pressure
groups in other countries, such as the Democratic Labour Party in Australia; third, the risk that communist nations would exploit the problem
for propaganda purposes and send arms to the IRA; fourth, the risk that
developing countries would see the problem as one of "colonialist repression"; fifth, the implications of the United Kingdom and Ireland joining
the EEC; and sixth, the concern of Britain's North Atlantic Treaty Organization (NATO) partners at the reassignment of soldiers to Northern
Ireland from Germany.[289]

From September 1971 the FCO also expanded its presence in Belfast.
The internment operation had demonstrated serious weaknesses in Britain's intelligence system. Two MI6 operatives, Frank Steele and Dennis

Trevelyan, were seconded to the Home Office and sent to Northern Ireland to improve matters. Their remit included strengthening systems for gathering, using, and sharing intelligence between the army and Special Branch. Some thirty years later Steele told a BBC reporter that he had been "expected to use his experience of conflict situations in the Middle East and Africa where he had spent most of his career ... to beat the IRA."[290] The high-level involvement of these two agents both illustrated and reinforced ministers' tendency to see Northern Ireland in terms of colonial analogies and precedents.

Steele and Trevelyan worked alongside Smith at UKREP and, like him, provided intelligence directly to UK ministers, bypassing Faulkner. Steele had no previous knowledge of Northern Ireland, which those who recruited him for the task told him they considered an advantage. He declared himself "horrified" at what he found. He had not been in Belfast long before concluding "the Unionist government seemed incapable of solving the problems facing Northern Ireland. The obvious answer was the introduction of Direct Rule from Westminster."[291] At first Steele harbored doubts about such a radical course of action, concerned at the risks. He was finally reassured that it would be feasible after a conversation with "a senior official from the Northern Ireland civil service" (presumably Bloomfield). According to a BBC reporter:

> The eminent Northern Ireland civil servant stunned his companions when he told them that Westminster would have to bring in Direct Rule. It was music to Steele's ears. "When a senior Northern Ireland civil servant with years of working for a Unionist Government, who was himself a 'Prod' and a Unionist, says this, then you start sitting up and taking notice," he said. Direct Rule seemed the only way forward, and by far the best way of making a fresh start. The problem was when to do it.[292]

Steele went on to tell the reporter that "the only good thing about [Bloody Sunday] was that it enabled us to bring in Direct Rule."[293]

Finally, the FCO had its ambassador in Dublin. As we have seen, Peck was sympathetic to the Irish position and receptive to Irish diplomats' ideas.[294] He passed these on in full to the head of the FCO, Sir Denis Greenhill, and to his counterpart Sir Philip Allen at the Home Office. Their import was that "the Paisleyite tail was wagging the Unionist dog and the Unionist tail was wagging the Conservative dog." Instead of pandering to unionism, Peck argued, Whitehall should ensure that the British government worked with the Irish to get a system of genuine Catholic participation in the government of Northern Ireland and so remove the causes of the violence.[295] In November, he called for a fundamental review of policy in Northern Ireland, which, echoing Lynch, he described as "a law-and-order obsession." He argued that the taoiseach was coming under political attack for cooperating with London without achieving anything for Nationalists in Northern Ireland, and that if Lynch's government fell, any likely successor would be more dogmatically republican, less pragmatic, and harder for Britain to deal with. He expressed concern that Lynch had recently lost his overall majority in the Dáil and was clinging to office at the pleasure of a handful of independent members. Peck shared army commanders' views that a political initiative was needed to give moderate Catholics an alternative outlet for their nationalist aspirations.[296]

Peck was not inhibited about discussing the details of internal discussions inside Whitehall with Lynch. In a personal note of a conversation with Peck on January 6, 1972, Lynch described him as suggesting that the official advice in Whitehall was "in the direction of a worthwhile political move but it seemed to be killed on reaching ministers who were influenced by the tough attitude of right-wing Tory backbenchers."[297] On March 9, Peck told a Dublin official that "press stories of split in Cabinet on political initiative are true. Line up not as given. PM for action. Exceptional and radical change. Big stuff."[298]

## Summary

Four types of factors contributed to the adoption of direct rule: those that required something to be done, those that favored the transfer to Westminster of responsibility for security, those that favored community government, and those that favored direct rule.

The deteriorating violence in Northern Ireland after internment, the continuing decline in Faulkner's authority, the alienation of Nationalist Ireland, the spread of the IRA's bombing campaign to England, the ending of bipartisanship at Westminster, Conservative backbench disquiet, and international and media criticisms cumulatively pressed UK ministers to be seen to do something. They resisted at first, intending to take an initiative only after the security forces had decisively overpowered the IRA. This waiting stance became increasingly uncomfortable after Wilson produced his fifteen-point plan in November 1971. By January, the Irish government and army commanders were both arguing that an initiative should begin before the IRA was defeated and while the Protestants were still afraid of it. Maudling was persuaded that a solution should be imposed if necessary. Other cabinet ministers dissented, but Bloody Sunday created a new urgency, convincing Heath that he could no longer continue as before. He faced strong political and diplomatic pressures for an immediate and important gesture of conciliation toward Nationalist Ireland. The Irish government and Labour opposition had produced their own proposals,

which closely matched and complemented each other. Heath had promised months before to bring forward a constitutional initiative when the
time was ripe; it had now become imperative.

The political and diplomatic reaction against Bloody Sunday called for
an exculpatory sacrifice. Heath had to choose between publicly acknowledging that he and his ministers had permitted a strategy of coercion that
had not only failed to stop the violence but fuelled it; publicly acknowledging that senior army commanders had made a deadly mistake; and ditch-
ing Faulkner. Immediately after Bloody Sunday, Faulkner predicted: "This
is London's disaster, but they will use it against us."[299] Heath later told him
"that this diminution in the powers, prestige, and authority of Stormont
was in reality simply a response to the criticism of our opponents, which
Mr. Heath and his colleagues neither substantiated nor supported."[300]

The transfer of security arose from demands made by Wilson, the Irish
government, the SDLP, and liberal Unionists. It would placate Nationalist
Ireland, enable the secretary of state to regulate the operation of internment as necessary to bring the SDLP to the negotiating table, and remove
a series of contentious issues from the political agenda. It can also be explained in terms of the army's competitive relationship with Stormont and
the RUC. Army commanders had been asking for it since internment.
It was the only way to achieve the integrated response required by their
counterinsurgency doctrine. It would take Unionist politicians off their
backs and, they hoped, clear the way for improvements in cross-border
security cooperation.

The case for community government was less compelling, and here
Heath found his colleagues harder to convince. Moderate Unionists and
the SDLP supported it, as did the Irish government and the Labour opposition. The Unionist Party was strongly opposed to it. Loyalist resistance
was intensifying, and there was no certainty that the SDLP, with its eyes
on a united Ireland, would cooperate in a coalition even if detailed arrangements could be agreed on. Some British ministers and officials shared
Faulkner's skepticism. If the attempt to negotiate a community government failed, or if it succeeded and the resulting coalition collapsed, direct
rule might have to be extended indefinitely. Heath nonetheless calculated
that it was worth being seen to make the effort. If the initiative succeeded,
it would address the roots of the problem, paving the way for a lasting
peace. Even if it only partially succeeded, it might at least stem the damaging torrent of criticism from Dublin and Wilson.

By November 1971, British officials had come to see direct rule as a
means to break out of the political impasse. They were influenced by five
discrete political interests: Nationalists who wanted to break the Unionist

Party's grip on power as a necessary step on the road to unification; Alliance and NILP moderate rivals of the Unionist Party; Faulkner's opponents within that party; external hard-line opponents, including Paisley; and the Labour opposition, seeking to build up the NILP or SDLP.

The activities of hard-line Unionists from September 1971 reinforced the shift in London, helping to persuade ministers that Faulkner's administration was incapable of serious constitutional change and no longer worth sustaining. It became evident that they would not be able to work with any of his likely successors since they would reverse or resist reform to an unacceptable degree.

It has been suggested that the decision-making process that led to direct rule conformed to the rational model described in chapter 2. Heath commissioned a fundamental policy review that identified and assessed a comprehensive list of options. The package was related to a plausible hypothesis about the causes and dynamic of the conflict; apparently comparable cases from other divided societies were examined and political and security dimensions were included in the analysis. Having reached preliminary conclusions, ministers took steps to explore alternative options in detail and to reduce residual uncertainties. The dramatic hiatus created by Stormont's suspension can be read as reinforcing this explanation.

But in reality the decision-making process from September 1971 was not at all tidy or comprehensive. Key ministers and senior officials did not believe that community government would be either attainable or sustainable; they also opposed it on philosophical and political grounds. Some continued to oppose direct rule, anxious that Britain might find itself saddled with an intractable problem indefinitely. Heath and Maudling were driven to overcome this resistance by immediate and painful political pressures.

After internment, power flowed back from Stormont to Whitehall, and within Whitehall from the Home Office to the MoD and FCO. The MoD wanted direct rule in order to free army commanders from the need to prop up an ailing Unionist government. The FCO wanted enough to satisfy the Irish government and avoid international disapproval. By commissioning the search for a radical initiative, Heath gave the senior officials in all three departments a stake in cutting the Northern Ireland government down to size and the opportunity to do so. Faulkner and the Unionist government no longer useful.

Consequently, Whitehall's priorities changed dramatically. Stormont became part of the problem rather than the instrument through which to solve it. Heath now saw himself as tackling a conflict between two equally irrational groups of Irishmen trapped in a primitive quarrel from which they could extricate themselves only through the intervention of progressive men of goodwill like himself, applying British standards of fair play. Ministers aligned their explanation of the problem with the new political realities within which they had to work.

Heath had to make strenuous efforts—and take some liberties in presenting his case—to press his dissenting colleagues into line in the critical period from March 3 to 23. The skeptics remained unconvinced, but he badgered and outmaneuvered them. They eventually accepted the need to act decisively, and to present a united front. None of them wanted the entire direct-rule package, but each got something: Maudling, release from a personal burden of work and criticism; Carrington, freedom for the army from Stormont's influence over security policy and operations; Douglas-Home, improved relations with Dublin, the potential for better intelligence gathering, and a step toward unification. Collectively, they could no longer be condemned for inaction.

The imposition of direct rule was a major risk. The next few weeks would be critical. But the heavy lifting had begun.

## Notes

1.　PREM 15/1002, "Northern Ireland: Political Reform," Cabinet Office, February 3, 1972.

2.　R. Deutsch and V. Magowan, *Northern Ireland: A Chronology of Events* (Belfast: Blackstaff, 1973).

3.　M. McGuire, *To Take Arms* (London: Macmillan, 1973), 20.

4.　I. McAllister, *The Northern Ireland Social Democratic and Labour Party* (London: Macmillan, 1977), 99.

5.　M. Farrell, *The Orange State* (London: Pluto, 1976), 283.

6.　Sunday Times Insight Team, *Ulster* (London: Penguin, 1972), 289.

7.　Compton Report: *Report of the Enquiry into Allegations against the Security Forces of Physical Brutality in Northern Ireland Arising out of Events on the 9th August 1971*, Cmnd. 4823 (London: HMSO, 1971).

8.　DEFE 23/119, Psychological Effects of Interrogation Techniques.

9.　M. Hayes, *Minority Verdict: Experiences of a Catholic Public Servant* (Belfast: Blackstaff, 1995), 137.

10.　*Irish News*, August 12, 1971.

11.　CAB 164/879, August 13, 1971.

12.　D. Bleakley, *Faulkner: Conflict and Consent in Irish Politics* (London: Mowbray's, 1974), 104. Bleakley's gesture was not a significant personal sacrifice in that his six-month term of office was in any case due to expire.

13.　McAllister, *Social Democratic and Labour Party*, 100.

14.　John Hume, reported in the *Irish Times*, August 16, 1971.

15.　McAllister, *Social Democratic and Labour Party*, 107.

16.   G. Murray and J. Tonge, *Sinn Féin and the SDLP: From Alienation to Participation* (Dublin: O'Brien Press 2005), 27.

17.   Farrell, *Orange State*, 282.

18.   Ministry of Defence, "Operation Banner: An Analysis of Military Operations in Northern Ireland," Ministry of Defence paper, July 2006.

19.   CJ 4/56, Smith to Allen, August 17, 1971.

20.   *The Times*, August 18, 1971.

21.   H. Kelly, *How Stormont Fell* (Dublin: Gill and Macmillan, 1972), 131.

22.   T. Hennessey, *The Evolution of the Troubles 1970–1972* (Dublin: Irish Academic Press, 2007), 198.

23.   NAS DT 2002/8/483, note by Eamonn Gallagher dated November 3, 1971.

24.   CJ 4/106, "Northern Ireland—The Next General Election," paper by R. Maudling, undated but evidently circulated in September 1971.

25.   CAB 128/48, September 21, 1971.

26.   B. Faulkner, *Memoirs of a Statesman* (London: Weidenfeld and Nicholson, 1978), 178.

27.   Callaghan, *House Divided*, 170.

28.   CAB 130/522, August 17, 1971.

29.   CAB 130/522, September 9, 1971.

30.   Faulkner, *Memoirs,* 147.

31.   Hansard, September 22, 1971, cols. 14–15.

32.   G. Fitzgerald, *Towards a New Ireland* (Dublin: Torc Books, 1973), 132.

33.   R. Maudling, *Memoirs* (London: Sidgwick and Jackson, 1978), 185.

34.   Government of Northern Ireland, *The Future Development of the Parliament and Government of Northern Ireland,* Cmd 560 (Belfast: HMSO, 1971), paragraphs 36–38.

35.   Hansard, September 22, 1971, cols. 14–15.

36.   Faulkner, *Memoirs,* 147.

37.   E. Heath, *The Course of My Life: My Autobiography* (London: Hodder and Stoughton, 1998), 422.

38.   Government of Northern Ireland, *The Future Development of the Parliament and Government of Northern Ireland,* Cmd. 560 (Belfast: HMSO, 1971), paragraphs 36–38.

39.   PREM 15/486, Trend to Heath, September 3, 1971.

40.   Heath, *The Course of My Life,* 430.

41.   CAB 130/522, minutes of October 6, 1971.

42.   CAB 130/522, November 12, 1971.

43.   CAB 134/3012, note from Sir Philip Allen, November 23, 1971.

44.   CAB 130/522, minutes of December 2, 1971.

45.   Cited in P. Dixon, "Contemporary Unionism and the Tactics of Resistance," in M. Bric and J. Coakley, eds., *From Political Violence to Negotiated Settlement,* (Dublin: UCD Press, 2004), 140.

46.   Hansard, November 25, 1971, col. 1586.

47.   CAB 130/522, minutes of December 2, 1971. The PUS, or permanent under secretary, is the highest official in a Whitehall Department.

48.   CAB 134/3536, Allen to ministers, December 23, 1971.

49. CAB 130/522, minutes of December 2, 1971.

50. CAB 130/522, minutes of December 13, 1971.

51. PREM 15/1000, January 10, 1972.

52. CAB 130/522, "Northern Ireland—Policy for 1972," memorandum by R. Maudling, January 18, 1972.

53. CAB 130/522, minutes of January 21, 1972.

54. CAB 130/522, minutes of January 27, 1972.

55. D. Hamill, *Pig in the Middle: The Army in Northern Ireland, 1969–1985* (London: Methuen, 1985), 93. After a protracted judicial inquiry led by Lord Saville, this verdict was effectively substantiated. Prime Minister David Cameron apologized to the bereaved. The full inquiry report is accessible at www.bloody-sunday-inquiry.org (accessed on October 17, 2010).

56. H.C. 220, the Widgery Report: UK Government, *Report of the Tribunal Appointed to Inquire into the Events of 30th January 1972* (London: HMSO, 1972).

57. Kelly, *How Stormont Fell*, 120.

58. Farrell, *Orange State*, 284.

59. J. Peck, *Dublin from Downing Street* (Dublin: Gill and Macmillan, 1978), 4.

60. B. White, *John Hume: Statesman of the Troubles* (Belfast: Blackstaff, 1984), 122.

61. J. Campbell, *Edward Heath: A Biography* (London: Jonathan Cape, 1993), 430.

62. Heath, *The Course of My Life*, 436.

63. K. Kyle, "How Direct Rule Came to Ulster," *The Listener*, March 30, 1972, 408.

64. M. McGuire, *To Take Arms*.

65. *The Times*, February 25, 1972. A copy of the article is filed with Heath's personal papers in PREM 15/1003.

66. CAB 128/48, minutes of February 22, 1972.

67. Hamill, *Pig in the Middle*, 97.

68. See, e.g., D.R.S. Gallagher, "The Failure of Attempts to Solve the Northern Ireland Problem 1972–80," PhD thesis, School of Politics, Queen's University, Belfast, 1984, 30.

69. D. Hurd, *An End to Promises* (London: Collins, 1979). Hurd was a private secretary to Heath who went on to become secretary of state for Northern Ireland.

70. CAB 130/522, minutes of February 2, 1972.

71. PREM 15/1002, "Northern Ireland: Political Reform," Cabinet Office, February 3, 1972.

72. Ibid.

73. Ibid.

74. Heath, *The Course of My Life*, 436.

75. R. Ramsay, *Ringside Seats* (Dublin: Irish Academic Press, 2009), 101.

76. Faulkner, *Memoirs*, 146.

77. CAB 164/1175, note of February 8, 1972.

78. CAB 130/560, minutes of February 10, 1972.

79. CAB 130/560, minutes of February 16, 1972.

80. PREM 15/1002, February 3, 1972.

81. CAB 130/560, minutes of February 17, 1972.

82. CAB 130/560, minutes of February 28, 1972.

83. Faulkner, *Memoirs*, 148.

242 THE BRITISH STATE AND THE NORTHERN IRELAND CRISIS

84. CAB 130/560, minutes of March 3, 1972.

85. CAB 164/1175, note of February 8, 1972.

86. PREM 15/1003, March 3, 1972.

87. CAB 164/1175, note of February 8, 1972.

88. CAB 128/48, minutes of March 7, 1972.

89. Excerpts from the unpublished diary of Lord Hailsham available from the Margaret Thatcher Foundation at www.margaretthatcher.org/archive.

90. CAB 130/560, minutes dated March 9, 1972.

91. CAB 128/48, minutes of March 9, 1972.

92. PREM 15/1004, minutes of March 13, 1972.

93. CAB 128/48, minutes of March 14, 1972.

94. PREM 15/1004, minutes of March 15, 1972.

95. CAB 130/560, minutes of March 22, 1972.

96. Faulkner, *Memoirs*, 152.

97. Ibid., 153.

98. Ramsay, *Ringside Seats*, 102.

99. CAB 128/48, minutes dated March 24, 1972.

100. CAB 130/560, minutes dated March 28, 1972. It is unclear how any concessions to Faulkner at this stage would have entered the public domain unless Heath had already given some prior commitment to someone outside the government machine to face him down. Wilson is the obvious candidate.

101. *The Listener*, April 22, 1976.

102. CAB 134/1347.

103. PREM 15/1003.

104. *Daily Telegraph*, March 20, 1972.

105. M. Dillon and P. Lehane, *Political Murder in Northern Ireland* (London: Penguin, 1973), 59.

106. Kelly, *How Stormont Fell*, 128.

107. S. Nelson, *Ulster's Uncertain Defenders* (Belfast: Appletree, 1984).

108. A. Boyd, *Brian Faulkner and the Crisis of Ulster Unionism* (Tralee: Anvil Books, 1972), 98.

109. *The Economist*, March 25, 1972, 17.

110. FCO 33/1608, Smith to FCO, September 10, 1971.

111. M.A. Murphy, *Gerry Fitt: Political Chameleon* (Cork: Mercia, 2007), 159.

112. Ibid., 176.

113. CAB 130/522, minutes of November 5, 1971.

114. CAB 134/3417, report of January 6, 1972.

115. PREM 15/1003, March 3, 1972.

116. Fitzgerald, *New Ireland*, 126.

117. White, *Hume*, 110.

118. J. Whyte, *The Reform of Stormont* (Belfast: New Ulster Movement, 1971).

119. Gallagher, "Failure," 20.

120. H. Calvert, *The Northern Ireland Problem* (London: United Nations Association, 1972), 8.

121. DEFE 23/117, November 9, 1971.
122. Maudling, *Memoirs*, 188.
123. CAB 130/560, minutes dated February 28, 1972.
124. P. Dixon, *Northern Ireland: The Politics of War and Peace* (New York: Palgrave, 2001), 101.
125. Heath, *The Course of My Life*, 422.
126. Hansard, March 24, 1972.
127. Campbell, *Heath*, 406.
128. Hansard, September 22, 1971, col. 45.
129. Kelly, *How Stormont Fell*, 132.
130. Faulkner, *Memoirs*, 150.
131. PREM 15/2192, letter of February 10, 1972.
132. CAB 130/560, minutes of February 25, 1972.
133. CAB 128/48, minutes dated March 24, 1972.
134. M. Laing, *Edward Heath, Prime Minister* (London: Sidgwick and Jackson, 1972), 224; Peck, *Dublin from Downing Street*, 145.
135. J. Callaghan, *A House Divided* (London: Collins, 1973), 158.
136. *The Times*, August 27, 1971.
137. Hansard, vol. 823, col. 228.
138. Ibid., col. 4.
139. Ibid., cols. 15–16.
140. Faulkner, *Memoirs*, 121.
141. Hansard, vol. 823, col. 22, September 22, 1971.
142. D. Wood, "The Westminster Scene," *Political Quarterly*, vol. 43, no. 2 (1972), 212–24.
143. Callaghan, *House Divided*, 170.
144. *The Economist*, October 2, 1971, 16.
145. A.T.Q. Stewart, "Northern Ireland," in *The Register of World Events 1971* (London: Chadwyck, 1972), 36.
146. Hansard, November 25, 1971, col. 1588.
147. Hansard, vol. 826, col. 1654, November 25, 1971.
148. Hansard, col. 1591, November 25, 1971.
149. PREM 15/1000, note of meeting on December 17, 1971.
150. Campbell, *Heath*, 429.
151. CAB 130/522, minutes of November 12, 1971.
152. CAB 130/522, minutes of November 26, 1971.
153. Dixon, *Northern Ireland*, 99.
154. PREM 15/1000, Heath to Maudling, December 19, 1971.
155. Faulkner, *Memoirs*, 142.
156. CAB 130/560, minutes dated February 10, 1972.
157. PREM 15/1002, note of February 16, 1972.
158. CAB 128/48, minutes of February 22, 1972.
159. CAB 130/522, minutes of November 26, 1971.
160. Hansard, vol. 833, col. 1137, March 20, 1972.

161. J. Haines, *The Politics of Power* (London: Cape, 1977), 129.
162. Compton Report.
163. *The Economist,* January 15, 1972.
164. *Daily Mail,* September 24, 1971.
165. Insight Team, *Ulster,* 306–07.
166. *The Times,* January 31, 1972.
167. L. Curtis, *Ireland: The Propaganda War* (London: Pluto, 1984), 45.
168. CAB 128/48, minutes dated February 4, 1972.
169. Dixon, *Northern Ireland,* 160.
170. Faulkner, *Memoirs,* 144.
171. *The Spectator,* February 12, 1972.
172. PREM 15/1002, Faulkner to Heath, February 16, 1972.
173. *The Times,* February 21, 1972.
174. *Financial Times,* March 7, 1972.
175. *The Spectator,* March 25, 1972.
176. CAB 130/522, minutes dated August 13, 1971.
177. Peck, *Dublin from Downing Street,* 29.
178. Ibid., 132.
179. *The Times,* August 12, 1971; *Irish Times,* September 3, 1971.
180. Heath, *The Course of My Life,* 424.
181. G. Fitzgerald, *All in a Life: An Autobiography* (London: Macmillan, 1991), 99.
182. Faulkner, *Memoirs,* 128–29.
183. NAI DT/2003/17/30.
184. CAB 133/406, September 28, 1971.
185. *The Economist,* October 2, 1971.
186. PREM 15/1034, October 7, 1971.
187. Heath, *The Course of My Life,* 423.
188. The case was submitted on December 16, 1971. It alleged that British forces had caused seven deaths since August 1971, in breach of Article 2 of the European Convention on Human Rights.
189. NAI DT 2002/8/495, November 18, 1971.
190. NAI 2002/8/416, minutes of meeting on November 29, 1971.
191. CAB 130/522, minutes of December 2, 1971.
192. NAI 2002/8/508, note of November 16, 1971.
193. NAI 2002/8/508, secret "note on discussion at dinner" on November 18, 1971, signature illegible.
194. *Irish Times,* October 23, 1971.
195. For an outline of the three-stage strategy, see the section on Dublin in chapter 4.
196. NAI 2002/8/508, Small to O'Sulleabháin, November 26, 1971.
197. NAI 2002/8/508, note of December 6, 1971.
198. PREM 15/1002, Armstrong to Angel, January 24, 1972.
199. *The Times,* February 1, 1972.

200. Peck, *Dublin from Downing Street*, 4.
201. Faulkner, *Memoirs*, 140.
202. Ibid., 145.
203. CAB 128/48, February 3, 1972.
204. R. English, *Armed Struggle: The History of the IRA* (London: Pan Books, 2004), 144.
205. *Sunday Telegraph*, March 12, 1972.
206. *Irish Times*, March 1 and 4, 1972.
207. *Irish Times*, March 15, 1972.
208. NAI 2003/16/462, "Report of a Meeting Held in Council Chamber, 11 February 1972."
209. Heath, *The Course of My Life*, 427.
210. Murphy, *Gerry Fitt*, 172.
211. DEFE 25/308, Elliott to Cable, December 28, 1971.
212. Heath, *The Course of My Life*, 435.
213. *Irish Times*, January 1, 2003.
214. Faulkner, *Memoirs*, 140.
215. Fitzgerald, *New Ireland*, 77.
216. Ramsay, *Ringside Seat*, 105.
217. Paper dated February 1, 1972, translated from the French by Ramsay.
218. The records of Schumann's meetings with Soames and Hillery remain classified.
219. K. Bloomfield, *A Tragedy of Errors* (Liverpool: Liverpool University Press, 2007), 26, supported by personal interviews.
220. Campbell, *Heath*, 297.
221. Hayes, *Minority Verdict*, 144.
222. NAI 2003/16/461, record of a conversation by Eamon Gallagher, January 24, 1972.
223. Hansard, vol. 823, col. 15, September 22, 1971.
224. Cited in Ferdinand Mount, "A Time to Moan and Weep," *The Spectator*, October 2, 2010, 34.
225. PREM 15/1003, March 3, 1972.
226. PREM 15/1002, Wolff to Heath, February 5, 1972.
227. Maudling, *Memoirs*, 191.
228. Campbell, *Heath*, 423.
229. Faulkner, *Memoirs*, 129.
230. Heath, *The Course of My Life*, 436.
231. P. Arthur, "The Heath Government and Northern Ireland," in S. Ball and A. Seldon, eds., *The Heath Government 1970–1974: A Reappraisal* (Longman: New York, 1993), 237.
232. Peck, *Dublin from Downing Street*, 112.
233. K. Bloomfield, *Stormont in Crisis: A Memoir* (Belfast: Blackstaff, 1994), 157.
234. Ibid., 162.
235. Hansard 6, vol. 87, col. 898, November 27, 1985.
236. Heath, *The Course of My Life*, 436.
237. *Sunday Times*, March 26, 1972.
238. CAB 128/48, minutes of September 22, 1971.

239. Hamill, *Pig in the Middle*, 33. As we have seen, this emphasis on an integrated response was central to the British army's counterinsurgency doctrine.

240. Kelly, *How Stormont Fell*, 132.

241. PREM 15/1004.

242. Wood, "Westminster Scene," 334; *Observer*, March 26, 1972.

243. CAB 134/3012, Home Office memorandum of March 12, 1971.

244. NAI 2003/16/465, note (signature illegible, apparently a senior DFA official) dated May 6, 1971.

245. CAB 134/3012, minutes dated May 20, 1971.

246. CAB 130/522, minutes of October 29, 1971.

247. CJ 3/105, November 8, 1971.

248. CJ 3/105, November 8, 1971.

249. J.A. Oliver, *Working at Stormont* (Dublin: Institute of Public Administration, 1978), 99.

250. Bloomfield, *Stormont in Crisis*, 157.

251. DEFE 13/924, Andrew to Maudling, March 8, 1972.

252. P. Bew, P. Gibbon, and H. Patterson, *The State in Northern Ireland 1921–72: Political Forces and Social Classes* (Manchester: Manchester University Press, 1979), 184.

253. Heath, *The Course of My Life*, 430.

254. PREM 15/1003, note of March 2, 1972, from Rothschild to Heath. This paper is an example of the radical (and impracticable) thinking that Heath encouraged, but it does not seem to have influenced the Cabinet's deliberations significantly.

255. *Belfast Telegraph*, February 12, 2002.

256. CJ 4/56, Burroughs to Maudling, April 14, 1971.

257. Gallagher, *The Northern Ireland Problem*, 13.

258. White, *Hume*, 112.

259. Hayes, *Minority Verdict*, 143.

260. DEFE 24/210, telex from Smith to Woodfield of December 18, 1971.

261. *Belfast News Letter*, March 19, 2007.

262. Bloomfield went on to thrive under direct rule. He became head of the Northern Ireland Civil Service in 1984 and received a knighthood in 1987. The IRA recognized his achievements by blowing up his house as he and his family slept in it in September 1988.

263. Ministry of Defense, "Operation Banner."

264. NAI 2003/16/461, handwritten note of a telephone call from E. Gallagher to the Office of the Taoiseach, signature illegible, recording that "a reliable source had assured him that the British Army in the North were pressing for the transfer of security to Westminster."

265. CAB 130/560, minute of March 22, 1972.

266. Hamill, *Pig in the Middle*, 98.

267. UK Government, *The Statement on the Defence Estimates*, Cmnd. 5976 (London: HMSO, 1975), Annex G, 103.

268. Hamill, *Pig in the Middle*, 26.

269. R. Evelegh, *Peace-Keeping in a Democratic Society: The Lessons of Northern Ireland* (London: Hurst, 1978), 3.

270. CJ 3/98, paper dated December 4, 1971.
271. Hamill, *Pig in the Middle*, 69.
272. Ibid., 39.
273. Chris Ryder, *The RUC 1922–2000: A Force under Fire* (London: Arrow, 2000).
274. Hansard, col. 274, February 1, 1972.
275. Hamill, *Pig in the Middle*, 86.
276. Ibid., 88.
277. P. Taylor, *Brits: The War against the IRA* (London: Bloomsbury, 2002), 88.
278. DEFE 24/210, minutes from Brigadier J.M.H. Lewis to DGI, December 22, 1971.
279. CAB 134/3011, minutes of meeting on March 31, 1971.
280. Cited in M. Urban, *Big Boys' Rules* (London: Faber, 1992), 22.
281. Dixon, *Northern Ireland*, 116.
282. Hamill, *Pig in the Middle*, 84.
283. Ibid., 103.
284. *The Times*, March 25, 1972.
285. Dixon, *Northern Ireland*, 120.
286. M. Carver, *Out of Step: Memoirs of a Field-Marshal* (London: Hutchison, 1989), 414.
287. NAI 2002/8/415, minutes of IDC meeting on June 16, 1971.
288. *Irish Times*, June 17, 1971.
289. DEFE 24/210, note from A.W. Stephens to AUS(GS), December 15, 1971.
290. P. Taylor, *Provos: The IRA and Sinn Féin* (London: Bloomsbury, 1998), 129.
291. Ibid., 130.
292. Taylor, *Brits*, 81.
293. Taylor, *Provos*, 130.
294. *Irish Times*, June 17, 1971.
295. FCO 33/1465, August 24, 1971.
296. Peck, *Dublin from Downing Street*, 136.
297. *Irish Times*, January 1, 2003.
298. Ibid.
299. "Brian Faulkner and Bloody Sunday," *Belfast Telegraph*, February 12, 2002.
300. Faulkner, *Memoirs*, 156.

# 6
# Negotiating Power Sharing, 1973

*There is nothing more difficult to arrange, more doubtful of success, and more dangerous to carry through than initiating changes in a state's constitution. The innovator makes enemies of all those who prospered under the old order and only luke- warm support is forthcoming from those who would prosper under the new.* —Machiavelli[1]

On March 23, 1972, Heath appointed William Whitelaw as first secretary of state for Northern Ireland, a cabinet post supported by three junior ministers and a new Whitehall department, the Northern Ireland Office (NIO). Whitelaw commandeered Faulkner's of- fices at Stormont Castle, next to the Northern Ireland parliament. As well as overseeing the Northern Ireland Civil Service (NICS) and Royal Ul- ster Constabulary (RUC) and providing political guidance for the army, Whitelaw had to deliver on Heath's commitment to building a new con- stitutional settlement that would "guarantee the elected representatives of the minority participation in the administration of the Province at Cabinet level." Whitelaw's efforts between March 1972 and December 1973 to turn that broad commitment into a practical reality, which involved negotiating with moderate leaders of Unionism and Nationalism, were formative in creating the organizational structures and patterns of understanding that underpinned British strategy in Northern Ireland for the next thirty years.

## The Problem: Violence

Whitelaw believed that imposing direct rule had opened up space for ne- gotiation, but that he had to make progress quickly. If, as the prevailing

249

Whitehall doctrine held, the violence resulted from a deficit in democratic representation, by the same logic a prolonged period of direct rule would increase the danger, not only from republicans. Army commanders warned ministers that they could not take on loyalists and republicans simultaneously. Estimates of Whitelaw's window of opportunity ranged from three to six months.[2] But before he could address the constitutional issue, he had to reverse the upsurge in republican violence.

The cabinet had hoped that the sharp hiatus created by Stormont's suspension would quickly drain popular support from the Irish Republican Army (IRA) and reduce to a politically acceptable level its capacity to inflict damage. This hope was not realized. The security situation deteriorated as the Provisional IRA pressed home what it saw as its tactical advantage. Eighty people had been killed from January 1 to March 24, 1972; 387 people were killed from March 25 to December 31. In the four months following the introduction of direct rule, 600 bombs were exploded, 2,057 people injured, and 192 murdered. In the month of March, security forces recorded 399 shooting incidents. By July this figure had risen to 2,718.[3]

*"Killing the IRA by Kindness"*

Whitelaw faced a tough dilemma. There could be no political progress as long as such intense violence continued, and to reduce it, he had first to reverse Nationalist disaffection; but conciliatory moves toward Nationalists would infuriate Unionists and could be claimed as victories by the IRA. On the other hand, if he did nothing he believed that he would "fail ignominiously."[4]

Shortly after the imposition of direct rule, Gerry Fitt, Paddy Devlin, and John Hume of the Social Democratic and Labour Party (SDLP) requested a meeting with UK officials Howard Smith and Frank Steele. This took place on April 11. According to Steele's record, "their main theme was that the SDLP was engaged in a struggle with the IRA and that we should help the SDLP in this struggle."[5] The SDLP advised the British that the army should avoid any confrontation that the IRA would exploit to bolster popular support, and that all internees should be released as soon as possible. If this advice were followed, they contended, "the IRA could be finally defeated within the next three weeks," since it was internally split and many of its supporters were weary of the struggle. Whitelaw acted on the SDLP's advice. Acutely aware of recent lessons in the costs of aggressive coercion, he instructed the army to keep a low profile, stopped signing internment orders, and released a flow of internees, which he regulated in response to changes in the level of violence.[6] By these means he hoped to strip the IRA of popular support and encourage the SDLP to enter negotiations.

A month into his new post, Whitelaw reported to his cabinet colleagues that the transition to direct rule had gone remarkably smoothly. The NICS and RUC had remained faithful, the anticipated Protestant backlash had not materialized, and the agreed-upon program of local government reform was continuing as planned. The only real problem, he maintained, was actually the fruit of this success, as both wings of the IRA had seen that they were at risk of losing support and had accordingly been "moved to increase their violent activities in an effort to prevent us from exploiting the advantage of our control of law and order by releasing internees." Whitelaw conceded that his low-profile approach was risking soldiers' lives and restricting the flow of intelligence to the security services, but assured his colleagues that army commanders had accepted this "as a necessary consequence of our political objectives."[7]

Looking ahead, Whitelaw defined three broad strategic options: to revert to vigorous military action, actively confronting the terrorists—essentially a return to the military security strategy; to allow shooting and bombing to take place without any military reaction; and a middle course, which he had already adopted, of using his political judgment to strike the correct balance between military and political objectives. This would entail "almost day to day the taking of political initiatives in the field of law and order with corresponding public relations activity."[8] He never had any intention of following the first or second course of action. He rejected the first because it would reverse Heath's declared policy direction and it would need more troops, which the Ministry of Defence (MoD) was reluctant to supply. He dismissed the second as politically unacceptable.

In contrast with the military security approach, which had provided the context for internment, the third option can reasonably be called a political security approach. As under Callaghan, army and police operations would be closely monitored, guided, and constrained, with an eye to their political implications. They would no longer be directed at propping up Faulkner but at engaging the SDLP in talks. If this approach succeeded, that negotiations were taking place, irrespective of the outcome, would help deliver Whitelaw's security objectives. He would have begun to create a virtuous circle in which there would eventually be no credible justification for violence.

During the first four months of direct rule Whitelaw took a series of steps that Faulkner characterized as "killing the IRA by kindness."[9] By June 1972, he had released over 500 internees and as a gesture to the SDLP lifted the ban on marches that Heath had demanded of Faulkner as a condition for introducing internment. When the Official IRA declared a cessation of hostilities on May 30, 1972, Whitelaw interpreted it as evidence that his conciliatory approach was succeeding.

Like the Officials, the Provisionals' Army Council reviewed its tactics in response to the changing mood in republican communities, but drew a very different conclusion. It decided that since the shootings and bombings had achieved their first objective, the fall of Stormont, they should be intensified. It had declared 1972 "The Year of Victory," and this aspiration seemed to be coming true.[10] It presented itself as directly confronting the traditional enemy, British colonialism. On April 14, 1972, the Provisionals exploded twenty-three bombs across Northern Ireland, sending a loud message that their campaign of terror would continue. Having established this, the Provisionals offered a ceasefire in June on the condition that Whitelaw would offer special status for certain convicted "political" prisoners, thus giving their offenses a degree of official legitimacy; "order the cessation of all harassment of the IRA"; and agree to meet Provisional representatives in person.[11]

The cabinet committee on Northern Ireland, now called GEN 79, considered the Provisionals' offer on June 16. Whitelaw told his colleagues that it would have been "folly" to agree to direct negotiations with the Provisionals, but the committee agreed that some understanding would have to be reached with them since "no solution seemed possible unless their point of view were represented. . . . Their cooperation could hardly be obtained without some semblance of a bargain."[12] The meeting concluded that Whitelaw should proceed as he saw fit. He at once offered concessions to all three demands.

He first authorized two of his senior officials, Frank Steele and Phillip Woodfield, to meet Provisional representatives to explore the logistics of a personal meeting. On June 20, Steele and Woodfield met David O'Connell and Gerry Adams. At the Provisionals' insistence Whitelaw had released Adams from internment to attend. Steele and Woodfield agreed that, during a ceasefire, Provisional volunteers would be permitted to carry weapons and walk about freely within their own areas without being subjected to arrest as long as they did not engage in "ordinary" criminal acts such as burglary. On the same day, Whitelaw granted special status for paramilitary prisoners, permitting them to wear their own clothes and to have extra visits and parcels.[13] Hume briefed Irish officials on his discussions with Whitelaw during this period, telling them that the British were also prepared to agree that, while the Provisionals would not formally be permitted to participate in the proposed political talks, the SDLP delegates could be accompanied by any representatives they wished to bring from their own constituencies—a device to bring the Provisionals into the discussions while publicly denying that they had been admitted.[14]

The Provisionals responded by suspending bombings and shootings starting at midnight on June 26. Steele and Woodfield encouraged Whitelaw to meet the Provisionals himself. Although his mainstream advisers warned him not to, Whitelaw was persuaded that a refusal would hand the initiative to the Provisionals.[15] He accepted Woodfield's assessment that O'Connell and Adams genuinely wanted a permanent end to the violence. He may have been reassured by Woodfield's observation that the Provisional representatives' conduct had been "respectable and respectful—they easily referred to Mr. Whitelaw as the secretary of state and they addressed me from time to time as 'Sir.'. . . Their behaviour and attitude appeared to bear no relation to the indiscriminate campaigns of bombing and shooting in which they have both been prominent leaders."[16]

Whitelaw arranged to meet Provisional representatives himself in secret on July 7 at the London home of NIO minister Paul Channon. The Provisional delegation included Chief of Staff Sean McStiofáin, Gerry Adams, and Martin McGuinness.[17] They traveled to London by British army helicopter and in a Royal Air Force flight, to the disgust of the British regular servicemen in attendance.[18] Whitelaw, who tried to set a conciliatory tone, was bitterly disappointed at the outcome: "The meeting was a non-event. The IRA leaders simply made impossible demands which I told them the British government would never concede. They were in fact still in a mood of defiance and determination to carry on until their absurd ultimatums were met."[19] Frank Steele was appalled, later commenting, "McStiofáin behaved like the representative of an army that had fought the British to a standstill. . . . He was in cloud-cuckoo-land."[20]

The failure of the meeting did not shift Whitelaw from his strategy of conciliation. That it had taken place at all reinforced his belief that the Provisional leadership was divided over tactics. The hard-line faction was believed to include McStiofáin; the moderates, O'Connell.[21] After the meeting, Adams has since indicated that he himself took "a fairly absolutist position," telling O'Connell that "unless there was going to be a political agreement with the British, it was not in the republican interest to be involved in a long, protracted truce."[22] His confidence was underpinned by the knowledge that 200 Armalite rifles—a new weapon, superior to those the British army normally used—had recently arrived in Belfast, smuggled aboard the *Queen Elizabeth 2* from New York; moreover, a consignment of RPG-7 rocket launchers and missiles was on its way to Ireland from Libya.[23]

The ceasefire ended on July 9 when the Provisionals' Belfast brigade fired on British troops in the Lenadoon housing estate in west Belfast.[24] Despite this, ministers clung to the hope that conciliation might yet succeed in splitting the Provisional leadership. During a chance encounter at a Buckingham Palace garden party a few days later, Whitelaw told the Irish ambassador that he was convinced that "O'Connell is a genuine moderate and that he can be counted on to exert a valuable influence. . . . If Stephenson [McStiofáin] could be got rid of then real progress with the IRA might be possible. . . . If you or we could pick him up this might be the right thing to do at this point in time."[25]

On July 10, however, Whitelaw reported to GEN 79 that the hard-liners had gained ascendancy over those who had secured the ceasefire. He argued that unless the security forces took firm action against the IRA, loyalists—notably the Ulster Defence Association (UDA)—likely would take the law into their own hands, requiring the army to fight both sides simultaneously. Whitelaw calculated that the Provisionals would seek to keep the level of violence sufficiently high to ensure that he could not end internment, but not so high as to risk losing popular support; they would be constrained by fear of a loyalist backlash, and of its effect on their supporters. Opinions were divided on objectives, strategy, and tactics within the Provisional Army Council, as was evident from intelligence sources and conversations between officials and republicans. There was a significant fault line between those who saw the armed struggle as politics by other means and those who viewed it as a war of attrition that could be won simply by inflicting sufficient damage on the British over a sufficiently long period, while tolerating as much suffering themselves as victory required. As for whether to revert to tougher tactics, Heath indicated that before doing so, "it was important to seek every opportunity of reducing tension in the hope that the more moderate leaders of the IRA would prevail and that a resumption of the ceasefire might enable the Government to continue their policy of reconciliation in the search for a political settlement."[26]

### Operation Motorman

Heath's optimism was soon punctured. Provisional hard-liners—now reportedly including Adams—calculated that they could negotiate from a position of greater strength after stretching the British further, and went on to call for "a war of the utmost ferocity."[27] On July 13, the Provisionals shot 3 soldiers dead in Belfast. Within a week they had murdered 6 more, bringing the total killed since 1969 to 100. They also brought back explosions. On July 21, they set off twenty-five car bombs in the centers of Belfast and Londonderry, killing 11 people and seriously injuring 130. Hoax warnings added to the chaos and reduced the effectiveness of emergency services. Television coverage showed rescue workers sweeping up scattered body parts from the wreckage of Belfast's central bus station.

The carnage of what came to be called Bloody Friday revolted moderate Catholic opinion, creating a new willingness in the SDLP to accept tougher security measures and engage in Whitelaw's quest for a political settlement. Dismayed and angered by the Provisionals' brutal rejection of the opportunity for negotiation that he had offered—at considerable risk to his reputation—Whitelaw now did a shameless U-turn, announcing "that a tough security response was essential to send an unmistakeable message to the IRA and to both communities in Northern Ireland."[28] From this point on, he pursued a twin-track strategy very similar to that for which the British had previously criticized Faulkner: on the one hand working toward a political settlement, on the other strengthening the capacity of the security services and the criminal justice system to deal with the IRA threat. He told Faulkner "that a new phase of policy had arrived, and that the Government now realized that the IRA would have to be beaten."[29]

Whitelaw's first action under the new dispensation was to move against the republican no-go areas, which he now characterized as "a symbol of weakness and failure in British rule."[30] For weeks he had resisted army commanders' requests to move into these neighborhoods in Derry and Belfast, from which republican barricades had excluded the police and army since internment. The soldiers had complained that this exclusion had permitted republican activists to set themselves up as an alternative local government, organizing basic public services and representing residents in dealings with the army and civil administration. Worse, it had enabled the Provisionals to reinforce their popular support base, recruit and train new members, stockpile arms, and prepare attacks without fear of interruption.

Enraged at the Bloody Friday killings, Whitelaw allowed the army to remove the barricades, which they did in Belfast on July 24 and in Derry on July 31; 4,000 extra soldiers were sent to Northern Ireland for the operation, which was called Motorman. They met little resistance. Even with the pain he had incurred as a result of Bloody Sunday, Heath had told the general officer commanding (GOC) that up to 100 deaths would be politically acceptable, a remarkable indicator of the change in the political context since February.[31] By giving advance notice of the operation, Whitelaw enabled Provisional activists to leave their areas and so reduced the risk of lethal confrontation. By ensuring that loyalist as well as republican barricades came down, he also reduced the credibility of complaints about sectarian bias, a lesson learned from the internment operation. Two people were killed during an exchange of gunfire. After Motorman, the army stepped up its patrols, house raids, and searches in republican areas and created a series of military bases in existing buildings there—precisely what Chichester-Clark and Faulkner had requested before direct rule, when the army had refused.

Operation Motorman did not immediately reduce the violence. On the same day, three Provisional car bombs killed nine people in the village of Claudy, near Derry. The monthly death toll remained within the range of twenty to fifty-five for the rest of the year, compared with a range of twenty-two to forty for the previous six months. The death rate among soldiers rose slightly. The Provisionals' bombing targets included the head-quarters of the Unionist Party in Belfast, which they blew up on September 2. But from a British perspective Motorman succeeded in that it enabled the security forces to establish a permanent presence in the republican areas from which they had previously been excluded, allowing them to disrupt Provisional operations and gather intelligence. It reduced the Provisionals' ability to undermine the development of political dialogue with the SDLP, which was Whitelaw's next goal. It showed republicans that the British meant business and assuaged Unionists' demands for firm action to restore the rule of law.

### The Loyalist Reaction

While he was trying to drain the Provisionals' popular support, Whitelaw also had to deal with the threat of violent protest from the loyalist side. This set a limit on how far he could go in meeting Nationalists' demands. Craig's Vanguard movement and the UDA mobilized Unionist outrage at direct rule by organizing a two-day protest strike, in which an estimated 200,000 people took part, and mass rallies at which paramilitary organizations paraded in uniform. But once they had registered their anger, the strikers went back to work, having demonstrated the strength of their numbers and made clear to Whitelaw that they would stoutly resist any attempt to move toward Irish unification.

Suspecting that Whitelaw was secretly seeking to negotiate a deal with the Provisionals, and to protest his refusal until then to occupy the republican no-go areas, the UDA began in June to build its own barricades around loyalist neighborhoods in Belfast. The cabinet minutes for July 10 record Whitelaw's concern that "unless the Government were seen to authorise more vigorous action by the security forces against the IRA, the UDA would be able to take the law into their own hands and the Army would find themselves fighting on two fronts against extremists of both factions."[32] These and other diffuse loyalist protests receded after Motorman. But loyalist paramilitary groupings responded to what they saw as Britain's failure to suppress the Provisionals by organizing atrocities of their own. Unable to target IRA members directly and unwilling to attack the security forces or civilian economic targets, the Ulster Volunteer Force (UVF) and elements in the UDA began randomly murdering Catholics, often on a tit-for-tat basis. The first of these murders was on April 15, and eighty more followed during 1972. They were often brutal; in some cases the victims were tortured. Faulkner later wrote:

> The arrival of the Protestant assassination gangs coincided with the collapse of confidence among the Unionist population in the will of the Westminster government to defeat the IRA and protect the rights of the majority. . . . It is sad but true that the real determination of Unionists not to join a united Ireland seems only to have been fully believed when Protestant assassins started killing Catholics.[33]

By December, the UDA's membership had reached an estimated 26,000, making it the largest nonstate paramilitary organization in the Western world.[34] Most were passive supporters rather than active combatants, but a hard core took the name Ulster Freedom Fighters (UFF), and threatened to murder Nationalist elected representatives. In January 1973, Whitelaw warned the cabinet that "the extreme Protestants have the capacity to create a situation in which many lives might be lost and which would certainly pose a major security operation [sic] for the British troops."[35]

When Whitelaw used his powers of detention against loyalists for the first time in February 1973, they responded with another mass strike, which Craig supported. Many areas were affected by cuts in power and public transport, and there was widespread intimidation. On February 7, police stations were attacked, four Catholics and a firefighter were killed, dozens of buildings were burned, and loyalists exchanged gunfire with the army. Although this upsurge crossed a new threshold for loyalist paramilitarism, it did not last long. Faulkner condemned it and it did not attract much popular support.

Loyalist paramilitaries were not a mirror image of the IRA. Their objectives were more limited and reactive. Beyond defending their streets from IRA attack, their main aim was to prevent Whitelaw from offering further concessions to republicans. They did not have a vision for constitutional transformation or access to significant international networks of supporters, and they could not strike from secure bases across the border. They depicted themselves as a defensive force, the legitimate heirs to the Ulster Special Constabulary (USC), with the primary role of reinforcing rather than fighting the police and army. They have been described as "localistic and politically primitive," and their relative incoherence led Whitelaw to underestimate their capacity to inflict damage.[36] But they had one significant asset which the IRA lacked: access to information, weaponry, and support from sympathetic individuals in the security forces, especially the Ulster Defence Regiment (UDR) and RUC.[37]

Loyalist paramilitarism constrained British strategy to the extent that army commanders could not fight both sides simultaneously,[38] a limitation reinforced by the government's dependence on the Protestant community for its foot soldiers. If the authorities confronted loyalist protests too aggressively, it could prove difficult to recruit and retain the personnel the UDR and RUC needed. On the other hand, the point was made at a meeting of the MoD's Northern Ireland Policy Group on June 1, 1972, that "the killing of IRA members by Protestants might be no bad thing from our point of view if it led to a cessation of violence."[39]

Whitelaw concluded from the pattern of events on the streets—including the loyalists' voluntary dismantling of their own barricades after Motorman—that he could safely proceed with his political initiative as long as he could persuade loyalists that he was commited to maintaining the union and preventing the IRA from gaining any further ground through violence.

### Detention without Trial

Direct rule did not end Catholic hostility to internment. The SDLP maintained its stand of not engaging with Whitelaw's political initiative until all internees had been released. But for both political and security reasons Whitelaw could not end internment until the IRA campaign had stopped. Thus, in effect, unless the SDLP softened its position, the Provisionals had a veto over political progress. On the Unionist side, Faulkner insisted that more effective security policies were the most crucial element in building an agreed-upon future government. He had accepted that internment in its original crude form would have to go, and as an alternative had proposed creating special courts to deal with terrorist offenses.

Faced with conflicting demands from the two sides, Whitelaw recognized that no political initiative would stop the violence without accompanying changes in security policy. Normal judicial procedures were ineffective against terrorist organizations willing to intimidate and murder witnesses and jurors. He needed some alternative to internment that would free the SDLP to negotiate. He accordingly introduced a new procedure, detention without trial, but faced an uphill task in convincing Nationalists that this was much different from internment. The main differences were that under the new system, introduced in December 1972, the power to detain passed from ministers to an independent quasi-judicial tribunal, and a separate appeal mechanism was created. The tribunal could authorize the detention of suspected terrorists for unlimited periods on the basis of evidence provided by the security forces.

For the longer term, Whitelaw set up a commission of legal experts under Lord Diplock to consider new judicial procedures to tackle terrorism. Diplock published his report on December 20. He endorsed detention without trial and recommended further changes in the law. Following this, Parliament passed the Emergency Provisions Act in July 1973, which introduced a new power of arrest for soldiers and allowed the police to hold suspects for seventy-two hours for questioning. Special courts were established, in which a senior judge would hear terrorist cases without a jury, but which otherwise retained as many of the features of normal court processes as practicable in what Diplock described as "the current atmosphere of terror."[40] These changes in security policy reflected Faulkner's thinking and encouraged him to engage with Whitelaw. More important for Whitelaw, they cleared the way for the SDLP to talk. They signaled a more sophisticated approach—selective control rather than brute force—that focused on detaining individual suspects rather than on overwhelming entire neighborhoods and, as far as practicable, treated terrorist crimes like any others, irrespective of their political motivation.

### IRA Setbacks

By December 1972, the Provisionals had been weakened by the loss of the no-go areas. They were facing articulate criticism from their own republican constituencies, confronting improvements in the training, tactics, and intelligence capabilities of the security forces, and suffering from the effects of internment. Even across the border, their fighters were not safe. Dublin was increasingly responsive to British requests for cooperation. Journalist Robert Fisk reported that the organization was "badly mauled, and in parts of Belfast beaten to virtual extinction."[41] There was growing war-weariness in republican neighborhoods and a widespread feeling that the Provisionals should end their terror campaign even if they retained their original role as neighborhood defenders of last resort. Some republicans wanted the armed struggle to end because they saw it as the only way the British army would leave.[42] Even Gerry Adams, normally upbeat about the republicans' capacity to persevere through severe hardships, has acknowledged that "by late 1972 the popular uprising had receded to some degree . . . the struggle had entered a defensive mode."[43]

Faced with the setbacks and with the progress Whitelaw was making in reducing Catholic disaffection, Adams as commander of the Provisionals' Belfast Brigade decided to take the struggle to the heart of the British establishment.[44] On March 8, 1973, Provisional volunteers from Belfast drove four car bombs to London. MI5 had learned about the operation in advance and two of the bombs were found and defused. But two others exploded, including one at the iconic Old Bailey courts complex. The extent of the resulting media coverage in Britain demonstrated that one bomb in London was worth a dozen in Belfast, especially if the target had great symbolic significance.

Adams had calculated that the London bombings would revive republican morale, which they did. But they did not have the huge effect he wanted on British public opinion or the government's strategic calculations, and they were soon offset by two morale-boosting successes for the security forces. On March 28, the Irish navy intercepted another consignment of guns and explosives on its way to the Provisionals from Libya. And on June 25, on the eve of elections to Whitelaw's new assembly, the army arrested thirty-five republican activists in Belfast, including Adams.

By summer 1973, there was evidence that Whitelaw's twin-track approach was working. During the six-month period from April 1, 1972, 283 deaths occurred as a result of the conflict, 163 of which have been attributed to republicans and 69 to various loyalists.[45] The corresponding figures for the six-month period from January 1, 1973, were 162, 78, and 56. Slow but steady progress on the security front had created a more positive context for political negotiations. Moderate Catholic opinion no longer supported illegal protests or sought to justify republican violence; the SDLP had signed up for dialogue and—albeit with strong qualifications—had acquiesced in the new security regime; the Provisionals were continuing to suffer major setbacks; moderate Unionist confidence was improving; and loyalist paramilitary violence had been contained.

## The Problem: Politics

Whitelaw recognized that his political initiative would be vulnerable to the weaknesses in Northern Ireland's party political system, which had been volatile even before direct rule had exposed it to further stresses. Success would depend on the ability of moderate elected leaders from both sides to mobilize the support of their parties and wider constituencies for his proposals, despite the fundamental irreconcilability of their constitutional aspirations, the harsh rhetoric each directed against the other, and a daily backdrop of death and destruction. This would have been a demanding challenge even for well-established, stable, and united political parties, which Northern Ireland's clearly were not. Of the potential partners for a community government in March 1972, only the Unionist Party had sturdy historical roots, and these had been seriously shaken by the external shocks and internal conflicts from which it had suffered since 1968.

Whitelaw and his officials accordingly took every opportunity to build up what they saw as the reasonable center parties, which they hoped would provide the core for the new administration—the SDLP, Alliance, and the Northern Ireland Labour Party (NILP); to promote moderation within the Unionist Party; and to confound the extremists, a category which they defined to embrace elected representatives such as Craig and Paisley as well as republican and loyalist paramilitaries.

## The SDLP

The SDLP of spring 1972 has been described as a loose coalition of trade union socialists, former civil rights campaigners, and constitutional nationalists that had yet to cohere and organize as a party that could deliver a negotiated deal and win elections. Its leading figures were still developing an agreed-upon manifesto and collective identity, while straining to hold together supporters from the rural border regions (who tended to emphasize the traditional nationalist agenda) with those from Belfast (who tended to emphasize trade union and socialist values). Like the IRA, the SDLP saw direct rule as a first step toward unification. With Stormont's suspension, they believed that they had brought the major political parties in Britain and Ireland around to their view that this was the only viable long-term solution. They thus focused on how and by when that outcome could best be engineered. As constitutional nationalists the SDLP enjoyed three great advantages over other Northern Ireland parties in the first year of direct rule. First, Whitelaw needed them. The secretary of state believed that he could not defeat the IRA without the SDLP's active cooperation and preferably full participation in government, and that the SDLP could attract support from both major traditions behind a progressive social and economic policy agenda. Second, the SDLP enjoyed national and international support. Its nonviolent strategy for a united Ireland was actively encouraged and promoted by the Irish government and the opposition parties in Dublin, by Harold Wilson and a substantial faction of the Labour opposition at Westminster, by grandees such as Ted Kennedy in the U.S. Congress, and by influential players at the United Nations and in the European Parliament. Third, Faulkner badly wanted a devolved administration back. This enabled the SDLP to pursue a harder bargain than if the leaders of Unionism had united around a tougher or more integrationist approach. After September 1972, Whitelaw took the Unionist Party's engagement largely for granted, while straining to lure the SDLP into negotiations.

With the imposition of direct rule, John Hume called on the IRA to end its terror campaign. Responding to Whitelaw's first concessions—the gradual release of internees and the lifting of the ban on demonstrations—and emboldened by popular Catholic revulsion at the continuing Provisional violence, the SDLP in May 1972 called off its boycott of public bodies, urging those who had withdrawn to return. Hume met Whitelaw on June 15, a meeting the secretary of state later described as a crucial breakthrough. It was the SDLP's first formal engagement with government

since walking out of Stormont a year earlier. Hume encouraged Whitelaw
to meet the Provisional leadership and accept their demand for special
status for their internees. He then helped to set up Whitelaw's meeting
with them. Both this and the failure of the meeting to deliver a peace
deal reminded Whitelaw how much his success depended on the SDLP's
strength and goodwill. Whitelaw told the Irish ambassador in London
that Hume "is behaving magnificently. Some of the others in his party
could be more helpful."[46]

Although the SDLP leaders would not yet agree to negotiate with
Faulkner, they were keen to influence the process of political policy development in London. They could already do so because they enjoyed direct
access to Whitelaw and Heath as well as to ministers in Dublin. In September 1972 the party produced a paper, "Towards a New Ireland," setting
out their proposals for a settlement. This helped to establish their collective identity as a modernizing party and reinforced their credibility.[47] The
SDLP's central demand was that the British government should work for
a united Ireland "on terms which would be acceptable to all the people of
Ireland."[48] They recognized that there would have to be a transitional period. During this time, London and Dublin would jointly control foreign
affairs, defense, security and policing, and the financial subvention from
London would continue. The two governments would each appoint a commissioner and this duumvirate would replace the secretary of state.

For the internal government of Northern Ireland during the transitional
period, the SDLP called for an eighty-four-member legislative assembly
elected by the single transferable vote (STV) method of proportional representation (PR). An executive of fifteen members would be elected from
the assembly, also by PR. These fifteen would elect a chief executive, who
would allocate departmental responsibilities among them. Security and
policing would fall under the direct control of a new department headed
jointly by the two commissioners. If necessary, the commissioners would be
able to call on military support from both sovereign governments. At the
all-island level, a new senate would be created with equal representation
from the Dáil and the new northern assembly. Its basic function would be
"to plan the integration of the whole island by preparing the harmonisa-
tion of the structures, laws, and services of both parts of Ireland and to
agree on an acceptable constitution for a New Ireland and its relationships
with Britain." The SDLP's proposals sought to reconcile their long-term
aspiration to a united Ireland with Whitelaw's offer of a share in power at
Stormont by making clear that their participation in the assembly would
be time-limited and conditional. The Nationalist majority in the new all-
island senate would ensure that this was so.

Satisfied with the ground they were gaining, the SDLP leadership per-suaded delegates at their annual conference in November 1972 that they should engage in formal negotiations with Whitelaw and the other parties. The SDLP performed well in its first regional election, to the reformed district councils in May 1973. The challenges of campaigning stimulated them into building a grassroots organization across the region. They won 83 of the 103 Nationalist seats; the balance went to the Republican Clubs (the political arm of the Officials), survivors from the old Nationalist Party, and assorted independents.

Whitelaw encouraged the SDLP to transform itself from a truculent opponent of Stormont into a constructive partner in negotiations. In re-turn for its leaders' collaboration, he recognized them as the authentic voice of the Catholic community. The SDLP's organizational achieve-ments and electoral success enabled British ministers for the first time to negotiate with elected representatives of the minority on equal terms with their Unionist counterparts in designing Northern Ireland's future politi-cal institutions.

## Sinn Féin

The Provisionals' political wing, Sinn Féin, considered the possibility of fighting the assembly election. However, it was an illegal organization with neither the experience nor the capacity for constituency campaigning. Its electoral prospects at the time were not promising. The republican leader-ship concluded that the movement should focus on the armed struggle and do nothing that might legitimate partition. As Adams observed, "we had succeeded in getting rid of Stormont and we just needed to keep up that momentum in order to get rid of the British altogether."[49] They decided to boycott Whitelaw's election.

## The Unionist Party

Direct rule came as one more disastrous blow to the morale and authority of the Unionist Party. Its leaders no longer had ministerial status, govern-mental powers, or access to the resources of the civil service. Party activists were deeply divided over personalities, issues, objectives, and tactics. In addition, the party suffered three major handicaps. First, the British and Irish governments mistrusted Faulkner. In a conversation in June 1972 with the Irish ambassador, Whitelaw said, "Craig is a diminishing influ-ence and Faulkner, as usual, is being devious."[50] The following month a Foreign Office minister told the ambassador, "What is badly needed is that somebody should emerge on the Protestant side who could give political leadership. Faulkner certainly cannot do this. He has been most unhelpful in the whole situation and must be regarded as of diminishing significance. There can be no question now of the restoration of confidence in him by Mr. Heath."[51] Second, Unionists lacked support outside Northern Ireland. With the exception of a handful of Conservative backbenchers, national and international opinion was against them; the national media and discourse of the British political elite depicted them as sectarian violators of Catholics' civil rights. Third, Faulkner showed that he was prepared to pay a substantial price to restore a devolved administration. This weakened his negotiating position and widened the fault lines in his own party. It also led Whitelaw to focus on wooing the SDLP.

In his first bitterness at what he saw as Heath's betrayal, Faulkner had refused to cooperate with Whitelaw and appeared to make common cause with Craig.[52] He was understandably suspicious of Heath's intentions.[53] He recognized that Heath was intent on distancing the Conservative Party from the Unionists, even if this meant that he could no longer rely on their votes at Westminster. Heath wrote a personal note to the Conservative Party's chairman that included this damning assessment of the Unionists' prospects:

> The Unionist Party, as we have known it, is a thing of the past. A number of small parties are already getting organized and their number will be added to by the break-up of the old Unionist Party. This process will no doubt be further encouraged by the use of proportional representation in the local government elections, with the further possibility of it being embodied in the electoral procedures for any central body agreed upon in a political solution.[54]

Far from expressing concern at this development, Heath told the chairman that "I do not believe that we can continue to maintain an alliance with a sectarian party based on and largely controlled by the Orange Lodges." He suggested that the Conservative Party should consider the possibility of fighting seats in Northern Ireland in its own right.

For the first four months of direct rule, Faulkner described his role as "leader of the constructive opposition" in the expectation that UK ministers would "sooner or later have to face the fact that their task is not just to bring reconciliation, so that Protestant and Catholic can live together in peace, but that it is also to deal with an armed and vicious rebellion."[55] He knew that Protestants were less likely than Catholics to support Whitelaw's efforts. In June 1972 an opinion poll found that 74 percent of Catholics but just 21 percent of Protestants thought the secretary of state was "doing a good job."[56] Collaboration with Whitelaw would create major political risks for him. To reduce them, he produced a broad and ambiguous statement of purpose around which he hoped to mobilize support for "the restoration of a meaningful Northern Ireland Parliament and Government."

Although Faulkner was outraged at direct rule, his priority was to return to power, and after the dust had settled, he came to see more advantage in working with Whitelaw than in fighting him. Many Unionist activists did not share this view, including Westminster MPs and members of the Ulster Unionist Council. With no powers of government or patronage at his command, Faulkner found it increasingly hard to maintain party discipline.

Operation Motorman persuaded Faulkner that Whitelaw had at last turned the corner, enabling him to engage with the British quest for a settlement. To free himself from the dependence on the Ulster Unionist Council that had plagued his predecessors, he created a new policy committee and appointed to it members representing all shades of opinion in the party, including even Craig. He persuaded the committee to publish a paper as a basis for discussion with Whitelaw in September. This called for a new Northern Ireland parliament, to be elected by the first-past-the-post method. Nationalist representatives would contribute to policymaking and overseeing departments through six committees, the composition of which would reflect the parties' strengths in the parliament. Opposition members would chair at least three of them. The majority party would form an executive comprising a prime minister and five or six ministers, each heading a department. It would control policing, intelligence gathering, and security. If Dublin would affirm Northern Ireland's right to self-determination and sign up for cooperation in ending terrorism, a cross-border intergovernmental council could be created with equal membership from north and south to address matters of mutual interest, particularly in the economic and social fields.[57] This paper in effect restated the position that Heath had rejected as insufficient six months previously, but it served its purpose as a basis for agreement within the party and negotiation with the British and other parties.

## Unionist Hard-Liners

Even while serving on Faulkner's new policy committee, Craig was promoting through the Vanguard movement his own concept of an independent Northern Ireland outside both the United Kingdom and Ireland. In May 1972 he issued a policy statement, "Ulster—A Nation," which set out his case for a unilateral declaration of independence (modeled on the unsuccessful example of the Smith government in Rhodesia/Zimbabwe) as a preferable alternative both to continuing direct rule, which in his view meant appeasement of the IRA, and enforced power sharing. In October he told the Monday Club, a Conservative pressure group at Westminster, that he could mobilize 80,000 men to oppose Whitelaw's policy; if necessary they would shoot to kill.[58] He rejected enforced power sharing in principle on the ground that Nationalists, by definition, sought to overthrow the state, and declared that he would accept nothing less than the full restoration of Stormont as it had been. Whitelaw thought Craig confused and inconsistent, and did not regard him as a serious threat.[59] Heath responded to Craig's threats during a visit to Belfast on November 16 and 17, 1972, by warning that a unilateral declaration of independence would cause a bloodbath throughout Ireland; he also threatened an immediate end to Northern Ireland's financial subvention from Westminster. Craig resigned from the Unionist Party on March 30, 1973, to transform Vanguard into a separate political party, the Vanguard Unionist Progressive Party. It stood for outright opposition to power sharing, the restoration of Stormont, and, as a fallback, full independence. Craig's defection enormously damaged the Unionist Party. Many influential members followed him and whole constituency associations defected en masse. More ominously for Faulkner, many who sympathized with Craig's opposition to power sharing remained inside the party to fight it from there. Craig's defection undermined Faulkner's negotiating position with Whitelaw, but without removing the internal threat to his leadership.

Faulkner's other most visible hard-line opponent, Ian Paisley, at first took the opposite tack to Craig, arguing for full integration with Britain. When Craig argued for an independent Northern Ireland, Paisley dismissed him and his supporters as "Protestant Sinn Féiners" who were out of touch with the real feelings of the Unionist community.[60] Opinion polls tend to confirm this. One found that only 3 percent of the electorate favored independence.[61] When Whitelaw finally agreed to meet Paisley for substantive talks in December 1972, Paisley made clear that he was not interested in discussing any political initiative until the IRA had been defeated. He called for stronger security measures, including military courts; the restoration of capital punishment for political murders; and the formation of a civil defense force to support the police and army.[62]

Faulkner also faced opposition on another front, among Unionist MPs at Westminster. With the transfer of authority from Stormont to Westminster, power and influence within the party shifted significantly to them. Six months into direct rule, their leader, Willie Orr, announced the creation of a coalition with Paisley and Craig to demand Stormont's immediate restoration.[63] This was contrary to party policy, and Faulkner persuaded Orr to backtrack, but the cracks in his relationship with his Westminster MPs were both very obvious and widening.

## Unionist Moderates

Faulkner also had to contend with disaffection and defections on his liberal flank, in particular to the Alliance Party, which he dismissed as putting forward "admirable non-sectarian sentiments which were music to the ears of British politicians."[64] Alliance unambiguously supported power sharing, though it was still small, politically inexperienced, and lacking in local constituency associations. In the first months of direct rule Whitelaw tried to build it up at the Unionist Party's expense. He succeeded in that some of that party's activists, led by Westminster MP Stratton Mills, transferred to Alliance after failing to have Vanguard members expelled. After a few months in office, however, Whitelaw recognized that relying on Alliance and other cross-community parties such as the NILP would not deliver sufficient Protestant support to secure a lasting settlement. Alliance's existence secured a separate voice for liberal Unionism in Whitelaw's negotiations, but it did so at the cost of weakening the moderate faction inside the Unionist Party.

In submitting its proposals to Whitelaw on the way forward, Alliance proposed a new assembly to be elected by the STV system. The assembly would establish committees the chairmen of which it would elect by the same method. The chairmen would also act as ministers, heading up civil service departments. Westminster would retain control over the RUC, but a second police force would be created to work alongside it, dealing with minor crimes and accountable to the assembly. The assembly would have no powers to enact security legislation. These proposals represented a compromise between those of the SDLP and the Unionist Party.

## Policy Development

During his first month in office, Whitelaw formulated a series of linked priority objectives: to deprive the terrorists of political support, destroy the IRA as an effective organization, plan social and economic reconstruction, and devise an agreed-upon constitutional settlement that would guarantee elected representatives of Nationalism a share in government.[65] As secondary objectives, he identified reducing the risks of a violent loyalist reaction, bringing direct rule to an end within a year, and withdrawing soldiers as quickly as practicable. Rather than publishing firm proposals immediately that risked attack from both sides, he decided first to seek the widest possible consensus on the broad principles that should govern a settlement. Although this staged process would take longer, he believed that it would give Northern Ireland's political parties time to adjust to the new realities. It would also force hard-liners to show their hands and enable him to marginalize them.

## Internal Consensus

Once Whitelaw had established the outline of his political security approach, he turned to the task of bringing the SDLP into negotiations, thereby discharging a commitment Maudling had first made in September 1971. He created a forward planning unit in the NIO to work on proposals for a constitutional settlement and convened an internal seminar for senior officials from the NIO and NICS. Working separately, each set of officials produced a paper identifying and assessing possible options. Surprisingly, given Heath's public commitment to power sharing, the NIO paper considered full integration with Britain as the best option, arguing that it would be virtually impossible to grant the minority participation on any basis that both sides would tolerate and that integration would solve the problem of minority exclusion, since both sides would accept Westminster rule as fair and unbiased.[66]

The NICS paper revealed a variety of opinions among the civil service heads of Northern Ireland departments, who had not previously been included in the policy development process. Some, like their NIO colleagues, favored full integration, but collectively they preferred some form of devolution, which they were accustomed to. They acknowledged the importance of securing Dublin's cooperation but shared their NIO counterparts' concerns that enforced power sharing was unlikely to be sustainable and would institutionalize sectarian divisions.

Whitelaw rejected his own officials' preferred option on the grounds that full integration would be unacceptable to Nationalist Ireland. It would not give the Irish government the political context it needed to cooperate on security and political development, it would not honor Heath's commitment to include minority elected representatives in government, and it would not restore peace. He added for good measure that full integration would be "administratively difficult" and that Northern Ireland had grown accustomed to "a more intimate form of government." He then concluded the seminar by declaring a consensus in favor of his own opinion that full integration was undesirable and that some form of devolution, with Westminster retaining control over law and order, offered the best prospects for peace in the longer term.[67]

## Consultation Papers

Whitelaw next published a green paper—a statement for consultation—that set out his broad rationale for the sharing of executive power.[68] Its main purpose was to show the leaders of the SDLP what might be on offer if they were to engage in negotiations, and ultimately in government, without causing Unionists to reject the concept of power sharing altogether.

Acknowledging that neither reform nor coercion had held the IRA back from terrorism and that internment had reinforced Catholic disaffection, the green paper asserted that the conflict required a high-level political solution that would bring elected representatives of the minority into government. It ruled out the SDLP proposals for phased unification and joint sovereignty but also dismissed the option, favored by some Unionists, of full integration into the United Kingdom. It then tentatively formulated the case for power sharing, including the concept of the Irish dimension, in deference to the SDLP's demand for action to express "the basic Irish aspirations of the Catholic community."

The green paper stated that "whatever arrangements are made for the future administration of Northern Ireland must take account of the Province's relationship with the Republic of Ireland; and to the extent that this is done, there is an obligation upon the Republic to reciprocate."[69] It did not present any specific proposals; at that stage the concept was little more than bait for the SDLP. It also enabled Whitelaw to test the breadth and intensity of Unionist opposition and Nationalist support without committing himself further. In the context of increasing Nationalist disenchantment with the Provisionals and improving Unionist confidence in his determination to confront terrorism, it was a subtle means to secure the traction he needed to engage with the SDLP without provoking a violent loyalist reaction.

Six weeks later the secretary of state was sufficiently confident in the way forward to put firmer proposals for political settlement to GEN 79.[70] Whitelaw had to work hard to convince Heath to give him the flexibility to negotiate the formation of the executive himself with the leaders of the assembly parties. But in the end, the cabinet agreed that significant powers should be devolved to a new Northern Ireland Assembly and Executive. Responsibility for all aspects of security should remain with London. Finally, there had to be a clear commitment to a Council of Ireland, in which the UK government would have a continuing interest by virtue of its security responsibilites.

Whitelaw submitted his final proposals on February 26, 1973, reminding his colleagues how difficult it would be to "avoid giving the extremists in both communities any plausible justification for taking their opposition into the streets and factories."[71] The Unionists would require a considerable devolution of powers, and the government also had to offer the minority "a prospect of an end to discrimination and second-class citizenship and of participation in government." The settlement must be proof against the outcome of the assembly election, which was highly uncertain. Consequently, the legislation should give the secretary of state maximum flexibility in constructing the executive. The cabinet agreed. Overcoming reservations from Heath, Whitelaw had secured the freedom he wanted to maneuver.

To smooth the passage for constitutional change, on March 8 Whitelaw held the first of what was declared to be a series of plebiscites on the union. In all, 591,820 people—57.5 percent of the electorate—voted for the proposition that Northern Ireland should remain part of the United Kingdom. With a Nationalist boycott of the plebiscite, only 6,463 voters supported the only alternative offered of "unification with the Republic outside the UK." The Provisionals responded by bombing government buildings in central London, killing 1 person and injuring some 250. The plebiscite was intended to demonstrate to Unionists that the union was secure, and to Nationalists and international opinion that it existed not by virtue of British force but by the free choice of the Northern Irish people.

On March 20, Whitelaw published a white paper converting the green paper's broad principles into concrete intentions.[72] There would be a single chamber assembly of some eighty members, elected by the STV method. Committees would oversee the work of each department, their composition reflecting the balance of parties in the assembly. The committee chairmen would act as the political heads of departments and collectively form the Northern Ireland Executive, which was no longer to "be solely based upon any single party, if that party draws its support and its elected representation virtually entirely from only one section of a divided community." Responsibility for policing and criminal justice were to be reserved to Westminster, at least for the time being. Other controversial matters—judicial appointments, public prosecutions, elections, and emergency powers—were to be excluded from devolution permanently. The office of secretary of state would continue, with the secretary formally appointing the executive, administering policing and criminal justice services, and overseeing UK interests in Northern Ireland. Westminster would replace the Special Powers Act and draft new legislation to protect human rights, outlaw discrimination, and provide for the investigation of complaints against the police. The UK government would invite representatives from the assembly parties and the Irish government to a conference to determine how best to realize the Irish dimension, addressing three broad issues: Dublin's formal acceptance of Northern Ireland's constitutional status, cross-border cooperation for mutual advantage, and concerted action against terrorist organizations.

The white paper package closely mirrored the proposals submitted in response to the green paper by Alliance and the NILP. Its careful wording, however, left open the questions of whether it was Catholics or Nationalists that the new executive would have to include and the extent to which they would be included. In theory, it allowed for the possibility of a cross-community government comprising Unionist, Alliance, and NILP members, to the extent that these parties could attract support from both Protestant and Catholic voters and field candidates from both sides. This deliberately loose formulation enabled Faulkner to avoid immediately having to confront his party with a U-turn on his previous robust undertaking not to share power with Nationalists. He even tried to present Whitelaw's proposals to the Unionist Party as being only incrementally different from the expanded committee system that it had already proposed itself.

## Legislation

Whitelaw moved quickly to implement the proposals, and the Northern Ireland Assembly Bill was enacted on May 3, 1973, providing for an election to a seventy-eight-member assembly. Between five and eight members would be returned for each of Northern Ireland's twelve Westminster constituencies. More detailed legislation swiftly followed. The Northern Ireland Constitution Act of July 18, 1973, reaffirmed Northern Ireland's status as part of the United Kingdom, which was made conditional on the outcome of future plebiscites rather than the will of the legislature. It also provided for the secretary of state to appoint a chief executive and up to eleven other assembly members, who would together form the Northern Ireland Executive, with powers devolved to them; arranged for cross-border agreements, including transfers of functions between public authorities in Northern Ireland and their southern counterparts; outlawed discrimination by any public authority on the ground of religious belief or political opinion; and created a new independent commission to advise the secretary of state on human rights issues.

The Constitution Act gave no automatic entitlement to devolution. It prescribed no formula either for determining whether or not devolution should take place or for what specific form it should take. There was no commitment to any of the four options for cross-community government that the green paper had described. The only firm requirement was that, in the opinion of the secretary of state, an executive could be formed "which having regard to the support it commands in the assembly and to the electorate on which that support is based, is likely to be widely accepted throughout the community."[73] The secretary of state would have the power both to appoint members to the executive and to decide whether or not to delegate responsibilities to them. The proposed coalition would be voluntary, but without it there would be no devolution.

The Constitution Act did not stipulate any special arrangements to ensure that the majority did not simply override the minority in the executive and assembly. Despite the Cabinet Office's earlier research into constitutional devices in divided societies, there was no provision, such as parallel consent or weighted majority, for ensuring that important decisions were made on a cross-community basis at either level. Whitelaw decided that his power to appoint the executive—and in the last resort to suspend it and the assembly—would provide sufficient protection.

### Election

Whitelaw did not know how much support each of the parties would command at the ballot box. There had been no elections in Northern Ireland since the Westminster election of June 1970, when the SDLP and Alliance did not exist as serious contenders. The results of that election could not have given him grounds for optimism, since it was memorable chiefly for Paisley's victory over the Unionist incumbent in North Antrim.

To make Whitelaw's project work, the leaders of Northern Ireland's parties would have to tackle four challenging tasks quickly in an already difficult political context, rendered extremely unstable by continuing terrorist violence: to build and sustain a solid coalition of support within their own parties, to win enough seats in the assembly election, to agree on the composition of the executive, and to agree on the form and substance of the "Irish dimension." Of the major parties only Alliance welcomed the white paper with enthusiasm. The SDLP and Unionist leaderships equivocated, reflecting tensions within their parties and the continuing strength of their more uncompromising rivals.

Faulkner talked up the guarantee of the union underpinned by the border plebiscite, the restoration of devolved government, the formation of the executive by negotiation, Whitelaw's explicit objective of marginalizing the IRA, and the restricted terms of the Irish dimension. He knew that, contentious as it was, power sharing was less obnoxious to Unionists than the threat from Dublin. One contemporary survey found that only 16 percent of Protestants versus 70 percent of Catholics favored the idea of a cross-border conference.[74] Once he had decided on engagement with Whitelaw as the best way forward, Faulkner deployed his considerable political skills with energy and commitment to allay the fears of the Unionist community. He tried hard to sell the changes outlined in the white paper. He seems to have been genuinely converted. In his memoirs he described it as "a cleverly flexible scheme, which avoided most of the objections which we had put to PR government or an institutionalized sectarian government, as there would obviously have to be a freely agreed coalition of parties."[75] He came to see it as a means to build a better, more inclusive society and as the best prospect for sustaining the union. He also calculated that if Unionists rejected it, the alternative was likely to prove much less attractive.

But selling the white paper to the Unionist community was hard uphill climbing. Faulkner resorted to verbal ambiguities and procedural manipulations that enabled him to keep going but undermined his credibility. His opponents accused him of collaborating in the destruction of the union by stealth, and of putting personal ambition before party and country. For all his enthusiasm and guile, Faulkner's collaboration cost him popular support, and his grip on the leadership slackened at each step in the process.[76] Although Whitelaw had deliberately kept specific targets for attack to a minimum, the white paper contained enough material for Unionist hardliners to exploit popular anxieties about the direction of events. Where the paper deliberately avoided offering detail, notably on the specifics for power sharing and the Irish dimension, they attacked it for its vagueness. After the Hunt reforms, radical changes in local government, an upsurge in Provisional violence, and direct rule, the white paper occurred to many Unionists to be just one more in a series of humiliations.

The assembly election was held on June 28, 1973. A majority of Unionist candidates accepted the white paper proposals with varying degrees of resignation, rather than campaigning actively for them.

In his election manifesto Faulkner declared that the party was "not prepared to participate in government with those whose primary objective is to break the Union with Great Britain."[77] This ambiguous phrase deliberately left unresolved the vital issue of whether Faulkner would enter into an executive with the SDLP. Many voters interpreted it to mean that he would not do so, a reasonable conclusion given the priority that SDLP leaders gave to ending the union. In an effort to impose discipline on the Unionist candidates, who were selected locally at constituency level, Faulkner asked them each to sign a pledge indicating that they supported the party's policy of making the white paper work. This ruse backfired as twelve candidates refused to sign; ten of them were elected.

In all, the Unionist Party won twenty-four seats with 29 percent of the poll. On the Nationalist side, the SDLP secured nineteen seats with 22 percent. Alliance won eight seats with 9 percent. Worryingly for Whitelaw, however, four Unionist factions opposed to power sharing attracted more support than either Faulkner's Unionists or the SDLP, winning a total of twenty-six seats with 30 percent. Although supporters of power sharing won a clear majority of seats in the assembly—by fifty to twenty-eight—a majority of the successful Unionist candidates opposed it. Given that the settlement required cross-community support, this outcome positioned them well to exploit divisions both within Faulkner's Unionists and between them and the SDLP, their potential partners in government. It was not a good foundation upon which to build an executive that was "likely to be widely accepted throughout the community."

On July 5, when Whitelaw reported to the cabinet on the implications of the election results, his assessment was mixed. On the one hand, all the major parties had engaged and the election had passed without serious incident, achievements that had looked improbable a year earlier. The SDLP had polled well; if they maintained party discipline they could deliver on Heath's requirement to have minority elected representatives in the executive. On the other hand, Alliance had done less well than he had hoped, and Unionists opposed to power sharing had won an uncomfortably large number of seats. Whitelaw assumed that there was no point in seeking to negotiate with Paisley and Craig, since in his view their primary objective was to obstruct progress.

Looking ahead, Whitelaw anticipated that the most promising possible coalition would comprise Faulkner's Unionists, the SDLP, and Alliance. If such an executive were formed, some of Faulkner's supporters would probably defect to Craig or Paisley. The process of negotiating an executive would prove difficult and protracted and its outcome was uncertain, but he considered that it was worth the effort. One possibility, which Whitelaw feared, was that Craig and the "extremists" who opposed the white paper might join a coalition with the SDLP, excluding moderate Unionists.[78] John Hume and Ivan Cooper of the SDLP had toyed with this possibility briefly after hearing Craig advocate independence, but it ran out of steam after the election.

### Executive

Whitelaw's next task was to steer his three target parties into a coalition. Initial soundings revealed that Faulkner was willing to work with the SDLP and Alliance but wanted the SDLP first to call off the rent and rates strike. Government ministers could not condone lawbreaking. On the SDLP side, there was strong resistance to working under Faulkner, the architect of internment, as chief executive. On October 5, 1973, Whitelaw chaired a first meeting of the leaders of the three potential partners at Stormont Castle. The other assembly parties were invited but declined. It was the first formal negotiation between the Unionists and the SDLP since Hume had led his colleagues out of Stormont over two years earlier. Faulkner gives a detailed account of their meetings, which lasted over seven weeks.[79] Whitelaw discharged his remit with skill. Despite intense political differences and personal antipathies, he built constructive working relationships between the Unionist and SDLP delegates.

Faulkner had entered the talks with serious reservations. Several of his assembly members had defected; many of those who remained were nervous. Inside the Unionist Party his opponents were calling for his resignation. In the assembly, Craig and Paisley were pursuing an obstructionist strategy to prevent the formation of an executive. But as the talks proceeded, and with some prodding from Whitelaw, Faulkner concluded that he could work with the SDLP, and that their aspiration to a united Ireland in the long term need not prevent them from contributing constructively to the everyday administration of Northern Ireland, which was what really mattered. He accordingly focused on practical priorities, bargaining particularly hard over the composition of the executive. He demanded a majority of seats, while the SDLP insisted on 50-50 representation.

At the end of October, Whitelaw reported to his cabinet colleagues that the talks were proceeding in a constructive atmosphere, but that the underlying mistrust was intense. Faulkner was under attack from hardliners in his own party, from dissident Unionists in the assembly, and from moderate leadership rival Roy Bradford. Although the SDLP delegation was presenting a united front, their backbenchers were restive and finding it difficult to appreciate why their negotiators were being so friendly to Faulkner.[80]

After six weeks, the delegations had still failed to agree on the party balance in the executive and on the powers and composition of the proposed Council of Ireland. To cut through the impasse, Whitelaw decided to present the parties with his own proposals, which would not be further negotiable. Faulkner's Unionists would have a majority of executive places as representatives of the larger population segment. In return they had to make concessions on the Council of Ireland and other issues of concern to the SDLP. Whitelaw warned Heath to be prepared for the talks to collapse. Yet within a day he had secured an agreement that provided for, first, an executive in which Faulkner's Unionists would have six seats to the SDLP's four; second, two additional ministers from the SDLP who would serve in government but not sit on the executive; third, a Council of Ireland supported by a permanent secretariat and an advisory forum of elected representatives; and finally, a conference that would include the British and Irish governments to determine the council's composition, scope, and functions.

On November 20, on the eve of the final breakthrough, Faulkner narrowly won a vote at the Ulster Unionist Council, with 379 to 369 members in favor of joining the coalition. It was enough to let the deal go ahead, but hardly an overwhelming endorsement. Worse was to follow. Five of the seven Unionist MPs at Westminster abandoned Faulkner for the dissident faction led by West in the assembly.

## Sunningdale

Whitelaw congratulated himself on having brought the rival party leaders over the threshold. But before he could return power to Stormont, he
needed an agreement on the nature and scope of the "Irish dimension."
The promised conference was held at Sunningdale in England on December 6–9, 1973.[81] The agenda covered the Council of Ireland, Dublin's
recognition of Northern Ireland's constitutional status, and cross-border
cooperation over security, including extradition.

The strength of Faulkner's hard-line opponents constrained Whitelaw's
concessions to Nationalism, but he did not otherwise take their policy proposals seriously or do much to include them or their constituency in his
quest for a settlement; he had already written them off as sectarian extremists and troublemakers who would never offer constructive contributions.
He decided not to invite them to Sunningdale, although the white paper
had undertaken that all assembly parties would be included and Faulkner
had argued that they should be. He accepted the SDLP and Alliance argument that they would disrupt the proceedings, and rejected Faulkner's
objection that they would make political capital out of their exclusion.

The delegates agreed to set up a Council of Ireland comprising seven
ministers each from the Northern Ireland Executive and the Irish government. It would be supported by a wider advisory body comprising thirty
members each from the Northern Ireland Assembly and the Dáil. This
went a small distance toward the SDLP's ambitious proposals for an all-
island senate, but crucially omitted the function of drawing up plans for
eventual unification. The Dáil and the assembly would decide which functions in practical fields, such as agriculture, tourism, and energy supplies,
should be allocated to the council. This meant that the Unionists could
veto any transfer of functions that did not meet their criteria for limited
practical cooperation.

On the wider constitutional front, Irish ministers flatly rejected Faulkner's request to amend the territorial claim in the Irish constitution. They
argued that this could be done only through a referendum, which they
might lose—and if they did, this would set back progress toward reconciliation. But they offered publicly to accept that, as a practical reality, there
could be no change in the status of Northern Ireland until a majority of
its people so desired. In response to Faulkner's concerns about extradition,
the two governments merely agreed to set up an advisory commission of
experts. These were the main elements in what came to be known as the
Sunningdale agreement.

Faulkner accepted the potentially expansive arrangements for the council of Ireland only under intense pressure from Heath. He persuaded him-

self that he could sell them to his party as merely cosmetic, potentially of practical value, and helpful to the extent that they would enable Dublin ministers to secure political support for firm action against the IRA. He told his supporters that he had thwarted Hume's efforts to bring the RUC under the council's control, and congratulated himself on reaching a settlement that would restore devolved government under his own leadership without jeopardizing the union.[82] But with every step he had taken toward the post of chief executive, his enemies had picked away at his support base. Like O'Neill, the predecessor whose grip on the premiership he had helped to loosen, Faulkner had complied with London's purposes at the cost of splitting the party he led and damaging his authority as its leader.

The SDLP delegates presented the outcome to their supporters very differently, as a substantial first step on the historic road to unification. One assembly member trumpeted it as "the vehicle that would trundle Unionists into a united Ireland."[83] Unfortunately for the future of the agreement, many Unionists chose to accept this assessment.

## The Alternatives

We have identified Whitelaw's goals and outlined the stepped process of maneuver and negotiation through which he sought to achieve them. Unlike the policy decisions examined in previous chapters, the strategy outlined in the white paper and extending into the Sunningdale agreement was hammered out in difficult discussions with elected representatives from the two sides in Northern Ireland. The British cabinet monitored the negotiations, keeping other options open in case they failed.

In a memorandum for GEN 79 dated February 1, 1973, Whitelaw ruled out three of the more radical alternatives as "impracticable at present": unification, independence, and repartition. But even as he was putting the finishing touches to the white paper, he identified two other alternatives to power sharing that he did consider viable: continuing direct rule and full integration.[84]

### Direct Rule

Whitelaw presented two arguments for continuing direct rule, which had originally been introduced only as an interim measure. First, many people on both sides in Northern Ireland thought that they were better off under it. Second, the political parties needed more time to adjust to the fundamental changes they would have to absorb before new, durable institutions could be created. Against the extension of direct rule, it was argued that the absence of local institutions encouraged "irresponsibility," the extension of a temporary solution would expose the government to criticism, the need to pass legislation for Northern Ireland would clutter up business at Westminster, and direct rule imposed "an unbearable strain" on UK ministers and their officials.[85] Despite these flaws, experience had shown that direct rule was workable and broadly acceptable to both sides, and it would at least suffice until a sustainable accommodation could be negotiated.

### Full Integration

Despite Whitelaw's peremptory rejection of integration at the officials' seminar in June 1972, he commissioned further work on how to accomplish it.[86] One of the options was that of legislative integration with administrative devolution—that is, legislation for Northern Ireland would be made at Westminster, but there would be a local devolved administration in Belfast with its own civil service and powers similar to those of the Greater London Council. Favoring this was that it would give the UK government full control over all salient security and political development policy issues without any risk of a constitutional challenge, and some Protestants would welcome it as helping to secure the union. On the other hand, it would be unacceptable to Nationalist Ireland as ruling out the possibility of unification. Labour might threaten to reverse it if they came to power, creating instability. The new structure of local government in Northern Ireland would then require substantial changes because it had been predicated on the existence of a local legislative assembly. Finally, it would drag Northern Irish affairs back into Westminster, cluttering up the government's legislative timetable and possibly impeding the conduct of parliamentary business.[87] Unstated was that integration would make it more difficult to pursue unification as the long-term solution favored by UK policymakers. During a meeting with the Irish ambassador on August 1, 1972, Heath "talked freely about reunification, which he is confident must come about. . . . Membership of the EEC will inevitably help in the direction of reunification."[88]

## Uncertainties and Paradigms

### Managing Uncertainties

When he first arrived in Northern Ireland, Whitelaw faced huge uncertainties. Would Faulkner hold on to the leadership of the Unionist Party? Would he make common cause with Craig or would he cooperate, and if so, on what terms? Would republicans settle for anything less than full British withdrawal? What would the SDLP settle for?

Once the immediate anxieties associated with direct rule had been set-tled—that is, the fear of a violent loyalist reaction and a refusal to collabo-rate on the part of the RUC and NICS—Whitelaw was better placed than Maudling had been to tackle these uncertainties. He controlled all the levers in the Stormont administration: security policy, internment, political development, and social and economic policy. And he was not distracted by other pressing national policy issues or looming scandal.

Building personal relationships with Northern Ireland's moderate polit-ical leaders, he disarmed them by arguing that the responsibility for mak-ing progress rested with them rather than the British government. Three features distinguished his public thinking during this period: unwarranted optimism over the power of reason and the triumph of moderation; a cor-responding denial of the strength and validity of political attitudes that he dismissed as "extremist," "hard-line," "irresponsible," or "sectarian"; and a conception of the British state's role and responsibilities as a disinterested intermediary.

## Reasonable People

Senior Whitehall officials continued to be skeptical about the moral jus-tification for community government and its workability, given the deep and widening divisions between the two traditions. Their doubts were reinforced by the SDLP's continuing refusal to enter negotiations with Faulkner. On the other hand, a survey published in August 1972 led one analyst to conclude that "after four years of violence . . . there has been a substantial swing towards non-sectarian voting."[89] Another poll conducted in February 1973 found that 44 percent of Protestants identified Faulkner as the leader most closely representing their views, compared with 13 per-cent for Paisley and 15 percent for Craig. On the Catholic side, 53 percent chose Hume or Fitt, compared with 6 percent for Máire Drumm, presi-dent of Sinn Fein.

But a less rose-tinted reading of these results would highlight that only 2 percent of Catholics liked Faulkner's policies and only 1 percent of Prot-estants Hume's. The only prominent politicians to gather equal support from the two traditions were David Bleakley of the NILP, with 7 percent of Protestants and 9 percent of Catholics, and Bob Cooper of Alliance, with 3 percent and 9 percent, respectively.[90]

Publicly, Heath chose to interpret the poll data favorably. He and Whitelaw had based their strategy on the emergence of a moderate cen-ter. Until the 1973 election, they continued to believe that a progressive political realignment was taking place. The old Unionist Party would col-lapse under the pressure of the transformation it was being forced to make;

moderate parties, namely Alliance and the NILP, would displace it; and the opportunity to share power at Stormont would encourage reasonable people to come forward from both sides who had previously avoided electoral politics because of its sectarian nature. But no hard evidence supported this, and Whitelaw's private predictions were more accurate. On June 9, he told Irish foreign minister Garret FitzGerald that he thought Official (Faulkner) Unionists would take twenty-five to thirty seats in the assembly (they actually took twenty-four), SDLP ten to fifteen seats (they took nineteen), Alliance ten seats (they took eight), and Paisley and Craig "quite a considerable number" (they took twenty-six).[91] In adopting the STV system, ministers were influenced by the fact that the moderate parties (SDLP, NILP, and Alliance) favored it, but correctly they were not convinced that it would actually work to those parties' advantage.[92] Proponents of STV were right to predict that it would damage the Unionist Party but mistaken in that the benefits went not to moderates but to extremists.

It was a serious flaw in Heath's logic to believe that a majority of Unionists would support the moderate center as he defined it (he considered Faulkner hard-line). Opponents of the white paper won more Unionist votes and assembly seats than its supporters did. On the Nationalist side, popular support for the armed struggle proved deeper and broader than ministers had appreciated. Whitelaw acknowledged this in his first report to the cabinet as secretary of state, but apparently concluded that the problem could be solved by building up the SDLP.[93] However, as one republican commentator later observed: "The moderate centre around whom the whole power-sharing scheme was to be constructed was painfully weak. . . . The White Paper presumed a substantial non-sectarian bloc in the centre to form the basis of the executive. It wasn't there."[94]

UK ministers' faith in the power of the moderate center led them to deny that the leaders of the Northern Ireland parties actually represented the views of the constituents upon whose support their electoral success and political careers depended. Heath actually said so in reporting to his Cabinet colleagues after a visit to the region in November 1972:

> He had canvassed a wide range of opinion, both within and outside political circles. He had formed the impression that the leaders of the political parties in Northern Ireland no longer represented a substantial section of public opinion. Although the extremists of either faction were probably irreconcilable he believed that a large body of opinion felt that the British Government had done everything possible to promote a satisfactory political solution; that the response from the leaders of the political parties in the Province had been inadequate; and that the Government should make up their own minds and proceed to put their decisions into effect.[95]

Heath dealt with any residual uncertainties he may have had by persuading himself that Northern Ireland's political elites would have a powerful incentive to cooperate across the sectarian divide, since they would not otherwise get any power at all; and that once they started to work together, norms and patterns of behavior would emerge that would enable power sharing to be sustained. Since Dublin had for all practical purposes acknowledged Northern Ireland's position in the union, there was no good reason for Unionists to feel threatened. He did not see the continuing fragmentation within Unionism as a problem because he interpreted it as a function of the progressive realignment toward moderation, which he welcomed and reported to GEN 79.[96] This was a leap of faith, not rational planning. It denied the solid evidence that was readily available for those who chose to see it.

The Unionist extremists who in Heath's grand design were to be marginalized as the transformation proceeded did not conveniently disappear, even though he excluded them from Sunningdale. Instead they gathered strength, convincing their constituents that the British government was planning to offer ever more concessions to the SDLP. Nor did republican support for the Provisionals' bombing campaign dissolve simply because British soldiers adopted a lower profile and Whitelaw released some internees. Republican communities continued to view the army as a hostile occupying force and the Provisionals to interpret British concessions as signs of weakness. Ministers reacted to the persistence of loyalist opposition by repeating Wilson's threats to review Northern Ireland's constitutional position. These tactics reinforced the insecurities that had led Unionists to shift toward harder positions in the first place.

The election results stripped away some of Whitelaw's illusions. The voting almost extinguished the NILP. Alliance polled less well than he had hoped. The opponents of power sharing did much better. After the election, the secretary of state had to accept that Faulkner would be the dominant player in the executive. Bearing in mind that direct rule had been introduced in part because London did not believe that Faulkner could survive as Unionist leader if he collaborated with any further reforms, it required a substantial leap of faith from Whitelaw to believe that power sharing could succeed.

As far as the Provisional IRA was concerned, Whitelaw had hoped by conciliation to drive a wedge between the moderate and extreme factions. But like Faulkner he had underestimated the scale and intensity of popular support for the armed struggle and the resilience of the Provisional leadership. In this he may have been misled by the briefings he received from intelligence officials such as Frank Steele, who advised him in April 1973 that relations between the army and the Catholic Bogside were "so good that one feels that they cannot be true.... There is gratitude and admiration for the work and restraint of the Army in very difficult conditions ... the Provisionals were now regarded as a nuisance and a hindrance to the much wanted return to normal life."[97] Steele may not have intended to deceive, but it seems clear from other evidence that his sources did not accurately represent the totality of local opinion.

### Britain's Role

Whatever intentions they may have had for the longer term, UK ministers' emerging policy of power sharing with an Irish dimension embodied two important changes in their perception of their own role. First, under direct rule they could no longer keep the problem at arm's length, operating through the buffer regime at Stormont; they now publicly and unambiguously carried full political responsibility for everything the government and its agencies did there. Second, and as a counterweight to taking on this extra responsibility, they formally acknowledged the limits to Britain's power by publicly accepting the case for an Irish dimension, whatever that might turn out to mean. Although Britain formally retained sovereignty over Northern Ireland, establishing the new executive depended on Dublin's consent, since the SDLP would participate only on the basis of a substantial Irish dimension. Britain was willing to pay this price in return for the possibility of improved cooperation in the security arena. It had become simultaneously colonial governor, pacifier, and conflict mediator, and the three roles did not always sit comfortably together.

## Politics

Heath and Whitelaw pressed ahead with the white paper package despite their own doubts about whether it could succeed, their officials' preference for integration as a more sustainable option, and clear evidence—including election results—that a majority of the Unionist electorate did not support it. They insisted on elaborating the Irish dimension even after it had become obvious that this was strengthening Unionist opposition to their proposals, a factor that increasingly threatened the success of the entire project. Why did they do this?

### The Backbenches

We saw in chapter 5 how Conservative backbench dissatisfaction increased after internment, pushing ministers toward a political initiative. Direct rule and the substitution of Whitelaw for Maudling satisfied most of Heath's critics, leaving Enoch Powell and his associates as the only articulate Conservative opponents of government policy. Powell was particularly incensed when the Provisionals embarrassed Whitelaw by revealing their secret meeting with him in July 1972, and demanded his resignation. This initiated a period of tension in the parliamentary party, as the dissidents attacked Whitelaw for what they described as his strategy of appeasement. Whitelaw described them as "a small but bitter and vociferous group."[98] He succeeded in keeping them small. By the time of the Commons debate on the white paper on March 29, 1973, only three Conservative backbenchers voted against him.

Although he failed to rally much support on the backbenches, Powell continued to maintain that direct rule had been no more than "a means of buying time in order to think what to do next."[99] He defined the problem in terms not of divided communities but of irreconcilable objectives. One side wanted to remain part of the United Kingdom, the other to join the Irish Republic: "Between those two objectives there is in the nature of things no compromise or reconciliation."[100] He argued that the government's proposals failed to address "the fundamental reality of the politics of Northern Ireland, which is that there are two nations which contend for a single territory."[101] Powell favored full integration as the only solution that could honestly resolve this impasse.

Other Tory MPs suggested that integration could be facilitated by redrawing the border to exclude predominantly republican areas, such as South Armagh and West Tyrone. Some, such as John Biggs-Davison, favored increasing Northern Ireland's representation at Westminster.[102] In response to the proposed Irish dimension, some called for a Council of the British Isles that would bring together not merely the two parts of Ireland but all Ireland and Britain in the context of the EEC.

Aligning himself with Powell, the new leader of the Unionist MPs at Westminster, James Molyneaux, attacked the white paper proposals as concessions to violence that would encourage more atrocities, and as undemocratic, since the secretary of state would appoint the executive and continue to engineer political developments. Molyneaux shared Powell's suspicions about the government's ultimate intentions: "some of the methods suggested in the white paper are so clearly seen to be unworkable that any resulting structure would be so unstable as to encourage the belief that it could be only temporary—perhaps it is only meant to be temporary."[103] Not all Unionist MPs agreed, and only three voted against the government.

Vocal though they were, the Conservative and Unionist dissidents did not so much influence the direction of government policy during this period as

THE BRITISH STATE AND THE NORTHERN IRELAND CRISIS

set boundaries beyond which ministers could not comfortably go in offering concessions to Irish Nationalism. As long as their personal positions were secure, it was more important to Heath and Whitelaw to retain Labour's support than to placate a handful of critics on their own backbenches. In the Conservative Party at large, Whitelaw won acclaim for his achievements. At the annual conference in October 1972, 4,000 delegates supported his strategy by more than ten to one, in contrast to the drubbing Maudling had received a year earlier.[104]

## The Opposition

Having suffered at Wilson's hands from November 1971 to March 1972, Heath attached great importance to bipartisanship in the Commons, which was restored with direct rule; the challenge was to sustain it. The direct-rule package of March 1972 had given Wilson most of what he had asked for: a commitment to phase out internment, the transfer of security, and guaranteed places for minority elected representatives in the Northern Ireland cabinet. Wilson happily took credit for these and many of the other proposals in the 1973 white paper, including the expanded assembly, PR voting, and the realization of the Irish dimension. Callaghan in turn claimed that he had planted these ideas in Wilson's mind. But the two Labour leaders still disagreed over strategy. Callaghan had been trying to build up the NILP, arguing that "the British Labour Party should pin its official support to the NILP [rather than the SDLP] because of its close links with the trade union movement which has always been a non-sectarian force in the North."[105] The NILP had been lobbying for some time for formal affiliation to the British party. Unfortunately for them, Wilson favored the SDLP. In October 1971, Labour headquarters issued a statement to say that affiliation at this time would be "politically inopportune."[106] There were a number of reasons for Wilson's choice. He shared the SDLP's view that unification was the only sustainable long-term solution, and wanted to support them in working toward it. Conversely he saw the NILP as a Unionist party that would obstruct progress toward unification. He also saw the NILP leaching members and authority to Alliance and the SDLP, and did not want to back a loser. Finally, the SDLP had one MP at Westminster (Fitt) with the prospect of more, who would generally vote with Labour, whereas the NILP had none and little prospect of getting one.

The SDLP continued to maximize its influence with Labour by working on Wilson both directly and through Dublin. Even as they refused to negotiate officially with Whitelaw, SDLP leaders acknowledged the importance of their close relationships with influential players in the Labour Party.[107] Heath would no doubt have recognized that if Wilson was not satisfied with Whitelaw's progress, he could induce the SDLP to hold out for a more attractive settlement under a future Labour government. Maintaining the bipartisan consensus was thus especially important during the period of Whitelaw's detailed negotiations with the Northern Ireland parties after June 1973.

Wilson cooperated as long as things were moving in his direction, pressing the SDLP to join the talks and advising them that they should not hold out for a better deal from a future Labour government.[108] During this period the left-wing *New Statesman* criticized a shift in Labour policy toward "a posture of unquestioning bipartisanship."[109] The *Irish Times* alleged that the Labour Party conference in October 1973 avoided discussion of the issue because of the delicate stage that Whitelaw's negotiations had then reached.[110] Setting aside Hume's reservations under pressure from Dublin, the SDLP eventually responded to Wilson's overtures by agreeing to accept Faulkner as chief executive.

It was scarcely surprising that Wilson should support government policy, since to a large extent he had made it; the white paper incorporated many of the ideas he had advanced before direct rule.[111] One of the party's Northern Ireland spokesmen, Stan Orme, boasted at the party conference in 1973 that the policies of the government had been forced on them by the Labour Party.[112] The one important element in Wilson's fifteen-point plan of November 1971 that Heath did not adopt was that the Dáil should be represented on a parliamentary commission to examine what would be involved in agreeing on the constitution of a united Ireland to be introduced over fifteen years. This point appears to have been personal to Wilson, though Callaghan had made the more realistic proposal for an all-Ireland council that would "go to work on such matters as unemployment, the future of the West of Ireland, and tourism,"[113] and this rather than Wilson's more radical proposal was eventually reflected in the Sunningdale agreement.

Throughout 1972 and 1973, Labour kept the pressure on Heath and Whitelaw to act quickly and curtailed legislative proposals that appeared to favor Unionists. Wilson delayed the legislation providing for a border plebiscite, for which Unionists had been calling.[114] He thwarted Whitelaw's efforts to increase Northern Ireland's representation at Westminster, threatening to terminate the bipartisan consensus if it went ahead.[115] However, despite the reservations of some of its backbenchers, Labour did not actively oppose security measures such as detention without trial and special courts.

Wilson's vigilance set boundaries that Conservative ministers could not cross. The record of Commons debates from the imposition of direct rule to the publication of the white paper suggests that the opposition shared the government's simple faith in the strength of moderation. Callaghan echoed Heath's rosy public optimism when he declared that by ending the Unionist ascendancy at Stormont, direct rule had paved the way for a new politics, in which Catholic and Protestant leaders could come together in "an Executive capable of agreeing on a programme of radical, progressive policies to meet the basic social and economic needs."[116] Merlyn Rees, his successor as Labour spokesman, maintained that "without PR the moderate parties will be obliterated. . . . PR is the way to ascertain, in the sort of society that exists in Northern Ireland, who are the true representatives of the people."[117] He declared that "the moderates in the North of Ireland must be liberated," but he did not identify the shackles that had been restraining them or how they were to be removed. By November 1972, apparently alarmed by the continuing violence on the streets, he was less confident, observing that if the electorate chose the "wrong" representatives—those who rejected the white paper—"this would . . . mean that there was no moderate majority in both communities . . . which is the basis on which we have been working for four years. . . . It would mean needing to face up to a complete reappraisal of policy by any British Government."[118]

Rees was more sympathetic to Wilson's Nationalist aspirations than Callaghan had been. He told the Irish ambassador that he saw merit "in giving the Assembly arrangements a life span of ten years, as he believes this would help condition minds in the direction of reunification."[119] Recording a subsequent conversation, the ambassador noted that if Labour came to power in 1973, Wilson would want to appoint an important political figure rather than a career diplomat to the Dublin embassy, "as this should help considerably in securing movement in the direction of reunification."[120]

Increasingly aware as the assembly election approached of the risk that the electorate might make the wrong choice, Labour spokesmen reverted to Wilson's tactic of making threatening noises. Callaghan said that Britain might have to reconsider its position if the electorate "sabotaged" the assembly: "Britain cannot bleed forever."[121] Wilson backed this up five days before the election, warning the electorate that if the principles in the white paper were rejected, "it might be necessary to reconsider the relationship between Britain and Northern Ireland." It apparently did not occur to either of them that the Northern Ireland electorate might view these statements as improper interference with the democratic process, or that they might prove counterproductive.

*Media and Public Opinion*

British public opinion was comfortable with direct rule. A survey in April 1972 showed that 61 percent—that is, 79 percent of Conservative and 51 percent of Labour voters—thought that the government had been right to impose it. However, respondents were not convinced that it would result in peace: 50 percent rated its chances as "none" or "not very good," as against 39 percent for "good" or "very good." In October 1973, as Whitelaw started his negotiations on the formation of the executive, a survey found that the issue continued to be salient, with 71 percent feeling "very strongly" or "fairly strongly" about the outcome of Britain's Northern Ireland policy. Among respondents, 47 percent supported pro-union solutions—24 percent for full integration, 23 percent for devolution—while 34 percent favored a united Ireland.[122]

The British national media were willing to accept ministers' contention that an agreed political solution could reduce the level of violence. After direct rule, the clamor for action subsided. Journalists and proprietors who had been happy to attack Unionist misrule were less keen to criticize their own government when things went wrong, especially in what they depicted as a war situation. Whitelaw was popular in the Conservative Party and in the country, Northern Ireland was no longer a matter of party political controversy, the failings of the military security approach had been well ventilated, and the issue attention cycle had moved on.

Editorials in *The Times* regularly and uncritically supported Whitelaw and his strategy. On June 16, the paper congratulated the secretary of state on his "determined and skilful approach," citing in particular his decisions to apply PR in the forthcoming local government elections and to convene the Darlington conference.[123] With the announcement of the Provisional ceasefire on June 22, the paper declared that Whitelaw's judgment had been "gratifyingly vindicated" and confidence "reinforced in his ability to handle whatever is in store."[124] Remarkably, when the ceasefire ended, there was no corresponding criticism, even when the Provisionals revealed that Whitelaw had met them in secret. The paper's only complaint was that Whitelaw had not rejected the Provisionals' demand for an all-Ireland plebiscite on the border.

By October 14, *The Times* was offering more qualified approval. On the positive side, Whitelaw had won the respect of party leaders on both sides, and a great deal of trust from "the detribalized citizens of the province" (a minority, as it later proved).[125] The Catholic mood was "less bitter," relations with Dublin were good, "censorious opinion in foreign capitals" had been placated, security operations were better coordinated, the republican barricades had been dismantled without bloodshed, the political deadlock had loosened, the Protestants had not risen up in anger, and public services had continued to run. On the other hand, the Provisionals had been encouraged by their success in toppling Stormont and had "not been detached from its sheltering population." There had been "no diminution of violence and lawlessness," "fear and despair and bewilderment" were more prevalent, and the signs of better conditions for political reconstruction were slight. The Protestant community was demoralized and its moderate leadership discredited, loyalist paramilitary preparations had intensified, and sectarian rioting had erupted again. In short, "those who now govern Northern Ireland are losing control of crucial sections of the Protestant community without having gained control of the Catholic community. The possibility must now be reckoned with that the political and military authorities in the province may find themselves lacking friends within it sufficient to enable them to succeed in their task."[126] The paper advised ministers not to delay their promised initiative, as it would fuel uncertainties and doubts.

Whitelaw's green paper was published two weeks later. *The Times* welcomed its substance as being "favoured by moderate, detribalized opinion in Ulster and by conscientious liberal opinion in Britain"; if its prospects were "far from good," it was "worth pursuing if only because any alternative looks worse and further indecision is dangerous." Progress was now urgent, and if the Northern Ireland parties could not agree on a settlement, then the government should terminate the negotiations and proceed at once to legislation of its own.[127] Whether by coincidence or good media grooming, this mirrored Heath's position at the time.

When the white paper eventually appeared, *The Times* considered it "a strong and ingenious attempt to harness by means of new institutions those forces of political moderation and reconciliation which have not yet been rendered ineffective in Northern Ireland," but qualified this welcome by pointing out that "enforced collaboration . . . can hardly be expected to bear very much political weight." If the involuntary coalition had to address contentious matters, "disintegration or paralysis would be likely to ensue, and then such matters would have to be resolved at Westminster."[128] It was far from a ringing endorsement.

### The International Dimension

The Irish government was surprised and pleased with the direct-rule package, which went further than Lynch had expected in meeting his demands. He promptly proclaimed it a victory for his policy of patient diplomacy,[129] and was determined that direct rule should not be permitted to evolve toward UK integration.[130] Irish officials continued to develop their strategy of working quietly toward unification behind the scenes. At the Department of Foreign Affairs, Eamon Gallagher produced a secret paper on Irish economic unity in which he contended that previous proposals for cross-border economic cooperation were insufficiently political and would not necessarily lead to eventual unification. They "would not satisfy the national instinct and would not therefore obviate the continuation of the present level of violence or its recurrence, if it should cease now, at a future date." Gallagher continued, "a move towards economic union could be brought under the EEC umbrella and therefore explained away to the majority on economic grounds while we and the minority could see it as having very definite political value."[131]

In the new political context created by the dissolution of Stormont, Lynch adopted more vigorous measures against the IRA, to the point that, when the British were trying to negotiate a ceasefire with the Provisionals in June 1972, they had to persuade Dublin to restrain action by the Irish security forces, which might have derailed the shift within the republican movement they were trying to encourage.[132] Lynch and his officials also intensified their contacts with Hume and the SDLP. Each exchanged information with the other on their meetings with the British. Lynch encouraged the SDLP to take up Whitelaw's invitation to negotiate formally with Faulkner, and as time passed, he became increasingly impatient with Hume's continuing insistence that internment must end before he would do so.[133] This impatience reflected an anxiety, reinforced when news emerged of Whitelaw's clandestine meeting with the Provisionals, that if the SDLP would not talk, the British might do a deal with republicans that would exclude moderate nationalism and create instability in the south.

Irish ministers and diplomats expended considerable energy in persuading the British to include them fully in the policy development process. Ambassador O'Sullivan told Foreign and Commonwealth Office (FCO) mandarin Kelvin White that it would be "absolute madness for Westminster to attempt a solution without in the process ensuring the goodwill and support of the Dublin government." White responded by conceding that "your government could sabotage a solution with which it disagreed."[134] After Motorman, Lynch wrote to Heath stressing the importance of pressing ahead with the political initiative and fully engaging with the Irish government. The British were keen to comply, but also concerned that including Dublin too visibly would excite Unionists' paranoia. Like Lynch, they preferred to cooperate behind the arras. The British ambassador privately copied a confidential record of the Darlington conference talks to the taoiseach, but UK ministers held to their position that to include the Irish formally in four-way negotiations at this stage would be a step too far for Unionists.[135]

On October 18, 1972, O'Sullivan lunched with Rees. The Labour spokesman asked him to do what he could to rescue Whitelaw, who, he said, "was in real difficulty and could conceivably throw in the sponge." Rees had in mind that Lynch should clarify publicly that there could be no question of coercing the Unionists into a united Ireland, persuade the SDLP to participate in the forthcoming local government elections, and undertake as part of any settlement to change the Irish constitution to remove its peculiarly Catholic ethos (although not the territorial claim). If Dublin would do this, Rees said, it would help him and Wilson to ensure that the Irish were included in the constitutional negotiations at an early stage.

On October 21, Lynch met Heath on the margins of a European summit in Paris. The taoiseach again argued for four-way negotiations and stressed the urgency of making progress. The minority must be given equal treatment, not only in the social and political spheres, but also in relation to policing and security. In response, the British ambassador on October 26 sent Lynch a personal prepublication copy of the green paper with a note requesting him in his public comment not to emphasize Dublin's desire to participate in negotiations or to work toward ultimate unification, since "your words would be eagerly seized upon by Protestant extremists to justify rejection of any reform measures and by the IRA to justify continuing violence."[136]

Whitelaw followed the note by meeting the Irish ambassador to London. It is characteristic of his modus operandi that rather than demanding cooperation, he "made a lengthy and rather emotional appeal for help from Dublin to get him off the hook." This mirrored Rees's extraordinary appeal on his behalf. Notwithstanding that delegates had overwhelmingly praised him at the party conference earlier in the month, Whitelaw depicted himself as under severe pressure from the Tory right—in particular Powell—to take penal action against Ireland. While the political context was not yet ripe for negotiations to include Dublin visibly, there would be no difficulty in arranging detailed talks between officials, with Ken Bloomfield acting for Whitelaw and Ken Whitaker, Lynch's personal adviser, for the taoiseach.[137] Thus the secretary of state enlisted both the Labour Party and the Irish government—a year earlier united in hostility toward Maudling—in supporting himself and his proposals.

Assured that the green paper would formally recognize the Irish dimension and open up the possibility of unification in the long term, Lynch gave Whitelaw some of what he had asked for. On the security front, he invoked the Offences Against the State Act, the Republic's equivalent of Stormont's Special Powers Act, to close Provisional Sinn Féin's headquarters in Dublin. In November, the vice president of Sinn Féin, Máire Drumm, was imprisoned for making an inflammatory speech; as Whitelaw had requested in July, Provisional Chief of Staff Sean McStiofáin was arrested and imprisoned for the offence of IRA membership; and the entire governing body of the state broadcasting corporation RTE was dismissed after transmitting an interview with McStiofáin in defiance of a ministerial directive. Other arrests followed in December, including of Rory O'Brady (a member of the Army Council and president of Sinn Féin) and Martin McGuinness (then commander of the Provisionals' Derry brigade).

Lynch and Heath met on November 24, 1972, at Downing Street to discuss how the forthcoming white paper should flesh out the concept of the Irish dimension. Lynch later described their conversation as "a closer meeting of minds than he had ever experienced before."[138] In press interviews, he declared that the Irish state would no longer pursue its negative international campaign against partition. Henceforth his government would take a positive approach to unification through developing joint north-south institutions. He indicated a willingness to change the Irish constitution to accommodate Unionists' fears and urged Nationalists to envisage a united Ireland gradually evolving by the year 2000.[139] The London correspondent of the *Irish Times* reported that the Irish "entered enthusiastically into negotiations and from this point onwards the British kept them very closely informed, usually in advance, of their proposals. Relations, recently so chilly, soon became warm, even excessively cosy."[140]

On January 1, 1973, Irish and British civil servants met to discuss the possible role and functions of the Council of Ireland in detail. At this level, the relationship turned out to be less easy. The Irish found the British "exceedingly cautious and circumspect" and accused them of wanting a "weak and ineffectual council . . . which could become an object of derision."[141] In February, Heath told GEN 79 members "that in considering the content of the white paper on future arrangements for Northern Ireland it was important to have regard to the probable reaction of the government of the Irish Republic. If our proposals were not acceptable to that government and if in consequence action against the IRA in the south was not pursued with vigor, our task would be immeasurably increased." This would be particularly the case if Labour sided with Dublin as it had in the months leading to direct rule.[142]

Heath had planned to meet Lynch again before finalizing the document, but this meeting had to be postponed when Lynch called a snap election for March 1. To the surprise of most observers, Fianna Fáil lost power for the first time in sixteen years. The two main opposition parties, Fine Gael and Labour, fought the election on a joint program and won, thanks largely to transfers between them under the Republic's PR system. The new government entered office just as the British were about to publish their white paper. Its main players were Taoiseach Liam Cosgrave, leader of Fine Gael; Brendan Corish, leader of the Irish Labour Party, who became tánaiste (deputy prime minister); and Garret FitzGerald of Fine Gael, who became minister for external affairs. On Northern Ireland, the new government broadly adopted Lynch's strategy. Faulkner welcomed the change away from Fianna Fáil as one that would ease tensions and open up the possibility of a new period of neighborly coexistence.[143]

Cosgrave and Corish met Heath and Douglas-Home at Downing Street on March 8 and 9. Cosgrave expressed the hope that the white paper would set out detailed proposals for cross-border cooperation.[144] However, Northern Ireland was not as high a personal priority for him as it had been for his predecessor. Like Lynch, he favored a low-key diplomatic approach; unlike him, he delegated responsibility for the issue to his minister for external affairs.

FitzGerald took the issue very seriously, bringing formidable intellectual energy to the post.[145] Formerly a journalist and lecturer, FitzGerald had the previous year published a book on the subject. Acknowledging his debt to the thinking of John Hume,[146] he had outlined various possible arrangements for power sharing at executive level. He shared the belief of the Alliance Party that PR voting would favor moderate candidates, assuming that extremists would tend to pass their vote down to more moderate candidates of the same community, and that some moderates on each side would transfer to moderates on the other side. He did not see power sharing as a permanent arrangement; like Maudling, he hoped that in time conditions would evolve to create the possibility of reverting to a "normal" parliamentary system along British and Irish lines.

FitzGerald also argued that by the start of 1972, "reunification seemed to have rather more prospect of realisation within a reasonable period than had existed at any time during the first forty years of existence of Northern Ireland," identifying a number of factors that had created this new situation: the "intransigence of the Unionist Government" in responding to earlier proposals for minority participation in government; the British government's failure to take a political initiative in the closing months of 1971; the reintroduction of the issue into the sphere of practical politics by Harold Wilson with his fifteen-point plan; the emergence in the Republic of a movement favoring a more liberal and pluralist society; and signs that liberal Unionists disillusioned by the conflict and by Britain's indifference to the union were opening up to the possibility of a new nonsectarian united Ireland.[147] FitzGerald concluded that the prospect for achieving reunification without violence was at least good enough to warrant serious consideration.

FitzGerald met Heath in London on March 15, the day after assuming office, to discuss the substance of the white paper. He reiterated Lynch's demand for an ambitious council of Ireland with clearly defined functions, maintaining that it was essential to secure the support of northern Nationalists. Heath replied with two distinct concerns, that Unionists would resent anything that looked like dictation from Dublin over the council's powers and functions and that the council might make decisions for which the British Treasury would have to foot the bill.

Heath published the white paper five days later, leaving these details to be tackled by the proposed conference. On FitzGerald's instructions Irish officials then trawled their civil service for possible functions for the council. To his disappointment, the replies were generally unenthusiastic. Most departments responded by defending their territories and policies: finance, for example, highlighted the need to protect the competitive edge that the Republic had gained as a result of its generous system of tax relief and business incentives, which could be compromised if tax policies and legislation were harmonized on an all-island basis.[148]

Another minister in the new Irish government had also published a book on the subject in 1972, Conor Cruise O'Brien, who did not endorse FitzGerald's dynamic vision for the Council of Ireland.[149] Formerly the Irish Labour Party's spokesman on the north, O'Brien had produced a scathing intellectual critique of traditional republican ideology, which included trenchant criticisms of the Catholic political establishment. O'Brien described himself as a "deadly enemy, politically speaking" of Hume.[150] He argued that the official doctrine of the Irish state effectively legitimated republican violence, made it politically impossible for the elected leaders of Unionism to agree to share power with Nationalists, and had created the preconditions for sectarian civil war in the north. For the foreseeable future, reunification was not a workable objective, and for the Irish government to pursue it in the context of the IRA's terrorist campaign was reckless. The only workable solution for the present lay in the reform of Stormont and economic reconstruction, which together might create a more positive environment for developing north-south relationships. O'Brien's was a lone voice of dissent in the Irish establishment; when at one cabinet meeting he queried the wisdom of insisting on a strong Council of Ireland in the face of implacable loyalist hostility, FitzGerald icily retorted by citing Hume's contention that the Protestants would accept the council without any difficulty.[151]

Under Cosgrave, qualified cooperation with Britain in the security arena continued. It was the Irish navy, tipped off by the British Intelligence Service MI6, which intercepted the *Claudia*, a fishing boat carrying five tons of weapons from Libya for the Provisionals. The haul included guns, anti-tank mines, gelignite, and ammunition. The British passed a secret dossier to the taoiseach providing detailed information on Provisional members and units operating in the border region. They included Martin McGuinness, who was identified as the officer commanding the Derry Brigade.[152] By this time not only were the British sharing top-secret information, they had also achieved a degree of north-south harmonization, in that both governments had instructed their security services not to pursue those perceived as being on the moderate or political wing of the IRA. Irish justice minister Paddy Cooney issued orders that David O'Connell—a leading member of the Provisionals' Army Council—was not to be arrested. Irish ministers were comfortable working with the British against the IRA as long as the release of information to the public was carefully controlled; the British ambassador noted that the Cosgrave administration was "pathologically determined to keep any cooperation with their British counterparts secret."[153] The British were glad to have the cooperation, but Dublin's insistence on secrecy complicated their task of reassuring Conservative backbenchers and Unionists that Dublin was in fact honoring its commitments.

On June 9, 1973, FitzGerald met Whitelaw in London for a detailed discussion of the Northern Ireland Constitution Bill and other issues of concern to the Irish, including Catholic representation in the senior ranks of the NICS, the reform of the RUC, and the behavior of the British army on the border. They also discussed the likely outcome of the forthcoming election.

Following that election, Cosgrave told a meeting of Conservatives at Westminster that although he wanted a united Ireland, to press for it in the prevailing climate of loyalist hostility would "dangerously exacerbate tensions and fears."[154] Drawing back from the expansive stand Lynch and FitzGerald took, Cosgrave initially accepted the British concept of a minimal role for the Council of Ireland. But Hume went to work on the Irish establishment over the summer. The SDLP took the view that equivocation like that from the coalition government could hurt it, even as success seemed possible. At a meeting on July 12, Hume told Cosgrave he was concerned at the "apparent drift of Government policy in the South. There appeared to be a definite policy of appeasement of the majority in the North."[155] Successive SDLP delegations eventually convinced Irish ministers that it would be in their interests to insist on a strong Council of Ireland with substantial powers, and to make clear that the new architecture of north-south relations was intended to be a transitional stage on the path to unification. As two political historians have noted, "the irredentism of the Republic's official ideology made it difficult for a southern government to be in open disagreement with the elected representatives of the 'beleaguered minority' in the north."[156] It is a measure of the success of Hume's lobbying that by September the Irish government—with the exception of O'Brien—had adopted the SDLP's line. O'Brien warned "that a Council of Ireland which was seen as a step in the direction of unity might only serve to exclude us from participation in it," but his colleagues pressed ahead regardless.[157]

Heath visited Dublin in person on September 17, 1973. It was an important symbolic event, the first official visit by a UK premier to Ireland since 1921. The main agenda item was the Council of Ireland. The talks went on for three hours longer than planned. As Hume had persuaded him to do, Cosgrave insisted that the Northern Ireland Executive must not be formed before the council, since the two were inextricably linked; that the council should have clearly defined and meaningful functions; and that it should be paralleled by a parliamentary tier comprising members of the Dáil and the assembly.[158] Heath did not close down the discussion on any of these points, although he did reject as unworkable the SDLP's most ambitious proposal, that the RUC should come under the council's control. He also speculated aloud whether in light of their more ambitious demands, the SDLP leaders were really ready for the responsibilities of government.[159] A meeting between officials followed on October 5. At this the British did not insist on limiting the council's reach, but emphasized that there was a serious political constraint in "how much could be sold to Unionists and at what pace and in what manner."[160]

On November 8, Whitelaw met FitzGerald in London, where he persuaded the Irish minister that Faulkner was indispensable for a breakthrough and warned that the Unionist leader had "absolutely nothing more to give." He insisted that the executive must be established before Sunningdale, arguing that it would otherwise be difficult politically to exclude Craig and Paisley from the conference.[161] FitzGerald tried unsuccessfully to persuade the British to appoint him as cochair of the conference.[162] They refused, and Heath took the chair alone.

Eight Irish ministers attended, led by the taoiseach. In comparison with the two governments, represented by large teams of civil servants, the northern parties were underresourced and (particularly the Unionists) underprepared. The SDLP could rely for the most part on the support of the Dublin delegation, whereas the Unionists found themselves at loggerheads

with Heath over critical issues.[163] British and Irish ministers joined to-
gether in pressing Faulkner to cede ground on the role and functions of the
Council of Ireland. Recognizing the risks to Faulkner, O'Brien and Paddy
Devlin of the SDLP tried to persuade them to hold back, unsuccessfully.

As we have noted, British ambassador Peck had advised Lynch as
far back as April 1971 to play the EEC card in negotiating with Heath.
Lynch had done so, and FitzGerald adopted the same tactic. Heath saw
the Council of Ireland sitting comfortably within the new framework of
international relationships that would be created when Britain and Ireland
acceded to the EEC.[164] This, he thought, would make it easier to sell the
concept to Unionists and to his own backbenchers, not as a step toward a
united Ireland but as a subsidiary component in the emerging grand architecture of European integration.

On the transatlantic front, British diplomats continued trying to avoid
criticism from prominent Irish-Americans, and to stem the flow of funds
and weaponry to the IRA. These active U.S. interests reinforced the importance of pursuing policies that could be presented so as to secure the
support of moderate Nationalist opinion and reduce support for armed
republicanism.

There was an interesting international twist to the role of the Catholic
Church in Irish politics when Heath visited the Vatican in October 1972.
Within the broad diplomatic strategy of favorably influencing Irish Catholic opinion, he had hoped to persuade the pope to condemn the IRA. His
advisers had briefed him to the effect that the pontiff's public statements
on Northern Ireland "have not always been as helpful as we would have
liked ... any denunciation of violence tends to be offset by long-standing
grievances which by implication go some way towards explaining and ex-
cusing the violence."[165] The prime minister did not make much headway.
Far from denouncing the IRA, the pope registered his disapproval of internment, but was more interested in criticizing British society for its per-
missive attitudes toward abortion and homosexuality.

### Key Ministers

### Heath

Heath has been credited as the chief architect of the Sunningdale settlement, with Whitelaw as his loyal lieutenant. The prime minister certainly
invested substantial political capital from January 1972 to December 1973
in tackling the problem. According to one commentator, his personal contribution "at the very least ... set the standards and established the parameters which were to shape British policy towards the wider Irish question
over the following two decades."[166] Heath set a fast pace. At an early cabinet

discussion, in May 1972, Whitelaw suggested letting the issue of Northern Ireland's future constitution sit until after the Royal Commission on the Constitution—which was then considering the future of relationships between the component parts of Great Britain—had reported at the end of the year. Heath would have none of it, and in summing up emphasized "that it was important to maintain the momentum of the Government's political initiative.... The Secretary of State for Northern Ireland should ensure that the work of his forward planning unit proceeded as rapidly as possible."[167]

As he himself conceded, Heath never fully understood the dynamics of Northern Ireland's political system, based as it was on differences over national allegiance rather than economic and social policies. He was as ready as Wilson had been to bully Northern Ireland's elected representatives toward accommodation, even when this was demonstrably counterproductive. When the SDLP dragged its heels about joining the Stormont Castle talks in September 1973, he announced that if the assembly failed to establish a power-sharing executive by March 1974, the best option would be full integration. When Wilson responded with a public letter of protest, Heath climbed down, indicating that Britain would never contemplate this option.[168] This left him with no credible fallback other than continuing direct rule should the talks fail.

In chairing the negotiations among the parties, Whitelaw showed more respect for the local leaders and a diplomat's sympathy for the difficulties they faced. By contrast, Heath would intervene to shove the process forward whenever it seemed to be stalling. Like Wilson, he was fond of reminding potentially awkward Unionists of their loyalty to Westminster and the extent to which Britain subsidized public spending in the region.[169] At Sunningdale, he pressured Faulkner into accepting arrangements for the Council of Ireland, which quickly led to the Unionist leader's downfall. His biographer noted, "Heath deceived himself, believing that reason as he saw it must eventually prevail. But he was exhausted in December 1973. He was facing the crisis of his Government. He desperately wanted to clinch the Irish settlement that seemed to be within his grasp."[170]

Heath's leadership style in cabinet has been described as aloof and authoritarian. He did not encourage debate, and "colleagues frequently remained silent until invited to speak."[171] Even the normally ebullient Whitelaw seemed subdued in his presence. In his account of the Sunningdale negotiations, Faulkner describes Heath as particularly impatient.[172] Bloomfield later described him as "a headstrong and excessively self-confident politician with many talents but few friends."[173] Heath himself acknowledged that "as 1973 wore on, I grew impatient with the failure of Northern Ireland's leaders to get their act together."[174]

## Whitelaw

Willie Whitelaw took up his new post with little knowledge or under-standing of the region and its peculiar politics. His first reaction was "one of shock at the depth of the divisions within the Northern Ireland community."[175] He held the Unionists primarily responsible, telling pub-lisher and diarist Cecil King that "the Augean stables were nothing to the mess he found at Stormont. Disproportionate ministerial salaries for Min-isters; jobs for the Protestant boys; every power of the Government used to depress the Catholics. Whitelaw obviously thought the Catholics had far more to put up with than he had realized."[176]

But Whitelaw's previous post as leader of the Commons had equipped him well to grasp the internal machinations of party politics and massage sensitive egos. As secretary of state he not only held the Conservative Party together on this potentially divisive issue but also maintained the biparti-san consensus. He used the same talents to overcome obstacles to accom-modation in Northern Ireland. Heath's biographer comments: "He was unquestionably the right man for the job, possessing a rare combination of human warmth, military experience, negotiating skill and toughness to overcome the bitterness of the Unionists and win the confidence of both communities."[177] Ken Bloomfield, who worked directly with Whitelaw on the political initiative, offers an equally appreciative assessment, describing him as "apparently spontaneous but infinitely cunning."[178]

Whitelaw's qualities and personal popularity among backbenchers en-abled him to survive the furor that greeted the Provisionals' revelation of their secret meeting with him in June 1972. If the Provisionals had en-gaged him in detailed negotiations—a possibility he was evidently pre-pared for—before letting out the secret, he could have found himself in great difficulties: "Clearly those ought to have been the IRA tactics. As it turned out, by returning to violence almost at once, they presented me with a considerable advantage. They proved that they were intransigent and that it was the British Government who really wanted an end to violence."[179]

Despite Faulkner's angry initial reaction to the imposition of direct rule, Whitelaw built up a constructive working relationship with the former premier, "which eventually grew into mutual respect and friendship."[180] Faulkner later offered the following assessment: "He came armed with all the wrong ideas about our problems and his policies for the first four months were an almost unmitigated disaster. But he had a priceless asset in his personality. He was a large genial and humane man, deeply affected by the sufferings of others ... it was not long before many began to feel a certain affinity for him—even when arguing with or attacking him."[181] By the time of the Stormont Castle talks in October 1973, Faulkner was able to appreciate Whitelaw's "sensitive and skilful" chairmanship, which played an important part in securing agreement on the formation of the executive.[182] This was despite the fact that Whitelaw personally believed that the only long-term solution was unification.[183]

On December 3, at a critical point on the eve of the Sunningdale conference, Heath withdrew Whitelaw to deal with the threat of a miners' strike in Britain. Thus the steward who against all the odds had brought the negotiations so far was unavailable at Sunningdale to temper Heath's impatience, remind him of the difficulties Faulkner faced, and finesse the presentation of the agreement to Unionism.

### The Pressure Balance

The white paper succeeded in its primary political objective of relieving domestic and international political pressures on Heath and his team. It addressed all the demands of the government's most influential critics— the Labour opposition, Dublin, and international opinion—without losing the support of Conservative backbenchers. If there were obstacles to progress, they could be depicted credibly as consequences of the intransigence of Northern Ireland's politicians; whatever the outcome, British ministers were congratulated for their perseverance in dealing with such unreasonable people under such difficult circumstances.

The process behind the Sunningdale agreement was more overtly political than any outlined in the previous chapters, in that it centered on negotiations with Northern Ireland's elected leaders. The British government had set the parameters in advance for the outcome it wanted, but remained open to the possibility that the negotiations would fail and an alternative approach would have to be adopted. Heath secured the opposition's support in the Commons and the cooperation of the Irish government largely by conceding most of what Wilson and Lynch had demanded. Thereafter, the opposition's principal effect was to ensure that there was no delay, backsliding, or increase in the Unionists' representation at Westminster.

### Structure and Doctrine

With direct rule, responsibility for Northern Ireland policy passed from the Home Office to the newly established NIO, which also took on key planning functions and personnel from the Cabinet Office, FCO, and MoD. The primary locus of decision shifted from the ministerial committee on Northern Ireland, supported by the ad hoc Northern Ireland officials group, to the secretary of state. The problem acquired its own dedicated bureaucracy.

## The Northern Ireland Office

The creation of the NIO was a watershed in the development of British policymaking. It finally and publicly buried the doctrine of nonintervention. The new department had a presence in both Whitehall and Belfast, and was responsible for all major strands of policy: political development, security, economic and social programs. It became the "effective apex and co-ordinator of the whole administrative machine."[184] It could be interpreted as strengthening the union, since it gave Whitehall an immediate interest in the administration of Northern Ireland. Some NIO officials—predominantly those drafted in from the Home Office and MoD—favored closer integration. But the NIO also contained a strand of senior officials recruited from the FCO, who favored Irish unification. Its political masters could task it either to strengthen or to dissolve the union.

With the full attention of a dedicated cabinet minister supported by a team of ministers and senior civil servants, the Northern Ireland question no longer had to compete for attention with other priorities in Whitehall. On the other hand, the NIO was a small player in relation to the big permanent departments that retained their respective interests in the issue: the MoD, FCO, and Treasury. And initially it depended on the Home Office for resources.

In its formative months, the NIO behaved more like a working group comprising senior personnel from discrete departments than a coherent autonomous entity. The Home Office's Northern Ireland planning unit provided the nucleus, including Neil Cairncross and Philip Woodfield. The NIO's most senior official, Permanent Under Secretary (PUS) Sir William Nield, was drafted in from the Cabinet Office. The FCO contributed Howard Smith (formerly UKREP), Frank Steele (Intelligence), and Dennis Trevelyan (Political Development). Other senior officials were brought in from defense, including Frank Cooper, "a veteran of dialectical wrestling matches with Archbishop Makarios," who replaced Nield as PUS in March 1973.[185] The NIO thus contained the views and represented the interests of the various departments with a stake in policy and provided a forum within which to reconcile them. But if issues arose that could not be resolved internally, the parent departments could override the NIO using their greater muscle in cabinet. Knowing this, NIO ministers and officials had a strong incentive to achieve consensus among themselves. On the other hand, if a secondee failed to get his way within the NIO, he could tacitly seek support from allies in his parent department. That ministers and senior officials divided their working weeks between London and Belfast complicated the task of creating and sustaining the new department. Detailed policy issues were allowed to drift as Whitelaw and his team focused on the day-to-day necessities of finding accommodation, equipment, and support staff, establishing their authority over the NICS, building critical relationships with key players in Northern Ireland, and maintaining continuity.

To take advantage of the new structure's greater capacity to coordinate the collection and application of intelligence across agencies—RUC Special Branch, Army Intelligence, MI5, and MI6—a new post was created within the NIO of director and controller of intelligence. Its first occupant came from the Special Intelligence Service MI6, under the overall control of the FCO. His unit, known as the liaison staff, was designed to put the collection, sharing, and use of security intelligence onto a proper footing after the debacle of internment. The liaison staff reported directly to UK ministers and occupied offices next to Whitelaw's at Stormont. They worked with another new unit, the Irish Joint Section (IJS), established by MI5 and MI6 in London. Their workings and the information they produced were restricted to a tight circle of ministers and senior Whitehall officials.[186] The new arrangements evidently satisfied the chief of general staff (CGS), who informed Defense Secretary Peter Carrington in June 1972 that "previous difficulties over the intelligence organisation in Northern Ireland had now been largely sorted out."[187]

The cabinet had established the policy parameters, including the stipulation that elected representatives of the minority should participate in the administration at executive level. After the initial settling-in period, the NIO had to deliver a political settlement that satisfied this condition by negotiating with the Northern Ireland parties, while the security forces contained the violence. Responsibility for developing political strategy and producing a constitutional settlement had now fully and formally passed from the elected representatives of the people of Northern Ireland to career civil servants from Whitehall, who acted as advisers to ministers representing constituencies in Britain. This meant that it could be done without bias between the two traditions or concern for the vulnerability of a Unionist government. On the downside, those making policy had no roots in either community, a superficial understanding of the complex issues they were required to address, and limited sensitivity to the full import of those issues for the Northern Ireland players. One Stormont permanent secretary (a Catholic) expressed concern that many senior NIO officials "revealed a less than adequate understanding of past political developments. . . . They knew almost no Irish history."[188]

The deficit in understanding and sensitivity was exacerbated as the newcomers did not attempt to integrate with the established NICS, which continued to deal with policy and administration in the social and eco-

nomic arenas. Senior NICS personnel ran their departments much as before, accountable to UK rather than Unionist ministers. But they were sub-
ordinated to the Whitehall newcomers in terms of the NIO's controversial
political development and security functions.[189]

Whitelaw and Nield sought to assure NICS senior officials that their
careers were secure, and that direct rule was intended only as a temporary
interregnum. Individuals who had shown a willingness to collaborate prospered. Bloomfield found himself cast in the role of native guide, advising
Whitelaw on constitutional development policy much as he had advised
Faulkner only a few months earlier.[190] He produced a first draft of the
green paper, which he presented to his NIO colleagues when they returned
from the Darlington conference.[191] But the two sets of civil servants did
not combine seamlessly, and an important element of continuity was lost.
Several senior officials from Faulkner's Cabinet Office were replaced by
Whitehall staff, including Bill Stout, the security adviser who had drawn
up the plans for internment. NICS staff were generally excluded from
posts that were considered politically sensitive or gave access to confidential information.

The newcomers tended to remain aloof from their NICS counterparts,
socializing with one another in the Culloden, a luxurious hotel on the
outskirts of Belfast. They enjoyed special allowances because of the alleged
hardships and dangers of their posting, and travelled to work at the taxpay-
ers' expense in official cars. Documents on political and security strategy
were classified as for "UK eyes only," meaning that they were not to be
shown to the natives of the NICS. The implication that they could not
be trusted with such material—and by extension that Northern Ireland
was not really part of the United Kingdom—created considerable resentment. Even Bloomfield, whose account of the transition is generally positive, smelled the odor of colonial rule; some of the incoming NIO staff
"approached their task like district commissioners set out to administer
a tribe of rather thick-headed savages."[192] Another NICS official recalls
overhearing a senior army officer say without any indication of embarrassment or irony, "Oh, the trouble with the Irish is that they're geneti-
cally inferior to the English."[193] However much Whitelaw sought to assure
the NICS permanent secretaries that he valued their opinions, he did not
permit them to deflect him from Heath's commitment to including Nationalists in the executive. But in that respect at least they were no more
impotent than their Whitehall counterparts. The NIO's political strategy
function rested primarily with Whitelaw's planning group. Its procedures
were relatively loose and unstructured. Whitelaw set an informal tone and
encouraged frank debate. No realistic option was ruled out; it was a time

for creative thinking rather than precedent and routine. The essential skills were those of imagination, negotiation, and consensus-building. Ministers and officials worked closely together, combining political and administrative skills and expertise. In the words of one commentator, the NIO for the first year of direct rule was "an adventure playground for constitutional experts and policy-makers."[194] A great deal depended on the personality of Whitelaw himself. When Heath prematurely withdrew him in December 1973, it created a huge void that impaired the process in its final stage and weakened its outcome.

In the course of the negotiations culminating in Sunningdale, the NIO was reluctant to offer the SDLP and the Irish government any substantial concessions in relation to policing and criminal justice. This resistance can be explained in part by the fact that these functions fell within the NIO's sphere of responsibility, and ministers were reluctant to lose control over them. Similarly, they resisted further concessions on internment, detention without trial, and the Diplock court system, and thus were driven to look for concessions in other areas of the council's work—which fell to the Northern Ireland executive.[195] This is one reason why Heath pressed Faulkner so hard at Sunningdale. The NIO were willing to push Faulkner into concessions in order to relieve the pressure on themselves.

## Defense

Senior army commanders at first welcomed direct rule wholeheartedly, believing that it would give them the strategic political direction and integrated control over all relevant policy areas as their counterinsurgency doctrine required. But the reality proved not to be as satisfying as they had anticipated. They still had to deal with two sets of ministers and officials, in the NIO and MoD. Within days they were complaining that it was even harder than before to engage ministers' attention.

During the first weeks of direct rule the arrangements for liaison between Whitehall departments broke down. GEN 47 had ceased to meet and the NIO had taken the opportunity, without consulting the MoD, to lift the ban on marches that the army had pressed Faulkner to introduce and retain.[196] By June, the CGS was telling Carrington that relations with the NIO were "generally good, apart from some clash of personalities at senior level: but difficulty was created by the fact that members of the Office were very hard pressed and spent much of their time in transit." The GOC added that "he now felt more remote from Stormont than before direct rule and that his contacts with Mr. Whitelaw were less frequent than with Mr. Faulkner."[197] Carrington agreed that the NIO must open up and give senior commanders direct access to Whitelaw.

Army commanders also were not happy with Whitelaw's use of his new powers. Under his political security approach, Whitelaw would fine-tune security operations and control the release of internees from day to day in response to events, accelerating or slowing the rate of release for political reasons. They were especially dismayed during the first four months by his conciliatory approach toward the IRA. According to one observer, the army "watched helplessly as its hard-earned military success was washed away and the Catholic areas, as one officer commented bit-terly, 'were handed back to the Provisionals on a plate.'"[198] Street patrols were reduced, stemming the flow of local intelligence. The practice of actively chasing suspected terrorists was dropped. Ministerial directives were issued to prevent soldiers from arresting named IRA members. By May, Whitelaw was releasing some forty internees per week, and the army knew that many of them were returning to their communities to reengage in paramilitary activity, including bombings and shootings. Army intelligence officers viewed Heath's decision to abandon intensive interrogation as a victory for their enemies and a propaganda setback. Casualties rose. In a single month twenty-eight soldiers were killed and over a hundred wounded.

At a meeting with Carrington on May 1, the CGS openly dissented from the view of one defense minister that the risk of releasing all internees was worth taking to bring the SDLP to the talks table. He argued that ending internment would have a serious effect on the security forces' morale, in particular that of Special Branch. Carrington supported him, adding that it would be intolerable to permit the creation of further no-go areas.[199] The commander of land forces, Major General Robert Ford, warned Car-rington that Whitelaw's low-profile policy was making the soldiers' job more difficult, and that the IRA was taking advantage of the army's in-activity to build more secure foundations in local communities.[200] Minis-ters argued that the soft approach was necessary to drain popular support from the IRA, but—despite Whitelaw's assurances to the cabinet—the commanders were not convinced. They could see no improvement on the streets and considered their new masters naïve.

The carnage of Bloody Friday enabled the army to shift Whitelaw back toward the more robust policy for which they had been lobbying. Motor-man was one early visible result. It was the army's largest military opera-tion since the Suez crisis of 1956. Extra soldiers, personnel carriers, and bulldozers were ferried in from Germany, bringing to 22,000 the number of troops in Northern Ireland—the most yet. Unlike internment, Motor-man was planned with close concern for its presentational effect. Ministers took exceptional precautions to minimize the risk of bloodshed, includ-

NEGOTIATING POWER SHARING, 1973

ing letting republican activists know in advance what was coming. They depicted the operation as liberating Catholic working-class communities from their paramilitary oppressors, rather than (as Faulkner had been demanding) establishing the state's authority in rebel areas.

Motorman was an important shift in the army's strategic approach, away from fighting a counterinsurgency campaign directed against entire communities and toward a counterterrorist campaign directed against the Provisionals as an organization.[201] NIO officials reported to their ministers that this shift had elicited cooperation from republican neighborhoods. After one visit to the Bogside in April 1973, officials indicated that most of its residents no longer believed that the army was deliberately harassing the entire community, understood the problems the army faced, wanted a return to normal law and order sustained by effective civilian policing, and in many cases regarded the IRA as a nuisance.[202] .

Independent of the decision to introduce direct rule and of Whitelaw's political security strategy, the army since internment had been taking steady steps to improve its capacity to tackle the IRA. Recognizing that its mission had evolved well beyond keeping the two communities apart, and that the military security approach was proving counterproductive, senior officers were adapting their tactics to meet the Provisional challenge assertively without alienating popular support. This ruled out indiscriminate actions, such as curfews, comprehensive search-and-arrest operations, and widespread interrogation. They now concentrated on intelligence-gathering and collecting evidence that could be used either to detain suspects or—after July 1973—secure convictions in the new Diplock courts. They developed more efficient patterns of patrolling that reduced soldiers' vulnerability to snipers. They expanded the role and duties of the locally recruited security services—the RUC, RUC Reserve, and UDR—which were increased in numbers and capacity. As part of this process the RUC introduced a system of special patrol groups, mobile units equipped to support the army in low-level public order situations.

Brigadier Frank Kitson's policy of making every company commander identify and tackle the IRA structures in his own local district was adopted throughout the region, leading each company to evolve a useful capacity as a low-level intelligence-gathering unit with a much better understanding of its opponents' relationships with republican communities.[203] Local commanders recruited informers from inside the IRA, including the Provisionals' Belfast quartermaster Eamon Molloy, uncovered and shot in 1975, and introduced new tactics for undercover intelligence gathering and preventing bombers from reaching their targets.[204] These included preemptive attacks on IRA activists.[205]

Early in 1973, the army decided to put its intelligence gathering onto a more secure foundation, leaving less to the initiative of local commanders. It established a new unit, known to the few who were aware of its existence as 14 Intelligence Company. Its members were attached to each of the army's three brigades, in Belfast, Derry, and South Armagh. Their mission was to operate inside republican communities, gathering intelligence, monitoring suspects, planting bugs in the homes of IRA activists and in weapons caches, and spreading misinformation.

When Gerry Adams and Brendan Hughes, as leaders of the Provisionals' Belfast Brigade, were arrested with fourteen of their comrades on June 25, 1973, Whitelaw invited the intelligence officers involved for a celebratory drink, telling them that they were "probably worth three or four Battalions to him."[206] The timing of the arrests was carefully calculated. Three days before the assembly election, Whitelaw wanted to strengthen the prospects of Alliance and SDLP candidates and to prevent the IRA from committing any atrocity that might encourage Protestants to vote for "extremists."

In February 1973, Sir Frank King took over the post of GOC. He decided to focus first on defeating the IRA in Belfast, using the army's new powers of detention to harass suspected IRA activists and planting misinformation to create insecurity in the IRA's ranks. As a result of these activities and improvements in its own training and tactics, the army felt that "by the end of 1973 we had the Provisionals well and truly gripped."[207] This was reflected in improving casualty figures. In 1973 the army lost 66 soldiers, down from 129 in 1972.

The army also developed its own propaganda capability, which extended well beyond responding to incidents in which soldiers had been involved to include matters of political strategy. On the publication of the white paper, the colonel responsible for the army's information policy produced a handling plan for the GOC, the stated aims of which were to maximize the coverage given to the favorable reactions of moderates and minimize the coverage given to unfavorable reactions from hard-liners and extremists. Unattributable briefings were to be used to "expose, discredit and demoralise extremist organisations."[208] In an interesting footnote to the moderate-extremist paradigm, Colonel Hutton explained: "For the purposes of this paper a 'moderate' is defined as someone who will, broadly speaking, support the proposals in the White Paper and who possesses or can be given sufficient stature to speak out in favour. 'Extremists' are defined as those opposed to a significant extent to the White Paper and able to get their views published."[209]

*Foreign and Commonwealth Office*

The MI6 operatives assigned to Northern Ireland did not share the view of some army commanders that the IRA could be defeated through a judicious combination of security measures and political concessions to the SDLP. As we have seen, Frank Steele was instrumental in arranging for Whitelaw to talk directly to Provisional representatives. He had no compunction about talking to "terrorists," later explaining to a BBC journalist that this, after all, had been the precedent set in Kenya and other colonies during Britain's previous colonial withdrawals.[210] Once Whitelaw's attempts to talk the Provisionals into a permanent ceasefire had demonstrably failed, the focus of the intelligence effort shifted to gathering tactical intelligence and covert operations; again, MI6 agents had extensive colonial experience to draw on.

On the political development front, Heath had requested that more FCO people should be put into the NIO because of their experience in drafting constitutions.[211] Their forte was diplomacy and negotiation. They brought a different perspective to the new department, more sympathetic than the Home Office to the aspirations of the Irish government and international opinion. Like the MI6 agents, many of them brought to their Northern Ireland assignment a pattern of understanding derived from experience in extricating Britain from colonial conflicts and unwanted responsibilities overseas.

Britain's diplomats also had the opportunity to influence policy through their lead role in discussions with the Irish government. In July 1972, the Irish ambassador to London arranged to meet the FCO minister responsible for Ireland, Anthony Royle, and his officials regularly twice a month to discuss and monitor developments.[212] The British were keen to keep these contacts out of the public eye; after their first meeting, Royle suggested to O'Sullivan that he should tell the press "what was far from the truth," namely, that the purpose of their meeting had been to discuss increased cultural cooperation between Britain and Ireland in the European context.[213] Ambassador O'Sullivan noted that FCO diplomats were particularly hostile toward Faulkner even in October 1972, when he was cooperating fully with Whitelaw's talks initiative.[214]

## Summary

Direct rule confirmed Heath's primacy in the decision-making process, supported now by Whitelaw and the NIO, rather than Trend and the Cabinet Office. By July 1972 the British had decided that they could not defeat the Provisionals by either coercion or conciliation alone. They had reformulated their priorities, which were now to reduce Provisional violence, drain popular support away from the armed struggle, engage Nationalist elected representatives in negotiations leading to the sharing of power, and secure Dublin's cooperation in all these objectives. They had to do this without provoking a loyalist backlash, as that would stretch the army beyond the resources that the MoD was willing to commit.

Whitelaw accordingly adopted a politically sensitive approach to security policy and operations, intended to bear down on the Provisionals without further alienating the Catholic community. His measures included better arrangements for the gathering, dissemination, and use of intelligence; new powers of arrest and detention; nonjury courts; and increasingly professional covert operations. When the Provisionals responded by stepping up their bombing campaign in England, the security forces hit back by infiltrating the organization, intercepting arms shipments, and arresting its leaders. By December 1972, the security forces felt that they were making good progress.

From September 1972 to March 1973, Whitelaw's political priority was to bring the SDLP to the negotiating table. They played hard to get, making the most of their influence over Irish ministers and diplomats and with the Labour Party at Westminster. For as long as there was the possibility of inducing the British to work proactively for unification, they had no incentive to take risks in pursuit of power sharing. Their continuing resistance to his blandishments stimulated Whitelaw to open up a potential pathway to eventual unification in the form of a public agenda for increasing cross-border cooperation. London also had its own reasons to improve its relations with Dublin, primarily to secure effective action against republican paramilitarism.

Heath needed a strategy that would ensure that he never again had to suffer the pain of a combined assault from the Labour opposition, the Irish government, and international opinion. The policy options of full integration and of continuing the previous policy of reinforcing the Unionist government were both unacceptable to Labour and Dublin, and a firm commitment to Irish unification was unacceptable to the Conservative Party. Helped by Whitelaw's genial manner and negotiating skills, the talks held the government's critics at bay for almost two years. But whenever there appeared to be some delay, Wilson reminded Heath of the need to sustain the momentum, and the prime minister elbowed Whitelaw.

Power sharing with an Irish dimension as a next step toward unification was the preferred policy option of both Dublin and Wilson. They envisaged that it would lead to unification over fifteen to twenty years. In the meantime, the Sunningdale agreement enabled Irish ministers to demonstrate their commitment to that goal without incurring any of the political risks or financial costs of trying to make it happen more rapidly. The agreement reflected the two sovereign governments' shared interest in stability—and creative ambiguity.

The NIO's initial inclination was to reject power sharing as unworkable and to propose full integration as a more practicable alternative. The green paper glossed over this. The substance of the white paper, however, determined that integration would not work because Nationalist Ireland would not accept it. For all their ministers' public declarations, NIO officials and Whitelaw privately continued to entertain doubts about whether the institutional apparatus that they had designed could be sustained. Nevertheless, power sharing with an Irish dimension became the core element in the NIO's bureaucratic doctrine as it settled into more routine methods of working.

Some have interpreted the Sunningdale agreement as a bold and idealistic attempt to tackle "the Irish problem" at its roots. It can, equally validly, be viewed as a pragmatic acceptance of lessons which the British army had acquired through hard learning—that military victory was impossible within the political constraints of public and international opinion, that a political initiative was needed to drain popular support from the IRA, and that the cooperation of the Irish government was needed to contain republican violence within tolerable limits.

By December 1973, Heath could congratulate himself on his apparent achievement. By a combination of willpower, diplomacy, and bluster, he had attained the result he had first formulated after meeting Lynch in September 1971. Direct rule was about to end, he would not have to resort to full integration, and he had done all this without provoking an unmanageable loyalist reaction. But events during 1974 were to destroy his creation and expose the flaws in his reasoning. By May the power-sharing executive had collapsed, destroyed by the hard-liners whose relevance he had discounted. The fate of his initiative turned out much as the Whitehall skeptics had predicted when it was first mooted in January 1972. In trying to reduce Nationalist alienation, Heath created fear and mistrust among Unionists, fatally damaging the one Unionist leader of the period who in a more propitious political context could possibly have led unionism into a lasting compromise.

## Notes

1.    N. Machiavelli, *The Prince*, trans. G. Bull (London: Penguin Classics, 1975), 51.

2.    *Financial Times*, April 27, 1973.

3.    British army operational statistics, cited in Ministry of Defence, "Operation Banner: An Analysis of Military Operations in Northern Ireland," Ministry of Defence paper, July 2006.

4.   W. Whitelaw, *The Whitelaw Memoirs* (London: Aurum Press, 1989), 92.

5.   CJ 3/98, F. Steele, note of meeting with SDLP on April 11, 1972.

6.   Personal interview with author.

7.   CAB 130/561, April 28, 1972. This assurance was true only to the extent that the commanders obeyed instructions; it is clear from the record that they did not approve of Whitelaw's approach.

8.   CAB 130/561, April 28, 1972.

9.   B. Faulkner, *Memoirs of a Statesman* (London: Weidenfeld and Nicholson 1978), 163.

10.   P. Taylor, *Provos: The IRA and Sinn Féin* (London: Bloomsbury, 1998), 135.

11.   PREM 15/1009 top secret "Note of a Meeting with Representatives of the Provisional IRA," P.J. Woodfield, June 21, 1972.

12.   CAB 130/560, June 16, 1972.

13.   Whitelaw used the term *special category status* rather than *political status* and included loyalists as well as republicans, but the effect was the same. Republicans claimed a propaganda victory and unionists were furious.

14.   NAI 2003/16/465, note of June 19, 1972, signature illegible.

15.   Whitelaw, *Memoirs*, 100.

16.   PREM 15/1009, note of June 21, 1972.

17.   Ibid. Woodfield had previously told Adams that it would be "much easier if Mr. McStiofáin were not included" in the delegation.

18.   P. Taylor, *Brits* (London: Bloomsbury Paperback, 2002), 122.

19.   Whitelaw, *Memoirs*, 100. The Provisionals' demands included a British commitment to withdraw by January 1, 1975, an acceptance that the people of Ireland voting as a unit should decide on the future of partition, an end to internment, and an amnesty for all political prisoners. In the interim, they asked for the release of all internees, the repeal of the Special Powers Act, the removal of the ban on Sinn Féin, and PR for all Northern Ireland elections.

20.   Taylor, *Brits*, 123.

21.   *Irish Times*, January 1, 2003.

22.   G. Adams, *Before the Dawn* (London: Mandarin, 1997), 200.

23.   E. Moloney, *A Secret History of the IRA* (London: Allen Lane, 2002), 115, 137.

24.   Taylor, *Brits*, 124.

25.   NAI 2003/16/465, note by O'Sullivan, July 14, 1972.

26.   CAB 130/560, minutes dated July 11, 1972.

27.   Moloney, *Secret History*, 113.

28.   Whitelaw, *Memoirs*, 101.

29.   Faulkner, *Memoirs*, 172.

30.   Whitelaw, *Memoirs*, 102.

31.   D. Hamill, *Pig in the Middle: The Army in Northern Ireland, 1969–1985* (London: Methuen, 1985), 115.

32.   CAB 130/560.

33.   Faulkner, *Memoirs*, 164.

34.   S. Bruce, *The Red Hand: Protestant Paramilitaries in Northern Ireland* (Oxford: Oxford University Press, 1992), 59.

35.   CAB 130/633, January 11, 1973.

36.   P. Bew and H. Patterson, *The British State and the Ulster Crisis* (London: Verso, 1985), 64.

37.   M. Urban, *Big Boys' Rules: The SAS and the Secret Struggle against the IRA* (London: Faber, 1992), 51.

38.   M. Carver, *Out of Step: The Memoirs of Field Marshal Lord Carver* (London: Hutchinson, 1989), 428.

39.   DEFE 13/9/6, secret note for the record, June 1, 1972.

40.   Diplock Report: Parliament, *Report of the Commission to Consider Legal Procedures to Deal with Terrorist Activities in Northern Ireland*, Cmnd. 5185 (London: HMSO, 1972).

41.   *The Times*, December 1, 1972.

42.   F. Burton, *The Politics of Legitimacy* (London: Routledge & Kegan Paul, 1978), 83.

43.   Adams, *Dawn*, 214.

44.   Moloney, *Secret History*, 118, 125. Gerry Adams disputes this account.

45.   Figures derived from M. Sutton, *Index of Deaths from the Conflict in Ireland*, available at www.cain.ulst.ac.uk (accessed November 8, 2010). They include deaths resulting from premature explosions, internal feuds, and accidental shootings. The residues are attributed to the British army, RUC, and unknown agents.

46.   NA 2003/16/465, note by Donal O'Sullivan, June 8, 1972.

47.   I. McAllister, *The Northern Ireland Social Democratic and Labour Party* (London: Macmillan, 1977), 121.

48.   Social Democratic and Labour Party, *Towards a New Ireland* (Belfast: SDLP, 1972).

49.   Adams, *Dawn*, 215.

50.   NAI 2003/16/465, note by Donal O'Sullivan, June 8, 1972. The complaint about deviousness was rich coming from Whitelaw.

51.   NAI 2003/216/465, note by Donal O'Sullivan, July 13, 1972.

52.   J. Campbell, *Edward Heath: A Biography* (London: Jonathan Cape, 1993), 542.

53.   Faulkner, *Memoirs*, 175.

54.   PREM 15/782, August 14, 1972.

55.   Faulkner, *Memoirs*, 166.

56.   P. Dixon, *Northern Ireland: The Politics of War and Peace* (New York: Palgrave, 2001), 122.

57.   Ulster Unionist Party, *A Unionist Blueprint* (Belfast: Ulster Unionist Party, 1972).

58.   Faulkner, *Memoirs*, 183

59.   CAB 130/561, memorandum of April 28, 1972.

60.   Hansard, vol. 838, col. 1104, June 12, 1972.

61.   *Belfast Telegraph*, February 19, 1973.

62.   *Irish Times*, January 1, 2003.

63.   Faulkner, *Memoirs*, 188.

64.   Ibid., 175.

65.   CAB 130/561, April 28, 1972.

66.   CAB 130/561, "The Range of Possible Options for a Future Settlement," NIO paper for Chequers Conference, June 3–4, 1972.

67.   CAB 130/56, note of meeting of June 3–4, 1972.

68.   Northern Ireland Office, *The Future of Northern Ireland* (Belfast: HMSO, 1972).

69. NIO, *Future,* paragraph 78.

70. CAB 130/561, memorandum by Whitelaw, December 12, 1972.

71. CAB 129/168, "Framework for a Settlement for Northern Ireland," paper by W. Whitelaw and minutes of meeting, February 26, 1973. Summarizing the discussion, Heath noted "that each of the solutions would be criticized by one group or another in Northern Ireland, and that several of them would not please Mr. Lynch."

72. Northern Ireland Office, *Northern Ireland: Constitutional Proposals,* Cmnd. 5259 (London: HMSO, 1973).

73. Northern Ireland Constitution Act 1973, section 2.

74. *Fortnight,* May 21, 1973.

75. Faulkner, *Memoirs,* 189.

76. J.F. Harbinson, *The Ulster Unionist Party* (Belfast: Blackstaff, 1972), 175.

77. G. Walker, *A History of the Ulster Unionist Party* (Manchester: Manchester University Press, 2004), 218

78. PREM 15, note of Heath-Whitelaw meeting, July 1, 1973.

79. Faulkner, *Memoirs,* 203–225.

80. CAB 130/633, October 31, 1973.

81. For a detailed participant's account of the Sunningdale conference, see Faulkner, *Memoirs,* 227–37.

82. See Faulkner, *Memoirs,* 236.

83. P. Bew and G. Gillespie, *Northern Ireland: A Chronology of the Troubles 1968–1999* (Dublin: Gill and Macmillan, 1999), 77.

84. CAB 130/633, memorandum by Whitelaw, February 1, 1973.

85. Faulkner, *Memoirs,* 203–25.

86. CAB 130/560, minutes of August 10, 1972.

87. CAB 130/633, memorandum by Whitelaw, February 1, 1973.

88. NAI 2003/14/466, note by Ambassador O'Sullivan of August 2, 1972.

89. Dixon, *Northern Ireland,* 133.

90. *The Times,* February 21, 1973.

91. NAI 2004/21/467, note of meeting, June 9, 1973.

92. CAB 130/560, minutes of May 15, 1972.

93. CAB 130/561, memorandum by Whitelaw, April 28, 1972.

94. M. Farrell, *The Orange State,* 308.

95. CAB 130/560, minutes of November 22, 1972.

96. CAB 130/633, note of January 11, 1973.

97. FCO 87/221, report of a visit to the Bogside by Frank Steele, April 5, 1973.

98. Whitelaw, *Memoirs,* 87.

99. Hansard, col. 83, November 13, 1972.

100. Hansard, col. 85, November 13, 1972.

101. Hansard, col. 1591, March 29, 1973.

102. Hansard, col. 758, May 24, 1973.

103. Hansard, col. 1632, March 29, 1973.

104. *Irish Times,* October 10, 1973.

105. J. Callaghan, *A House Divided* (London: Collins, 1973), 152.

106. *Daily Telegraph,* October 8, 1971.

107. P. Dixon, "A House Divided Cannot Stand: Britain, Bipartisanship, and Northern Ireland," *Contemporary Record* (1995), 166.

108. *The Guardian,* July 24, 1973.

109. *New Statesman,* September 21, 1973.

110. *Irish Times,* October 3, 1973.

111. Dixon, "A House Divided," 166.

112. *Belfast Newsletter,* October 1, 1973.

113. Callaghan, *House Divided,* 154.

114. *The Guardian,* October 28, 1978.

115. C. King, *The Cecil King Diary 1970–1974* (London: Jonathan Cape, 1975), 276.

116. Callaghan, *House Divided,* 184.

117. Hansard, col. 1098, June 12, 1972.

118. Hansard, col. 57, November 13, 1972.

119. NAI 2003/16/465, note by O'Sullivan, July 28, 1972.

120. NAI 2003/16/467, note by O'Sullivan, October 18, 1972.

121. Hansard, June 14, 1973, col. 1750.

122. *Irish Times,* October 5, 1973.

123. *The Times,* June 16, 1973.

124. *The Times,* June 22, 1973.

125. The writer gave no indication of how sizable this segment might be, which parties they might vote for, or what the "tribalized" citizens thought.

126. *The Times,* October 14, 1972.

127. *The Times,* October 31, 1972.

128. *The Times,* March 21, 1973.

129. J. Peck, *Dublin from Downing Street* (Dublin: Gill and Macmillan, 1978), 145.

130. Lynch wrote that any attempt at "integrating Northern Ireland fully into the UK would be disastrous." See J. Lynch, "The Anglo Irish Problem," *Foreign Affairs,* vol. 50, no. 4 (July 1972), 601–17.

131. NAI 2003/16/466, secret paper by Gallagher, May 8, 1972.

132. CAB 130/560, June 22, 1972.

133. Bew and Patterson, *The British State,* 52.

134. NAI 2003/16/465, note by O'Sullivan, July 13, 1972.

135. NAI 2003/16/466, September 29, 1972.

136. NAI 2003/16/467, Peck to Lynch, October 26, 1972.

137. NAI 2003/16/467, O'Sullivan to McCann, October 27, 1972.

138. Dixon, *Northern Ireland,* 137.

139. *Irish Times,* November 25, 1972.

140. Cited in Dixon, *Northern Ireland,* 137.

141. *Irish Times,* January 1, 2004.

142. CAB 130/633, minutes of February 19, 1973.

143. Faulkner, *Memoirs*, 187.

144. CAB 128/51, minutes of meeting on March 15, 1973.

145. H. Patterson, *Ireland since 1939: The Persistence of Conflict* (Dublin: Penguin, 2006), 268.

146. G. FitzGerald, *Towards a New Ireland* (Dublin: Torc Books, 1973), 125.

147. Ibid., 146.

148. *Irish Times*, January 1, 2004.

149. C.C. O'Brien, *States of Ireland* (London: Panther, 1974).

150. C.C O'Brien, *Memoir: My Life and Themes* (London: Profile Books, 1998), 341

151. O'Brien, *States of Ireland*, 349.

152. *Irish Times*, January 2, 2004.

153. *Irish Times*, January 2, 2004

154. *The Times*, July 3, 1973.

155. NAI 2004/21/467, note of meeting on July 12, 1973.

156. Bew and Patterson, *The British State*, 58.

157. NAI 2004/21/467.

158. *Irish Times*, September 18, 1973.

159. *Irish Times*, January 1, 2004.

160. *Irish Times*, January 1, 2004.

161. The white paper had indicated that "the leaders of elected representatives of Northern Ireland opinion" would be invited to the conference.

162. *Irish Times*, January 1, 2004.

163. Faulkner, *Memoirs*, 228.

164. *Irish Times*, January 1, 2003.

165. *Irish Times*, January 1, 2004.

166. P. Arthur, "The Heath Government and Northern Ireland," in S. Ball and A. Seldon, eds., *The Heath Government 1970–1974: A Reappraisal* (Longman: New York, 1993), 237.

167. CAB 130/560, minutes of May 15, 1972.

168. T.E. Utley, *Lessons of Ulster* (London: Dent, 1975), 108.

169. J. Campbell, *Edward Heath: A Biography* (London: Jonathan Cape, 1993), 546–47.

170. Campbell, *Heath*, 552.

171. K. Bloomfield, *Stormont in Crisis: A Memoir* (Belfast: Blackstaff, 1994), 187.

172. Faulkner, *Memoirs*, 234.

173. K. Bloomfield, *A Tragedy of Errors* (Liverpool: Liverpool University Press, 2007), 42.

174. E. Heath, *The Course of My Life: My Autobiography* (London: Hodder and Stoughton, 1998), 440.

175. Whitelaw, *Memoirs*, 90.

176. King, *Diary*, 193–94.

177. Campbell, *Heath*, 433.

178. Bloomfield, *Stormont in Crisis*, 173.

179. Whitelaw, *Memoirs*, 101.

180. Ibid., 89.

181. Faulkner, *Memoirs*, 160.

182. Ibid., 205.

183. King, *Diary*, 207.

184. Bew and Patterson, *The British State*, 45.

185. Bloomfield, *Stormont in Crisis*, 192. Makarios was a leader of the Greek Cypriot resistance to British rule and subsequently president of Cyprus.

186. Taylor, *Brits*, 114–15.

187. DEFE 13/916: Secret note of Ministry of Defense on Northern Ireland Policy Group meeting, June 1, 1972.

188. P. Shea, *Voices and the Sound of Drums: An Irish Autobiography* (Belfast: Blackstaff, 1981), 191.

189. NIO officials took a particular interest in social and economic issues of particular political salience, such as integrated education and the location of inward investment.

190. Bloomfield, *Stormont in Crisis*, 173.

191. Ibid., 178.

192. Ibid., 170.

193. Taylor, *Brits*, 114.

194. Arthur, "Heath Government," 250.

195. Bew and Patterson, *The British State*, 59.

196. DEFE 13/916, minutes of May 1, 1972.

197. DEFE 13/916, minutes of June 1, 1972.

198. Hamill, *Pig in the Middle*, 103.

199. DEFE 13/916, minutes of May 1, 1972.

200. Hamill, *Pig in the Middle*, 107.

201. Taylor, *Brits*, 126.

202. FCO 87/221.

203. Hamill, *Pig in the Middle*, 121.

204. Taylor, *Brits*, 128.

205. Ibid., 130.

206. Ibid., 156.

207. Hamill, *Pig in the Middle*, 133–39.

208. CJ 4/301, memo from Col. G.W. Hutton to GOC, February 25, 1973.

209. Hamill, *Pig in the Middle*, 121.

210. Taylor, *Brits*, 119.

211. CAB 130/560, minutes of meeting on May 12, 1972.

212. NAI 2003/16/465, note from O'Sullivan to McDonagh, July 13, 1972.

213. NAI 2003/16/465, note from O'Sullivan to McDonagh, July 13, 1972.

214. NAI 2003/16/467, note by O'Sullivan, October 4, 1972.

# 7

# Comparing the
# Four Case Studies

*The instinctive reaction of most Ministers when confronted
with an issue is not to think in terms of analysing a complex
problem to seek out the optimum solution but instead to see it
in political terms.* —Clive Ponting[1]

The case studies set out in the previous four chapters have examined
some of the processes of reasoning, patterns of understanding,
political pressures, and organizational factors that helped to shape
British policies for managing political violence in Northern Ireland between 1968 and 1973; the interests and principles that underpinned them;
how policymakers tried to resolve value conflicts, dilemmas, and uncertainties; and why policies evolved as they did. Tables 7.1–7.4 summarize
the conclusions according to the models of analysis outlined in chapter 1.

## The Rational Model

The rational model seeks to explain British policies as the outcomes of
systematic decision-making processes, directing attention to the changing
nature and intensity of the violence and to political developments inside
Northern Ireland. It identifies ministers' objectives, options, and calculations. This model clearly fails to provide a full and credible explanation of
the policies Britain adopted in any of the four cases.

In the first case (chapter 3), as ministers have since openly admitted,
they intervened in Northern Ireland "knowing nothing about the place. . . .
It wasn't so much deciding what policy to have as being able to excuse

**Table 7.1     Reform, October 1968–October 1969**

| | |
|---|---|
| *Rational Model* | |
| Nature of disorder and disaffection | Protest marches and counterdemonstrations leading to intercommunal rioting; attacks on public facilities; collapse of policing. |
| Deaths 1969 | 14 |
| Bombs planted 1969 | 10 |
| State of political leadership | Fragmentation of Unionist Party; forced resignation of O'Neill. |
| | Emergence of assertive Nationalist leaders outside party system. |
| Policy objectives | End disorder; create an effective police force supported by Catholics; avoid further entanglement. |
| Options considered | Reinforce Stormont; reform police and local government; direct rule; withdrawal. |
| | |
| *Cognitive Process Model* | |
| Uncertainties | Future development of Northern Ireland's party political system and culture. |
| Cause of violence | Discrimination against Catholics; poverty and unemployment; Unionists' response to peaceful protest. |
| Motives of protesters | Secure equal rights for Catholics. |
| Political dynamic | Unionist fragmentation a necessary part of modernization. |
| Own role | Bringing an outdated political system up to British standards. |
| | |
| *Political Model* | |
| UK Parliament | Labour backbenchers hostile to Unionists, pressing for reform; conservatives supporting government; end of precedent of nonintervention. |
| UK media and public opinion | Support for civil rights campaign and condemnation of Unionist misrule. |
| International factors | Dublin presses for British withdrawal and concessions to nationalism. |
| Pressure balance | For civil rights; against Unionists. |
| Key ministers | Callaghan, Wilson: both hostile to Unionists; Wilson interventionist and in favor of a united Ireland. |
| | |
| *Organizational Model* | |
| Locus of decision | Callaghan and Wilson. |
| Structure | Home Office lead; separation of Northern Ireland Civil Service from Whitehall; separation of Royal Ulster Constabulary (RUC) from police forces in Britain. |
| Routine | Noninvolvement. |
| Doctrine | Home Office; nonintervention; MoD; minimal intervention; Army; if intervening, primacy over RUC. |

**Table 7.2    Coercion, April 1970–August 1971**

*Rational Model*

| | |
|---|---|
| Nature of disorder and disaffection | Intercommunal rioting; republican no-go areas; rioting against army; Irish Republican Army (IRA) bombing and shooting campaign; Ulster Volunteer Force (UVF) bombs and sectarian assassinations; Social Democratic and Labour Party (SDLP) campaign of civil disobedience. |
| Deaths 1970 1971 pre-internment | 25 in 12 months. 34 in 7 months. |
| Bombs planted 1970 1971 total | 170 1,515 |
| State of political leadership | Unionist Party increasingly restive; Paisley elected to Westminster; Chichester-Clark replaced by Faulkner; formation of Alliance and SDLP. |
| Policy objectives | Sustain a cooperative administration at Stormont; defeat the IRA; avoid a loyalist backlash. |
| Options considered | Reinforce Stormont; constitutional reform; direct rule; repartition; independence. |

*Cognitive Process Model*

| | |
|---|---|
| Uncertainties | Severity of pressures on Faulkner; Nationalist reaction to internment; ability of security services to catch enough key IRA activists. |
| Cause of violence | IRA-led insurgency; risk of mass loyalist reaction. |
| Insurgents' motives | Overthrow the state. |
| Political dynamic | Moderate Unionist leaders under threat from hard-liners; IRA to be defeated before constitutional reform can be pursued. |
| Own role | Conditional support for devolved administration. |

*Political Model*

| | |
|---|---|
| UK Parliament | Conservative government sympathetic to army; backbenchers and activists pressing for tougher security measures; Labour compliant. |
| UK media and public opinion | Antirepublican; demands for tougher security measures; Troops Out movement. |
| International factors | Arms trial and IRA cross-border activity reduce Dublin's credibility. |
| Pressure balance | Antirepublican; pro-army. |
| Key ministers | Maudling, Carrington, Heath: all hands-off. |

*Organizational Model*

| | |
|---|---|
| Locus of decision | Ostensibly Stormont, but with UK veto on all important issues. |
| Structure | Stepped return of control over security to local commanders; increasing influence of Ministry of Defence in Whitehall; tensions between army and Stormont/Royal Ulster Constabulary. |
| Routine | Military security approach to policing republican areas; plans for internment drawn up in advance. |
| Doctrine | Home Office yielding on nonintervention; Cabinet Office exploring radical alternatives; army applying counterinsurgency doctrine; Foreign and Commonwealth Office concern for Anglo-Irish and international relations. |

**Table 7.3 Direct Rule, September 1971–March 1972**

*Rational Model*

| | |
|---|---|
| Nature of disorder and disaffection | Nationalist mass protests against internment; Social Democratic and Labour Party (SDLP) boycott of regional administration; intensification of Irish Republican Army (IRA) campaigns and extension to England; emergence of Ulster Defence Association (UDA); loyalist bombings and assassinations. |
| Deaths | |
| 1971 after internment | 140 in 5 months. |
| 1972 before direct rule | 80 in 3 months. |
| Bombs planted 1971 | 1,515 |
| State of political leadership | Faulkner losing grassroots support to both flanks; formation of Democratic Unionist Party (DUP) and Vanguard; defections to Alliance; greater coherence within SDLP; divisions within Provisional IRA. |
| Policy objectives | Secure Dublin's cooperation; open dialogue with SDLP; defeat IRA; break up Unionist monolith; avoid loyalist backlash. |
| Options considered | Comprehensive review of all options, including withdrawal; then focusing on alternatives for constitutional reform. |

*Cognitive Process Model*

| | |
|---|---|
| Uncertainties | Unionist reaction; whether sufficient to win over Nationalist Ireland; whether Northern Ireland Civil Service (NICS) and Royal Ulster Constabulary (RUC) would cooperate. |
| Cause of violence | IRA insurgency with mass Catholic support because of discrimination and exclusion from power. |
| Protesters' motives | SDLP, to secure a fair deal for the minority; IRA, to overthrow the state and force British withdrawal. |
| Political dynamic | Unionists incapable of leading progressive change; SDLP amenable to negotiated settlement; IRA leadership divided. |
| Own role | Neutral intermediary, steering both sides into a fair settlement in line with British standards. |

*Political Model*

| | |
|---|---|
| UK Parliament | Conservative backbenchers concerned at Maudling's inaction and sympathetic to army; Labour critical of internment; Wilson's fifteen-point plan ends bipartisan consensus. |
| UK media and public opinion | Strongly critical of internment, interrogation procedures, and Bloody Sunday; anti-Unionist. |
| International factors | Dublin criticizes Heath and endorses Wilson's proposals; international condemnation over Bloody Sunday. |
| Pressure balance | Cumulative pressure to act; anti-Unionist. |
| Key ministers | Heath in lead, with Carrington and Maudling. |

*Organizational Model*

| | |
|---|---|
| Locus of decision | Heath pushing his preferred solution through cabinet. |
| Structure | Cabinet-led policy review; Whitehall distances itself from NICS; Northern Ireland planning teams in Home Office, Ministry of Defence (MoD), and Foreign and Commonwealth Office (FCO); UK Representative undermines Stormont. |
| Routine | Plans for direct rule in place since 1969. |
| Doctrine | Home Office advocates direct rule; MoD counterinsurgency doctrine requires integration of military and civil administration; FCO supports Nationalist position. |

**Table 7.4 Power Sharing, April 1972–December 1973**

*Rational Model*

| | |
|---|---|
| Nature of disorder and disaffection | Intensification of Provisional Irish Republican Army (IRA) campaign; Social Democratic and Labour Party (SDLP) boycott ends; Vanguard mass rallies; loyalist bombings, assassinations, and strikes; sectarian gun battles; rioting. |
| Deaths | |
| 1972 after direct rule | 387 in 9 months. |
| 1973 | 252 |
| Bombs planted 1972 | 1,853 |
| 1973 | 1,520 |
| State of political leadership | Faulkner's authority slipping as he tries to sell Heath's policies; majority of Unionist Assembly members oppose power sharing; tensions within SDLP; Provisional IRA settling into long war. |
| Policy objectives | To July 1972: drain popular support from IRA; from July 1972: defeat PIRA. Secure Dublin's cooperation; negotiate agreed settlement; promote moderate parties and marginalize hard-liners; avoid loyalist backlash. |
| Options considered | Devolved coalition government with Irish dimension; full integration; continuing direct rule. |

*Cognitive Process Model*

| | |
|---|---|
| Uncertainties | Faulkner's reaction and leadership of Unionist Party; power of loyalist protest; bottom lines of IRA and SDLP. |
| Cause of violence | IRA insurgency with mass Catholic support because of discrimination and exclusion from power. |
| Insurgents' motives | Prevent an agreement and force British withdrawal. |
| Political dynamic | Victory of progressive parties inevitable with UK support. |
| Own role | Neutral intermediary imposing just settlement. |

*Political Model*

| | |
|---|---|
| UK Parliament | Bipartisan consensus restored but requiring continuous maintenance; Wilson blocks increase in Northern Ireland MPs. |
| UK media and public opinion | Support for Whitelaw and his initiative; urgency. |
| International factors | Dublin works with Labour and SDLP; Britain and Ireland join European Economic Community (EEC); closer high-level relationships with Dublin. |
| Pressure balance | For power sharing with an Irish dimension. |
| Key ministers | Heath supported by Whitelaw and Carrington. |

*Organizational Model*

| | |
|---|---|
| Locus of decision | Cabinet directed by Heath. |
| Structure | Northern Ireland Office (NIO) created to coordinate security policies and operations, political development, and civil administration; creation of Intelligence Director. |
| Routine | NIO drawing on other departments; army pressure to return to military procedures; Foreign and Commonwealth Office experience in colonial withdrawals. |
| Doctrine | NIO establishing its own in line with Heath's directive. |

it."[2] For public consumption they articulated a series of objectives associated with the principles of fairness and the process of modernization, but their motivation was primarily political and organizational: to reduce the power of the Unionist Party and the Stormont administration, to dampen criticism of themselves, and to minimize the scale and extent of the army's reluctant intervention.

In the second case (chapter 4), although British officials had made contingency plans for internment, the crucial decision to permit Stormont to introduce it was again made hastily, in reaction to a crisis—the impending collapse of Faulkner's government. UK ministers were not convinced that internment would help defeat the Irish Republican Army (IRA). They did not even expect it to prolong Faulkner's survival for more than a few months. But they were not ready to introduce direct rule immediately and reasoned that it would be better to implement internment before rather than after direct rule. This would enable them to avoid criticism from the Unionists and their Conservative supporters for not permitting it but also to blame Faulkner if it failed. As unwilling conscripts, British ministers and officials put little effort into ensuring that the policy succeeded or mitigating its worst features.

On the surface, the imposition of direct rule (chapter 5) in the third case meets some of the rational model's criteria. Heath initiated a comprehensive policy review that, at one stage, identified no less than sixteen possible options. As a result of this review, ministers decided to work toward a voluntary coalition if the Northern Ireland parties could be induced to agree. But this was not the policy that they followed. The events of January and February 1972—in particular Bloody Sunday and its aftermath—created political pressures that overturned their previous calculations. Heath's priorities changed dramatically. He discarded the conclusions of the review in order to win back the cooperation of Nationalist Ireland, which insisted that it would not even negotiate possible solutions until the Stormont regime was abolished. Contrary to the expectations of the rational model, Heath had not thought through the steps that might lead from direct rule to the political settlement that he wanted, the obstacles to progress, or how they might be overcome. Meanwhile, his cabinet colleagues and senior officials remained deeply skeptical about the prospects for power sharing. But once Heath decided to impose direct rule, he closed his ears to Faulkner's last-minute proposals, refused to negotiate with the Unionist leader, and dealt with the differences among his colleagues not by rational argument but by appealing to their collective ego.

In the fourth case (chapter 6), the policy that emerged after Sunningdale was clearly not the product of a single rational decision-maker but the outcome of a lengthy process of negotiations with Northern Ireland's "moderate" political parties, the Labour opposition, and the Irish government. The outcome was not the first preference of any of the participants but a compromise that they all, with varying degrees of reluctance, could accept. Those responsible for the violence and disorder were deliberately excluded from the negotiating process.

## The Cognitive Process Model

The case studies identify a number of important ways that British policymakers conceptualized and simplified the problem as they struggled with its uncertainties and complexities. They held unwarranted optimism about policies they favored and denied or downplayed both the capabilities of their opponents and the legitimacy of their views. They entertained politically expedient explanations of the causes of the violence and adopted familiar templates for solutions, which they referred to approvingly as British norms, British standards, and normal politics. They demonized those who did not accept these norms as extremists, hard-liners, bigots, and terrorists, and idealized those who agreed with them as reasonable, moderate, and men of goodwill. Finally, they reframed the role of the British state variously as sovereign authority and neutral intermediary to suit the case they were making and the political context.

### Managing Uncertainties

In each of the four cases the British undertook some research to reduce the risks and uncertainties of policy change but still took huge leaps into the unknown. They handled this in part, as mentioned above, by being overly optimistic. It required considerable suspension of disbelief to conclude that the disbandment of the Ulster Special Constabulary (USC) and disarming of the Royal Ulster Constabulary (RUC) would enable the army to disengage more rapidly, that internment would hasten the defeat of the IRA; that Unionists would quickly acquiesce in direct rule, and that a sustainable coalition government, comprising elected representatives with incompatible constitutional aspirations, could be created at all, never mind within two years.

In the first case, Callaghan acted on the belief—although he apparently did not really believe—that there was little probability of mass disorder again and that policing reforms could be implemented in time to allow the army to be withdrawn within six months. In the second case, Heath chose to accept Faulkner's assurances that internment would accelerate the destruction of the IRA despite clear and accurate warnings to the contrary from army commanders, the Irish government, and Nationalist elected representatives. In the third case, Heath persuaded himself that a progressive political realignment was already taking place that, under direct rule, the British government could encourage and accelerate. He pressed the cabinet into agreeing to impose direct rule without any clear idea as to how this would enable them to achieve their objectives and despite the strong reservations of other ministers and officials. In the fourth case, Heath pinned his faith to the development of normal politics, conducted by moderate leaders, despite the evidence of recent history and contemporary surveys of public opinion.

In each instance, key ministers and their advisers harbored private reservations about the prospects for the strategies they promoted in public. They were particularly skeptical about the workability of power sharing, and their doubts persisted long after it had become official policy.

### Causes of Disorder

In 1969, Labour ministers relied heavily on information provided by the Northern Ireland Labour Party (NILP) and the British national media. These sources directed their attention toward Northern Ireland Civil Rights Association (NICRA) demands and the failures of policing at the expense of less visible but equally important developments, notably tensions within the Unionist Party. Callaghan gratefully adopted the legitimate grievances hypothesis, which attributed the unrest to Stormont's failure to respond positively to complaints about discrimination in the local government franchise, employment, and the allocation of public housing. To these he added the unusually high levels of unemployment and deprivation in parts of Derry. The optimistic corollary was that once Catholics' social and economic grievances had been resolved, the protests would stop.

When the disorder continued to intensify despite the reforms, the incoming Conservative administration developed a new explanation, which it overlaid onto the legitimate grievances hypothesis: that the IRA had exploited the original grievances and transformed the protests into a violent assault on the authority of the state. So it was appropriate to apply a coercive remedy, in the form of the military security approach to policing. Without any palatable alternative, ministers discounted an increasing body of evidence—including advice from their own officials on the ground— that this approach was exacerbating the problem.

In response to domestic and international protests over the internment operation, ministers again revised their diagnosis. After his two meetings with Lynch in September 1971, Heath adopted the explanation advanced by Nationalist Ireland that the violence was rooted in the minority's exclusion from decision-making, reinforced by the one-sided application of the military security approach. Since the Unionist government could not survive without such an approach and had already made clear that it would not admit Nationalist representatives into the Stormont cabinet, this created a strong argument for direct rule.

Three months into direct rule, ministers again changed their diagnosis. Whatever its origins, the Provisional IRA campaign had assumed a life of its own and robust security policies would be needed to end it. The political initiative could proceed with a view to draining popular support for the Provisionals, but security measures would also have to be strengthened; in future, they would be directed more discriminatingly at active insurgents, applying selective rather than brute force.

Two characteristics of ministers' changing patterns of understanding are worth noting. First, they were readily discarded in response to events and changes in the political pressure balance at Westminster. Second, they discounted the extent to which British policies had become their own cause. The military security approach that paved the way for internment resulted from the predictable failure of the Hunt reforms to produce a police service capable of delivering effective civil policing in republican districts. The consequences of the incompetent implementation of internment contributed to the decision to impose direct rule. This then enabled Faulkner's Unionist opponents to capitalize on the anxieties of the protestant community, leading to the rejection of the white paper proposals and ultimately to the failure of the power-sharing experiment.

### British Standards

In 1969 British policymakers' understandings of Northern Ireland were rooted in a conception of political life based on their own experiences. Labour and Conservative ministers alike assumed that the main problem with the government of Northern Ireland was that it was not British enough. They believed that most Catholics were predisposed to give allegiance to the regime, if only it would behave evenhandedly. The idea that a segment of the population identified with another nation-state was alien to them. They viewed the conflict as an anachronism that persisted because of discrimination and backwardness, and were seemingly oblivious to centuries of conflict between Protestants and Catholics in Britain and Ireland, the continuing inheritance of discrimination against Irish people in Britain, and the gerrymandering that plagued the political system in Britain at least into the 1980s.[3]

Hunt's recommendations for the future of policing in Northern Ireland assumed that the RUC should be brought into line with mainland forces. Neither ministers nor senior officials showed any appreciation for why things had been done differently in Ireland, or of the possibility of using other models to organize policing, such as the Republic's. Callaghan's proposal for a community relations commission was derived from English experience in the field of race relations; neither side in Northern Ireland had asked for any such body, and one of the first acts of the power-sharing executive in 1974 was to abolish it.

That said, Conservative ministers did not apply their template to the army's policing role, where it might actually have been useful, even to the limited extent of requiring soldiers to respect citizens' basic human rights. The military practices that paved the way for internment owed more to overseas colonial practices—at times and in places where human rights were not an issue and the armed forces were not exposed to critical media scrutiny—than to patterns of civilian policing in Britain. It is highly unlikely that heavily armed paratroops would have been used to maintain public order in a parallel context in London. To fill the policing gap, the army adopted more comprehensively oppressive measures than Stormont and the RUC had ever used. The British army and intelligence services, accountable to British ministers, were responsible for the Falls curfew, the ill treatment of internees, and the civilian deaths on Bloody Sunday. It was ironic that ministers of a devolved administration in Ireland were dismissed from office for having failed to live up to British standards.

Colonial models were also applied in considering the possibility of withdrawal. During the previous twenty years the British political establishment had overseen the evacuation of British administrators and armed forces from most of the nation's colonies and dependencies: India and Pakistan, the Middle East, Cyprus, and east Africa.[4] Nationalists and others depicted Northern Ireland as England's first colony and withdrawal as long overdue. As we saw in chapter 1, there is a valid case to be argued for applying the colonial paradigm as one of a number of models that contribute to understanding the preconditions for the conflict. Lessons from Britain's experience with former colonies suggested that the solution should be a duly planned and phased withdrawal; the white paper package opened up a pathway for moving in this direction, if and when it became expedient to do so.

The tendency to look to British models extended to the scale and status of the Stormont government. Callaghan questioned why such a small population needed its own parliament, with lawmaking powers and a paramilitary security force, when a county council with none of those things would be the norm for a region of comparable size and population in England. Heath and Maudling used the same comparison to argue their case for stripping Stormont of its security powers and status. They neglected both their Irish history and their contemporary geography. In the European Economic Community (EEC) context, Heath was happy to respect Luxemburg (for example) as a fully autonomous nation-state, with an area of 998 square miles (compared with Northern Ireland's 5,456) and a population of some 340,000 (compared with 1.6 million).

UK ministers convinced themselves that politics in Northern Ireland should conform to the British left-right model, even though, in a global context, Britain's system was rather exceptional. Meanwhile, the minority whose interests they claimed to be advancing looked not to Britain but to Ireland for their norms, where party politics were based only to a limited extent on class divisions. Heath overrode objections from at least one of his ministers that the institutional arrangements needed to permit power sharing were fundamentally inconsistent with the Westminster model of parliamentary democracy.

If British party leaders were serious about developing a new politics in Northern Ireland patterned on the British model, they might have at least tried to persuade their own parties to fight elections there. Both the Conservative Party and the Labour Party were associated with parties in the region, with which they could have developed UK-wide partnerships. Labour could have affiliated with the NILP, but despite Callaghan's efforts chose not to. The Conservatives could have worked with and through the Unionist Party but chose to reject it as too sectarian because of its links to the Orange Order. Heath toyed with the idea of building up a separate Conservative Party machine in the region but did not follow through.[5]

*"Reasonable People"*

Linked to the concept of British standards was that of reasonable people, meaning those political activists, commentators, and voters in Northern Ireland who sought to comply with the norms of the British political establishment. Hunt expressed the opinion that his proposals would "be widely accepted by reasonable men and women in Northern Ireland."[6] This suggests a failure to appreciate that Nationalists rejected the RUC not just because it had implemented ministerial decisions that effectively discriminated against their community but because it represented, served, and sought to defend a state the very existence of which they opposed. Whether the RUC included the USC or not, armed or unarmed, this fundamental objection remained. Correspondingly, many Unionists supported the RUC uncritically, seeing it as their one reliable line of defense against republican subversion.

In the second case, Heath regarded Faulkner as the last available Unionist leader who—narrowly and lacking anyone better—fell within his definition of reasonableness, albeit tainted by his membership in the Orange Order. It was thus worth taking the risk of internment to prevent his government from collapsing. After internment, however, the British premier seems to have been influenced by Lynch's depiction of Faulkner as intransigent, sectarian, and irrationally obsessed with the military defeat of the IRA. The British came to believe that without increasingly tough (and hence counterproductive) coercive measures, Faulkner's government would fall. He would then be replaced by an extremist who would refuse to cooperate with them. Thus, it was preferable to impose direct rule on Faulkner, who would at least react responsibly.

A central goal of Heath's strategy in the third and fourth case studies was to depoliticize the Northern Ireland administration by removing big contentious issues, such as partition and internment, from the agenda. Once this had been done, he argued that the moderate leaders of the two sides would cooperate in tackling social and economic issues. The extremists would then either convert to reasonableness or become irrelevant. From this perspective, "extremists" such as Ian Paisley and "terrorists" such as Martin McGuinness were merely the dangerous legacy of a primitive past standing in the way of a sensible, just, and durable settlement.[7] Unfortunately for Heath, large swaths of the population and their political representatives fell outside this Anglo-centric definition of reasonableness. Heath acceded to the demands of Alliance and the Social Democratic and Labour Party (SDLP) that Craig and Paisley should be excluded from the Sunningdale conference. Far from receding into the shadows, they drew strength from their exclusion and denounced Faulkner as a traitor, bent on collaborating with the British in offering still more concessions to their republican enemies. Nor did popular support for the IRA melt away because soldiers adopted a lower profile on the streets. Republicans continued to see the British army as an occupying force, and interpreted British concessions as harbingers of the victory that their doctrine assured them was historically inevitable.

### Britain's Role

Wilson's government depicted itself as the champion of progress, dragging Northern Ireland into the modern age. Callaghan declared it was his mission to induce Unionists to implement the reforms necessary for the army to withdraw as quickly as possible without risking further disorder. This was not the only possible choice of role. Stormont argued and Home Office doctrine decreed that the British government should provide whatever police or army reinforcements were necessary to restore order, and not to interfere in devolved policy areas. Nationalists, on the other hand, argued that Britain should dismantle its puppet regime and withdraw.

When they came to power, the Conservatives at first accepted the Home Office's doctrine on relations between the two jurisdictions. While publicly they continued to depict themselves as champions of reform, they increasingly acted as a detached sovereign government sustaining the devolved administration. By delegating authority to Stormont and army commanders, they relieved themselves of a considerable burden.

After internment, the British dropped the doctrine of minimal intervention and re-created themselves as neutral intermediaries working for an equitable political settlement. Where previously he had portrayed himself as supporting the devolved government against republican terrorism, Heath then described nationalism and unionism as equally legitimate—if primitive—worldviews requiring institutional reconciliation. The British state would no longer defend the union and respect the right of the electorate in Northern Ireland to determine its own constitutional status.

Heath acknowledged the practical limits to Britain's sovereign and military power by accepting the case for an Irish dimension to the governance of Northern Ireland. He did not, however, fully appreciate that the British state was not just an intermediary but an active participant in the problem. Its security forces were deployed in Northern Ireland, and an essential element in the conflict—the clash over sovereignty—could be resolved only at the level of the two national governments.

## The Political Model

The case studies reveal that major policy transformations occurred only after a significant shift in the balance of political pressure, when the conflict generated criticisms so intense and sustained as to cause ministers pain and anxiety. Three of the factors contained in the political model emerge from the case studies as especially influential: the personal contributions of key ministers, the balance of pressure in the Commons, and—in the last two cases—the influence of the Irish government.

### Key Ministers

All the most influential ministers directly concerned with policy in Northern Ireland over the four cases personally favored a united Ireland as the best long-term outcome. None saw power sharing as more than an interim solution. Wilson was the most interventionist and the most committed to unification. He personally drafted the Downing Street Declaration, which stripped the Unionist government of control over security and committed London to a reform program irrespective of Stormont's views. He continued to shape government policy as leader of the opposition after internment, making common cause with Nationalist Ireland in calling for a new political initiative in consultation with Dublin. When this was not quickly forthcoming, he goaded Heath into action by producing his own fifteen-point plan, which foreshadowed the transfer of security powers, the inclusion of Nationalist elected representatives in the Stormont cabinet, and the Irish dimension. After direct rule, he continued to denounce any delays in carrying the initiative forward, ensured that Northern Ireland's representation at Westminster was not increased, and effectively closed off the option of legislative integration.

Yet even as prime minister, Wilson did not act decisively until events with political consequences forced him to do so. He worked within the level of support that he could command in the cabinet and in the Commons. Callaghan constrained him. Both men accepted the legitimacy of NICRA's initial demands, wanted to weaken the Unionist Party, and favored a united Ireland in the long run, but they disagreed over how deeply to intervene and how hard to press the Unionist government. Callaghan shared his officials' concerns about the implications of forcing through reforms against Unionist opposition. He wanted to build up the NILP, whereas Wilson favored the SDLP. When Wilson dismissed Callaghan from the Northern Ireland portfolio in November 1971, he freed himself to propagate proposals for reunification that Callaghan considered unworkable and dangerous.

When the Conservatives came to power in 1970, Heath considered that Wilson had made matters worse by undermining Stormont's authority. So he left it to Chichester-Clark and later Faulkner to oversee the implementation of the strategy that the two governments had agreed upon. This meant that political and security policies were made by Unionist politicians and army commanders, who each had their own distinctive priorities. It created the political context for the military security approach, and for introducing internment without due diligence.

Heath reacted to the national and international furor over the internment operation by losing confidence in Faulkner. Jack Lynch—like him, the head of a national government seeking admission to the EEC—came to look like a more reliable source of advice and a more useful ally. From September 1971 Heath personally set the parameters and forced the pace for policymaking. He required Maudling to take successively bigger steps, pressing Faulkner into including minority elected representatives in the regional administration (September 1971), voluntary coalition (November), the transfer of security powers and mandatory coalition (January 1972), and finally direct rule (February). He relentlessly imposed his vision for power sharing on a skeptical cabinet and forced it through to implementation, resisting every attempt by Whitelaw and others to allow the Unionist establishment more time to adjust to his overthrow of their political universe.

Heath could steamroll the skeptics in part because he refused to accept the underlying reality of a political system based on differences over national allegiance rather than economic and social issues. Whether this was a strength is a matter of judgment. But eyewitnesses agree that he never developed relationships of mutual respect and understanding with the leading players in Northern Ireland as Whitelaw had done. Convinced of his own superior logic and confident in the authority of his office, he forced Faulkner to swallow proposals for the Council of Ireland that predictably resulted in his downfall.

Maudling is commonly depicted as intellectually gifted but detached and lethargic. He allowed Chichester-Clark and later Faulkner to claw back much of the power over security policy and operations that Wilson had deliberately stripped from Stormont. He declared that he wanted to engage Northern Ireland's Nationalist politicians in negotiations, yet like Heath and unlike Whitelaw, he failed to establish a meaningful personal relationship with any of them.

After direct rule Whitelaw was by far the most influential of Heath's ministers. He used his ample personality and diplomatic skills to good effect in overcoming huge obstacles to accommodation. He earned Faulkner's respect, built good working relationships with SDLP leaders, and defied the expectations of his officials by getting the leaders of at least three of the main parties to agree on the formation of a power-sharing executive.

### The Balance of Pressure

By 1968 the Campaign for Democracy in Ulster[8] (CDU) had been pressing for over three years for the Labour government to intervene in Northern Ireland, but it was only when the disorder on the streets prompted the national media to give sustained and sympathetic coverage to NICRA's demands that it began to make headway. It successfully killed off the Commons precedent of nonintervention, ensured that Callaghan acted quickly to reform the police in the summer of 1969, and called ministers to account for the delivery of reform.

After February 1971, Conservative ministers were subjected to very different pressures. Amid demands from his backbenchers for Maudling's resignation, Heath agreed to give Faulkner a greater say in determining security policies. By August ministers were again required to do something visibly tough; internment was the least unattractive of the various coercive measures that their critics demanded.

Labour did not object to internment until the balance of media opinion judged that it had failed. The bipartisan consensus to which both Callaghan and Maudling had attached such importance then collapsed. Maudling found himself trapped between Labour's demands for constitutional reform and Faulkner's insistence that he could not share power with Nationalists. The publication of Wilson's fifteen-point plan in November generated new urgency but also made it harder to convene talks between the Northern Irish party leaders. The dramatic events of January and February 1972 created an alarming new context for the cabinet's deliberations. They finally convinced ministers that a radical initiative was imperative and required bipartisan support. The criticisms to which they had been subjected rattled ministers and left them determined to show Faulkner who was in charge. Imposing direct rule achieved Heath's goal of restoring the bipartisan consensus. Thereafter he was careful to proceed in close consultation with Wilson, and the 1973 white paper incorporated most of Wilson's proposals from November 1971.

Comparing the effects of political pressures at Westminster across the four case studies, we can conclude that organized factions of backbenchers enjoyed significant influence over government policy when the following conditions were satisfied: that the stands they took were reinforced by strong media and public concern, that they enjoyed substantial support in their party at large, and that the prime minister was personally willing to take their proposals seriously. Even then it took time and strategic maneuvering to achieve results. For their part, ministers were prepared to go to great lengths to maintain bipartisan consensus, recognizing that any policy that the opposition actively resisted was unlikely to succeed. Divisions between government and opposition tended to undermine public support, could be exploited by factions in Northern Ireland for their own advantage, and impaired the army's morale. Moreover, if a policy introduced by a government today could be reversed by another party in government tomorrow, its prospects were appreciably diminished.

That said, the influence of Unionist MPs was weaker than might have been expected, not only because they were so few but also because they were divided among themselves and had neglected to build up networks of allies as the CDU had done. They were ambivalent about the future of Stormont. As Westminster MPs, they stood to gain in stature and authority to the extent that the subordinate parliament was diminished.[9]

COMPARING THE FOUR CASE STUDIES

333

*The Irish Government*

The events of August 1969 stimulated a return to traditional republican sentiments in Dublin. London did not fear Irish military power and recognized the political pressures that prompted the taoiseach to take an assertive nationalist public stance. But the Irish played on three British concerns: that their words and deeds might stimulate further disorder, that Irish diplomats might embarrass the United Kingdom or undermine British interests internationally, and that Lynch was vulnerable to defeat by hard-line republicans within his own party, which would make Britain's problem worse. Labour ministers saw these concerns as favoring a policy of reform rather than merely reinforcing the RUC.

In the second case, the incoming Conservative administration accepted their officials' advice to avoid words and actions that might encourage republican sentiment in Dublin. As the violence continued, however, Conservative ministers came to share Stormont's view that the Irish government was part of the problem rather than the solution. From June 1970 to September 1972, evidence of Irish ministers' republican sympathies tended to reduce their credibility in the eyes of Conservative ministers. At the same time, the British army was learning from bitter daily experience how valuable it would be to have wholehearted cooperation from the Irish in the security arena. After internment, the Ministry of Defence (MoD) convinced Heath that such cooperation was essential to defeating the IRA, and that it was worth paying a price for it. After his two meetings with Lynch in September 1971, Heath's view of the problem changed. He concluded that for any solution to be durable, the Irish government must support it. It was around this time that he commissioned the policy review that paved the way for the 1973 white paper. Although it was not immediately obvious to the wider world, Lynch's strategy of private and patient diplomacy had enabled him to assert the interests of Nationalist Ireland in a way that Britain could act on. Lynch successfully regulated the flow of security cooperation to retain London's confidence without provoking more criticism than he could handle from his own side, while keeping the British hungry for more.

Reinforcing Lynch's wooing of Heath, the government machine in Dublin sought to shape British policy through the British ambassador, the British Labour Party, and international opinion. It scored an important goal in November 1971, when Wilson engaged directly with all main Irish political party leaders to develop his fifteen-point plan. Dublin's influence was again evident in January 1972; when Heath showed signs of backsliding from his commitment to take a political initiative, Lynch threatened to publish proposals of his own. The British premier thus faced the prospect of a critical alliance between the Westminster opposition and a national government without whose cooperation he could achieve neither his military nor his political objectives. Bloody Sunday interrupted the process. For a few weeks Lynch could not be seen to collaborate. Yet even during this period Lynch secured his party's support for a strategy that implicitly accepted the reality of partition.

In the new context of direct rule, Lynch delivered incrementally on his promise of a tougher attitude toward the IRA, although still falling short of the fulsome cooperation the British would have liked. Having helped to create and finance the SDLP, he induced its leaders to enter into Whitelaw's talks process, dropping their earlier precondition that internment must end first. Lynch and Heath had another groundbreaking meeting in November 1972, when they discussed how the white paper would flesh out the concept of the Irish dimension. Lynch was determined that the Council of Ireland should be serious and meaningful. Again, he was not immediately successful, but as a result of this conversation Heath initiated work that culminated in the substantial gains made by Nationalist Ireland at Sunningdale. Irish strategy did not change significantly after Lynch's election defeat in March 1973. FitzGerald continued to try to maximize the role and functions of the Council of Ireland as the central component in a process that could eventually result in unification.

Over the four cases, there was a broad shift in the allegiance of the British state from Belfast to Dublin. Although Callaghan in 1969 wanted to weaken the Unionist Party, he did not consider that the Irish government had any positive role to play in Northern Ireland other than reforming its own affairs to make the prospect of unification less unattractive to unionism. By 1973, Heath had abolished the Belfast administration and was working in partnership with Dublin to pressure the Unionists into taking a step that many on both sides saw as leading toward unification.

## The Organizational Model

At a high level of generality, the development of British policies toward Northern Ireland over the four cases can be seen as part of a broad thrust toward the centralization and bureaucratization of the state apparatus. The reforms in local government initiated by Terence O'Neill paralleled changes already under way in England that effectively transferred power from local to national elites and from political parties' constituency associations to government departments. The Local Government Act 1972 transformed local government in England, wiping out historical administrative districts. The dissolution of the Unionist government can be understood in organizational terms as part of that process.

## Home Office

In 1968 the Home Office had unchallenged lead responsibility for relationships with Northern Ireland. It had a strong tradition of nonintervention and saw its primary function as representing Stormont's interests in Whitehall. There were no senior staff devoted to the issue and officials depended on their counterparts in the Northern Ireland Civil Service (NICS) for information and advice. This organizational context favored the option of reinforcing the RUC without imposing any political conditions and of withdrawing the troops as soon as order was restored. But when the army went in, the soldiers' presence on the streets shifted the locus of decision-making from the organizational to the political arena, from Home Office bureaucrats to the prime minister.

The Downing Street Declaration of August 1969 heralded a new form of relationship between the national and regional levels of administration. It stripped Stormont of its political autonomy and control over security. Henceforth the Unionist government would be much reduced, a client regime under constant supervision. Nevertheless, the doctrine of nonintervention lived on in ministers' determination to avoid direct rule, in their desire to pull the army out as soon as they could, and in their not immediately legislating to transfer responsibility for security formally to Westminster.

The doctrine lived on also in the Conservatives' deliberately and quietly transferring authority back to Stormont after they came to power in June 1970, both reducing and concealing the level of political oversight that they exercised from London. But because Northern Irish issues were now liable to be raised at Westminster, the Home Office had to stay ready to brief ministers and prepare for possible interventions at short notice. Officials had to have draft legislation ready for rapid introduction in response to an emergency, such as the collapse of the devolved government. After 1969, the Home Office maintained a staff of around twenty, who monitored developments in Northern Ireland and their political implications, coordinated policy activity with the MoD and Foreign and Commonwealth Office (FCO), liaised with the UK Representative (UKREP) and army commanders, and kept contingency plans for direct rule updated.

The doctrine was further dissolved in stages from February 1971, when the first British soldiers were killed. Following the crisis over Chichester-Clark's resignation, the Home Office established a high-level interdepartmental strategy group, which met from time to time and identified a range of long-term options, including direct rule and unification. When Heath decided to take action in September 1971, this group and its preparatory work were available as a foundation for future policymaking. The department then created a small full-time staff team to support the group; its tasks included drawing up legislation and detailed plans for direct rule.

Unlike their predecessors in the Home Office, working only occasionally on Northern Ireland alongside a host of other miscellaneous issues, the members of this team did not see their role as representing or supporting the Unionist government but as potentially transforming the Northern Ireland constitution. Ministers now looked to them rather than Stormont to take the lead in political development planning. One of their first recommendations was that direct rule should be considered not just as a last resort to prevent Stormont from falling into the hands of extremists but as a deliberate tactic to break the political impasse. This was a paradigm shift in official doctrine.

They also identified a range of options for transferring responsibility for security policy and operations back to Westminster. Their work heavily influenced ministers' discussions from November 1971, generating powerful momentum toward direct rule. Heath's dramatic initiative in February 1972 was already backed up by the necessary legislation, detailed plans, and a core group of staff, all lying conveniently at hand.

### Northern Ireland Office

With direct rule, the Home Office's key officials and responsibilities passed to the Northern Ireland Office (NIO). The problem now had the full attention of a dedicated and influential cabinet minister and a team of supporting ministers and senior civil servants. Its staff included experts in defense and diplomacy with extensive experience in the subtle arts of, first, tackling colonial insurgencies and, second, negotiating withdrawal from troublesome colonies. It had a full presence in Belfast and no longer depended on the NICS for information and advice. Its role included ensuring that all the administration's activities in Northern Ireland—specifically security operations and political development—were properly integrated and coherent.

The creation of the NIO was a watershed. It demonstrated Heath's determination to stick with the problem until it was resolved, and transferred the primary burden of finding a solution from the political arena (a cabinet committee) to a dedicated bureaucratic organization. It opened up new opportunities for integration across the different strands of public service delivery and improved use of intelligence. Above all, it expanded the brainpower available to address the problem and interact with Northern Ireland's competing political players.

*Ministry of Defence*

As the troops moved onto the streets in Northern Ireland in the summer of 1969, the MoD took its place beside the Home Office at the Whitehall policymaking table. Its senior officials and commanders were not tied to the doctrine of nonintervention, and as each day passed, their presence tended to contradict it. But they had their own reasons for minimizing the army's involvement. It was not consistent with the army's sense of its own mission, it drew resources away from essential commitments to NATO and elsewhere, and there was an increasing risk of confrontations with loyalists that would require a larger and longer intervention.

While the MoD at first wanted to avoid direct rule, it did not support Stormont's contention that the army should simply support the civil authority. Commanders did not want to take directions from RUC officers or their political masters at Stormont. The Downing Street Declaration reflected the ministry's position rather than the Home Office's in distinguishing between security operations, for which the GOC would be accountable to Westminster, and normal police duties, for which the chief constable would be accountable to Stormont. The Hunt reforms were intended to clarify and strengthen this distinction. In disbanding the USC and disarming the police, they gave the army a monopoly on the legitimate use of armed force. They were presented as civilizing the police along British lines, but in practice, they effectively militarized the maintenance of order in republican communities.

Under the Conservatives, power flowed from Whitehall to army commanders on the ground. Defense ministers generally took the view that it was not for them to second-guess operational decisions. So the army followed its habitual routines without much political oversight. These fueled the resistance of republican communities, contributing to the escalation of violence, which in turn led to the decision to intern. They also produced internment's worst excesses.

When internment failed to deliver the results Faulkner had predicted, commanders quickly took the opportunity to lobby ministers for the transfer of security responsibility back to Westminster. Whatever the substance of any new political initiative, the MoD argued that control over all areas of government activity should be centralized in line with longstanding counterinsurgency doctrine. Direct rule was the only obvious means to that end. Moreover, it would get Unionist politicians off their backs and provide the strategic political direction that had been lacking. The secretary of state would construct a unified administration in which all agencies of government—the RUC, civil service departments, the army, and intelligence services—would work toward the common objective of ending the violence and facilitating a political settlement.

Four months into direct rule, Operation Motorman marked the start of a new phase in the army's campaign, from indiscriminate counterinsurgency measures directed against entire republican communities to selective counterterrorism measures targeting the Provisional IRA. Required by Whitelaw to account closely for the political implications of their actions, commanders adapted their routine tactics and procedures to meet the challenge of tackling terrorism assertively without alienating entire communities. They concentrated on infiltration, intelligence gathering, and the harassment of individual IRA volunteers, seeking to collect evidence that could be used either to detain them without trial or preferably secure convictions in court.

### Foreign and Commonwealth Office

The events of 1969 also brought the FCO into the policymaking process. The department's principal interests lay in ensuring that the problem did not impair Britain's international relations, particularly its relationship with the Republic, and British ambassadors fed Dublin's views into the Whitehall policy machine.

The FCO's contribution is perhaps most remarkable, however, for what it did not do: press the Irish government hard to crack down on the IRA. This was apparently because British diplomats took the view that it would be counterproductive to hector or bully Irish ministers. This reflected a concern about creating turbulence within Fianna Fáil, the assumption being that Lynch was preferable to anyone who might replace him. Avoiding public confrontations between ministers, British and Irish diplomats preferred to work together behind the scenes.

The FCO expanded its role and the capacity it brought to bear on the issue during the summer of 1971. The additional personnel included Secret Intelligence Service (MI6) agents with backgrounds in decolonization. It did not take them long to conclude that direct rule was an essential next step. This expansion in the FCO's involvement coincided with Heath's first meetings with Lynch, and the department went on to contribute a substantial proportion of the senior personnel who set up the NIO and helped steer Whitelaw's political negotiations.

### UKREP

By March 1971, UKREP had established itself as an authoritative source of advice to UK ministers on the performance of the Stormont government and on Catholic opinion. Its actions and advice contributed to Stormont's decline. When Chichester-Clark asked for troop reinforcements in 1971, UKREP advised them to offer only a cosmetic increment; they did, and Chichester-Clark resigned. Fuller reinforcements were provided shortly afterward in response to representations from Faulkner, again in an attempt to shore up a Unionist leader whose authority was crumbling precisely because of his willingness to collaborate and compromise. UKREP advised Maudling that the fragmentation of the Unionist Party might result in strengthening more moderate parties such as Alliance. Five months before Maudling announced it in the Commons as government policy, UKREP had invited him to consider the option of guaranteeing Catholic elected representatives an active role in the Stormont executive. It seems improbable that the Nationalist leaders UKREP spoke to were unaware that his thoughts were moving in this direction, or that this knowledge would not have influenced their actions as they built up the SDLP into a party that could fight and win elections. If they rejected Faulkner's offer of committee chairs at Stormont, they would eventually get full seats on the executive as of right. Why settle for less—or talk to Faulkner at all?

After internment, British ministers increasingly depended on UKREP for advice as Faulkner's credibility declined. From September 1971, they commissioned him to harvest ideas for a political initiative from "men of goodwill"; extremists were ignored, however much popular support they might have. Based on his conversations with SDLP leaders and liberal Unionists—including Ken Bloomfield from Faulkner's office—UKREP came up with the idea of direct rule as a break with the past that would open up new possibilities in the search for a settlement.

## Learning and Adaptation

The rational model expects decision-makers to adjust their assessments of available options appropriately and without delay in response to new information. In a sequence of decisions, a process of learning occurs, characterized by increases in intellectual breadth and sophistication.

The cognitive process model expects learning to be constrained as new information is squeezed into established patterns of understanding and calculation without logically necessary adjustments being made. Existing assumptions and beliefs persevere despite evidence that objectively discredits them. Lessons are systematically biased by such characteristics of human inference as the tendency to give disproportionate weight to recent events personally experienced, to avoid policies that have recently failed, and to talk up the prospects for policies that are politically expedient.

The political model predicts that electoral, party, and diplomatic pressures are required to drive changes in policy, but might also delay and
distort them. It focuses on shifts in the balance for and against current
policies. Adaptation occurs when the coalition protecting current policy
loses sufficient power to the coalition demanding change.

Finally, the organizational model expects change normally to take the
form of incremental structural, doctrinal, and procedural responses to
events in the problem field and its political context. The cumulative effect
of these responses may be great, especially if they take place in rapid succession. Occasionally, in reaction to a critical performance failure—such
as Bloody Sunday—radical change may occur very quickly. In such cases,
an unsuccessful program may be replaced by a new one, but this will often
be assembled from elements in an existing repertoire. If no such elements
are available, the power relationships between the responsible units may be
altered, the problem may be transferred from one unit to another, or a new
unit may be created specifically to deal with it.

The four case studies show that all three models of learning and adaptation have some explanatory value. Critical assumptions that the British
had made about the nature and causes of the conflict and the capacity of
the Northern Ireland government to absorb Protestant reactions to reform
were adjusted during 1970 in response to events in the problem field and
improved information. But there was resistance to using this new information, and it was partially assimilated into old paradigms without the lateral
and upward expansions in understanding that, logically, it required. Ministers acknowledged the strength of Protestant fears and recognized the
dangers created by the army's presence in republican areas but repeatedly
failed to incorporate these perceptions into a new pattern of understanding grounded in the pivotal importance of national, historical, and territorial issues as preconditions for the violence.

As the IRA stepped up its attacks, British policymakers adopted a new
but arguably even more inadequate explanatory model based on the hypothesis of deliberate insurgency. They thus missed an opportunity to tease
out the subtle linkages that had evolved among deprivation, perceptions
of discrimination, the activities of the army, and IRA tactics. Again, when
they dropped the insurgency model in favor of the divided society hypothesis, they neglected evidence of major obstacles to accommodation that
political scientists had already described in published articles.

In the first case, there was little scope for UK ministers to learn from previous experience because they had none. The Unionists and the RUC did, but
their advice was discounted as biased. Policy was made on the hoof as Callaghan and Wilson tried to keep a step ahead of their critics in the CDU.

With the reform package in 1969 new information channels were opened up through UKREP and the personal contacts with influential members of the minority made by UK commanders, officials, and ministers. These created new opportunities for learning. However, the change of administration in June 1970 interrupted the process. The incoming ministers lacked even the limited experience of their predecessors. By distancing himself from the issue, Maudling discarded many of the learning opportunities that Labour's interventions had created.

The army, left largely to its own devices, naturally focused on military matters. Standard operating procedures were refined; new patrol groupings, tactics, and equipment were introduced. Even in this narrow field, difficulties in coordination with the RUC concealed important lessons. Radical changes were needed but not made in the organization of intelligence, in public relations, and in deployment patterns. However, the army learned two important lessons that it used to influence policy in favor of direct rule: that it could not hope to restore order without constitutional reform and cross-border cooperation, and that the continuing existence of the Unionist government at Stormont was an obstacle to both.

In the third case there was an attempt at the highest level to review policy systematically in line with the rational model. Carrington and Heath lifted their sights from the immediate military goal of defeating the IRA to the longer-term objective of achieving a lasting peace. There was also lateral expansion in the belated recognition of the potent threat presented by the Nationalist population's intense hostility toward Stormont. But these advances in intellectual sophistication were ultimately less crucial to introducing direct rule than the political pressures applied by the Irish government and the Labour opposition in the wake of Bloody Sunday, along with the bureaucratic interests of the MoD and the army.

In the fourth case, the pace of learning accelerated rapidly. For the first time, London had a full team of ministers and senior officials devoted to the issue, located partly in Belfast and controlling all the levers of power in the region. It took the NIO some time to settle down, but this concentration of people, authority, and resources created the potential for faster and deeper learning. One of the first lessons Whitelaw learned was that he could not stop the insurgency by conciliation alone; the solution would have to lie in firm and discriminating action against terrorism combined with generosity toward the nonviolent elected representatives of the Nationalist community.

In all four cases, the stimulus for change lay in dramatic, highly visible, and widely criticized failures of performance, which created discomfort for the governing party and embarrassment for key ministers. Research was commissioned and analyses conducted, but the real momentum for change came from accumulations of political pressure.

## Summary

The Northern Ireland government responded coercively to illegal but non-violent civil rights protests in 1968, whereas the British government, when faced with a more serious problem of terrorist violence in 1972, offered a far-reaching package of concessions. When the disorder first morphed into violent insurgency in 1971, London permitted the incompetent implementation of coercive measures that inflamed Nationalist opinion, yet when the violence deteriorated further, it offered more concessions, including the opportunity for power sharing. The nature and levels of disorder helped shape policy outcomes, but they did so through the intermediation of, first, political pressures generated by the parties to the conflict and their advocates; second, the organizational responses that they stimulated from street level to the highest levels of decision; and third, their interpretation through policymakers' understandings, misunderstandings, hopes, and calculations.

The rational model is clearly inadequate to explain any of the four policies or the process of policy evolution. The cognitive process model provides a richer explanation. Once policymakers' patterns of understanding are known—in this case, successively, the legitimate grievances, insurgency, and divided society hypotheses—policy becomes more amenable to evaluation. These patterns of understanding, however, were subject to political pressures. The hypotheses that ministers adopted were, in every case, urged on them by other players in the political game: the CDU, Unionist ministers, the Labour opposition, the Dublin government, army commanders, and diplomats. They tapped political sources for feedback on their performance and to assess the various options available, and they allowed political pressures to resolve value conflicts and uncertainties in their own calculations. Policies were also determined by organizational factors, notably the locus of decision, along with the agency selected to deal with the problem, its doctrines, and its standard operating procedures. By leaving it to the army to solve the problem during 1971, ministers effectively decided that policy would be coercive; later, by assigning it to diplomats, they decided that the outcome would be a negotiated agreement.

In light of the case study findings, it makes sense to deploy all four models of analysis rather than relying predominantly on any one of them. There may be tensions among their respective assumptions and lines of argument, but there is value in drawing on the essential elements of each to construct an integrated model that explains the reality better than any of the four on its own. Such a model would look for a group of decision-makers at the top of the policymaking system whose collective thinking is influenced by its members' diverse interests and strengths and by an array of external political and diplomatic pressures. This group depends for information, advice, and implementation on a series of loosely coordinated bureaucracies, which each have their own distinct interests and considerable autonomy. Policies are largely determined through a boundedly rational process of collective deliberation and negotiation that accounts for political and organizational factors as well as events in the problem field. A cognitive process model, incorporating political pressures and organizational factors, provides a more plausible account of learning and adaptation than any of the separate models on their own.

Under an integrated model of analysis, the interesting questions concern which conditions and problem characteristics favor which factors in the policy development process. In terms of the choice between concession and coercion, one possible approach looks at the changing balance between the factors favoring each type of outcome. In Northern Ireland during the study period, the principal factors for concession were the breadth and intensity of the minority community's support for disorder; the extent to which policymakers' fear of Catholic violence exceeded their fear of Protestant violence; policymakers' belief that the disorder was rooted in the deprivation, discrimination, and exclusion from power suffered by the minority; the balance of opinion in the Labour Party; a pro-minority stance in media and public opinion in Britain; a shift in the locus of decision-making from the Home Office to the Cabinet Office; the increasing influence of the MoD and FCO; and the recent failure of coercive actions. Factors tending to favor coercion were the breadth and intensity of the majority's protest against republican violence; the extent to which policymakers' fear of loyalist violence exceeded their fear of republican violence; policymakers' belief that the violence resulted from deliberate insurgency, and that the residents of the areas from which the IRA operated would be glad to get it off their backs; the balance of opinion in the Conservative Party; heavily publicized attacks on soldiers; a pro-army balance in media and public opinion in Britain; the delegation of political influence to the Unionist government; and the recent failure of concessions to deliver peace.

British policymakers consistently wanted to minimize their involvement in Northern Ireland; what varied was their perception of how best to do this. In August 1969 they believed that reforming the police was essential to enable the soldiers to disengage; in August 1971, that they had to prop up Faulkner's government to avoid direct rule; in February 1972, that drastic action was need to prevent full-scale civil war; by 1973, that only power sharing with an Irish dimension would provide the basis for a sustainable devolved administration.

The four case studies have not, of course, covered all the factors that shaped policy. A psychoanalytic study of key policymakers, for example, could add a further dimension to understanding, as could a comparative cross-regional study of developments in the political economy. Chance incidents, unlikely combinations of events, coincidences of timing, and surprising coups by key actors all played their parts. Who could have predicted the seismic developments of January and February 1972, all happening within six weeks of Maudling's submitting a proposal to the cabinet for imposing a radical political initiative?

There are alternative ways of applying and combining the methodological insights derived from the four models of analysis. For example, political factors such as the position taken by the Irish government could be incorporated into the problem field as matters requiring interpretation and understanding in the same way as this study has incorporated the motives of party and insurgent leaders in Northern Ireland. Such an approach would produce more complex tradeoffs, requiring resolutions between political and substantive goals. The linkages between organizational doctrines and the patterns of understanding of key policymakers also could be more thoroughly explored. In analyzing and explaining government policies for the management and resolution of violent conflicts, all relevant factors should be included.

Northern Ireland should be compared with other conflict regions only with great caution. Even so, the approach in this study offers a potential framework to examine other governments' approaches to the management and regulation of conflict in deeply divided societies. Most immediately, it provides an instrument with which to address the subsequent development of Britain's policies toward the conflict in Northern Ireland. It also has direct applicability to other instances in which nation-states seek singly or together to manage or resolve conflicts in deeply divided national or subnational regions. With some refinement, the same general approach could be applied usefully in analyzing the policies of powerful nations seeking to influence developments in client states.

The ideas of interaction between policy and problem, of policy as a dynamic balance between factors favoring coercion, reform, and constitutional change, and of the interplay among rational, political, organizational, and cognitive process factors all promise to add value to any explanation and assessment of states' strategies. They should also help policymakers to become more aware of the context for their own decisions and choices, enabling them to produce better strategies and achieve better outcomes.

# Notes

1.    C. Ponting, *Whitehall: Tragedy and Farce* (London, Sphere Books, 1986), 63.

2.    R.H.S. Crossman, *The Diaries of a Cabinet Minister,* vol. 3 (London: Cape, 1977), 623.

3.    The legacy of religious conflict in Britain lives on, for example, in that the 1701 Act of Settlement still prohibits any Catholic from becoming king or queen, or marrying the heir to the throne. For an account of gerrymandering in local government in London in the 1980s, see A. Hosken, *Nothing like a Dame: The Scandals of Shirley Porter* (London: Granta, 2006). As leader of Westminster Council, Lady Porter initiated a "homes for votes" strategy to ensure that the Conservatives would win the 1990 local elections. Council homes in eight key marginal wards were put up for sale under the council's right-to-buy policy, thus attracting more voters inclined to vote Conservative; the poor and homeless, more likely to vote Labour, were placed in "appropriate wards." The Law Lords subsequently found that Lady Porter and other Conservative councillors had been guilty of disgraceful gerrymandering."

4.    Many of Britain's former colonies are now the sites of conflicts that some political scientists have compared with Northern Ireland; see chapter 9.

5.    The Conservative Party eventually organized in Northern Ireland in the late 1980s. Its support peaked in the 1992 Westminster election at 5.7 percent of the votes cast; it secured only 0.5 percent in the 2007 Assembly election.

6.    Hunt Report: *Report of the Advisory Committee on Police in Northern Ireland,* Cmd. 535 (Belfast: HMSO, 1969), paragraph 18.

7.    P. Dixon, *Northern Ireland: The Politics of War and Peace* (New York: Palgrave, 2001), 101. In May 2007, the Northern Ireland Assembly jointly elected Ian Paisley and Martin McGuinness as first minister and deputy first minister.

8.    As indicated in chapter 3, the CDU was a pressure group built around the Labour Party at Westminster and local constituency levels that campaigned for electoral reform in Northern Ireland.

9.    P. Norton, "Conservative Politics and Stormont," in P. Catterall and S. McDougall, eds., *The Northern Ireland Question in British Politics* (London: Macmillan, 1996), 137–39.

# 8

# Evaluation

*Rationality resides in results.*       —A. Wildavsky[1]

B y December 1973 the British intervention had been a partial success. The insurgency had not deteriorated into a full-scale internal war. It had been contained spatially and in its intensity. In most areas, public services continued to be delivered as before. Anglo-Irish relations had improved. London and Dublin had both signed up for the power-sharing constitution and the Sunningdale agreement as the way forward.

Irrespective of the collapse of the 1974 executive, subsequent developments can be interpreted as evidence in favor of the power-sharing strategy. By 2006 it had been endorsed by all the main political players in the region, including the Democratic Unionist Party (DUP), Sinn Féin, and loyalist paramilitaries. By 2007 the army had withdrawn and a power-sharing devolved administration had been established. The conflict had ceased to be a source of international embarrassment for Britain and was even being celebrated as a model for conflict resolution in less fortunate regions.

On the other hand, the violence had persisted for over thirty years. By 1998 it had claimed some 3,700 lives, more than 90 percent of them after direct rule. The annual death rate did not return to its 1971 level until 1977; it then held until 1994 at between 61 and 124.[2] While full-scale civil war may have been avoided, the insurgents and their supporters proved resilient and adept at integrating violence, propaganda, diplomacy, and political action in pursuit of their objectives. During this period there was no effective community policing in many districts. The quality of Anglo-Irish relations rose and fell as ministerial priorities changed in London and Dublin. Britain continued to be criticized for failing to meet international human rights standards.

This chapter evaluates British policies during the formative period from 1969 to 1973 to identify what worked, what failed, and why. It does not aspire to assess later policies except to the extent that they illuminate what preceded them. It reviews the evidence from the four case studies, considers how policy evolved later, compares the 1973 agreements on power sharing and the Irish dimension with those of 1998, and reviews published assessments of two alternative policy options.

## The Evidence of the Case Studies

From the evidence of the case studies, could the British have achieved a settlement earlier? Did their interventions make the problem better or worse?

*Reform*

The Labour government in August 1969 had several objectives: to end the disorder on the streets, reduce perceived discrimination by Protestants against Catholics, make the Royal Ulster Constabulary (RUC) more professional and acceptable to Catholics, avoid political criticism for having neglected the Catholic minority, minimize UK intervention, and sustain the devolved administration. Wilson and Callaghan succeeded in turning the rising tide of criticism they faced in the national media and on their Westminster backbenches. They forced Stormont to tackle the issues raised by the civil rights campaign and kept the Stormont administration in existence. But they clearly failed to prevent further disorder and minimize the army's intervention. Their attitudes and actions widened the already dangerous rift in the Unionist Party, rendering Stormont incapable of the confident and cooperative leadership upon which the ultimate success of the reform strategy depended.

The radical restructuring of the RUC did not make it acceptable to republicans, nor did it give the RUC the capacity to meet the public order challenges that predictably ensued: tackling sectarian riots, responding to shooting incidents, and gathering intelligence on insurgents and their organizations. Chief Constable Arthur Young's attempts to police republican neighborhoods failed ignominiously and were soon allowed to lapse. This was partly because the general officer commanding (GOC) would not subject soldiers to the risk of accompanying unarmed police officers on patrol without themselves bearing arms. The unarmed and restructured RUC was neither authorized nor equipped to deal with large disorderly crowds or with the aggressive republican campaign of violence that surfaced within six months of the soldiers' appearance on the streets. So the army was required to take on these roles. Yet its very presence stimulated disorder and gave republicans the opportunity to draw on ancient animosities, depicting the soldiers as occupiers and oppressors rather than peacekeepers. Callaghan had anticipated the danger but failed to prevent the outcome. Bew has described the decision to send in the troops while leaving the Stormont administration intact as "the greatest mistake of British policy during the Troubles," as it allowed the Irish Republican Army (IRA) to present the army as the tool of the Stormont ascendancy regime.[3]

In 1975, a Labour government ditched the Hunt model of unarmed policing and required the RUC once again to adopt paramilitary practices and equipment, much as it had done from its inception in 1921. From then on, police officers routinely carried guns and patrolled the streets in armored vehicles. They were authorized to use plastic and rubber baton rounds against rioting crowds.

As for complaints of discrimination, Callaghan's reforms were too little, too late. They tackled the problem in local government and public housing but failed to address the more intractable areas of regional government and general employment. Most of the reforms did not produce tangible results for individuals until after the imposition of direct rule. Whatever popular goodwill they may have engendered in republican communities was soon lost as a result of the military security approach to policing and the popular perception that the Conservatives were biased toward the Unionists. The various reform programs eventually addressed all the original grievances of the Northern Ireland Civil Rights Association (NICRA), but other complaints quickly surfaced—over policing, unemployment, and deprivation—and both sides suffered from the authorities' failure to suppress paramilitary violence. Proportional representation (PR) voting was introduced for local government elections, but by then, most of the councils' powers had passed to nonelected statutory bodies appointed by Northern Ireland Office (NIO) ministers. Under direct rule, minority leaders enjoyed equal status with their majority counterparts, but only because both were equally excluded.

Bloomfield maintains that Wilson should have pressed the Unionist government harder for reform before the civil rights protests led to violence on the streets.[4] It was not as if nobody had told them. The Northern Ireland Labour Party (NILP) and others had been warning of the consequences of inaction long before 1968.[5] Bloomfield also argues that the British should have introduced direct rule as soon as the soldiers went onto the streets in August 1969, as their reform strategy then subjected the Unionist leadership to intolerable political pressures. Unionist ministers could not deliver order without the means to do so, nor could they secure the support of their grassroots activists for reforms that struck at their power base in local government and stripped them of the means to tackle republican violence.

But Faulkner's argument is also credible, that London's mistake lay in depriving Stormont of its security powers and publicly humiliating Unionist ministers. Wilson undermined and demoralized the reformists in the Unionist Party and encouraged extremists on both sides to resort to disorder and violence. The British needed a strong devolved administration to deliver the support of the Unionist community for the delivery of the reforms, but instead they destroyed it. Wilson could have left Stormont's security responsibilities intact and induced the Unionists to introduce reforms by more diplomatic means. But after August 1969 this was not seriously attempted. Responsive to political pressures in Westminster and to his own agenda for diminishing Unionists' authority, Wilson created a context in which Stormont's enemies—whether in the NILP or People's Democracy (PD)—concluded that they could successfully destroy the vehicle through which the reforms were to be implemented. As Paul Dixon has argued, Wilson's threats of intervention served "to undermine rather than bolster O'Neill's position within Unionism. Rather than pulling the Ulster Unionist Party (UUP) behind O'Neill's 'trust the British' position, these threats suggested that the British could not be trusted with the security of the Union."[6]

Meanwhile, the Whitehall civil servants posted to Northern Ireland in August 1969 set about developing their own contacts and agendas. They opened up a direct line to London for minority representatives, further undermining Stormont's authority and losing an opportunity for the Northern Ireland Civil Service to develop its own understanding of Nationalist and republican views. By dealing with them directly, the British encouraged Nationalist leaders to discount any possibility of reconciliation through Northern Ireland's established political institutions. The leaders of the protest movement had no incentive to seek an accommodation with the Unionists as long as the UK government was willing to pressurize and undermine Stormont.

## Coercion

The Conservative government's objectives by July 1971 were to defeat the IRA, avoid political criticism for failing to do so, and minimize the depth and length of the UK intervention. The internment policy clearly failed on all three counts. It was followed by an intensification in the violence and a flow of new recruits into the IRA. It provoked damaging national and international criticism, further deepened the fissures in the Unionist Party, and expanded and stiffened Catholic hostility toward Stormont. Maurice

Hayes offers this unambiguous verdict: "Of all the stupid things that government could do [internment] was probably the worst . . . an enormous political misjudgement."[7] Hennessey describes internment as "Heath's greatest error."[8] Even the Ministry of Defence has agreed; in 2006 an official review report concluded that internment was "a major mistake."[9]

It remains legitimate, however, to ask whether internment was wholly misconceived in principle or just badly planned and implemented in practice. The chief of general staff (CGS) of the time has since argued that if it had been properly planned and presented, it would have not caused such a damaging reaction.[10] According to the MoD's own assessment, the operation yielded some short-term security benefits. It cost the Provisional IRA an estimated 50 officers and 107 volunteers. Of the twelve men selected for "in-depth interrogation," ten provided large quantities of valuable information, leading to some three-quarters of the IRA arms and explosives finds over the following three months.[11] The rate at which arms and explosives were discovered increased dramatically: 115,000 rounds of ammunition were discovered from August 9 to the end of December, compared with 41,000 between January 1 and August 8.[12] The interrogations reportedly enabled security forces to identify a further 700 IRA members and revealed details of the two factions' structures, planned operations, arms dumps, safe houses, communications and supply routes, propaganda tactics, and relations with other groups.[13]

Although army commanders had been skeptical about internment beforehand, once it had been introduced they argued strongly that known paramilitaries should not be released until the IRA stopped its violence. Defence Minister Peter Carrington, who had insisted that Faulkner should be seen to take responsibility for the policy, was satisfied that it had helped "bring the poison of terrorism to the surface," where it could be cleaned up.[14] Faulkner himself remained convinced that by December 1971 the tougher security measures, of which internment was one, were paying off and, had they been consistently and firmly pursued, would have resulted in the defeat of the IRA within a year.[15]

While Heath and Wilson blamed Faulkner for internment's failure, they both accepted the need for some such policy, albeit with better procedural safeguards. When Whitelaw discontinued internment in 1972, he replaced it with detention without trial, a more sophisticated method of locking up IRA activists, which Wilson endorsed as opposition leader and which persisted until 1975. In Dublin, Lynch and Hillery acknowledged that they would have been willing to introduce internment themselves in the south as part of a package including power sharing; their opposition to it was rooted in practical politics, not principle.[16]

Much of the political damage could have been avoided if the initial operation had been better prepared and presented. That it was not reflects the fact that it was introduced before Whitehall officials had completed their planning. It was introduced in haste. Moreover, UK policymakers continued to be ambivalent about it. Army commanders were not prepared to argue for it on military grounds, and diplomats opposed it. Carrington refused to take the political responsibility for it, which was properly his under the Downing Street Declaration.

UK ministers may have wanted Faulkner's buffer regime to survive, but they did little to ensure that an operation intended to sustain his faltering regime actually did so. Vital missing elements included effective procedures to protect internees' basic rights during arrest, detention, and interrogation; a coherent public relations strategy directed at nationalist and international opinion; a complementary political and diplomatic strategy including the Irish government; proper targeting to ensure that only the most dangerous activists were interned; the inclusion of loyalist paramilitaries on the same basis as republicans; a determined effort to stop IRA leaders escaping across the border; and serious negotiations at ministerial level to secure support from Dublin.

Foreign Secretary Alec Douglas-Home took no effective action to secure the Irish government's cooperation or even acquiescence. He left critical conversations with the Irish to his ambassador in Dublin, who personally opposed the policy and did not have the authority to offer the taoiseach anything in return, even if he had wanted to. By April 1971, around the time of Chichester-Clark's resignation, influential personnel in the Foreign and Commonwealth Office (FCO) and MoD had lost confidence in the strategy of working through Stormont and had begun to look forward to the time when they could free themselves from their Unionist subordinates.

These problems were compounded by the fact that, also due to the lack of national political leadership, the work of developing an effective police service had lost momentum. The RUC had been stripped of its arms but had not been directed or resourced to deliver civilian policing in republican districts, to develop any capability to deal with disorderly crowds or public disturbances, or to tackle the increasingly aggressive tactics of the IRA campaigns. The Ulster Defence Regiment (UDR) had been established as a potential source of reinforcement, but it was equally unfit to meet the republican challenge. Urgently needed action to build a comprehensive integrated intelligence service had not been taken.[17]

More broadly, reflecting the division of responsibilities between Westminster and Stormont, there was no effective attempt to coordinate the activities, policies, and structures of the army with those of the RUC, to integrate the activities of the security forces with those of the civil administration, or to reduce Nationalists' alienation. Consequently, when the IRA forced the pace from spring 1971, the authorities could not produce a coherent response combining security and political measures. Lacking strategic political direction, the army tried to apply its experience in colonial counterinsurgency campaigns. Similarly, RUC Special Branch drew on the presumed lessons of the IRA cross-border campaign of the 1950s, when internment had apparently succeeded. On the political front, Maudling failed to prevent stalemate and inertia.

### Direct Rule

The goals of the Conservative government by February 1972 were dramatically different from seven months earlier: to retrieve control over security policy and operations from Faulkner, restore the bipartisan consensus at Westminster, repair relations with Dublin, bring Nationalist elected representatives into dialogue aimed at producing a lasting settlement, defeat the IRA, and do all this without provoking a loyalist backlash. As a dramatic gesture that humiliated the Unionist Party, direct rule helped persuade Nationalist Ireland that the Conservatives were serious about radical reform. It signaled a definitive break with the past and opened doors to new possibilities. It thus largely achieved its political and diplomatic objectives. It also gave UK ministers direct and visible control over security policy and operations. This last was something of a misrepresentation, however, in that London had already held effective control over security since August 1969, even if Maudling and Carrington chose to pretend otherwise or to neglect their responsibilities.[18] What mattered was not the formal transfer of responsibility but the suspension of the devolved administration. Future security policy decisions could be made without regard for their implications for the survival of a compliant Unionist leadership.

Direct rule addressed a fundamental contradiction that had been at the heart of British policy since August 1969: between sustaining a strong devolved administration at Stormont, on one hand, and operations away from it and implementing sufficient reforms to secure Nationalist Ireland's acceptance of it, on the other. But Heath continued to underestimate Faulkner's vulnerability to hard-line rivals. Many Unionists believed that they had nothing to gain from Whitelaw's process of dialogue and much to lose. They saw the British government as offering one concession after another to republican violence and were not impressed by the concept of draining away the IRA's popular support or strengthening the union by securing minority consent for it.

It is debatable whether a sustainable negotiated settlement could have been reached earlier without direct rule. Hayes rejects the suggestion that it would have been better to proceed in a more incremental way, building on the committee system proposed by Faulkner in 1971 and his further proposals to Heath in March 1972. He argues that outside events forced Heath's hand, particularly the reaction against internment and Bloody Sunday and the alienation it produced across the Catholic community. On the other hand, Gerry Fitt, who had been campaigning since 1966 for the abolition of Stormont and as Social Democratic and Labour Party (SDLP) leader had welcomed direct rule, later told a biographer that "in retrospect, it may have been better not to call for the abolition of Stormont but reform it from within."[19] We now know from the official records that other UK ministers and senior officials until the last minute advocated a compromise that would have permitted Faulkner to remain in office. Even after Bloody Sunday neither the cabinet collectively nor the Whitehall machine felt forced by events to introduce direct rule. Faulkner offered further concessions, including an effective veto for the UK government over individual internment orders. Some senior mandarins and ministers would have accepted this, but Heath by then had made up his mind and closed his ears to further discussion. He depicted the issue as one of personal control and domination. A momentum had been created that could not be reversed.

On the security front, direct rule was a partial success in that the Official IRA declared a ceasefire that later became permanent. However, the Provisionals intensified their campaign in anticipation of imminent success; Whitelaw's conciliatory approach gave them the opportunity to regroup, retrain, and reorganize without shedding any popular support. There was also a decline in public order. Protestant and intercommunal rioting became more frequent.[20] Shooting incidents increased, from 399 in March to 2,718 in July. By then, as the MoD itself said later, "it was reasonable to observe that a firmer stance against the IRA would have generated a better environment for political development. The 'low profile' approach had failed, an explosive situation was developing and control was being lost."[21] Former CGS Lord Carver has commented:

> The Government achieved some success in detaching support from the IRA both in the Republic and in Northern Ireland, but at the cost of building up a Protestant reaction, indirectly encouraging the formation of Protestant armed bodies, on the excuse that the Army was neither protecting the Protestants nor pursuing the IRA vigorously enough, and also at the expense of some loss of control over and suppression of the activities of the IRA.[22]

A year earlier the UK Representative (UKREP) had criticized Faulkner for seeking a military solution alongside incremental constitutional reform;

twenty-four years on the MoD would claim that the success of Operation Motorman made Whitelaw's political initiative possible. Four months into direct rule, Whitelaw authorized the military occupation of the no-go areas that Unionists had been demanding since before Chichester-Clark resigned over the issue. According to the MoD, Motorman "confirmed that the British Government would not be seen to be beaten, and broke the cycle of violence that characterised the early years of the campaign. Operation Motorman may be seen as a turning point in the campaign, changing it from a counter insurgency to a counter terrorist operation. Never again would the instances of violence approach the 1972 levels."[23] While it is true that the annual death toll declined after Motorman, it stayed at over 100 until 1978 and topped that figure again in 1979, 1981, 1982, 1987, 1988, and 1991.[24] If Motorman paved the way for political progress, it is at least arguable that a comparable operation—though on a more modest scale—should have been undertaken in March 1971, when Chichester-Clark asked for it, and that this could perhaps have reversed the slide toward internal war.

On the political front, the MoD concluded that suspending Stormont achieved little.[25] UK ministers still found themselves having to deal with Faulkner and an unreformed Unionist Party. Whitelaw eventually lured the SDLP into negotiations, but ultimately failed to deliver a political solution. Republicans succeeded in ending one-party rule but also got a massive expansion in the British army presence, military occupation of their neighborhoods, the formalization of detention without trial, and the exclusion from power of all elected representatives.

Focusing on the immediate priorities of restoring bipartisan consensus at Westminster and securing Dublin's cooperation in the battle against the IRA, UK ministers discounted the obstacles to an agreed-upon settlement. They underestimated the intensity and tenacity of the division between the two sides, neglected the structural consequences of partition for Northern Ireland's political system, dismissed Unionists' concerns, and denied the intractability of the national question. Under severe political and diplomatic pressures from September 1971 to March 1972, Heath succumbed to wishful thinking. Steinbruner describes the process: "When a set of beliefs is under pressure from inconsistent information being processed in a short time frame, it is possible to maintain consistency without changing the beliefs by casting them in a long-range time frame and adopting the inference of transformation; namely that the immediate situation will succumb to a favourable trend over time."[26] Heath coped by persuading himself that once his bold initiative had broken the logjam, modernization would inevitably follow; how could the tide of history be stopped or men of goodwill fail to work together?

What was the alternative to direct rule? The most obvious in the political context of February 1972 was the incremental strategy for reform described in the cabinet's November 1971 paper as green paper plus. Ministers initially favored this option and could have added to it the elements Faulkner offered in March 1972 and the further concessions he later said he would have been prepared to make. It is at least arguable that the net costs and risks of such an approach would have been less than those Heath chose to incur, and the net gains greater and faster in coming. The army by December 1971 had reported substantial success in Belfast and had identified additional practical measures to take against the IRA's cross-border operations. They and the Irish ministers alike were telling Carrington and Heath during January 1971 that they should introduce their political initiative quickly, before the Protestants lost their fear of the IRA. Ministers could have used the IRA's bombing campaign in England from February 1972 to stiffen public resolve behind more rigorous security measures, including the obvious but as yet untaken step of proscribing the IRA.

Under the above scenario, Heath would have proceeded by agreement with Faulkner. He could have used the many levers available to him to ensure effective UK control over internment and other politically contentious security operations. As the security situation improved, he could have required Stormont to take further steps toward constitutional reform. He did not need Faulkner's agreement to appoint a secretary of state, equip him with a team of creative civil servants, or strengthen the intelligence services in Northern Ireland. An agreed-upon package such as this might have avoided the turbulence, violence, and Unionist alienation that followed the abrupt imposition of direct rule; avoided the risks of being seen to succumb to violence; preserved the framework of devolved government as a cocoon within which more inclusive political institutions could be nurtured; and, through the new secretary of state, given the leaders of the Nationalist community direct access to the highest level of decision-making.

The secretary of state would have had to press Stormont hard to maintain the momentum of reform, as Callaghan had done, but he would have been well placed to do so. Whatever the constitutional niceties, Westminster had always effectively controlled both the army and the flow of funds to Stormont, and ultimately could legislate on any Northern Ireland issue that it wished. It might have taken some time to persuade the SDLP to engage in talks, but that was the case anyway. Once they had accepted that London was not going to suspend Stormont, it is likely that they would have accepted that it was in their interests to do so. Until they did, the British could fairly have taken the position that they were excluding themselves from the possibility of power by their refusal to engage.

This is not to argue that the more gradual alternative would have produced a better outcome, merely that direct rule was not made inevitable by the facts on the ground. It was shaped more by political and organizational factors than by rational calculation. That this alternative was not adopted reflects the depth of ministers' disenchantment with Faulkner and the high value they attached after August 1971 to improving relationships with Dublin. What might have happened is pure speculation.

### Power Sharing

Shortly after assuming office, Whitelaw defined his objectives as defeating the IRA, devising an agreed-upon constitutional settlement that would guarantee Nationalist elected representatives a share in government, ending direct rule within a year, and accomplishing all this without provoking a loyalist backlash. He succeeded to the extent that the Officials terminated their campaign within two months, the SDLP agreed within eight months to engage in talks, and the loyalist reaction was violent but containable. Under Whitelaw's close political supervision, there were improvements in the legal framework for detention, security policies, and operations. The policy of gaining Dublin's cooperation yielded some dividends. By November 1973, the Provisionals had suffered serious setbacks, Dublin and the Labour opposition continued to support the white paper proposals, and those Northern Ireland political parties that had opted to participate had reached agreement on the terms for power sharing.

On the other hand, the talks process had excluded the IRA, loyalist paramilitaries, and a majority of Unionist elected representatives. Each of these groups had the capacity to undermine the outcome. Loyalists had begun to develop their own paramilitary structures and prepare for a mass protest campaign. As it turned out, they were to overthrow the settlement within five months.

By any hard criteria, the policy of imposing power sharing with an Irish dimension failed in 1974. Neither the settlement, which was designed to bring constitutional nationalism in from the cold, nor the executive, which was supposed to attract widespread support from across the community, was endorsed by the elected representatives of the majority or by those responsible for the violence on both sides. The Council of Ireland never met. The army would not withdraw for another thirty-three years. The trust that was necessary for power sharing to succeed did not exist, and opponents of the settlement had the will and capacity to destroy it.

One Stormont official had predicted Heath's failure. Norman Dugdale, permanent secretary at the Department of Health and Social Services, contributed a personal paper in August 1972 to Whitelaw's internal deliberations. Dugdale sought to inject a sense of realism into the NIO's blue skies thinking. He realized that it would be counterproductive to press for fundamental change too quickly:

> By raising false expectations on the one side and exacerbating real fears on the other, those who hanker for an early political settlement may only be increasing the instability of an already unstable and volatile situation. Inconvenient as it would be from the standpoint of Westminster or Whitehall, realism may require a prolongation of the present interregnum, possibly for several years, until new opportunities and fresh groupings of political forces emerge in Northern Ireland.[27]

Even this was optimistic. In any future constitutional settlement, Dugdale argued that the authority and functions of the devolved administration should be clearly defined from the outset, and that the sovereign parliament should then respect them. This was precisely what Wilson and Heath had failed to do.

Structural factors aside, Bloomfield has drawn attention to a series of process failures in Heath's management of the Sunningdale conference in December 1973. First was the decision, made against Faulkner's advice, to exclude the Unionists who had opposed the white paper, even though their combined electoral strength was greater than Faulkner's. Second was the decision to remove Whitelaw from the NIO on the eve of the conference, depriving the critical final negotiations of his diplomatic and relationship skills and understanding of the complexities in play. Third was that Heath personally "treated Faulkner and his Unionist colleagues with something approaching brutal contempt," bullying them into submission over the Council of Ireland and exposing them to abandonment by their party.[28] Fourth was Heath's letting the Nationalists pocket substantial gains without offering Faulkner's Unionists anything equivalent in return.

It is now widely accepted by independent analysts that Heath pushed Faulkner too far, too fast.[29] The Irish and British governments threw their combined weight behind Hume, and neither tried to protect the Unionist leader.[30] Realizing what was happening, SDLP delegate Paddy Devlin told the Irish delegates, "Look, we've got to catch ourselves on here. Brian Faulkner is being nailed to a cross."[31] Dermot Nally, FitzGerald's senior official adviser, tried to curb his enthusiasm, but to no avail.[32] The two governments assumed that whatever Faulkner accepted he would be able to sell. By failing to insist on clear limits to the expansion of the Council of Ireland, the British inflated Nationalist aspirations and reinforced loyalist resistance. Whatever the substantive merits of the Sunningdale package, as Hayes notes, "There was no time given for new attitudes to develop. Whitelaw made his move in setting up the Executive too quickly. . . . There was no time to involve followers, no time to build a solid base of support across the community."[33] Another senior mandarin, Sir Frank Cooper (subsequently permanent under secretary at the NIO), has recorded his view that the Sunningdale structures were too advanced for their time: "To try and introduce it into one of the most disturbed societies that we can find anywhere must be doomed to failure ... the whole thing was too complex, too dependent on people behaving reasonably."[34]

Heath consistently miscalculated where the center of Unionist politics lay; discounted the breadth and depth of popular support for those he disliked, such as Paisley and Craig; and overestimated the electoral strength and potential of those he regarded as progressive, such as Alliance. The evidence of opinion polls suggests that the majority of Protestants were prepared to accept power sharing in principle in 1973 but strongly opposed the Sunningdale agreement because they saw it as a step toward Irish unification. Both the SDLP and the Irish government publicly proclaimed as much, and UK ministers privately wanted to move in the same direction. The agreement thus gratuitously handed the Unionist opponents of power sharing an important political advantage.

As for the republican side, Heath apparently assumed that Nationalists and republicans would turn against violence once they saw how reasonable the British government was being. But their general acquiescence in a strategy of armed resistance was not predicated primarily on the experience of Unionist misrule and discrimination; its roots lay deeper. From a republican perspective, Stormont's dissolution was not evidence of British fair play but the first in a series of successes for their strategy of armed struggle. The imposition of direct rule demonstrated the power of the bomb and bullet.

## Policy Developments since 1974

There are several valuable political histories of Northern Ireland since 1973.[35] My purpose here is not to produce another but to identify weaknesses in Britain's approach to the 1973 agreement as revealed by later developments.

### The Collapse of the Executive

Whitelaw established a power-sharing executive that met for the first time on January 1, 1974. Widely acclaimed as a final settlement and fresh start by ministers and media commentators in Britain, Ireland, and the United States, the executive survived only until May 28, 1974. As skeptics in Whitehall had foreseen, the power-sharing institutions proved incapable of surviving the tensions generated by the clash between protesting Unionism and insurgent Nationalism. Faulkner did not have the necessary political support to sustain the deal that Heath had pressured him into making.

Setting aside their longstanding differences over policies and tactics, Faulkner's opponents—Craig, Paisley, and West—created a new umbrella body, the United Ulster Unionist Council (UUUC); its first meeting coincided with the opening of the Sunningdale conference. The UUUC brought together all the Unionist opponents of the white paper proposals, including some Unionist Party assembly members. It challenged the executive's legitimacy on the ground that it offended the principle of cross-community support, since a majority of elected representatives from the Unionist side had rejected it and were not represented on it. When it was concluded, the Sunningdale agreement—particularly the arrangements for the Council of Ireland—provided Faulkner's rivals with further powerful ammunition. Three days after the executive's first meeting, the Ulster Unionist Council, the governing body of the Unionist Party, rejected the Council of Ireland by 427 votes to 374. Three days later Faulkner resigned as party leader. On January 16, the Irish High Court dealt a further blow to the agreement when it ruled that Dublin's acceptance of the consent principle clashed with the claim to sovereignty in the Irish constitution. The constitution had to prevail.

Faulkner held on to his role as chief executive, hoping that the tide of Unionist opinion would turn before he had to face the voters again. But this hope was soon dashed. Attempting to resolve a damaging miners' strike in Britain, Heath called a Westminster election on February 28, 1974. UUUC candidates standing on a platform of opposition to Sunningdale won eleven of Northern Ireland's twelve seats; Faulkner's supporters won none. Nationally, Labour narrowly defeated the Conservatives. Heath briefly explored the possibility of striking a deal with the seven Ulster Unionist MPs now led by West, but dropped the attempt after they insisted on an end to the power-sharing institutions.[36] Wilson returned to office and appointed Merlyn Rees as secretary of state.

The developments effectively sealed the fate of the executive, the members of which were still struggling with the unaccustomed challenges of working together after years of bitter antagonism. Under the aegis of another new body, the Ulster Workers' Council (UWC), the UUUC and a variety of loyalist paramilitary and workers' groups opposed to Sunningdale called a general strike, starting on May 14, protesting the government's continuing refusal to review the Sunningdale agreement in light of the Unionist electorate's overwhelming rejection of it. The crisis intensified on May 17, when bombs exploded in Dublin and Monaghan town (in the Republic), killing thirty-three people.

The members of the executive divided over how they and Rees should respond to the strike. In a revealing reversal of traditional positions the SDLP argued for coercive measures, including the arrest of loyalist leaders and tough army action, while Faulkner's Unionists called for negotiations with the strike leaders, among whom were their former colleagues. Rees refused to negotiate with men he described as fascists, setting aside increasing evidence that the strike enjoyed substantial popular support. But at the same time he held back from instructing the security forces to act against them. Adding intimidation to their arsenal, the UWC quickly succeeded in seriously disrupting economic activity across the region. Within two weeks, they effectively controlled Northern Ireland's electricity and fuel distribution networks. With Wilson and Rees still refusing either to negotiate with or to arrest the strike leaders, the executive cracked under the strain of its members' divided loyalties. Faulkner and the Unionist members resigned on May 28, prompting Rees to reintroduce direct rule.[37]

Over the next three months a cabinet subcommittee chaired by Wilson conducted yet another in-depth policy review. Ministers again examined all the options, including withdrawal, repartition, and independence, before concluding again that any of these would make matters worse. Policy thus remained essentially as it had been: to introduce power sharing with an Irish dimension when the time was ripe. Wilson personally wanted to work toward British withdrawal as quickly as practicable, but there was still no consensus on this in the cabinet or in Whitehall. Ironically in light of the Irish constitution's territorial claim, when the Irish government learned that Wilson had prepared a secret plan for withdrawal over a five-year period, Foreign Minister FitzGerald became so alarmed that he asked U.S. national security adviser Henry Kissinger to intervene.[38]

*Revival Initiatives*

For the next twenty-four years, successive secretaries of state tried to engineer an agreement between the leaders of the two sides that would allow devolution to be restored on the basis of power sharing. In May 1975, Rees convened a constitutional convention, elected in a similar manner to the assembly, which he invited to produce its own proposals for a settlement. Unionists opposed to power sharing won 55 percent of the poll, Faulkner's supporters less than 8 percent, and Alliance just under 10 percent. Predictably, the convention produced a report that called for a return to the former majoritarian system, reformed only to the extent that Faulkner had suggested in June 1971. Rees responded by binning the report and dissolved the convention in February 1976.

In 1982, Conservative Secretary of State James Prior created a new assembly, effectively a hybrid of the 1973 assembly and the 1975 convention, to which he offered the possibility of what he called rolling devolution. The assembly was to be given legislative and executive powers if and when the two sides could agree through a 70 percent vote on how they should be exercised. Until then, it would have limited advisory and scrutiny functions. Prior declared that in discharging this limited remit, the moderate leaders of the two sides would learn to work together on social and economic matters. This fragile hope was dashed even before the assembly met. Standing in a regional election for the first time, Sinn Féin won 10 percent of the vote. This raised fears among ministers and SDLP leaders that unless constitutional nationalism made some visible headway soon, Sinn Féin could soon overtake the SDLP as the main voice of the minority community. Sinn Féin then boycotted the assembly on the ground that it was irrelevant to the pursuit of reunification, and the SDLP decided to do the same. The assembly met for the first time in November 1982. Fifty-nine Unionist members attended and nineteen Nationalists stayed away. The three participating parties (Unionist Party, DUP, and Alliance) produced proposals for devolution on the basis of majority rule, which London again rejected. By 1985 the assembly had become little more than an arena for Unionists' protests against British political and security policies. In June 1986, Prior's successor Tom King dissolved it.

In parallel, under the auspices of the Irish government, the main parties in the Republic and the SDLP—the elected representatives of Nationalist Ireland, excluding Sinn Féin—met in Dublin in May 1983 as the New Ireland Forum. Fitt had stood down from the leadership of the SDLP to protest its increasing shift toward a Nationalist agenda and had been replaced by Hume. The forum issued a report in May 1984 that amplified Hume's proposals for a unitary Irish state to be achieved by consent[39]—in effect, British pressure on unionism. It also explored two possible alternatives: a federal Ireland and Anglo-Irish joint authority. Then prime minister Margaret Thatcher bluntly rejected all three. Behind the scenes, however, she agreed to a program of work on Anglo-Irish cooperation that resulted in a major initiative the following year.

### The Anglo-Irish Agreement, 1985

Thatcher, prime minister since May 1979, was widely seen as the most pro-union British leader since the Troubles began.[40] An informed observer could have been forgiven for thinking, as Unionist leader and member of parliament Jim Molyneaux did, that under her leadership the potential for achieving further agreement at nation-state level was slight. Yet by 1984

officials in the FCO and Cabinet Office had persuaded her—in the face
of resistance from the NIO—to develop a formalized working partnership
with Dublin, where FitzGerald had become taoiseach.[41] The Anglo-Irish
Agreement was signed on November 15, 1985. In it the two governments
confirmed the principle that any change in Northern Ireland's status would
only come about with the consent of a majority of its people. The agreement
established a standing Inter-Governmental Conference to address political and security issues of common interest, including cooperation against
terrorism, Thatcher's main concern. For as long as the Northern Ireland
parties failed to agree on restoring devolution, the conference would also
provide a framework within which the Irish government could represent
the minority's interests. Officials from Dublin would maintain a secretariat
in Belfast to liaise with their NIO counterparts.

The SDLP welcomed the agreement, for which Hume had lobbied the
Irish government hard, but Unionists were furious. The Unionist Party had
not been consulted, no advance attempt had been to secure even their acquiescence, and they saw it as a first step on the road toward the forum's
concept of joint authority. An estimated 250,000 people gathered at Belfast City Hall to protest.[42] All fifteen Unionist MPs resigned their seats
to fight by-election campaigns on a manifesto of opposition to the agreement under the slogan "Ulster says no."[43] There were riots and a loyalist
campaign of intimidation against police officers. The sense of injustice was
not confined to Unionists. Irish senator Mary Robinson resigned from the
Irish Labour Party to protest its support for the agreement, maintaining
that since it was unacceptable to all shades of Unionist opinion, it could
not possibly contribute to peace and stability.[44] One lasting legacy of the
agreement, however, is that it formalized and intensified cooperation between the two nation-states at the heart of the dispute, committed them
both to determined efforts to resolving any differences between them, and
created a mechanism for consultation on potentially contentious issues before serious damage had been done.

### Including Republican Paramilitaries, 1989

The 1985 agreement was not intended to be the end of the matter, but
rather—at least for the Nationalists—a means to pressure Unionists.
O'Leary and McGarry have described it as "part of a jointly designed British and Irish Machiavellian master-plan to coerce Unionists into accepting
a power sharing devolved government together with an Irish dimension,
knowing that the intergovernmental conference could survive whatever
strategy the Unionists would use to undermine it."[45] Four years later, it had
not produced any visible progress toward that result. Unionists remained

adamant in their opposition, while Nationalists were disappointed at the pace and scale of reform.

With attempts to restart negotiations with the constitutional parties continuing to fail, the Conservatives began to explore the possibility of negotiating peace directly with the IRA. Like Whitelaw in 1972, ministers wanted to strengthen and encourage those in the IRA leadership who they believed were genuinely committed to a political alternative to the armed struggle. Unlike in 1972, Sinn Féin was by now a well-organized political party with strong internal discipline, participating in elections and capable of attracting substantial popular support. A dialogue was already under way between John Hume and Gerry Adams that the SDLP leader hoped would lead republicans to give up the armed struggle.

In November 1989, Secretary of State Peter Brooke indicated in a newspaper interview that he found it "difficult to envisage" the military defeat of the IRA, nor did he believe that a restoration of devolved government would "cause terrorism to falter." Drawing a somewhat misleading analogy with Britain's withdrawal from Cyprus in the 1950s, he said that the government would respond "with flexibility and imagination" if the IRA stopped its violence.[46] In October 1990 Thatcher personally authorized a resumption of secret conversations with republicans. Brooke made a conciliatory speech on November 9 in which he declared that "the British Government has no selfish strategic or economic interest in Northern Ireland; our role is to help, enable and encourage."[47] This message was not substantively different from what Heath had said in November 1971, but it fell on less bullish republican ears.

In parallel with efforts to secure an IRA ceasefire, Brooke and his successor Paddy Mayhew pressed ahead with a new round of talks among the Northern Ireland parties. This was intended to encourage both the IRA and Unionists toward accommodation. If either refused to play or overplayed their hand, they risked being excluded from a final deal. On March 26, 1991, Brooke told the Commons that the talks would address three distinct strands: new institutions of government within Northern Ireland, north-south relationships, and relationships between the British and Irish governments. Nothing would be agreed until everything was agreed. No settlement would neglect the Irish dimension, but adding an east-west dimension provided token compensation for unionism. Talks began in earnest on April 29, 1992, with the participation of the UUP, DUP, SDLP, and Alliance. From the government's perspective they made some progress, in that the UUP explicitly accepted both power sharing and an Irish dimension in principle. However, the DUP demanded that the Irish government should drop its "illegal, criminal and immoral" territorial claim to the north as a precondition for discussing the Irish dimension,[48] while the SDLP insisted on a form of joint authority incorporating a six-member executive with three members appointed by London, Dublin, and Brussels. Neither would give way, and the talks were suspended in November 1992.

The IRA continued to set off bombs and kill people in England; they exploded a huge bomb in London on April 24, 1993, causing an estimated £350 million in damage. Despite this, persuaded by intelligence information that there was a substantial faction in the republican movement that wanted to give up violence in favor of politics, the British continued with their efforts to engage the IRA in dialogue. They wanted to ensure that the republican leadership could get as much of their movement as possible behind any agreement. When the talks with the mainstream parties stalled, British officials passed their republican contacts a detailed assessment of the progress so far and an outline of a possible settlement.

On December 15, 1993, the two governments published a joint declaration intended to bring Sinn Féin into a new round of multiparty talks without driving the Unionists out.[49] The declaration was deliberately ambiguous and offered each side something. At its heart was an invitation to all "democratically mandated parties which establish a commitment to exclusively peaceful methods" to participate in a dialogue with the two governments on the way forward.[50] Its deeper significance lay in that a Fianna Fáil government had openly committed the Irish state to the principle that unification should be achieved only with the consent of a majority of the electorate in the north.[51]

The joint declaration succeeded in that neither the Unionist Party nor Sinn Féin instantly rejected it. The republican leadership bought time by asking the governments for "clarification" while initiating an internal debate on the merits of a tactical shift from armed struggle to democratic politics. The IRA announced "a complete cessation of military activities" on August 31, 1994, justifying this to its supporters by emphasizing the potential for advancing the reunification project through a new powerful republican coalition that would include the Irish diaspora in Britain and the United States.[52] The loyalist paramilitaries announced a parallel ceasefire on October 13.

The two governments' next public move was to flesh out their thinking in two framework documents, which they published on February 22, 1995. These set out the British government's proposals for a first strand of internal settlement and their joint proposals for north-south and east-west institutional arrangements. The second strand included a Council of Ireland with considerable "executive, consultative and harmonising functions."[53]

The two frameworks outlined most of the provisions of the eventual agreement, which a majority of Northern Ireland's parties endorsed in 1998. A lengthy process of negotiations followed among the two governments and the parties, including Sinn Féin, although the DUP walked out in protest as soon as Sinn Féin joined. There were many setbacks, crises, and interruptions. On February 9, 1996, the Provisionals set off a bomb in London's Canary Wharf financial district that killed two people and caused over £85 million in damage. Others followed, most spectacularly in Manchester in June 1996, when 200 people were injured. It is unclear to what extent the Sinn Féin leadership had authorized these explosions, but the available evidence suggests that they were organized by Provisional dissidents opposed to Adams's strategy of political negotiation.[54]

On May 1, 1997, Labour returned to power at Westminster under Tony Blair with a majority of 147 seats. The IRA reinstated its ceasefire on July 20 and political talks resumed on October 7. The two governments and Northern Ireland's main parties (except the DUP) collectively negotiated a new constitutional agreement, completed on April 10, 1998.[55] This provided for a power-sharing devolved administration that included Sinn Féin, subject to its electoral performance. The issue of IRA disarmament was not resolved, but the agreement committed all parties "to exclusively democratic and peaceful means of resolving differences on political issues." Unsurprisingly, given the complexity of the issues and the suspicions among the participants, the document contained a host of safeguards, vetoes, and ambiguities.[56]

The crucial transformation at the core of the Good Friday Agreement (GFA) was that Nationalist Ireland—including Sinn Féin—formally accepted that the union would continue for as long as it was supported by a majority of the electorate in Northern Ireland. In return, those Unionists who supported the GFA accepted specific arrangements for power sharing and institutionalized cross-border cooperation. It was harder for Unionists to accept the two governments' subsequent insistence that, as compensation for having ceded ground on the constitutional issue, Sinn Féin should be given a series of concessions related to contentious security issues, including the release of paramilitary prisoners, the future of policing, and the decommissioning of IRA weapons.[57]

Voting in a referendum on May 22, 1998, the northern electorate endorsed the agreement by a majority of 71 percent. Nationalists voted for it overwhelmingly, Unionists narrowly.[58] In a parallel referendum in the south, 94 percent supported the agreement and approved the requisite amendments to the Irish constitution. In the ensuing assembly election on June 25, the SDLP and the Unionist Party emerged as the largest parties on the two sides, with 22.0 percent and 21.2 percent of first preference votes, respectively. They were closely followed by the DUP, which continued to oppose the agreement (18.0 percent), and Sinn Féin (17.6 percent).

In an attempt to spoil the GFA, an IRA splinter group on August 15 set off a bomb in the town of Omagh that killed twenty-nine people—the worst single incident in Northern Ireland since the Troubles began. Nevertheless, after many further rounds of negotiation, a power-sharing executive was formed and met for the first time on December 2, 1999. In accordance with the GFA, ministers were appointed from all four of the largest parties in proportion to their representation in the assembly. With the exception of two DUP ministers—who took up their posts as heads of departments but boycotted executive meetings to protest Sinn Féin's participation—they sat together in government. The new North-South Ministerial Council met for the first time on December 13.

As in 1973, the settlement proved to be unstable, as the hard-line rivals on both sides constrained the extent to which the leaders of the two moderate parties could accommodate each other. There was a high level of mistrust and conflict between Unionist and Sinn Féin ministers, particularly over the "decommissioning" of IRA weaponry. When the IRA did not deliver on it as the Unionists had understood they would, the executive collapsed after only ten weeks. It was restored in June 2000 only after the IRA initiated a process for "putting its arms beyond use." The executive continued fitfully for two more years. Eventually, with Unionists accusing the republican movement of chronic bad faith, London reinstated direct rule on October 14, 2002, to prevent another collapse.[59]

### Reconciling the Extremes, 2003

In 2003 Blair adopted a new tactic. Instead of building an accommodation around the center parties, as successive secretaries of state had tried to do since Whitelaw, the British would instead try to engineer an agreement between the DUP and Sinn Féin. They reasoned that UUP and SDLP leaders were always going to be vulnerable to attacks from hard-liners, but if the more uncompromising parties could strike a deal, it would be virtually unassailable.[60] They called an election to the assembly for November 26, 2003, even though there was no immediate prospect of its sitting. For the first time ever in a Westminster or assembly election the DUP topped the poll, with 25.7 percent of first preference votes as against 22.7 percent for the Unionist Party. After the election three UUP assembly members reinforced the shift by transferring to the winning team. In a parallel shift on the Nationalist side, Sinn Féin (23.5 percent) outpolled the SDLP (17.0 percent).

Through 2004 and 2005, Blair and his team pursued the elusive deal between the extremes. The main issue of contention continued to be IRA decommissioning.[61] Under pressure from the British, Irish, and U.S. governments, the IRA eventually completed its decommissioning process in September 2005. On April 6, 2006, Blair announced that the assembly would be convened on May 15, giving it a few weeks to prepare for government. It would then be required to elect a first and deputy first minister, one from each tradition and equal in status and authority, and to form an executive. If and when it did this, power would automatically be devolved. But if the assembly failed to agree on an executive within a reasonable time scale, its members would cease to be paid and devolution would be deferred indefinitely. In that event, the two governments would implement "Plan B," which they hinted would mean strengthening the Anglo-Irish partnership. This was intended as a threat to the DUP—seen as the more recalcitrant partner—that the provisions originally set out in the Anglo-Irish agreement of 1985 would be renewed and extended.[62]

Pressing ahead, the two governments convened a conference at St. Andrews in Scotland in October 2006, which all the main Northern Ireland parties attended. The governments consented to a modest series of revisions to the GFA, mainly in response to requests from the DUP, and set out a timetable to restore devolution by March 26, 2007.[63] They also agreed to call a fresh election that would further strengthen the DUP and Sinn Féin, as Secretary of State Peter Hain publicly predicted. The election was held on March 7, 2007. The DUP increased its share of first preference votes to 30.1 percent and Sinn Fein to 26.2 percent. The SDLP declined to 15.2 percent, and the once dominant Unionists suffered the humiliation of coming in fourth, with under 15.0 percent.

Secure in their electoral support, the leaders of the two largest parties declared that the electorate had given them a mandate to strike a deal. They agreed to appoint old enemies Ian Paisley as first minister and Martin McGuinness as deputy first minister. Devolution was restored on May 8, 2007, with all four parties gathered around the executive table.

## Sunningdale and the Later Agreements

Whyte describes the intention behind the concept of power sharing with an Irish dimension, first outlined in 1972, as aspiring "to give each community what it was perceived as most wanting."[64] For Unionists, this meant a solid guarantee of the union; for Nationalists, equal treatment within Northern Ireland and recognition of their belonging to the Irish nation. Writing in 1990, Whyte had identified two main obstacles to realizing the concept. A majority of Unionists had so far rejected it, and even if the constitutional parties agreed to it, paramilitary violence would continue. By 1998, the political talks and the separate but linked peace process—Britain's negotiations with the IRA—were well on the way to removing them.

Despite the flaws in the process that Whitelaw oversaw and in the outcome he achieved, the first secretary of state in 1973 delivered a package including many of the elements of the deal that all the major parties eventually accepted; the UUP and loyalist parties signed up to the GFA in 1998 and the DUP assented to most of its provisions with the supplementary St. Andrews agreement in 2006. Both agreements incorporated a declaration of British neutrality over the union, respect for the principle of majority consent, close cooperation between the British and Irish governments, institutional arrangements based on power sharing with a north-south institutional dimension, and attempts to balance the ethnic and national identity claims of both Nationalists and Unionists. So why did Unionists in 1998 and 2006 accept changes similar to those that had provoked them to protest and violence in 1974? What do the later agreements tell us about the strengths and weaknesses of Sunningdale? Let us consider the differences between the two packages.

The first is in the participants. In 1972 and 1973, extremists on both sides were excluded. Whitelaw kept out not only the IRA but also, at the request of the SDLP and Alliance, the various Unionist factions opposed to his proposals. In 1997, Blair went to great lengths to ensure that Sinn Féin and their loyalist counterparts were both included.[65] The DUP initially opposed the 1998 agreement, but by 2006 the electoral arithmetic had changed. The DUP had achieved primacy and the IRA had put its weapons beyond use. The DUP thus was able politically to renegotiate the 1998 agreement and accept the principle of power sharing, even when power was to be shared with people they had previously denounced as terrorists and "apologists for terrorists."[66] On the Nationalist side, Sinn Féin had achieved primacy over the SDLP. Thus, as long as they could maintain internal cohesion, the leaders of the major parties on each side could reach tactical agreements without fear of being undermined by other less conciliatory parties from their own side.

The second difference involved Unionist attitudes. In 1972 and 1973, the British required the Unionists to give up their cherished institutions, share power with dissidents who aspired to destroy their constitution, and engage in negotiations that Nationalists had declared would result in the termination of the union. By 1998 the Unionist Party—particularly its leader, David Trimble—had accepted that the old Stormont could not be restored, felt confident about the future of the union, and pragmatically recognized that the price for devolution would be compliance with the sovereign government's insistence on power sharing with an Irish dimension. Trimble dropped the integrationism of his predecessor James Molyneaux. With power devolved to Scotland and Wales, devolution would no longer set Northern Ireland apart from the rest of the United Kingdom. While the DUP's elected representatives vocally opposed the GFA, they did not as in 1973 set out to disrupt the assembly, and in due course took their seats on the executive. Far from leading mass protest rallies, the political representatives of loyalist paramilitary organizations participated in the talks, endorsed the agreement, and even criticized the DUP's hostility to it. There was no longer a UWC to reinforce the DUP's rhetorical complaints with the threat of economic disruption and the theater of street disorder.

A third factor was nationalist and republican attitudes. In 1972 the Provisional leadership believed that they stood on the brink of victory and the SDLP that a united Ireland was imminent. Neither had any motivation to settle for anything less. By 1998 the SDLP had moderated the scale and pace of its ambitions. It also had decided that Sinn Féin must be included in the executive to maximize the overall influence of nationalism. Republican leaders were weary of combat and accepted that violence was not going to force the British to withdraw. They had experienced electoral success, but also recognized that the IRA's violent actions were setting a limit to this, and were ready to persuade their core supporters that a strategy of democratic politics—stiffened as necessary by the threat of reverting to force—had a greater prospect of achieving their long-term goals. To the extent that the IRA's ceasefire held—and when they breached it, they did so mainly in England—the public in Northern Ireland experienced an immediate benefit from the talks. This increased popular support for Sinn Féin, which in turn encouraged a majority of republican activists to support the leadership's political strategy.

Changes in the British government were a fourth factor. As prime minister from May 1997, Tony Blair made it a personal priority to secure a settlement and assigned his close personal adviser Jonathan Powell, a career diplomat, to build and sustain a constructive working relationship with republican leaders. Blair insisted on including them in the talks without requiring the IRA first to lay down its weapons or declare its campaign over, even though this caused the DUP to walk out. He personally intervened at critical moments to prevent the process from breaking down, most visibly in the last two days of the 1998 negotiations. He and Powell deployed their considerable presentational skills, the authority of the prime minister's office, and a string of verbal ambiguities to sell the deal to Unionists, who remained to the end both skeptical and anxious.[67] Unlike Heath, Blair was determined to include in the talks all parties that had a sufficient popular mandate—not to mention the capacity to set off bombs in England—and were willing to participate. He had an empathy that Heath lacked and exhibited an understanding of Irish political leaders' concerns and aspirations. Again unlike Heath, he showed great patience. Of course, it helped that he had a secure Commons majority, the support of the opposition and the Irish government, and, crucially, ten years in which to complete the task.

Fifth was the Irish government. Taoiseach Bertie Ahern came to office only a month after Blair and adopted a similarly pragmatic and determined approach to the political negotiations. There was by then much greater acceptance among the Irish political elite that unification was neither imminent nor in the best interests of the Irish state, unless it could be achieved with the genuine consent of unionism. Ahern committed himself to changing the Irish constitution and accepted limitations to the role and scope of cross-border institutions, two things that FitzGerald had explicitly refused to do during the Sunningdale negotiations. Meanwhile, Anglo-Irish relations had greatly improved in terms of sophistication, mutual understanding, and shared perspectives on the conflict. The two governments had agreed in advance on a framework for the eventual settlement and had published it. As the legitimate authorities in the nation-states to which the competing communities had given their allegiance, they had settled their competing claims to sovereignty between themselves. They then steered the parties toward the outcome, which they had already scripted. Acting together and with the party leaders, they carefully choreographed events, to the extent that Sinn Féin leaders delivered speeches that incorporated material drafted by Jonathan Powell, while Blair's speeches incorporated material from Sinn Féin.

While the Irish government was still more receptive to overtures from the SDLP than from the Unionist parties, the close working relationships between the two governments made it harder for the northern parties to exploit differences between them. During the talks in January 1998, the governments were able to fine-tune their previous proposals by producing a heads-of-agreement paper, which accepted that the powers of the Council of Ireland as outlined in the 1995 framework would have to be diluted. Once completed, the GFA had the status of an international treaty and was underpinned by national legislation in each jurisdiction

Because of the governments' close working relationship, the Unionists had a greater incentive to reach an agreement. In 1973, the alternative had been direct rule, which they collectively preferred to power sharing. In 1998 and again in 2006, the alternative with which they were threatened was an extension and intensification of the Anglo-Irish Agreement, possibly leading toward joint authority. A pro-union form of direct rule was no longer on offer. Moreover, as secretary of state from 2005 to 2007, Peter Hain initiated a number of policy changes intended to render direct rule obnoxious to Unionists, including the introduction of domestic water charges and the abolition of selective secondary education.

Perhaps the main legacy of Sunningdale is that it shook up settled opinions on both sides and opened up the path for a new relationship between the two governments. It helped to clarify what was politically feasible, what the obstacles to a sustainable accommodation were, and how they might be overcome. It took many years before the IRA indicated that it was ready and willing to give up violence, but when it did so, the two governments and the local parties could draw on the lessons of 1973 and 1974 in charting the way forward. Many years of preliminary work, starting in 1989, cleared the path for the formal multiparty negotiations that began in earnest in Belfast on September 15, 1997. This included relationship building among British and Irish ministers and officials and key players in the local parties, especially the Unionist Party and Sinn Féin.

The later multiparty talks were internationalized, chaired by U.S. senator George Mitchell rather than the British secretary of state. Unionists initially objected that Mitchell would be susceptible to the influence of Irish America, but in time the senator became respected by all the parties for his skill, patience, and fairness.[68] Unlike Whitelaw, he did not have to manage pressures from the UK political system or comply with instructions from an impatient prime minister, and he was able to stay with the process until the deal was struck.

In addition, by 1998 both the United Kingdom and Ireland had settled into membership in the European Union. The boundaries of national sovereignty within the union were less impermeable, much legislation for both states was made or determined at the European level, and programs of cross-border cooperation had become the norm across Western Europe. The south had developed a more outward-looking political culture in which its leaders were more concerned about prosperity and their influence in Europe than in preserving de Valera's pastoral vision or liberating the economy from dependence on Britain. By 2006, the international context had again changed dramatically, as the attitude of the U.S. political elite toward the IRA hardened after the al-Qaeda attacks on New York and Washington of September 2001. President George W. Bush's special envoys, Richard Haass and Mitchell Reiss, were less willing than their predecessors had been to overlook IRA criminality, and hence better able to secure the confidence of unionism.

As for the terms of the agreement, there were several main differences in substance from 1973 to 1998. The Irish government agreed to amend its constitution to convert what the Unionists denounced as a territorial claim in Articles 2 and 3 into an aspiration for unity between the people of the island. The British secretary of state would have no role in selecting Northern Irish ministers. Each political party would have an automatic right to a given number of posts in the executive, proportionate to its seats in the assembly. Voting procedures in the assembly would ensure veto rights for each of the two sides based on a system of designation as Unionist, Nationalist, or other. There were unambiguous boundaries to the scope and functions of the North-South Council; to balance the north-south institutions, there would also be a British-Irish Council, on which all the devolved UK administrations would be represented. The British government would take steps to promote the use of the Irish language, reduce its military presence, and rescind its emergency powers. Finally, the Anglo-Irish agreement of 1985 would be replaced by a new British-Irish agreement, which would operate with greater openness and deal only with those matters not devolved to the assembly.

Other problematic issues were referred to new bureaucratic structures for action. New independent commissions would be established to promote and protect equality and human rights. An independent commission with international representation would consider the future of policing, alongside a parallel review of the criminal justice system. With the agreement, there also would be an accelerated program to release paramilitary prisoners. The leadership of the Unionist Party thus could distance itself from the policing and criminal justice reforms to the extent that it could say that these were matters for the British government.

The later negotiating process comprised two strands: the peace talks with the IRA and the political talks with the parties. Because Sinn Féin enjoyed the legitimacy of substantial electoral support, the British could include them in mainstream negotiations. Because the British could maintain the position—some would say fiction—that Sinn Féin was separate from the IRA, they could say that they were not negotiating with the IRA.[69] Sinn Féin, meanwhile, could say that it could not make commitments on behalf of the IRA; this is reflected in the wording of the GFA, which merely commits the participating parties to "use any influence they may have to achieve the decommissioning of all paramilitary arms within two years ... in the context of the implementation of the overall settlement."[70]

It took the best part of five years to negotiate the GFA and nine years more to bring it to full implementation, as amended in 2006. This supports our conclusion that Heath in 1972 and 1973 was well advised by those like Whitelaw who wanted to take the process more slowly, allowing time for the parties to adjust to the new realities.

## Others' Assessments

Unsurprisingly, British policies have been attacked by partisan proponents of full integration and of unification. Unionist politician Robert McCartney has condemned the 1998 agreement and by implication British policy since 1972 as being "to appease Sinn Féin/IRA and avert mainland bombings by creating transitional institutions of government leading to Irish unity, while sedating gullible and greedy Unionists with the illusion of devolved democracy."[71] McCartney attacks the devolved institutions on the grounds that ministers are not subject to collective responsibility, there is no proper opposition in the assembly, and no means of improving matters.

On the republican side, Sinn Féin chairman Pat Doherty has emphasized that the GFA is "an accommodation, not a settlement . . . for Irish republicans, the cause still persists—the British Government's claim of jurisdiction over part of our country . . . it is this denial of the Irish people's right to self determination, freedom and independence which is the core, outstanding issue which must be resolved." The value of the GFA is not as a resolution to the problem but as a vehicle that opens up "a constitutional route to Irish unity."[72] From another perspective, former PD activist Eamon McCann has criticized the "creative ambiguity of the GFA as a form of dishonesty, allowing both republicans and Unionists to avoid facing up to the full implications of what they have signed up for."[73] Doherty's statement appears to bear this out.

From an academic perspective, Richard Rose famously wrote of Northern Ireland in 1971 that "in the foreseeable future, no solution is immediately practicable."[74] He identified a range of options in terms of different governing coalitions comprising ideal types of citizen, but all of them problematic. Closest to the policy that the British adopted in 1973 is "a coalition between fully allegiant and compliant protestants and fully allegiant and repressed Catholics." Rose predicted that this would stimulate a successful loyalist challenge, as in 1974 it did. Returning to the issue in 1975, Rose was no more optimistic: "The test of a policy designed to create public order in the midst of internal war is not whether it conforms to comfortable liberal assumptions, but whether it produces order."[75]

We have looked at why Heath's initiative failed by exploring the differences between Sunningdale and the GFA. But how these and other factors are to be interpreted remains controversial. Paul Dixon has identified four alternative perspectives focusing on, first, Unionist opposition to the Sunningdale package of power sharing with an Irish dimension, on the ground that this would lead toward unification; second, unionist opposition to the Irish dimension alone; third, the failure of the incoming Labour government to stand up to the UWC strike; and fourth, a political context too polarized to sustain such radical innovation. Dixon concludes that the British government at least "has to share responsibility for creating the climate of constitutional uncertainty and complaint in which the unbalanced Sunningdale settlement failed. Unionist fears that power-sharing and Sunningdale represented an attempt to manipulate Northern Ireland out of the Union were 'reasonable' (rather than paranoid) given British policy during this period."[76] Hennessey supports this position, maintaining that the fundamental flaw in the Sunningdale settlement is that it failed to deliver the long-term constitutional stability that Unionists required in return for assenting to power sharing.[77] From a more explicitly Unionist perspective, Anthony Alcock has argued that Sunningdale failed because it ducked the border issue, leaving intact the Republic's "constitutional irredentism."[78]

From a perspective more sympathetic to Nationalism, McGarry and O'Leary have argued that most of the conditions that cross-national studies suggest are required for the success of a consociational settlement were absent in 1972.[79] The implication is that the settlement was bound to fail unless more favorable conditions could be created. Specifically (like Alcock), these two authors highlight the resolution of the border issue.[80] Since it goes to the heart of the political science debate over consociationalism, I will return to this argument in chapter 9.

Some commentators, predominantly among those that favor unification, have criticized British policy as inconsistent, contradictory, and reactive.[81] As we have seen from the case studies, this is a tenable assessment of the formative years from 1969 to 1972, but it is harder to sustain in relation to the doctrine of power sharing with an Irish dimension. The genesis of the Sunningdale formula may have been messy and the agreement flawed, but it had a certain intellectual coherence.[82] It is easy with hindsight to declare that the British should have adopted a more proactive approach from the start, introducing direct rule in 1969 to pave the way for a solution that had yet to be devised. But it was far from obvious at the time that such a radical constitutional upheaval would have prevented the deterioration that followed in 1970 through 1972, and logical to conclude that direct rule would create instability and make it harder to disengage.

While policy until 1972 may have been consistent only to the extent that it focused on minimizing Britain's intervention, it has had a broad continuity since 1973.[83] In retrospect it is apparent that the five years covered in this study were the formative period for a strategic doctrine that has evolved considerably over time, and which continues to underpin British policy. Having investigated all the major theoretical options, London had by 1972 concluded that other alternatives, including withdrawal, independence, repartition, and full integration, were not politically or diplomatically feasible.[84] Neither was a return to simple majority rule. The broad components of the new orthodoxy, were, first, British sovereignty subject to the principle of majority consent; second, military support as required under national control for the regional police service to maintain order; third, Anglo-Irish diplomatic and security cooperation; fourth, bipartisanship at Westminster; fifth, a north-south institutional dimension; and sixth, devolution to an administration in which power would be shared between the two sides. The details of the arrangements for devolution would have to be agreed on between elected representatives of the two sides, and at a minimum would include an administrative assembly with oversight over civil service departments, an executive drawn from assembly members, mutual veto over contentious issues, PR elections, and the retention of Westminster control over "excepted" matters, including international relations, defense, national security, taxation, and elections.

Dixon has criticized British security policies as having a persistent and structural bias against the Nationalist side, in part because of the state's reliance on Protestants to man the police and UDR. Successive British governments permitted disproportionate influence to those who used violence, and in an effort to demonstrate its determination to defeat the IRA, the state itself deployed excessive violence. This undermined British efforts to win over public support and promote political accommodation. Meanwhile, the British political elite's flirtations with unification and willingness to include the IRA in negotiations undermined the security forces and created ammunition for Unionist hard-liners. More broadly, UK ministers failed to understand the communal pattern of politics in Northern Ireland, and thus tended to push moderate Unionist leaders too far, too fast. Their threats—in particular Wilson's—were counterproductive.

## Direct Rule

Some analysts have argued in favor of alternative policy approaches. The most easily doable seem to be permanent direct rule and shared authority. Continuing direct rule indefinitely would retain the first four elements in the NIO's doctrine but drop devolution. Although it has never been the preferred option of any of the parties to the conflict, direct rule was in force for over thirty years from 1972 and remains Britain's obvious fallback position. The Anglo-Irish agreement of 1985 added an Irish dimension, with formal arrangements for consultation with Dublin.

Both governments and each of the parties in the Northern Ireland executive maintain that the region is better governed by local elected representatives. As depicted by analyst Derek Birrell, however, direct rule had advantages over power sharing, particularly in relation to the development of the 1998 agreement: "Direct rule facilitated the introduction of radical measures to assist in the peace process, the search for a political settlement, tackling social and economic disadvantage, and post-conflict recovery and stability."[85] Birrell argues that it is doubtful whether a coalition at Stormont could ever have agreed on the legislation necessary to implement the agreement or on the equality and human rights provisions that helped to seal the deal. Direct rule opened up the potential for north-south cooperation and, Birrell contends, helped protect the UK financial subvention to Northern Ireland, which in 2005 exceeded £5 billion.[86]

Birrell goes on to argue that direct rule provided greater stability and a more coherent program of government, underpinned by agreed-upon values and a consistent political ideology. It was relatively efficient, whereas the executive's complex and rigid decision-making procedures and blocking mechanisms since 2007 have, he argues, slowed down decision-making and created policy deadlocks. Nor has devolution fully addressed the problem of the democratic deficit, since there is no effective opposition.

But even if it is accepted that direct rule was necessary to engineer the accommodation, it does not follow that it is better than the devolved arrangements to which it gave birth. The extent to which direct rule ministers acted consistently and coherently is debatable, and it seems perverse to suggest that the colonial system of direct rule by ministers from Britain was structurally more democratic than government by the elected representatives of the people of Northern Ireland.

### Shared Authority

Shared authority was not examined during Heath's fundamental policy review. It did not emerge as a serious contender until it was included as one of three options in the report of the New Ireland Forum. As set out in that report as "joint authority," it would mean that London and Dublin would have equal responsibility for Northern Ireland, although equal sharing is not intrinsic to the concept. Prime Minister Thatcher dismissed it brusquely at the time. Among the objections were that it would violate the principle of majority consent; Unionists would reject it as a staging post toward unification; it would create the risk of disputes and deadlocks between the two sovereign powers; and it would invite potential insurgents to create a crisis, perhaps ultimately requiring British and Irish security forces to confront each other.

O'Leary and McGarry have argued that shared authority is a fairer and more logical alternative to internal power sharing than direct rule, which they deem inconsistent with the self-determination of the Nationalist community.[87] In their view it is more equitable than any solution that fails to confront the national question or leaves Northern Ireland purely British, and better reflects the reality that the conflict can ultimately be settled only through continuing partnership between the two nation states. Without the Anglo-Irish agreement of 1985, the GFA would not have been possible. In their first detailed proposal for shared authority in 1993, O'Leary and McGarry envisaged that a shared authority council would be established, comprising seven members, five elected in Northern Ireland and one each appointed by London and Dublin. It would appoint ministers to run government departments and take ultimate responsibility for security. There would also be an assembly with limited powers to legislate and responsibility for overseeing the work of civil service departments. The United Kingdom and the Republic together would guarantee the sustainability of the internal settlement. Each community would enjoy self-government in the religious, cultural, and educational domains; proportionality would operate throughout govern ment and the public sector; consensus would be required in contentious policy domains, such as security; and each side would have veto powers to protect its essential identity. Safeguards would be provided to reassure Unionists that these institutions would be durable and not a staging post toward reunification.[88]

O'Leary and McGarry subsequently conceded that this design would not secure cross-community consent and the two governments would be unwilling to impose it. They have, however, continued to maintain that Unionists would have less to fear from a form of shared authority such as this than from the GFA, which includes provision for an eventual referendum on unification.[89] They have also argued that shared authority can exist in covert form without being formally declared. There is already an element of it in the GFA, which could simply be allowed to expand over time. Also or alternatively, the threat of gradually expanding Dublin's input in British decision-making could be used to persuade unionism to make or accept concessions to nationalism. The gradual emergence of shared authority could in time be complemented by further reforms in the internal government of Northern Ireland at regional and local levels.[90]

Like McGarry and O'Leary, Joseph Ruane and Jennifer Todd depict shared authority as the logical response for those who (like them) explain the conflict as arising from the failure to complete historical processes of state and nation building in Britain and Ireland. They argue that it would in principle achieve equity between the national aspirations of the two competing communities in a way that merely internal solutions would not. It would balance the support given by the British state to Unionists with comparable support from the Irish state for Nationalists. Ruane and Todd also point out, however, that shared authority would fail to correct for the fundamental imbalance between Britain's willingness to withdraw under the right conditions and Ireland's historical commitment to unification. There would be an asymmetry between the two states' levels of engagement. Thus, without strong limits and safeguards, Unionists would be justified in seeing each step toward sharing authority as moving toward eventual Nationalist majority rule.

Coming from a similar theoretical background, O'Duffy notes that Britain from July 1972 adopted a dual approach, combining security measures to weaken the IRA with the offer of power sharing to cultivate support among moderate Nationalists. He argues that "the crucial error in this 'twin-track' strategy, stemming from the unwillingness to face the conflicting national questions, was to assume that the militants within each bloc could be suppressed to facilitate a constitutional settlement. This view stemmed ultimately from the wishful thinking that the conflict was purely internal, rather than between Britain and Ireland."[91] According to O'Duffy, Sunningdale failed primarily because it did not address Britain's and Ireland's competing claims to sovereignty.[92] The Irish government failed to dilute or qualify the territorial claim in the Irish constitution, partly because it was not politically secure enough to do so and partly because it still considered unification a realistic objective within fifteen to twenty years. Intent on finding an internal solution, the British did not seriously consider the possibility of "a symmetrical exchange of constitutional claims to sovereignty."[93] The dispute between the two states was eventually made manageable only when their relative status had been made more equal as a result partly of Ireland's growing economic independence, wealth, and membership in the European Economic Community (EEC). O'Duffy does not suggest that shared authority was available in 1973. His analysis does, however, confirm that close Anglo-Irish cooperation was essential to the negotiation of the GFA, and that equally close cooperation may be required to sustain the 1998/2006 accommodation against possible future shocks.

Once they had acknowledged that their first prescription for shared authority was unworkable, McGarry and O'Leary produced an alternative proposal in 1995. This built on the two governments' joint declaration of December 1993 and predicted with some accuracy the main components of the 1998 agreement.[94] While it is important not to read too much into this, O'Leary was one of a group of academics consulted by the Labour opposition in developing its Northern Ireland policies after 1994, and as such might have had some inside access to the policy development process.[95]

There are four main differences between O'Leary's and McGarry's blueprint and the outcome embodied in the GFA. They proposed using the Sainte-Laguë rule rather than d'Hondt for selecting ministers and assembly committee chairs. They wanted the principles of proportionality and power sharing to be enforced at the local as well as the regional government level. They wanted the cultural insignia of both traditions to be either equally protected or equally unused, including national anthems and flags. Finally, they proposed that the British-Irish intergovernmental conference should have the power to veto any law or policy that either government considered fundamentally to threaten the basic rights of either community. They argued that a settlement such as this would achieve the same practical results as shared authority without violating the principle of majority consent. Their subsequent assessment of the GFA is overwhelmingly positive.[96]

## Conclusion: Achievements, False Hopes, and Misunderstandings

Overall, the evidence assembled in this chapter suggests a mixed record of achievement. In relation to their own original objectives, British policies had by the first anniversary of Sunningdale contributed to reforming local government and policing, removing Stormont's paramilitary policing capability, terminating majoritarian rule, and weakening the Unionist Party. They enabled the SDLP and Alliance to emerge as vehicles for expressing nationalist reformism and antisectarian unionism. They also secured an Official IRA cease-fire, demonstrated that the parties of the center could reach an agreement on power sharing, restored the bipartisan consensus at Westminster, and improved relations with Dublin.

On the other hand, local government had transferred most of its powers and responsibilities to unelected quasi-nongovernmental organizations, appointed by British ministers on the advice of their civil servants. Although reformed, the RUC still did not have the capability to deal with the public order and security challenges it faced and had not been accepted by the Nationalist side; the army continued to lead policing republican districts. The new political context created by the dissolution of Stormont had permitted hard-liners to mobilize Unionist resistance to reform and power sharing. The Provisionals had developed the capacity to sustain a paramilitary and propaganda campaign that continued despite a substantial military deployment and determined efforts to weaken it. The power-sharing executive had collapsed and the assembly had been suspended. Larger and more lethal loyalist paramilitary formations had emerged that could successfully resist policies that they strongly opposed. Indices of disorder did not show a convincing and sustained drop until 1977, after the abandonment of the explicit search for a political settlement.

If direct rule contributed anything to the eventual settlement, it was a long time coming and exacted a high price. Both sides perceived the suspension of Stormont as a victory for republican violence, which stimulated both republicans and loyalists toward greater aggression. Direct rule deprived elected representatives of a statutory forum for their aspirations and grievances, removed any remaining possibility of presenting a process of constitutional reform as evolutionary within established institutions, and struck another blow at the Unionist Party as a vehicle for delivering majority assent to a new dispensation. It strengthened Unionist hard-liners, destroyed what remained of Unionists' trust in the British government, yielded a major concession to Nationalism without any return, and led Nationalists and Unionists alike to anticipate further radical steps leading toward unification. Heath presented direct rule as advancing progressive modernizing objectives, but it served the purposes of the British elite rather than the people of Northern Ireland, drew heavily on Britain's historical experiences in managing colonial conflicts,[97] and treated the established institutions of government in Northern Ireland as dispensable once they had ceased to serve Britain's purposes.

While individual agencies drew on their own experiences, the Whitehall system as a whole failed to recognize and hence to avoid dangers that had already been identified in published works by political analysts. British ministers did not comprehend the emotional significance for Nationalist Ireland of the blood sacrifice, or appreciate the complexity of relationships inside republican communities. In 1969 as in 1919, the British responded to insurgency in Ireland with an incoherent combination of conciliation, coercion, and irresolution. They would almost certainly have fared better if they had adhered consistently to the framework of law and due process that they purported to be defending.

Labour and Conservative leaders alike subscribed to the view that the Northern Ireland electorate was more moderate than its political representatives, although they never explained why the electorate voted for candidates who were more extreme than themselves. On the basis of this misperception, Wilson imagined he could steer Unionists into a united Ireland over fifteen years, Whitelaw plotted to detach and build up the liberal wing of the Unionist Party in 1972, and Heath dreamed of constructing a new political dispensation within a year. All these miscalculations had deadly consequences. Faulkner later commented:

> Willie Whitelaw and his team ... misunderstood Ulster politics and applied Westminster attitudes to a different political situation. [Their policy] underestimated the strength of Unionist sentiment and miscalculated the position of the real political "centre," which was represented by my colleagues and I [*sic*]. New parties with a "clean hands" approach could not hope to achieve the political leadership which was necessary in order to deliver support for any settlement. It was some months before the Government came to realize this.[98]

The idea of achieving a stable power-sharing government with an Irish dimension within one or two years was a convenient fantasy, grounded in the unsubstantiated belief that politics in Northern Ireland could be "modernized" within a few years. There was no reason to believe that, with London's political initiative, a left-right divide would replace communal issues as the basis for electoral competition, that border referenda would reorient politics toward an economic and social agenda, that moderate parties would thrive under a new consensual dispensation with PR voting, or that security policies would cease to be controversial simply because London assumed formal responsibility for them. If thirty-six years is a sufficiently long experimental period, Northern Ireland's recent history has demolished all four of these beliefs.

Even when they grasped that the salient issues in Northern Irish politics were constructed around national allegiance and identity, British ministers continued to discount the power and reach of republicanism and unionism as unifying ideologies, to underestimate the strength and resilience of paramilitary formations, to deny the scale and intensity of popular support for them, and to depict the people of Northern Ireland on both sides as irrational. They regarded the conflict as an anachronism that could be cured through a healthy dose of British good sense rather than a largely structural consequence of the partition settlement that London had itself engineered, imposed, and sustained.[99]

When he told the Commons that he had always found the Irish extremely difficult to understand, Heath probably meant to criticize the Irish.[100] But his statement highlighted his own failure to grasp the realities underpinning the conflict. In his memoirs he attributes it to "the bitter, tribal loathing between the hard-line elements in the two communities, springing from an atavism which most of Europe discarded long ago." This "inspired the Protestant majority to discriminate shamelessly against their fellow citizens for almost half a century." Catholics had been "denied adequate housing, jobs and social services, and poorly represented as a result of gerrymandering."[101] From this lofty perspective the fault appeared to lie within unionism only. Modernization was inevitable, and he was its chosen instrument. This self-serving explanation discounted Unionists' fears of abandonment and absorption into a Catholic Irish state; neglected Protestants' experiences of poor housing, unemployment, and unresponsive public services; and swept magisterially over the issue of clashing national identities.

The exasperated condescension of British ministers is apparent in each of the four cases. Wilson dismissed Unionist elected representatives as "atavistic" and "reactionary." An aside in a discussion paper Maudling circulated in November 1971 exclaimed, "If only we were dealing with reasonable people!"[102] In his definitive paper justifying direct rule in March 1972, the home secretary wrote: "Sometimes it seems almost as if the people of Northern Ireland or at any rate their political leaders (which in realistic terms includes the IRA) are possessed of a death wish."[103] The FCO specialized in patronizing the Irish: Bloomfield describes the "patrician arrogance" that even he as a professional colleague and political moderate encountered among British diplomats intent on withdrawing from an expensive and embarrassing commitment without much concern for the views of either side.[104] Ambassador Peck's memoirs show no sympathy for Faulkner's dilemma and disdain for Northern Ireland's established constitutional status.[105] As the British political parties came to see Northern Ireland increasingly as an alien system, they withdrew their support from their sister organizations there. Labour denied affiliation to the NILP and Wilson put his weight behind the SDLP. Heath condemned the Unionist Party as sectarian and asked the chairman of the Conservative Party to consider running candidates against it.

For all their declarations about fairness and democracy, British governments, Labour and Conservative, made clear that they would ignore the wishes of the Northern Ireland electorate if it chose leaders whose views they found unacceptable, or if its elected leaders came up with policy proposals with which they disagreed. They were prepared to suspend Stormont rather than permit Craig or Paisley to take control. They made no secret of their preference for Alliance and the SDLP over the Unionists and the DUP. Whitelaw deliberately introduced constitutional arrangements permitting him to create a government that excluded those whose views, conduct, and character he disliked. British political leaders successively undermined O'Neill, Chichester-Clark, and Faulkner, then complained that there was nobody reasonable available to lead the Unionist community. They dismantled the Ulster Special Constabulary (USC), then abolished the devolved government on the ground that it was incapable of maintaining security without the British army. They banned republican political organizations, so depriving republicans of any nonviolent outlet for their legitimate aspirations.

The first UK representative in Belfast was not wrong when he wrote to the home secretary in 1969, "The basic problem of Anglo-Irish relations down the centuries is that relations with Britain have been at the heart of Irish politics while the Irish problem has always been at the periphery of British interests. . . . For the past hundred years or thereabouts, Ireland has been like a mosquito buzzing about our ears which we have tried from time to time and without much success to swat. We have wished that the Irish problem would go away so that we can concentrate on what interests us."[106] The most consistent element in British policy since 1968 has been the desire to avoid, minimize, or end entanglement in "the Irish bog."

When required to intervene, Britain sought to satisfy the irreconcilable demands of both sides by resorting to diplomatic ambiguity and carefully crafted verbal formulations. On the one hand, ministers affirmed that Northern Ireland was an integral part of the United Kingdom; on the other, that they would not stand in the way of unification if the people of Northern Ireland assented. Although this has seemed fairer than coming down definitively on either side, ambivalence helped to exacerbate and sustain the conflict by encouraging republicans to believe and Unionists to fear that violence and the threat of violence—especially in England— would eventually secure British withdrawal. Unionist hard-liners capitalized on the discrepancy between London's indifference to the Union and the rhetorical enthusiasm with which politicians in Dublin pursued their goal of unification. Republican activists came to believe that the British had no heart for the struggle and would inevitably withdraw as long as the IRA sustained its armed campaign.

Bloomfield concludes that from the 1960s on, successive British governments showed "a lack of firmness in recognizing and addressing the legitimate grievances of substantial numbers of people under their ultimate jurisdiction, succeeded by an ambiguous reaction to the subsequent violence, which has led ultimately to the disastrous radicalisation of Northern Ireland politics."[107] If the inconsistencies in British policies and actions were rooted in irresolution, this was perhaps not so much a moral failing as a consequence of the misperceptions, miscalculations, and false hopes identified in this study.

It is possible to take the argument further. There is at least a credible case to be made that the British government helped to create and sustain the IRA and its campaign of violence through a cumulative sequence of policies, actions, and declarations. In 1969 they stripped the devolved government and police of their authority and introduced British soldiers onto the streets in Catholic districts. In 1970 they failed to give the army strategic political direction and permitted it to pursue the military security approach to policing republican districts. In 1971 they permitted internment on an indiscriminate scale, directed solely at republicans, and authorized the ill treatment of internees. In 1972 they suspended the devolved administration. This encouraged republicans and loyalists to believe that a united Ireland was imminent. Whitelaw then allowed the Provisionals to recoup, rearm, and train an influx of new volunteers. In 1973 the British engineered a power-sharing coalition into being with the promise of cross-border institutions, but from the start this lacked democratic legitimacy. It was opposed by a majority of the Unionist electorate and by republicanism. Its collapse created a governance vacuum in which extremists and paramilitary formations thrived.

Although there is substance to the above criticisms, it has to be asked whether other states would have performed better. Whatever the flaws and inconsistencies in British policy, the mainstream IRA and loyalist campaigns of violence have ended and the main paramilitary organizations have laid down their weapons. Republicanism and loyalism have endorsed the accommodation. Northern Ireland's five main parties are working together in a power-sharing assembly and executive. The Irish government, the Irish electorate, all the significant political parties in the United Kingdom and Ireland, and the republican movement have formally endorsed the principle of majority consent. While the DUP and Sinn Féin as the largest parties on the two sides aspire to irreconcilable models of national integration, they are working together at Stormont on everyday policy issues, including health and education. DUP ministers are operating power-sharing and cross-border institutions; former IRA volunteers are serving as government ministers. In 2010, the leaders of the two parties agreed on arrangements for the devolution of policing and criminal justice.[108] Men Whitelaw depicted as terrorists and bigots have moved into his offices at Stormont Castle. British soldiers have withdrawn, and the army has dismantled its bases.[109] There is robust, enforceable legislation against discrimination, whether in employment or the provision of goods and services. In accordance with the GFA, independent commissions protect equality and human rights.

On the darker side, many of the preconditions for conflict remain much as described in chapter 2. The parties on the two sides of the executive still hold mutually incompatible objectives. Sinn Féin remains committed to ending the union and the DUP to defending it. Both have a track record

of dogged perseverance. Incompatible ideologies have been institutionalized as the basis for party politics. Members of the assembly are required to
register themselves as either Unionist or Nationalist. There is evidence that
political life "is characterized by growing political extremism and diminishing prospects for better community relations."[110] The national question
continues to shape the political agenda and determine positions on salient
issues. Small splinter groups of republican dissidents have demonstrated
their capacity and willingness to kill soldiers and set off bombs, risking
civilian lives. The most dangerous are trying to disrupt civil policing and
to provoke an overreaction from the authorities.[111] In 2009–10, the police
recorded 50 bombing and 79 shooting incidents and 127 casualties as a
result of paramilitary-style attacks; 169 people were arrested for and 36
charged with terrorist offenses.[112]

The heads of the executive parties can lead only so far; that there are now
two well-established parties on each side makes it more difficult to offer
tradeoffs and concessions across the divide. At the community level, most
children are still educated apart. Five years into the GFA, 94 percent of
Protestant children attended de facto Protestant schools, while 92 percent
of Catholic children attended a Catholic school.[113] In public housing, 92.5
percent was segregated.[114] At many urban interfaces there were so-called
peace walls, high barriers constructed to protect each side from attack by
the other; in 2007 they stretched for a total of thirteen miles, predominantly in inner Belfast. Political opinions were as polarized as they had
been forty years earlier, as 75 percent of Catholics described themselves as
Irish rather than British, while 75 percent of Protestants described themselves as British rather than Irish. In party affiliation, 77 percent of Catholics described themselves as closest to Sinn Féin or the SDLP, while 71
percent of Protestants described themselves as closest to the DUP or UUP.
Eighty-nine percent of Protestants wanted to remain part of the United
Kingdom; Catholic opinion was divided, with 39 percent for staying in
the United Kingdom and 47 percent for joining the rest of Ireland.[115] By
way of comparison, in 1968, 76 percent of Catholics described themselves
as Irish rather than British or Ulster, while 71 percent of Protestants described themselves as British or Ulster rather than Irish; at a time when
neither the SDLP nor Sinn Féin existed in their present form, 78 percent
of Catholics described themselves as closest to a Nationalist party or the
NILP, while 79 percent of Protestants described themselves as closest to a
Unionist party.[116]

Support for cross-community parties had declined. In the Stormont
election of 1969, 9.4 percent of electors voted for the NILP or the Ulster
Liberal Party. In the assembly election of June 1973, the first to use PR

voting, this proportion—now including Alliance—rose to 11.9 percent. By the assembly election of March 2007, it had fallen to 7.0 percent, shared between Alliance and the Green Party. As in 1972, elections were contested primarily on issues that divided the electorate along ethnonational lines.

Perhaps the most obvious risk to the accommodation lies in the possibility of a dispute between the two patron states that are its ultimate guarantors. Developments that could destabilize their partnership include economic decline, creating social unrest and curbing public spending; events that allow the opponents of accommodation to exploit popular fears, such as contentious parades; electoral victory in either state for a party allied to one side or the other;[117] the ending of bipartisanship at Westminster; gradual loss of interest by one or both national governments; and a demographic shift, creating the possibility of a majority favoring unification without the acquiescence of unionism. These risks may be increased by continuing dissident violence, elite insecurity caused by fragmentation within parties and the success of rival parties, and failure to resolve thorny issues such as policing policies and the management of Orange parades.

Despite the continuing political divisions, violent events, and dangers, the people of Northern Ireland have clearly benefited from the agreements. Although the Troubles might have been small by international standards, the violence was concentrated over a small geographical area, primarily at the interfaces between republican and loyalist communities. The people who lived there suffered twenty-seven years of violence, fear, and grief. They were denied opportunities that other regions take for granted. For all the policy failures of their first few years, the British government eventually secured a peace deal that offered the IRA a path away from violence, negotiated an agreement that both sides have now accepted, and formally resolved the international border dispute. Since 1998, the region has enjoyed a level of peace, order, and stability unknown for thirty years. There is much to be thankful for.

It should not be concluded that power sharing with an Irish dimension was always the right solution but that 1973 was the wrong time. The agreements of 1998 and 2006 were built on much more complex foundations, notably resolute, persistent, and constrained action by the security forces; close collaboration between the two governments based on a shared vision for an attainable outcome; stringent measures to eliminate discrimination; and high levels of public spending to maintain services, support personal incomes, and create employment.[118] We cannot know whether this outcome or something similar could have been achieved more quickly by other means, or for how long the accommodation will hold. There is a continuing tension in that republicans view the settlement as a staging post toward unification, which Unionists by definition resist.[119] But the ending of the violence makes it at least worth exploring whether there might be lessons in Northern Ireland's experience for other places, and for the development of better approaches to managing and resolving conflict in divided societies.

## Notes

1.    A. Wildavsky, *Speaking Truth to Power: The Art and Craft of Policy Analysis* (Boston: Little, Brown, 1979), 10.

2.    M.T. Fay, M. Morrissey, M. Smyth, and T. Wong, *The Cost of the Troubles Study: Report on the Northern Ireland Survey: The Experience and Impact of the Troubles* (Londonderry: INCORE, 1999).

3.    P. Bew, *Ireland: The Politics of Enmity 1789–2006* (Oxford: Oxford University Press, 2007), 496.

4.    K. Bloomfield, *A Tragedy of Errors* (Liverpool: Liverpool University Press 2007), 20.

5.    C.E.B. Brett, *Long Shadows Cast Before* (London: Bartholomew, 1978), 139.

6.    P. Dixon, *Northern Ireland: The Politics of War and Peace* (New York: Palgrave, 2001), 103.

7.    M. Hayes, *Minority Verdict* (Belfast: Blackstaff, 1995), 132. Hayes was at the time chair of the Northern Ireland Community Relations Commission.

8.    T. Hennessey, *The Evolution of the Troubles 1970–1972* (Dublin: Irish Academic Press, 2007), 345.

9.    Ministry of Defence, "Operation Banner: An Analysis of Military Operations in Northern Ireland," Ministry of Defence internal paper, July 2006.

10.    M. Carver, *Out of Step: Memoirs of a Field-Marshal* (London: Hutchison, 1989), 408.

11.    DEFE 23/160, Stephens to Moore, January 21, 1972.

12.    Parker Report: *Report of the Committee of Privy Counsellors Appointed to Consider Authorised Procedures for the Interrogation of Persons Suspected of Terrorism,* Cmnd. 4901 (London: HMSO, 1972), paragraph 20.

13.    Ministry of Defence, "Operation Banner."

14.    Hennessey, *Evolution of the Troubles,* 221.

15.    B. Faulkner, *Memoirs of a Statesman* (London: Weidenfeld and Nicholson, 1978), 197.

16.    Ibid., 202.

17.    D. Hamill, *Pig in the Middle: The Army in Northern Ireland, 1969–1985* (London: Methuen, 1985), 69.

18.    In a personal interview with the author, one senior civil servant at the heart of the decision-making process in Stormont at the time described the notion that Faulkner was giving the army orders as "absolute balls—a face-saver." Army commanders were never in any doubt that their political direction came from Westminster.

19.    Cited in M.A. Murphy, *Gerry Fitt: Political Chameleon* (Cork: Mercia, 2007), 180.

20.    K. Peroff and C. Hewitt, "Rioting in Northern Ireland: The Effects of Different Policies," *Journal of Conflict Resolution,* vol. 24, no. 4 (1980), 608.

21.    Ministry of Defence, "Operation Banner."

22. Carver, *Out of Step*, 423.

23. Ministry of Defence, "Operation Banner."

24. M. Smyth, "Lost Lives," in M. Cox, A. Guelke, and F. Stephen, eds., *A Farewell to Arms* (Manchester: Manchester University Press, 2006), 8.

25. Ministry of Defence, "Operation Banner."

26. J.D. Steinbruner, *The Cybernetic Theory of Decision* (Princeton, NJ: Princeton University Press, 1974), 117.

27. CAB130/561, Annex 4 to Whitelaw's note of October 3, 1972. Dugdale's perspective was unusual. Born and educated in England, he was a Greek scholar and published poet of distinction.

28. Bloomfield, *Tragedy of Errors*, 43.

29. See, e.g., A. Jackson, *Home Rule and Irish History* (London: Phoenix, 2004), 316.

30. M. Kerr, *Imposing Power-Sharing: Conflict and Co-Existence in Northern Ireland and Lebanon* (Dublin: Irish Academic Press, 2005), 62. Interviewed by Kerr, Hume described the SDLP's influence over Dublin at the time as "total."

31. B. White, *John Hume: Statesman of the Troubles* (Belfast: Blackstaff, 1984), 152.

32. Obituary of Dermot Nally, *The Times*, February 19, 2010.

33. M. Hayes, *Minority Verdict: Experiences of a Catholic Public Servant* (Belfast: Blackstaff, 1995), 202.

34. Cited in P. Bew, H. Patterson, and P. Teague, *Between War and Peace: The Political Future of Northern Ireland* (London: Lawrence and Wishart, 1997), 40.

35. See, e.g., T. Hennessey, *A History of Northern Ireland 1920–1996* (Basingstoke: Macmillan, 1997).

36. PREM 16/231, memorandum by Robert Armstrong, March 4, 1974.

37. Detailed accounts of the UWC strike and the fall of the executive are given in R. Fisk, *The Point of No Return* (London: Deutsch, 1975), and P. Devlin, *The Fall of the Northern Ireland Executive* (Belfast: Devlin, 1975).

38. Bew, *Politics of Enmity*, 518.

39. The New Ireland Forum Report is available at http://cain.ulst.ac.uk/issues/politics/nifr.htm (accessed October 16, 2010).

40. This is not a huge claim, as Wilson, Heath, and Callaghan all personally favored reunification. Thatcher's unionism owed more to her English Nationalism than to affection for the Unionist Party.

41. For an account of interdepartmental differences in Whitehall over the 1985 agreement, see Bew, Patterson, and Teague, *Between War and Peace*, 53.

42. Dixon, *Northern Ireland*, 205.

43. The number of Northern Ireland's seats at Westminster increased from twelve to seventeen in June 1983. Ironically, in view of Wilson's track record on the matter, this was agreed by a Labour government under Jim Callaghan. The Unionists' gesture proved costly in that they lost one seat, to SDLP deputy leader Seamus Mallon.

44. Senator Robinson went on to become president of Ireland in 1990 and UN high commissioner for human rights in 1997.

45. B. O'Leary and J. McGarry, *The Politics of Antagonism: Understanding Northern Ireland* (London: Athlone Press, 1996), 238.

46. *Irish Times*, November 4, 1989.

47.    Dixon, *Northern Ireland*, 225.

48.    DUP paper for Brooke-Mayhew Talks, cited in T. Hennessey, *The Northern Ireland Peace Process* (Dublin: Gill and Macmillan, 2000), 63.

49.    British and Irish governments, The Downing Street Declaration, December 15, 1993, available through www.cain.ulst.ac.uk/events/peace/docs (accessed September 15, 2010).

50.    *Irish Times,* November 4, 1989.

51.    At Sunningdale the Irish had been represented by a Fine Gael government, traditionally less Nationalist in orientation.

52.    Hennessey, *Peace Process*, 84.

53.    The full text of the Framework Documents is reprinted in Cox, Guelke, and Stephen, *Farewell to Arms*, 496–507. Paragraphs 24 to 38 cover the north-south institutions.

54.    E. Moloney, *A Secret History of the IRA* (London: Penguin, 2002), 441.

55.    This agreement has become popularly known as the Good Friday Agreement, although many Unionists prefer to call it the Belfast Agreement.

56.    For fuller accounts of the negotiating process and the 1998 agreement, see Dixon, *Northern Ireland*; P. Bew, P. Gibbon, and H. Patterson, *The State in Northern Ireland 1921–72* (Manchester: Manchester University Press, 1979); and H. Patterson, *Ireland since 1939: The Persistence of Conflict* (Dublin: Penguin, 2006). For more comprehensive assessments of the agreement, its implementation, and implications, see A. Aughey, *The Politics of Northern Ireland: Beyond the Belfast Agreement* (London: Routledge, 2005); and Cox, Guelke, and Stephen, *A Farewell to Arms*.

57.    Bew, *Politics of Enmity,* 549.

58.    Evidence from exit polls suggests that 96 percent of Catholics and 55 percent of Protestants favored the agreement. Anticipating the danger that a majority of Protestants might reject it, Blair published an open letter on the morning of the referendum, to the effect that Sinn Féin could be in the devolved executive only if the IRA ended all forms of paramilitary violence and the threat of violence. This condition was not part of the agreement and Blair was not in a position to deliver on this undertaking.

59.    The proximate reason for the final collapse was an allegation that republicans had planted a spy at the heart of the devolved government. In a curious twist, the alleged spy, a Sinn Féin administrator at Stormont, Denis Donaldson, was later unmasked as a British informer. He was shot in April 2006; it is a republican tradition to execute informers.

60.    Personal interviews by the author with British officials, December 2004.

61.    The two governments also reported continuing evidence of IRA criminality. For example, £26.5 million was stolen from the Northern Bank in Belfast in December 2004, and republican Robert McCartney was murdered, apparently by IRA members, in February 2005.

62.    In reality there was no Plan B (personal interviews by the author with British officials, December 2004).

63.    As far as the internal arrangements within Northern Ireland were concerned, the changes consisted of largely presentational gains for the DUP at no real cost to Sinn Féin. The d'Hondt system continued for the selection of ministers and committee chairs; the first minister was still required to share power with a deputy first minister from the other side; and assembly members still had to designate themselves as Unionist, Nationalist, or other. Perhaps the most significant change was that the first and deputy first ministers would no

longer have to be selected jointly with explicit cross-community support. The changes in the north-south arrangements gave Sinn Féin some modest gains, which were matched by parallel steps to strengthen the east-west framework.

64.   See J. Whyte, *Interpreting Northern Ireland* (Oxford: Clarendon Press, 1990), 224.

65.   Two loyalist political parties associated with paramilitary organizations—the Progressive Unionist Party and the Ulster Democratic Party—were included in the talks that resulted in the 1998 agreement. Unlike the DUP, they stayed in the process after Sinn Féin joined.

66.   A further distinction is that the 2006 agreement was between the two governments, reached after consultation with the Northern Irish parties. While the governments presented it as if it were a multiparty agreement, the DUP announced that they had neither signed it nor committed themselves to its implementation.

67.   For a detailed if self-serving account of Blair's personal role in the talks process, see J. Powell, *Great Hatred, Little Room: Making Peace in Northern Ireland* (London: Bodley Head, 2008).

68.   See, e.g., D. Trimble, *To Raise Up a New Northern Ireland* (Belfast: Belfast Press, 2001), 1.

69.   Personal interview by the author with senior British officials, December 2004.

70.   The text of the 1998 agreement was circulated to voters in Northern Ireland and is reprinted in Cox, Guelke, and Stephen, *Farewell to Arms*, 459–83.

71.   R. McCartney, *Reflections on Liberty, Democracy, and the Union* (Dublin: Maunsel, 2001), 202.

72.   UTV news report, February 20, 2010.

73.   Eamon McCann, *Belfast Telegraph*, November 6, 2008.

74.   R. Rose, *Governing without Consensus* (London: Faber, 1971), 21.

75.   R. Rose, *Northern Ireland: Time of Choice* (Washington, DC: American Enterprise Institute, 1976), 62.

76.   Dixon, *Northern Ireland*, 154–57.

77.   Hennessey, *Peace Process*, 18.

78.   A. Alcock, "Northern Ireland: Some European Comparisons," in B. Hadfield, ed., *Northern Ireland Politics and the Constitution* (Buckingham: Open University Press, 1992), 160.

79.   For a fuller discussion of these criteria, see chapters 1 and 9.

80.   J. McGarry and B. O'Leary, *Explaining Northern Ireland* (Oxford: Blackwell, 1995), 324–26.

81.   See, e.g., P. O'Malley, *The Uncivil Wars: Ireland Today* (Belfast: Blackstaff, 1983), 205–06; M. Tomlinson, "Walking Backwards into the Sunset: British Policy and the Insecurity of Northern Ireland," in D. Miller, ed., *Rethinking Northern Ireland*, (Essex: Addison-Wesley Longman, 1998).

82.   Bew, Gibbon, and Patterson, *Northern Ireland*, 162.

83.   M. Cunningham, *British Government Policy in Northern Ireland 1969–2000* (Manchester: Manchester University Press, 2001), 154. This is also the view of Dixon, *Northern Ireland*, 284.

84.   Comprehensive academic assessments of the various theoretical solutions are set out in Whyte, *Interpreting Northern Ireland*, chapter 10; and O'Leary and McGarry, *The Politics of Antagonism*, chapter 8. From time to time ministers have reviewed the options again and reached the same conclusion.

85.   D. Birrell, *Direct Rule and the Governance of Northern Ireland* (Manchester: Manchester University Press, 2009), 243. This is a comprehensive account of direct rule as a distinctive system of administration.

86.   The amount by which total public spending exceeded taxes and revenues collected in Northern Ireland—over 20 percent of the region's gross domestic product (Northern Ireland Department of Finance and Personnel statistics).

87.   McGarry and O'Leary, *Explaining Northern Ireland*, 371.

88.   B. O'Leary, T. Lyne, J. Marshall, and B. Rowthorne, *Northern Ireland: Shared Authority* (London: Institute for Public Policy Research, 1993); McGarry and O'Leary, *Explaining Northern Ireland*, 370–72; O'Leary and McGarry, *Politics of Antagonism*, 287–95. For a critique see P. Mitchell, "Futures," in P. Mitchell and R. Wilford, eds., *Politics in Northern Ireland* (Oxford: Westview, 1999), 276–81.

89.   Mitchell has argued that this is disingenuous of O'Leary and McGarry, since Unionists calculate that irrespective of any hypothetical vote on unification, they cannot be coerced into a united Ireland. See Mitchell, "Futures."

90.   B. O'Leary, "The Character of the 1998 Agreement: Results and Prospects," in R. Wilford, ed., *Aspects of the Belfast Agreement* (Oxford: Oxford University Press, 2001), 49.

91.   B. O'Duffy, *British-Irish Relations and Northern Ireland: From Violent Politics to Conflict Regulation* (Dublin: Irish Academic Press, 2007), 92.

92.   Ibid., 96.

93.   Ibid., 102.

94.   See McGarry and O'Leary, *Explaining Northern Ireland*, 374–75.

95.   His contribution is acknowledged with others' in M. Mowlam, *Momentum: The Struggle for Peace, Politics, and the People* (London: Hodder and Stroughton, 2002), 18. Mowlam was appointed secretary of state when Labour returned to office in 1997.

96.   For a comprehensive defense of the GFA against all major lines of attack, see McGarry and O'Leary, "Argument" and "Response," in R. Taylor, ed., *Consociational Theory: McGarry and O'Leary and the Northern Ireland Conflict* (London: Routledge, 2009).

97.   For a detailed analysis of British strategy in Malaya, Kenya, and British Guiana, see F. Furedi, *Colonial Wars and the Politics of Third World Nationalism* (London: Taurus, 1994).

98.   Faulkner, *Memoirs*, 175–76.

99.   See, e.g., Dixon, *Northern Ireland*, 2001.

100.   Hansard 6, vol. 87, col. 898, November 27, 1985.

101.   E. Heath, *The Course of My Life: My Autobiography* (London: Hodder and Stoughton, 1998), 422.

102.   CAB 130/522, note by officials circulated under Maudling's minutes of November 10, 1971.

103.   PREM 15/1003, Maudling, memorandum of March 3, 1972.

104.   Bloomfield, *Tragedy of Errors*, 219.

105.   J. Peck, *Dublin from Downing Street* (Dublin: Gill and Macmillan, 1978), 135.

106.   CJ 3/18, Oliver Wright to the Home Secretary, October 19, 1969.

107.   Bloomfield, *Tragedy of Errors*, 238.

108.   The RUC was reconstituted and restructured as the Police Service of Northern Ireland (PSNI) in November 2001. Northern Ireland's stringent equality legislation was al-

tered to permit recruitment procedures that guaranteed that at least 50 percent of new officers come from a Catholic background.

109. The security service MI5 retains a substantial presence in Northern Ireland. In 2007 it took over responsibility for antiterrorist intelligence activity as part of the arrangements for devolving responsibility for policing.

110. A. Oberschall and L.K. Palmer, "The Failure of Moderate Politics: The Case of Northern Ireland," in I. O'Flynn and D. Russell, eds., *Power Sharing: New Challenges for Divided Societies* (London: Pluto, 2005), 81.

111. Independent Monitoring Commission, *Twenty-First Report,* HC 496 (London: HMSO, 2009).

112. Police Service of Northern Ireland, *Annual Statistical Report No. 5*, April 2009–March 2010, available at www.psni.police.uk.

113. B.C. Hayes, I. McAllister, and L. Dowds, "In Search of the Middle Ground: Integrated Education and Northern Ireland Politics," research update, April 2006, available through www.ark.ac.uk (accessed September 15, 2010).

114. *The Independent*, April 6, 2004.

115. Northern Ireland Life and Times Survey 2007, available through www.ark.ac.uk (accessed September 15, 2010).

116. Rose, *Governing without Consensus*, 235 and 485. (The Protestant figure excludes those who said they were closest to the NILP.)

117. For the 2010 Westminster election the Unionist Party and the Conservative Party jointly selected candidates, prompting the one remaining Unionist MP at Westminster to leave the party in protest and stand successfully as an Independent.

118. For a detailed account of supporting economic policies, see Cunningham, *British Government Policy.*

119. Unionists see the agreements as final, although the DUP would like to improve the devolved structures and processes, for example by reducing the number of departments and replacing mandatory with voluntary coalitions.

# 9

# Lessons?

*Try again. Fail again. Fail better.*     —Samuel Beckett[1]

Toward the end of his seminal account of political violence in Ireland from 1919 to 1921, Charles Townshend offers this assessment: "British government in Ireland has shown the uncanny knack of getting the worst of both worlds; of appearing to rest on force while seldom exerting enough force to secure real control. By contrast, armed resisters have repeatedly used 'physical force' as an adjunct to 'moral insurrection' and secured the benefit of both combined."[2]

In surveying the strategic options open to governments, I described in chapter 1 a common pattern of events that matches closely the sequence of events in Northern Ireland from August 1969 to July 1972. First, the state responded to peaceful protest with limited concessions. These failed to stop the disorder. The authorities then reacted to renewed disturbances with a rhetorical emphasis on law and order and increasing coercion. Factions among the protesters yielded, but a committed minority organized clandestinely and attempted to secure popular support for inflating the limited protest into internal war. A spiral of insurgency began, in which state repression and rebel violence fed off each other. Then the state, having driven its opponents underground, inflamed their enmity, and cemented their organization, suddenly relaxed its coercion and reverted to a policy of concessions.[3]

As in the earlier period described by Townshend, the Irish Republican Army (IRA) directly challenged the authority of the British state, attacked its moderate Nationalist rivals, and successfully provoked coercive responses from the security forces, so escalating the conflict and narrowing policymakers' options. In both periods, Britain responded with a military security approach including curfews, mass searching, and internment. This was demonstrably counterproductive and strengthened the rebels.

In 1919, London clung to the belief that most Irish people were not intrinsically hostile to Britain but that many had been intimidated or misled into supporting extremism. On this assumption, ministers built a two-track strategy of suppressing insurgents while offering concessions to moderates. But "no real attempt was made to assess the strength and outlook, or even to prove the existence, of this moderate group on which the whole policy hinged. . . . The dual policy also faced the formidable difficulty, shown by all guerrilla experience, of rooting out extremists without injuring the ordinary population."[4] Bloomfield makes a similar point: "For much of the nineteenth century, British treatment of Ireland swung like a pendulum between coercion and concession. . . . An administration unswervingly stern in its principles and actions might have inspired fear and obedience; an administration consistently benign in its approach and methods might have inspired loyalty and affection."[5]

The earlier pattern repeated itself in the spiral of violence in Northern Ireland between 1969 and 1972. The policy pendulum swung in February 1971 toward coercion and again in February 1972 toward concession. When the first British soldiers were killed, UK ministers permitted the army to adopt a series of increasingly repressive and indiscriminate tactics against a community misperceived as universally republican; after Bloody Sunday, the emphasis swung back to conciliating nationalism. There was a parallel inconsistency in the army's routines. As one set of soldiers roughed people up in the streets and in their homes, others tried to win hearts and minds and to divert young people toward constructive leisure activities. These contradictions in strategy and operations undermined ministers' own propaganda efforts, demoralized the security forces, encouraged the IRA to believe that victory was in sight, and led loyalist counterinsurgents to develop their own paramilitary structures.

The analysis in the previous chapters confirms Townshend's argument from Irish history and the findings of previous cross-national studies, that coercive actions by state security forces are themselves a major cause of disorder. When spontaneous protests provoke coercive responses, the result is likely to be more capable and resilient insurgent organizations. The state then has to make more concessions—possibly including changes in the constitution itself—to restore order. There is a recurring pattern in the evolution of policy toward violent conflict. First, disorder occurs and the state intervenes to pacify it. When the violence increases, policy shifts toward coercion. When that also fails, the state offers to negotiate changes in the rules of the game by altering the constitution. If this offer is rejected, the authorities conclude that the problem is insoluble and settle for merely managing it. Where the violence is cross-communal, they offer limited concessions to whichever side threatens to cause the greatest damage. The swings of the pendulum continue until one side yields or both tire of the struggle.

The above dynamic suggests another lesson: that it is important to identify the risk of such a spiral as early as possible, take steps to reduce it, and avoid any actions that increase it. When all other avenues have been exhausted and there is no alternative to coercion, it should be used discriminately, avoiding overreaction and minimizing confrontation. Coercion should stay as close as possible to the norms and procedures of rights-based civil policing. If as a last resort, because of an inability or failure to provide a sufficient force of suitably trained and equipped police officers, soldiers have to be used, their routines and behavior should as far as possible reflect the routines and values of civil policing. Popular perceptions will be formed in the first hundred days of a military intervention, and they will be crucial to its outcome.[6]

There is a third lesson. The agencies of the state are each equipped to discharge specific functions. In crude terms, police forces exist to enforce the law, civil servants to implement political decisions within an established constitutional framework, armies to fight wars, diplomats to negotiate with other states. So ministers will get a different solution depending on which agency they select to tackle a problem. Mainstream civil servants will tend to favor the status quo or limited reforms; armies to apply coercive routines; diplomats to seek negotiated solutions; intelligence services to gather information, infiltrate, and conduct covert operations; constitutional lawyers to propose institutional change. Thus, when the Home Office took the lead, the response was to reform policing without encroaching any more than ministers demanded onto the territory of the Northern Ireland government. The army adopted a military security approach built from prior routines and organizational doctrine and, when this failed, pressed ministers to free them from the constraint of propping up the Unionist government. When Heath turned to the Foreign and Commonwealth Office (FCO) for advice in August 1971, the emphasis shifted to negotiating an agreed-upon approach with the Irish state. In the fourth case study, the creation of the Northern Ireland Office (NIO) was intended to integrate all these organizational perspectives within a single comprehensive campaign success. So it is important for ministers—or the equivalent political level policymakers in other jurisdictions—to choose carefully which arms of the state to deploy, and to ensure that they are properly oriented and equipped for their tasks. If more than one agency is used, ministers also need to implement clear arrangements governing how they work together so that there are no gaps and they are not undermining each other.

## The Ministry of Defence Review

I have identified three general lessons for policymakers facing any challenge of sustained internal disorder. In 2006, the Ministry of Defence (MoD) published a review of Operation Banner, the army's thirty-seven-year-long intervention in Northern Ireland, to identify lessons specifically for the army for similar campaigns in the future. The review report concludes that there were few directly repeatable but many general lessons for future operations.[7] It highlights the importance of understanding local culture, accurate and timely intelligence, the integration of policies and operations across all government agencies, and the capacity to adapt quickly in response to events.

### Local Culture

The republican community accorded the IRA a status and legitimacy comparable with that of a national army. Many British commanders, especially those in Northern Ireland on short spells of duty, never fully grasped this or understood the "deep-seated beliefs, myths and feelings held by the local population."[8] Because of this, the authorities failed to conduct an effective propaganda campaign. The report concludes that this was their greatest mistake. It allowed the Provisionals to exploit popular resentments without any credible response.

Those on the MoD review team do not seem to have fully absorbed their own lesson. Rather than concluding that the people of Northern Ireland might have had a valid perspective on the world, they comment: "They showed a strong tendency towards intransigence and entrenched views. . . . Moderate political opinion, compromise and often logic has largely been marginalised."[9] This suggests a further learning point. It is not enough simply to have an intellectual awareness of the importance of local culture; it is vital also to work with the grain of community traditions and values, however outmoded and irrational they may appear. Restoring peace should not be confused with imposing one's own worldview.

### Intelligence

The MoD report emphasizes the importance of gathering, sharing, and acting on full and accurate intelligence: "The insurgency could not have been broken, and the terrorist structure could not have been engaged and finally driven into politics without the intelligence organisations and processes that were developed."[10] The process of building an effective intelligence infrastructure began only after internment. Royal Ulster Constabulary (RUC) Special Branch had never been fully equipped for the challenges it faced, and the Hunt reforms had further incapacitated it. The Ulster Special Constabulary (USC), which had been an important source of routine information, had been disbanded, and the Ulster Defence Regiment (UDR), which replaced it, was not allowed any role in gathering intelligence, even at the lowest level. UK ministers refused to share their security service capabilities with the devolved administration. Once the Unionists were out of the way, however, the path was clear for a more intensive effort.[11] After the introduction of direct rule, there was a rapid expansion in the numbers of UK personnel employed in intelligence collection, analysis, and dissemination.

The corollary, also noted in the report, is that many of the methods used at first were intrusive and counterproductive. Individuals were stopped and searched by soldiers in the streets or detained for screening. Social gathering places, such as public bars, were aggressively checked. However useful these methods might have been in gathering information, they cost community support, itself a vital ingredient in  intelligence gathering.

*Integration*

One of UK ministers' most egregious mistakes was their failure to act on "the need for substantive, multi-agency action . . . in order to address the underlying causes of the unrest."[12] Before direct rule, no effective action was taken to coordinate the activities of the security forces with the civil administration or to reduce Nationalists' alienation from Stormont. Wilson and Callaghan made no secret of the fact that they had forced the Unionists to reform. Consequently, when the IRA forced the pace in spring 1971, the authorities could not produce a coherent strategic response. As we saw in chapter 5, commanders lobbied hard to transfer responsibility for security away from Stormont in the hope that direct rule would create a single unitary source of political authority and strategy. But direct rule did not live up to their expectations. Successive secretaries of state insisted on doing things for political reasons without factoring in their security implications. Whitelaw, for example, would release batches of internees, who went on to reoffend: "The terrorists took advantage of this confusion and viewed it as a sign of weakness."[13]

One conclusion that the MoD report does not set out is that commanders' expectations of what could be achieved through the creation of a unified chain of command were never realistic. Northern Ireland in the 1970s could not be placed under military rule as Cyprus had been in the 1950s. The high-level political development work of the NIO was intrinsically complex and untidy. Solutions had to be negotiated rather than imposed.

Since a purely military solution was impossible, diplomats and politicians were required to practice their subtle arts, more nebulous than soldiering, and this inevitably had an impact on security policies and operations.

### Learning

The review stresses the importance of organizational learning: "Conflict is complex, adversarial and evolutionary, which suggests that in the longer term the advantage goes to the side whose military and non-military processes adapt and evolve fastest."[14] The army gradually evolved new tactics for dealing with recurrent problems such as street riots, gun ambushes, and roadside bombs. Mass rioting, for example, was eventually countered by the skillful placement of shield walls, containing rioters on their home ground to reduce property damage, moving in on them from behind, allowing routes for them to disperse, and restricting the use of tear gas and baton rounds. There were similar developments in covert operations. More suitable light armored vehicles were produced and helicopters used to cover ground patrols. In some areas, the entire population was subjected to movement controls and surveillance.

The army started to gain the evolutionary advantage once it had developed "a very closely linked loop responsible for the development of counter terrorist response measures, all of whose components were effectively under command of HQ Northern Ireland."[15] This included all aspects of intelligence, forensics, research and development, tactical and organizational innovation, the conduct of operations, procurement, training, review, and feedback. Commanders may not have been able to persuade their ministerial masters to create a single campaign authority or to stop acting like politicians, but they did manage to improve coordination of the elements that were already under their control.

## Lessons: Political Development Strategy

### Comparable Cases?

I have identified a number of general lessons for the management and resolution of political violence and for security policies. They are potentially applicable to any internal conflict. What about political development?

John Darby, one of the first scholarly commentators from Northern Ireland to attempt a balanced account of the preconditions for the Troubles, has warned that "any theory which is not based on a painstaking analysis of the Ulster background . . . cannot hope to understand either the nuances or the essence of the problem. This applies to decision-makers as well as to researchers. . . . Northern Ireland is at least as remarkable for its peculiarities as for its general characteristics."[16] Constitutional solutions must address the discrete circumstances of each individual case. Before considering what lessons there might be for political development strategies in other regions, we should establish whether Northern Ireland is in fact comparable and, if so, on what basis.

Political historians who have written about the conflict favor comparisons with Ireland at an earlier period rather than with other places. As we have seen, Townshend's analytic approach to history enables us to identify recurrent patterns of behavior, from which later policymakers could have learned. A.T.Q. Stewart has identified repetitive patterns in communal rioting in Northern Ireland and in the policy responses to them, such as tinkering with the police: "If they were unarmed it was recommended that they should be armed; if they used their arms, it was recommended that they should be disarmed."[17]

Ethnonational division, political violence, and instability are not so exceptional, however, and our four case studies have served to validate the findings of cross-national research as outlined in chapter 1. But even if we accept that comparative analysis in political science has helped to identify the preconditions for and dynamic of the conflict in Northern Ireland, it remains a matter of debate how much this theoretical knowledge can contribute to designing workable solutions. The sources of the conflict may be similar, but there are many other variables working to determine its outcomes, including the capacities and calculations of the insurgent organizations, changing public attitudes, the behavior of external actors, and the economic and cultural contexts. Key individuals and events too can change the course of history.

Standing up for political science and its quest for regularities, McGarry and O'Leary have insisted that Northern Ireland *is* properly comparable with other deeply divided regions in terms both of diagnosis and prescription. They classify the conflict as an ethnonational war like those in Lebanon, Cyprus, and Sri Lanka.[18] From a similar theoretical perspective, O'Duffy argues that cases comparable to Northern Ireland are to be found, but found only "where one or more external states have national sovereignty disputes over territory, governance and civil, cultural rights of individuals and 'identity' groups."[19] He cites Palestine, Kashmir, Sri Lanka, Cyprus, and Lebanon.

On the other side of the argument, David Trimble counsels caution, identifying a number of important differences between Northern Ireland and Palestine.[20] The Irish republican movement had a stable integrated paramilitary and political command structure for over twenty-five years, whereas the Palestinian leadership has been too fragmented even to engage in a coherent process of negotiation. After 1972, the two external state actors involved, Britain and Ireland, had a shared vision for achieving stability and ending the violence, whereas Israel and its neighbors did not. The British state has had a much more substantial power advantage over the IRA than Israel has had over its assembled enemies.

Other differences are that in Northern Ireland the two sides have much in common. Both are Christian and English-speaking, share cultural norms and values, and have lived on the island under common institutions of law and government since the seventeenth century. There is a relatively high level of integration in geography, at work, and in civil society, higher education, shopping, and leisure activities. There have always been open elections and considerable freedom of expression. The British state has sustained economic activity at a relatively high level, has administered the region with relative equity and efficiency, and has patiently pursued a political settlement. The Irish government has never been in a position to challenge Britain militarily or itself to assume responsibility for the resolution of the conflict.

From the debate to date it seems fair to conclude that useful lessons can be identified and potentially transferred from Northern Ireland, but that this must be done with care and discrimination, accounting for all relevant preconditions and contextual factors. Some lessons are more likely to apply to future outbreaks in Northern Ireland than to other regions. Many are at a high level of generality. Some are tactical. Some relate to the process of and conduct of negotiations, which is beyond the scope of this book.

One of the lessons that is commonly drawn is that the accommodation in Northern Ireland offers a model settlement that other regions might usefully adapt to their own circumstances. In the light of what has been said above, it is important to register the limits to this claim. The changes agreed to in 1998 to Northern Ireland's constitutional architecture were clearly not solely responsible for ending the violence. British agents and intermediaries had been talking in secret to IRA leaders about the terms of a possible peace deal at least as early as 1986, and the IRA's campaign of sustained violence had effectively ended by 1994. Indeed, the republican movement had begun a gradual transition toward electoral politics in 1981, with the adoption of the "Armalite and the ballot box" strategy.[21] This shift can be traced back to the electoral success of IRA prison hunger striker Bobby Sands MP, and over time reflected the security services' increasing ability to infiltrate the IRA, cut off its arms supplies, and disrupt its operations.

Nor is it the case that the British army ever defeated the IRA militarily. Rather, in its own words, "it achieved its desired end-state, which allowed a political process to be established without unacceptable levels of intimidation. Security force operations suppressed the level of violence to a level which the population could live with, and with which the RUC and later the PSNI [Police Service of Northern Ireland] could cope. The violence was reduced to an extent which made it clear to the PIRA [the Provisionals] that they would not win through violence."[22] Cooperation between the Irish and British states further limited the IRA's capacity to achieve its objectives, and this was institutionalized in the Anglo-Irish Agreement of 1985. The British then opened up an opportunity to talk privately, initially through intermediaries, which offered the IRA an avenue toward peace without the indignity of surrender, and substantial rewards for abandoning violence. The offer was eventually accepted by the dominant faction in republicanism but created a split in the movement that persists.

The talks led eventually to the 1998 agreement. It was not created by political scientists from some blueprint derived from the academic literature on consociationalism but grew through tough negotiations involving the two governments, the IRA, and the political parties. The agenda for the negotiations was driven by events, political and diplomatic pressures, and other factors. The talks covered a wide range of disputed issues, not merely the architecture of political institutions and electoral systems. But political science, the evidence base, and lessons for practice that researchers have accumulated since 1968 clearly contributed to the crafting of the two governments' framework documents, and these in turn closely foreshadowed the institutional components in the agreement. The possibility of a consociational or similar accommodation provided an exit route from violence for the IRA and arrangements tolerable to both sides for the governance of a territory the national status of which continues to be disputed.

If Northern Ireland has benefited from research in other regions, what contribution can it offer to refining theories of conflict resolution and management? Given the status of consociational theory as a dominant paradigm for work on deeply divided societies, let us consider the lessons claimed by writers from that tradition. Does Northern Ireland's experience support the argument that consociational theory delivers the best solutions for comparable conflicts?

## Consociationalism

McGarry and O'Leary examined a comprehensive series of possible constitutional solutions and concluded that "consociation is the best means of stabilizing the Northern Ireland conflict, on the grounds of equity and of adherence to democratic values."[23] Even in regions where consociation had to be imposed, they argued that it was preferable to the likely alternatives of internal war or the repression of one community by the other. It offered a workable alternative to repartition or federation in regions like Northern Ireland where the two sides were demographically intermingled. It did not require them to abandon their national allegiances or adopt a shared vision of the good society, merely to agree to work together in the routine business of government.

McGarry and O'Leary acknowledged Lijphart's conclusion that most of the conditions required for consociation to work were conspicuously absent from Northern Ireland.[24] In a tribute to the Dutch master's seminal work, they called their 1993 volume on Northern Ireland *The Politics of Antagonism*, which they described as an attempt to understand why the region had failed to develop a "politics of accommodation." Lijphart had identified a number of conditions "conducive to the establishment and maintenance of consociational democracy," namely, a commitment by the political leaders of the two communities to maintain and improve the political system; political cohesion within each of the communities; a tradition of elite accommodation; external threats that the communities perceive as a common danger; a multiple balance of power among the communities, so that they are of roughly equal size and none has a majority; a multiparty system with segmental parties; some overarching loyalties, such as a common sense of national identity; and an absence of extreme socioeconomic inequalities between the communities.[25]

As we have seen, most of these conditions were not satisfied in Northern Ireland.[26] The political leaders of the two sides do not have a shared commitment to maintain and improve the political system, neither side favors power sharing within the United Kingdom as its first choice, and organizations on both sides have been willing to use disorder and violence to advance their constitutional objectives. The Social Democratic and Labour Party (SDLP) and Sinn Féin want to end the union, while Unionists have variously preferred a return to majority rule, full integration with the United Kingdom, or independence. Sinn Féin ministers remain resolved to detaching Northern Ireland from Britain as quickly as practicable, and the party's MPs do not take their seats at Westminster. Democratic Unionist Party (DUP) ministers participate in meetings of the north-south ministerial council but remain determined to resist any developments that might be interpreted as moving toward unification by stealth.

As regards political cohesion, the leaders of each community must be able to compromise with each other without losing the support of their activists and voters. Unionist leaders O'Neill, Chichester-Clark, Faulkner, and Trimble all lost their leadership positions because their party was internally fragmented and fissiparous. On the Nationalist side, the SDLP succeeded in bringing together the various strands of constitutional nationalism, but it has struggled to reconcile its Nationalist and social democratic tendencies in the context of criticism from hard-line republicans for being "Catholic Unionists." Northern Ireland now has a dual two-party system, characterized by intense competition between the two main parties on each side. The leaders of all the major parties have deployed the fear of fragmentation to their advantage in negotiating with the two governments, arguing that if they make too many concessions, their hard-line rivals will overthrow them. Tony Blair was willing to offer Sinn Féin more concessions between 1998 and 2003 because he took this danger seriously; on the other side, the Unionist Party split over the deal and suffered electoral damage as a result. Having profited repeatedly from the destruction of Unionist Party leaders who had compromised with Nationalism, Ian Paisley was determined to avoid suffering the same fate himself; the DUP leader was highly cautious about power sharing with Sinn Féin until 2006, maintaining that it would be morally wrong to sit in government with unrepentant terrorists. Even with IRA weaponry decommissioned and after a string of decisive electoral victories, the DUP waited until 2010 before formally agreeing to the transfer of responsibility for policing back to Stormont. On both sides, continuing threats from hard-line rivals have meant that leaders cannot afford to be seen to compromise on the essential issues that divide them, especially when an election is in the offing. Since 1992, there has been an average of one election per year.[27]

As for elite accommodation, the tradition has been one of open and destructive hostility. The state was born into violence as the Anglo-Irish War spilled across the border. From the 1920s to the 1960s, Nationalists boycotted Stormont and Unionists let them. After Sunningdale, a negative tradition emerged as Britain's repeated attempts to engineer moderate coalitions broke down. DUP leaders in 2006 knew well the fates of the moderate Unionist Party leaders whom they had helped to topple. In contrast to O'Neill and Faulkner, the uncompromising Ian Paisley had reigned supreme at the DUP since 1970, while Gerry Adams and Martin McGuinness had helped lead the republican movement continuously since 1972.

As regards external threats, not only has there not been any common threat, but each side sees itself as vulnerable to a different outside power. Unionists resent the nationalism of the Irish state and the international diaspora that has supported it. Republicans resent Britain's continuing involvement in Northern Ireland, upholding the division of their nation with the ultimate threat of armed intervention.

As for the balance of power, the boundaries of the jurisdiction had been fixed by 1925 in such a way as to ensure that Unionists would hold the balance of power for the foreseeable future. Northern Ireland until 1972 was ruled by a party representing the majority community that had enjoyed electoral hegemony for fifty years and would continue to do so unless the rules were changed. Northern Ireland now has a power-sharing system, but one of the two sides still has a clear electoral majority.

With respect to overarching loyalties, both sides are Christian, but as we saw in chapter 2, their denominations tend to distinguish and divide them. There is for many on both sides an overarching hostility toward the cosmopolitan social and cultural values associated with England, for example on sexuality and abortion, but this is rooted in the separate denominational traditions rather than cutting across them. There are shared experiences of trauma and loss associated with the Troubles, but this feeds blame as well as a desire for reconciliation.

Finally, while there have been socioeconomic inequalities between the two sides, both have suffered poverty and deprivation and both include a prosperous middle class. Perceptions of inequality and discrimination have been more divisive than the realities. Narratives about discrimination and fecklessness have been exploited for political advantage and have taken on special salience in Northern Ireland's particular political and cultural environment.

Despite the overwhelming absence of favorable conditions, British policymakers have maintained that Northern Ireland's leaders will make devolution work, since otherwise they will have no power at all; that a tradition of cooperation will emerge over time as elites work together on uncontroversial social and economic issues; that there is no longer any credible reason for either side to feel at risk from the other; and that although the present arrangements may not fully conform to all the standards of conventional democracy, they do provide stable devolved administration, ministers are accountable to the local electorate, and the elites can themselves improve the arrangements by agreement over time. Irrespective of favorable conditions, the Good Friday Agreement (GFA) will have succeeded if it permits the conflict to be contained long enough for the parties to change the political culture of the region so that the dispute between unionism and nationalism no longer carries the risk of spilling over into intense and prolonged violence.[28]

By 2001 McGarry and O'Leary were claiming the GFA as a victory for consociational thinking.[29] They argued that the unanticipated breakthrough to peace had been made possible because the agreement cleverly combined consociational arrangements within Northern Ireland with a robust external dimension along the lines of the shared-authority solution that they had themselves previously advocated. They conceded that the external dimension fell short of their original prescription, as outlined in chapter 8, but predicted that the GFA would deliver an equally successful outcome.

Starting from a similar theoretical perspective, Kerr has compared attempts to introduce power-sharing structures in Northern Ireland and Lebanon, concluding that consociation is not a reliable vehicle for long-term ethnic conflict resolution so much as "a tool for conflict regulation provided that a stable external environment exists to guarantee the political structures."[30] Like McGarry and O'Leary, Kerr finds that previous analysts underestimated the significance of neighbouring kin-states and the international community. In both of his cases, the success of consociation depended on other states applying positive pressures. In Northern Ireland, the accommodation continues to depend on "how the British government exercises its sovereignty in the interests of preserving consociation . . . as opposed to supporting idiosyncratic British or Unionist interests. . . . If these external parameters were to shift to the detriment of the status quo in Northern Ireland, or the two governments were to disengage from the process to any significant degree, the GFA would collapse."[31]

Several other lessons have been drawn from the Northern Ireland political process. External actors, in this case the U.S. government, can play an important part in mediating an internal settlement. An agreement may have to cover a range of potentially destabilizing issues, such as policing, language rights, and demilitarization. Proportional representation voting systems will not necessarily assist moderate candidates.[32] An automatic mechanism for allocating key posts, such as the d'Hondt rule, can be valuable in that it avoids the need for potentially destabilizing negotiations between party leaders where trust is lacking.

### Counterarguments

Some critics of consociation have argued that it cannot work or work for long in Northern Ireland because of underlying structural factors that generate the unfavorable context described in the preceding section. Until these change, attempts to sustain consociational institutions will inevitably fail. The critics argue that the very process of imposing consociational arrangements in 1973 and 1998 and the intermittent operation of these arrangements from 1999 to 2007 has deepened the division between the two sides, ensuring that the national question remains electorally dominant for the foreseeable future.

As early as 1975, Barry was questioning Lijphart's basic assumptions.[33] He refutes the depiction of Switzerland and Austria as consociational democracies, questions whether Belgium and the Netherlands really carry the theoretical weight Lijphart attributes to them, and concludes that the relevance of the consociational model for other divided societies is doubtful. Divisions based on ethnic identity are more likely to resist consociational solutions than those based on class or religion. This is in part because religious and class conflicts occur between organized groups—such as church congregations, trade unions, and political parties—whereas ethnic conflict is between social groups that do not require formal structures or appointed leaders to identify their enemies or work up a riot. If ethnic group leaders achieve positions of authority and then offer to compromise with the leaders of the other side, they run the risk of being undercut and supplanted by more hard-line rivals. Barry concludes that Northern Ireland cannot be a consociational system as defined by Lijphart because the leaders of the two sides are not committed to preserving the constitution, and any agreed-to institutions are thus intrinsically unstable.

There is also an empirical case against consociational prescriptions, namely, that they have produced more failures than successes: Northern Ireland in 1973, Cyprus, Lebanon, Malaysia, Fiji, Angola, Sierra Leone, and Sudan.[34] On the other side of the scorecard, there are few examples of consociational constitutions that have survived for long. Lijphart himself conceded that only Belgium and Switzerland fully conformed to his model, and Barry has challenged even this modest claim.[35]

More recently, O'Leary's assertion that the GFA is a victory for consociational theory has been attacked by Dixon, who challenges O'Leary on much the same ground as Barry's critique of Lijphart: that this claim requires such substantial adjustments in Lijphart's definition of a consociational system that the term can no longer meaningfully be applied.[36] The GFA does not provide for a consensual grand coalition but for ministers to be appointed on the basis of a mechanistic formula; the construction of the executive does not depend on any deals between elites; and apart from political appointments to the executive and in the assembly, there is no explicit proportionality in the distribution of public funds and jobs. Dixon goes further, arguing against O'Leary's and McGarry's brand of consociationalism in principle on the grounds that it is intrinsically segregationist and undemocratic, since it effectively reinforces the divisions between communal groups and strengthens the elite leaderships upon which the politics of accommodation depend. By contrast, Dixon characterizes the GFA as an integrationist form of power sharing, designed to remove obstacles to cross-community cohesion.[37]

Other analysts accept that the GFA *can* properly be characterized as consociational, given the developments that have taken place in consociational thinking since Lijphart's original formulation, but unlike Dixon complain that it does in fact tend to institutionalize and entrench Northern Ireland's social divisions and helps to sustain sectarian ideologies. Horowitz maintains that the GFA has produced a system in which "by appealing to electorates in ethnic terms, by making ethnic demands on government, and by bolstering the influence of ethnically chauvinist elements within each group, parties that begin by merely mirroring ethnic divisions help to deepen and extend them."[38] Horowitz's concerns have been echoed by commentators in Belfast who, like the New Ulster Movement of the early 1970s, aspire to build a new integrative culture, transcending both Britishness and Irishness.

The above commentators have also criticized the arrangements for the executive, arguing that the use of a mechanistic formula for allocating ministerial posts guarantees the authority of office to all parties that win enough seats in the assembly, irrespective of their suitability for governing or willingness to behave cooperatively. There is no effective scrutiny of ministerial decisions and no effective opposition. Ministers have little incentive to cooperate across party or communal boundaries, and so have not been able adequately to tackle contentious issues such as parading and community relations.

The proponents of integrative power sharing call for changes in legislation that would have the effect of encouraging pre-election compacts across the communal divide, a redistribution of power to local government, and policies designed to promote overarching political allegiances.[39] Other elements in the integrative model could include weighted majority voting without the need for members to designate themselves as Unionist or Nationalist; providing for the executive to be formed on the basis of a voluntary coalition rather than the d'Hondt formula; unspecified incentives from the two national governments to reward political leaders for collaborative behavior and for tackling extremism; and changing the assembly voting system from single transferable vote to alternative vote in single-member constituencies because (it is argued) this would favor candidates drawing support from both sides.[40] Dixon speaks for this integrative tendency when he calls for "a comprehensive and inter-related programme of reform aimed at undermining communalism."[41] Such a program would include integrated education, desegregated public housing, a more proactive approach to tolerance and community relations and policies to grow awareness of a shared cultural heritage.

O'Leary and McGarry object to the integrative approach on the grounds that it neglects the roots of the problem by denying the salience of sovereignty and allegiance, that consequently it is biased toward the British status quo, and that it would be inequitable and impractical to force people to integrate education and housing against their wishes.[42] It would clearly be desirable to have a common Northern Irish identity, and one may emerge over time; until it does, the operation of the power-sharing institutions will help to grow it.[43]

At the level of party politics, another stated objection to the integrative approach is that nonaligned parties have so far failed to muster much electoral support, despite much maneuvering and encouragement from the British government, particularly in the early 1970s. Some integrative commentators have contended that this is a negative consequence of the arrangements set out in the GFA.[44] However, the only significant party to draw support on a balanced basis from both sides, Alliance, had already been gradually losing electoral support since 1973.[45] Moreover, with the devolution of policing and criminal justice in 2010, the DUP and Sinn Féin agreed to appoint Alliance's leader, David Ford, as minister of justice, an office that—as the SDLP complained—the party would not have secured had the d'Hondt formula been applied.

Although Dixon merely notes the point in passing, the substantial external dimension to the negotiation and implementation of the GFA provides another important ground for challenging O'Leary's claim to a victory for consociational theory. The interstate dimension is arguably so substantial that it requires a new paradigm. O'Duffy hints at this when he suggests that in cases such as Palestine, Kashmir, Sri Lanka, Cyprus, and Lebanon, the fundamental sovereignty dispute between the neighboring nation-states must be resolved before internal consociational accommodations can be achieved. These states must also agree on mechanisms of self-determination, a constitutional framework for power sharing, and means to protect minority rights. Only then can the conflict be resolved. This process requires flexibility on the part of the nation states so as to reduce the intensity of the differences between the two sides, protect their competing national identities, and "pluralize sovereignty in terms of federal, confederal and consociational practices."[46] If, as O'Leary argues, the roots of the Troubles lie in the historical conflict between Britain and Ireland, and if the British-Irish dimension is a more important part of the solution than the internal political architecture, then we are dealing not so much with a consociational solution to the problem of a deeply divided society as with a binational treaty solution to a longstanding frontier dispute.[47]

The British government has had an interest in publicly downplaying the importance of the interstate dimension because of the difficulties it creates for Unionist leaders, and because it has wanted to demonstrate that the GFA belongs to the people of Ireland, as displayed through the parallel referenda in 1998. The fact remains, however, that the framework for the GFA was thrashed out between the two governments over a period of years starting in 1991. The process acquired new momentum with the advent of new governments in both states in 1997. Prime Ministers Blair and Ahern choreographed the multiparty negotiations and formalized the outcome in an international treaty. It would not have happened without the active engagement of the highest levels of leadership in both states.

There are clearly important limitations on the extent to which the Northern Ireland political agreements can properly be described as consociational. The serious negotiations that eventually resulted in an accommodation did not begin until the British government and the republican movement both accepted that they could not prevail by force. The devolved institutions are sustained by an interstate framework, without which they would not exist.

## Conclusions

Great care must be exercised in identifying and extrapolating lessons from Northern Ireland to other conflict regions, particularly when it comes to political development policy prescriptions. Indeed, one of the learning points from this study is that there is no off-the-shelf solution for such conflicts. Preventing, managing, and resolving them is a craft, not a science. Any lessons should be drawn only within a wider intellectual framework of historically informed context-specific analysis and assessment.

Having said that, the Northern Ireland case provides potentially useful material for consideration by analysts, policymakers, and mediators working on other conflicts that are legitimately comparable. They fall into this category where and only where the following conditions are met: a society deeply divided along ethnonational lines; a substantial proportion of the population on both sides that is willing to accept, support, or use violence as a means to assert its identity claims; identification of the rival sides with different kin-states; and a parallel sovereignty dispute between these states.

Any presumed lessons should be applied with sensitivity and care, taking account of differences in the preconditions, precipitants, context, and dynamics of the conflict under consideration. Subject to the caveats above, the research presented in this book contains material and reaches conclusions to sharpen the senses and expand the repertoire of those working to prevent, manage, and resolve conflicts in other places, be they policymakers, military commanders, diplomats, or mediators. It demonstrates the importance of having, or quickly acquiring, a sound knowledge and understanding of the historical background to the particular case, of eth-nonational disputes in general, and (where power sharing is contemplated) of consociational theory and its limitations.

Perhaps the most important lesson of the book is that policymaking for conflict resolution needs to be evidence-based and self-aware. Policymak-ers should develop the capacity to protect the integrity of rational decision-making processes from ignorance, misunderstanding, bias, false optimism, mistaken preconceptions, transient political pressures, rigid organizational procedures, missing capabilities, lack of imagination, and time pressures. If an outside power intends to intervene in an internal conflict in a divided society, its policymakers should equip themselves, preferably in advance, with full and accurate background information. They should have a scien-tific understanding of the preconditions for the conflict and the political worldviews of the organizations and ideologies on both sides, including symbols and myths that may seem primitive and irrational; as the MoD review noted, this was a fundamental weakness of British policymaking in the 1970s. They should maximize their influence over their political and diplomatic environment, enabling them to manage pressures to act hastily and counterproductively. Willie Whitelaw performed relatively well in this respect, Reginald Maudling badly. They should ensure that they deploy appropriate organizational capacity, structures, and routines, avoiding (for example) using soldiers to do the work of police officers. Wilson and Cal-laghan could arguably have prevented the insurgency altogether if they had sent police reinforcements to Londonderry in 1969 instead of soldiers.

Terminating a well-organized insurgency that has popular support re-quires not only military power and effective intelligence operations but also political authority, a persuasive message, deep understanding, good coordination, sustained concentration, and a clear vision of both the cur-rent situation and an attainable peaceful future.

## Notes

1.    S. Beckett, *Worstward Ho* (New York NY; Grove Press, 1983).

2.    C. Townshend, *Political Violence in Ireland* (Oxford: Clarendon, 1983), 410.

3.    H. Eckstein, "On the Causes of Internal Wars," in E.A. Nordlinger, ed., *Politics and Society* (Englewood Cliffs, NJ: Prentice Hall, 1970), 302.

4.    C. Townshend, *The British Campaign in Ireland 1919-1921* (Oxford: Oxford Univer-sity Press, paperback edition, 1978), 203.

5.    K. Bloomfield, *A Tragedy of Errors* (Liverpool: Liverpool University Press 2007), 218.

6.    Ministry of Defence, "Operation Banner: An Analysis of Military Operations in Northern Ireland," Ministry of Defence internal paper, July 2006, paragraph 856.

7.    Ministry of Defence, "Operation Banner," paragraph 104.

8.   Ministry of Defence, "Operation Banner," paragraph 820.

9.   Ministry of Defence, "Operation Banner," paragraph 108.

10.   Ministry of Defence, "Operation Banner," paragraph 818.

11.   One possible explanation lies in the well-recorded unwillingness of the national and regional levels to share information with one another, a process that worked both ways. Another is that Unionist leaders and community activists were themselves the objects of British intelligence gathering.

12.   Ministry of Defence, "Operation Banner," paragraph 805.

13.   Ministry of Defence, "Operation Banner," paragraph 406.

14.   Ministry of Defence, "Operation Banner," paragraph 823.

15.   Ministry of Defence, "Operation Banner," paragraph 856.

16.   J. Darby, *Conflict in Northern Ireland: the Development of a Polarised Community* (Dublin: Gill and Macmillan 1976), 196.

17.   A.T.Q. Stewart, *The Narrow Ground* (London: Faber and Faber, 1977), 151.

18.   B. O'Leary and J. McGarry, *The Politics of Antagonism: Understanding Northern Ireland* (London: Athlone Press, 1993), 18.

19.   B. O'Duffy, *British-Irish Relations and Northern Ireland: From Violent Politics to Conflict Regulation* (Dublin: Irish Academic Press, 2007), 3.

20.   D. Trimble, "Misunderstanding Ulster," 2007, available at www.davidtrimble.org (accessed September 16, 2010). Trimble was the leader of the Unionist Party during the 1998 negotiations and subsequently first minister.

21.   Martin McGuinness used the term, also however reassuring the military faction that "we recognise that only disciplined revolutionary armed struggle by the IRA will end British rule." Cited in *Republican News*, June 28, 1984.

22.   Ministry of Defence, "Operation Banner," paragraph 855

23.   J. McGarry and B. O'Leary, in J. McGarry and B. O'Leary, eds., *The Future of Northern Ireland* (Oxford: Clarendon, 1990), 295.

24.   A. Lijphart, "Consociational Democracy," *World Politics*, vol. 21, no. 2 (1969), 207–25; "The Northern Ireland Problem: Cases, Theories, and Solutions," *British Journal of Political Science*, vol. 5, no. 3 (1985), 83–106; foreword to McGarry and O'Leary, *The Future of Northern Ireland*.

25.   The list of favorable conditions was originally set out in A. Lijphart, *Democracy in Plural Societies* (New Haven, CT: Yale University Press, 1977), chapter 3.

26.   For a fuller account of Northern Ireland's unfavorable conditions, see J. McGarry and B. O'Leary, *Explaining Northern Ireland* (Oxford: Blackwell Publishers, 1995), 320–26.

27.   Whether to local government, regional assembly, Westminster, or the European Parliament.

28.   Personal interviews by the author with NIO officials, August 2006.

29.   See, e.g., J. McGarry and B. O'Leary, "The Character of the Agreement," in J. McGarry and B. O'Leary, eds., *The Northern Ireland Conflict: Consociational Engagements* (Oxford: Oxford University Press, 2004), 49.

30.   M. Kerr, *Imposing Power-Sharing: Conflict and Coexistence in Northern Ireland and Lebanon* (Dublin: Irish Academic Press, 2005), 2–3.

31.   Ibid., 111.

32. O'Leary and McGarry have calculated that, if a party list system had been in place in 1998, the Ulster Unionist Party would not have been strong enough to strike a deal.

33. B. Barry, "Political Accommodation and Consociational Democracy," *British Journal of Political Science,* vol. 5, no. 4 (October 1975), 477–505.

34. J. McGarry and B. O'Leary, eds., *The Politics of Ethnic Conflict Regulation* (London: Routledge, 1993), 36; T. Sisk, "Power Sharing," in G. Burgess and H. Burgess, eds., *Beyond Intractability,* Conflict Research Consortium, University of Colorado, Boulder, 2003, available at www.beyondintractability.org (accessed September 16, 2010).

35. For a comprehensive account of the development and contemporary relevance of consociational theory and its limitations, see R. Taylor, "Introduction: The Promise of Consociational Theory," in R. Taylor, ed., *Consociational Theory: McGarry and O'Leary and the Northern Ireland Conflict* (London: Routledge, 2009).

36. P. Dixon, "Why the Good Friday Agreement in Northern Ireland Is Not Consociational," *Political Quarterly,* vol. 76, no. 3 (2005), 357–367.

37. The term *integrationist* as used by Dixon should not be confused with the constitutional policy option, advocated by some Unionists, of integrating Northern Ireland more fully into the United Kingdom. For clarity I prefer the term *integrative* to describe the position taken by Dixon and other commentators.

38. D. Horowitz, *Ethnic Groups in Conflict* (Berkeley: University of California Press, 2000), 291.

39. I. O'Flynn and D. Russell, "Introduction," in I. O'Flynn and D. Russell, eds., *Power-sharing: New Challenges for Divided Societies* (London: Pluto, 2005), 5.

40. These elements have been identified by Horowitz and others. O'Leary disputes the final point in particular. See "The Character of the 1998 Agreement," 58.

41. P. Dixon, *Northern Ireland: The Politics of War and Peace* (New York: Palgrave, 2001), 305.

42. O'Leary and McGarry, *Politics of Antagonism,* 307.

43. J. McGarry and B. O'Leary, "Argument," in Taylor, *Consociational Theory,* 83.

44. R. Wilson, "Towards a Civic Culture," in I. O'Flynn and D. Russell, eds., *Power Sharing: New Challenges for Divided Societies* (London: Pluto Press, 2006), 206.

45. Alliance achieved the following shares of first preference votes in assembly elections: 1993, 9.2 percent; 1998, 6.5 percent; 2003, 3.7 percent; 2007, 5.2 percent. See CAIN Web Service, available at cain.ulst.ac.uk (accessed October 16, 2010).

46. O'Duffy, *British-Irish Relations,* 201.

47. This was political scientist Frank Wright's position as long ago as 1987. See F. Wright, *Northern Ireland: A Comparative Analysis* (Dublin: Gill and Macmillan, 1987).

# List of Abbreviations

| | |
|---|---|
| CDU | Campaign for Democracy in Ulster |
| CGS | chief of general staff |
| CLF | commander of land forces |
| CPRS | Central Policy Review Staff |
| CSJ | Campaign for Social Justice |
| DCDA | Derry Citizens' Defence Association |
| DEA | Department of External Affairs |
| DUP | Democratic Unionist Party |
| EEC | European Economic Community |
| FCO | Foreign and Commonwealth Office |
| GFA | Good Friday Agreement |
| GOC | general officer commanding |
| IJS | Irish Joint Section |
| IRA | Irish Republican Army |
| JIC | Joint Intelligence Committee |
| JSC | joint security committee |
| MoD | Ministry of Defence |
| MP | member of parliament |
| NATO | North Atlantic Treaty Organization |
| NCO | noncommissioned officer |
| NICRA | Northern Ireland Civil Rights Association |
| NICS | Northern Ireland Civil Service |
| NILP | Northern Ireland Labour Party |
| NIO | Northern Ireland Office |
| NUM | New Ulster Movement |
| PD | People's Democracy |
| PR | proportional representation |
| PUS | permanent under secretary |
| RIC | Royal Irish Constabulary |
| RUC | Royal Ulster Constabulary |
| SDLP | Social Democratic and Labour Party |
| STV | single transferable vote |
| UDA | Ulster Defence Association |

UDR       Ulster Defence Regiment
UFF       Ulster Freedom Fighters
UKREP     UK Representative
USC       Ulster Special Constabulary
UUC       Ulster Unionist Council
UUP       Ulster Unionist Party
UUUC      United Ulster Unionist Council
UVF       Ulster Volunteer Force
UWC       Ulster Workers' Council

# Index

Page numbers followed by *t* and *n* indicate tables and footnotes, respectively.

# United States
# Institute of Peace Press

Since its inception, the United States Institute of Peace Press has published over 150 books on the prevention, management, and peaceful resolution of international conflicts—among them such venerable titles as Raymond Cohen's *Negotiating Across Cultures*; *Herding Cats* and *Leashing the Dogs of War* by Chester A. Crocker, Fen Osler Hampson, and Pamela Aall; John Paul Lederach's *Building Peace*; and *American Negotiating Behavior* by Richard H. Solomon and Nigel Quinney. All our books arise from research and fieldwork sponsored by the Institute's many programs. In keeping with the best traditions of scholarly publishing, each volume undergoes both thorough internal review and blind peer review by external subject experts to ensure that the research, scholarship, and conclusions are balanced, relevant, and sound. With the Institute's move to its new headquarters on the National Mall in Washington, D.C., the Press is committed to extending the reach of the Institute's work by continuing to publish significant and sustainable works for practitioners, scholars, diplomats, and students.

Valerie Norville
Director

# About the
# United States Institute of Peace

The United States Institute of Peace is an independent, nonpartisan institution established and funded by Congress. The Institute provides analysis, training, and tools to help prevent, manage, and end violent international conflicts, promote stability, and professionalize the field of peacebuilding.